The Great Patrioti[c War of the] Soviet Union, 194[1-45]

This book consists of extracts from key documents, along with commentary and further reading, on the 'Great Patriotic War' of the Soviet Union against Nazi Germany, 1941–45.

Despite the historical significance of the war, few Soviet documents have been published in English. This work provides translations of a range of extracts from Soviet documents relating to the titanic struggle on the Eastern Front during World War II, with commentary. This is the only single-volume work in English to use documentary evidence to look at the Soviet war effort from military, political, economic and diplomatic perspectives. The book should not only facilitate a deeper study of the Soviet war effort, but also allow more balanced study of what is widely known in the West as the 'Eastern Front'.

This book will be of much interest to students and scholars of military history, Soviet history, and World War II history.

Alexander Hill is an Associate Professor in Military History at the University of Calgary, Canada.

Soviet (Russian) study of war
Series Editor: David M. Glantz
ISSN: 1462-0960

This series examines what Soviet military theorists and commanders learned from the study of their own military operations.

1 **Soviet Documents on the Use of War Experience, Volume I**
   The initial period of war 1941
   Harold S. Orenstein, translator and editor, with an Introduction by David M. Glantz

2 **Soviet Documents on the Use of War Experience, Volume II**
   The Winter Campaign 1941–1942
   Harold S. Orenstein, translator and editor, with an Introduction by David M. Glantz

3 **Red Armor Combat Orders**
   Combat regulations for tank and mechanized forces 1944
   Joseph G. Welsh, translator and editor, with an Introduction by Richard N. Armstrong

4 **Soviet Documents on the Use of War Experience, Volume III**
   Military operations 1941 and 1942
   Harold S. Orenstein, translator and editor, with an Introduction by David M. Glantz

5 **The Nature of the Operations of Modern Armies by V.K. Triandafillov**
   William A. Burhans, translator, edited by Jacob W. Kipp, with an Introduction by James J. Schneider

6 **The Evolution of Soviet Operational Art, 1927–1991**
   The documentary basis, volume I, operational art 1927–1964
   Harold S. Orenstein, translator, with an Introduction by David M. Glantz

7 **The Evolution of Soviet Operational Art, 1927–1991**
  The documentary basis, volume II, operational art 1965–1991
  Harold S. Orenstein, translator, with an Introduction by David M. Glantz

8 **Winter Warfare**
  Red Army orders and experiences
  Richard N. Armstrong and Joseph G. Welsh

9 **The Bear Went Over the Mountain**
  Soviet combat tactics in Afghanistan
  Lester W. Grau

10 **The Battle for Kursk 1943**
   The Soviet General Staff study
   David M. Glantz and Harold S. Orenstein, editor and translator

11 **Kursk 1943**
   A statistical analysis
   Niklas Zetterling and Anders Frankson

12 **Belorussia 1944**
   The Soviet General Staff study
   David M. Glantz and Harold S. Orenstein, editor and translator

13 **The Battle for L'vov, July 1944**
   The Soviet General Staff study
   David M. Glantz and Harold S. Orenstein, editor and translator

14 **Stalin and the Soviet–Finnish War, 1939–40**
   Alexander O. Chubaryan and Harold Shukman, editors

15 **The Battle for the Ukraine**
   The Red Army's Korsun'-Shevchenkovskii Operation, 1944
   David M. Glantz and Harold S. Orenstein, editor and translator

16 **The Soviet Strategic Offensive in Manchuria, 1945**
   'August Storm'
   David M. Glantz

17 **Soviet Operational and Tactical Combat in Manchuria, 1945**
   'August Storm'
   David M. Glantz

18 **The War Behind the Eastern Front**
   Soviet Partisans in North-West Russia 1941–1944
   Alexander Hill

19 **Soviet Air Force Theory, 1918–1945**
   James Sterrett

20 **The Great Patriotic War of the Soviet Union, 1941–45**
   A documentary reader
   Alexander Hill

The Great Patriotic War of the Soviet Union, 1941–45

A documentary reader

Alexander Hill

Routledge
Taylor & Francis Group
LONDON AND NEW YORK

First published 2009
by Routledge
2 Park Square, Milton Park, Abingdon, Oxon OX14 4RN

Simultaneously published in the USA and Canada
by Routledge
270 Madison Ave, New York, NY 10016

First issued in paperback 2010

Routledge is an imprint of the Taylor & Francis Group, an informa business

© 2009 Alexander Hill

Typeset in Garamond by Wearset Ltd, Boldon, Tyne and Wear

All rights reserved. No part of this book may be reprinted or
reproduced or utilized in any form or by any electronic, mechanical,
or other means, now known or hereafter invented, including
photocopying and recording, or in any information storage or
retrieval system, without permission in writing from the publishers.

British Library Cataloguing in Publication Data
A catalogue record for this book is available from the British Library

Library of Congress Cataloging in Publication Data
Hill, Alexander, 1974–
The great patriotic war of the Soviet Union, 1941–45 : a
documentary reader / Alexander Hill.
p. cm. – (Cass series on the Soviet (Russian) study of war)
1. World War, 1939–1945–Soviet Union–Sources. 2. World War,
1939–1945–Campaigns–Eastern Front–Sources. 3. Soviet
Union–History, Military–Sources. I. Title.
D764.H52 2009
940.53'47–dc22
2008024833

ISBN13: 978-0-7146-5712-7 (hbk)
ISBN13: 978-0-415-60424-6 (pbk)
ISBN13: 978-0-203-88637-3 (ebk)

To the victims of the Great Patriotic War

Contents

Acknowledgements	xi
Introduction	1
1 Lenin, Stalin and the West 1917–39	5
2 The Icebreaker controversy and Soviet intentions in 1941	22
3 Barbarossa	40
4 The Battle of Moscow	68
5 The tide turns: the Battle for Stalingrad	91
6 The Battle of Kursk and the race for the Dnepr	117
7 The siege of Leningrad	141
8 Lend-Lease aid, the Soviet economy and the Soviet Union at war	163
9 The Soviet Partisan Movement	193
10 The 'Ten "Stalinist" Crushing Blows' of 1944	220
11 From the Vistula to Berlin: the end of the Reich	247
12 The Soviet invasion of Manchuria	273
Conclusion	283

Chronology of key events	292
Glossary	304
Notes	314
Bibliography	331
Index	341

Acknowledgements

This reader has benefited from the work of many Western and Russian and Soviet scholars whose works are provided in the introduction and bibliography, as well as of course interaction with the students I have taught over the seven years of my post-doctoral academic career to date. Before turning to thanking specific individuals, a number of organizations and their staff have made significant contributions to this reader. Over a number of years I collected published materials specifically for this reader from the Russian National Library in St Petersburg and the library of the School of Slavonic and East European Studies in London in particular. Funding provided by the University of Calgary allowed the purchase and acquisition of many of the materials used to write this reader, and many of the later chapters were written during a semester-long part-funded sabbatical during the second half of 2007. A course release provided by the Centre for Military and Strategic Studies during 2006 facilitated the writing of some of the earlier chapters.

As regards specific individuals, thanks certainly go to colleagues in Russia who have provided assistance over the years, and in particular, in alphabetical order, Sergei Kudriashov, Nikita Lomagin and Mikhail Suprun. David Glantz was able to find time during his busy writing schedule to look over a draft of this reader minus introduction and conclusion. On specific issues I would like to thank Arthur G. Volz for pointing out two errors in Nikolai Simonov's figures on T-34 production in *Voenno-promishlennii kompleks SSSR*, one of which I was aware of and the other not! I would also like to thank Sofia Klimachevskaia-Djavakhia for assistance in the translation of medical terminology in Chapter 7. My family have always been supportive of my academic endeavours, even when living thousands of miles away, and I am grateful for their continued support. The standard caveat on accuracy applies with this reader as any other work – whilst I am grateful for any assistance received any errors remain my responsibility.

Alexander Hill
May 2008

Introduction

The Great Patriotic War of the Soviet Union, or, in Western terms, the war on the Eastern Front during the Second World War, saw horrendous carnage over a vast geographical area and over a sustained period of time. Two ideologically opposed regimes equipped with the modern weaponry that could be provided in huge quantities by modern industrial states fought a struggle for their very existences at the expense of millions of combatants, both volunteers and conscripts, along with their civilian populations. Both sides saw the war as inevitable. Whilst for Hitler German destiny lay in eastward expansion, for Stalin a clash with fascism, an extreme expression of capitalism, was similarly inevitable. Nazi Germany struck first as Stalin and the Soviet Union tried to buy time to rearm and reorganize in the light of war experience, and, although not explicitly, make good the damage done by the Great Purges. That German forces and their allies got so deep into the Soviet Union, and that it took Soviet forces so long to eject them from Soviet territory despite the relative initial lack of preparedness of Germany for a sustained war, is certainly testimony to the quality of German arms in the broadest sense. However, given Soviet long-term preparation for war, a qualitative parity in many aspects of equipment and numerical superiority without lower quality at least in armour and artillery, it is perhaps surprising that German forces got as far as they did. They did not capture Moscow and Leningrad and enslave the Soviet peoples for many reasons. In addition to firing Soviet will to resist through brutal, racially driven occupation policy, after having squandered resources to halt the German advance Soviet forces were able to recover a material superiority borne out of long-term planning and a complete neglect of the Soviet consumer sector of the economy, with a little help from their new allies, and then increasingly effectively use these resources to defeat their opponent. Whilst Red Army losses remained colossal throughout the war, the Red Army became a far more effective fighting machine as the war progressed, that bore the brunt of the fighting against German land forces.

Whilst the secondary literature available in English on the Soviet war effort during the Great Patriotic War has increased significantly in the last decade or so, thanks particularly to David Glantz, it remains difficult for the reader to examine the Soviet Union at war through documentary sources in English translation.[1] This documentary reader has therefore been written in order to give students and a wider audience access to a range of documents for the Soviet Union during the Great Patriotic War in translation and with commentary. Such material has been available more widely in English for Nazi Germany at war for some time,[2] and providing this material for the Soviet Union should therefore facilitate not only a deeper study of the Soviet war effort for many students of the war but also more balanced study of what is widely known in the West as the Eastern Front through documentary materials for both protagonists.

This reader has been developed whilst teaching a final-year undergraduate seminar course on the Great Patriotic War, for the first time at Newcastle University, UK, whilst a temporary lecturer there during the 2002–03 academic year, and subsequently from 2004–05 onwards at the University of Calgary, Canada, where the course has developed a more operational flavour given the strength of the department in and student enthusiasm for military history. Whilst the focus is operational, the operational military history is set very much in its diplomatic, political, economic and to a lesser extent social context. This contextual material certainly and necessarily broadens the perspective of students keen to focus on the operational history to the exclusion of other dimensions to the history of the Soviet Union at war, and has proved successful in doing so particularly where it is obviously tied to the operational history rather than the latter being tacked on, almost as an afterthought, to the broader material.

The 12 chapters in this reader are intended, in the first instance, to provide the focus for 12 seminars, with additional seminars on, for instance, Russia during the First World War and the revolutions of 1917 and Civil War and foreign 'intervention', should time allow and should students require broader context.

Whilst this reader has been written primarily with student use in mind, be this in upper-level undergraduate or graduate courses, it has also been borne in mind that those outside the academic world with an interest in the Soviet war effort, whether avid readers of the English-language literature on the subject per se or wargamers and modellers, are also poorly served with 'primary' source materials for the Soviet side. It is therefore hoped that such an audience will find this reader of value in providing a depth of understanding or food for thought, be it for wargaming, modelling activities or otherwise, that is difficult to gain from the English-language secondary literature and more 'popular' publications deriving their information from undisclosed or dubious sources.

This reader was written to be used in conjunction with one or both of what are currently the best of the general histories of the Great Patriotic War readily available in English. David Glantz and Jonathan House's *When Titans Clashed* provides an excellent overview of Soviet operations during the Great Patriotic War, and works well alongside Evan Mawdsley's *Thunder in the East*, which provides more of the strategic context, including diplomatic and economic dimensions to the war, and benefits from a further ten years of published research and publication of archival materials. Both of the above have been cited frequently in the text supporting the documents presented in this reader, and should be referred to regularly where broader context is required. Details of these two works, and additional materials on the war as a whole mentioned below, are provided at the end of this introduction. Further reading specific to particular chapters is provided at the end of each chapter.

As regards additional materials to be used alongside this reader, students wishing to start with a summary of the course of the war and seeking a little more economic and social context might benefit from starting with or referring later to Barber and Harrison's *The Soviet Home Front, 1941–1945*, unfortunately out of print at the time this reader was in preparation but still widely available through libraries. Indeed, Richard Overy's *Russia's War* might also serve as a useful introduction to the Soviet Union at war, providing an excellent synthesis of the English-language literature up to the point it was written. Other English-language works dealing with the war as a whole that should be considered include, of the less recent literature, Alexander Werth's *Russia at War*, in which readers can benefit from sections drawing on the keen insight of a journalist based in the Soviet Union during the war, and John Erickson's dense two-volume history of the war consisting of *The Road to Stalingrad* and *The Road to Berlin*. More recent works, benefiting directly or indirectly from documents released from Soviet archives from the late 1980s onwards, include Geoffrey Roberts's *Stalin's Wars*, an interesting rehabilitation of Stalin as war leader, and Chris Bellamy's *Absolute War*. Of the Soviet 'memoirs' dealing with the war as a whole available in English, perhaps most useful remains Shtemenko's *The Soviet General Staff at War, 1941–1945*. Finally, for reference purposes, readers might like to consult David Glantz's three-volume reference history of the Red Army at war, the first two volumes of which, *Stumbling Colossus* and *Colossus Reborn*, have been published to date.

Core basic reading

David Glantz and Jonathan House, *When Titans Clashed: How the Red Army Stopped Hitler* (Lawrence, KS: University Press of Kansas, 1995).

Evan Mawdlsey, *Thunder in the East: The Nazi-Soviet War 1941–1945* (London: Hodder Arnold, 2005).

Additional basic reading

John Barber and Mark Harrison, *The Soviet Home Front 1941–1945: A Social and Economic History of the USSR in World War II* (London: Longman, 1991).

Chris Bellamy, *Absolute War: Soviet Russia in the Second World War* (New York: Alfred A. Knopf, 2007).

John Erickson, *The Road to Stalingrad: Stalin's War with Germany: Volume One* (London: Weidenfeld and Nicolson, 1975).

John Erickson, *The Road to Berlin: Stalin's War with Germany: Volume Two* (London: Weidenfeld and Nicolson, 1983), as well as other imprints.

Richard Overy, *Russia's War* (London: Allen Lane, 1998) and other imprints.

Geoffrey Roberts, *Stalin's Wars: From World War Two to the Cold War, 1939–1953* (New Haven, CT: Yale University Press, 2007).

S.M. Shtemenko, *The Soviet General Staff at War, 1941–1945* (Honolulu, HI: University Press of the Pacific, 2001), and earlier imprints by Progress Publishers.

Alexander Werth, *Russia at War, 1941–1945* (London: Barrie and Rockliff, 1964), and other imprints.

For reference

David M. Glantz, *Stumbling Colossus: The Red Army on the Eve of World War* (Lawrence, KS: University Press of Kansas, 1998).

David M. Glantz, *Colossus Reborn: The Red Army at War, 1941–1943* (Lawrence, KS: University Press of Kansas, 2005).

1 Lenin, Stalin and the West 1917–39[1]

The Soviet Russian republic that came into existence after the Bolshevik seizure of power of October 1917, and that would become the Soviet Union in 1924, was born into a hostile international environment. In late 1917 the Bolsheviks had to deal with the German threat that had played a crucial role in both bringing down the Tsarist regime and weakening the Provisional Government. Peace with Germany with the Treaty of Brest-Litovsk in March 1918 came at the temporary price of vast swathes of Russian imperial territory, including the Ukraine, and marked the longer-term separation of the Baltic Republics and Finland from the former Empire. The peace also brought the Bolsheviks into direct confrontation with the *Entente*, determined to preserve an Eastern Front in the war against the Central Powers. British and French input into the Civil War undoubtedly prolonged the fighting, and would not be forgotten quickly by Soviet leaders.

Whilst by 1921 the Bolsheviks found themselves nominal masters of much of the former Russian Empire, they faced a population and particularly peasantry weary of the excesses of the politics of War Communism and the bloodshed of war, prompting the Bolsheviks under Lenin's leadership to take a step back from propelling the fledgling republic towards communism, a key dimension of which, for many within the Party, was 'forced', or at least intensified industrialization. War Communism was replaced by the semi-capitalist New Economic Policy (NEP).

There was an uneasy peace not only in Soviet society and within the Communist Party, but also between the Soviet Union and the capitalist world. Whilst both sought to normalize relations and particularly trade, the Soviet Union was aware of the latent hostility towards the upstart republic, and the capitalist world of the fact that for the Bolsheviks the international revolutionary project was on hold rather than off the agenda. Under Lenin's leadership, the development of the Soviet military power required to spread 'revolution' by force, as attempted in Poland in 1920, was increasingly of secondary importance to stability, both internally and in relations with other powers. This situation was to remain under the collective leadership following Lenin's death in January 1924.[2] With the rise of Stalin, however, the pursuit of military power for use against an abstract capitalist threat would become a key justification for the ending of NEP and the associated projects of forced collectivization and industrialization from 1928 onwards, Stalin's 'revolution from above'.

International relations and the 'revolution from above'

For the Soviet Union, eventual conflict with the capitalist world was always inevitable, even if, in the short term, undesirable. The capitalist threat to the Soviet Union was, however, at least in Soviet eyes, to become more significant with the apparently increasing prospects of revolution in capitalist countries associated with depression in the 1920s:

> DOCUMENT 1: *From the report of the Chairman of the Council of Peoples' Commissars A.I. Rikov at the IVth Congress of Soviets SSSR, 18 April 1927*
>
> Soviet foreign policy has recently been developing in conditions in which there has been a growth in active hostility towards the Soviet Union from a whole host of countries.... Recently a number of [British] conservative newspapers have repeated that it is necessary to 'encircle the Soviet Union', 'destroy the Bolshevik menace', 'establish a *cordon sanitaire*', and alike....
>
> (Source: A.F. Kiselev and E.M. Shchagin, 1996, p. 667)

> DOCUMENT 2: *From the speech of V.M. Molotov at the tenth plenary session of the Executive Committee of the Comintern, 9 July 1929*
>
> The situation is now such, that in all of the core capitalist countries of Europe events are in progress, signifying the rise of revolutionary mood....
>
> From what I have said, it follows that the most important responsibility of communist parties is ... preparation for new revolutionary struggles on a massive scale....
>
> Now, more than ever before, the tactic of coming to terms with reformers, the tactic of coalition between revolutionary organisations and the organisations of the reformers is unacceptable and damaging....
>
> In conditions of the current period the question of strengthening the struggle against social democracy has gained special significance. The struggle with social democracy, and in particular with its left wing,... cannot but be the centre of attention for communist parties....
>
> The increase in international revolutionary mood and the successful conduct of socialist reconstruction in the USSR is indicative of the weakening progress of capitalism.... It means that now the danger of a new imperialist war and a new intervention against the Soviet Union is intensifying.
>
> (Source: A.F. Kiselev and E.M. Shchagin, 1996, pp. 671–672)

Fearing revolution, capitalist powers were portrayed as likely to seek to destroy the Soviet beacon for communism across Europe in order to forestall revolution, although there is little or no evidence of concrete preparations. The Soviet 'war scare' of 1927, which stemmed from a series of apparently unrelated events and, in particular, the Arcos crisis with Britain, was sufficiently serious to result in a British break in diplomatic relations with the Soviet Union.[3] The Soviet response was both to strengthen the Soviet economy and defence sector and to make certain that the Soviet rear in future 'war' against the capitalist world was secure:[4]

DOCUMENT 3: *Extracts from an article by Stalin on the threat of war, 28 July 1927*

It can scarcely be doubted that the main issue of the present day is that of the threat of a new imperialist war. It is not a matter of some vague and immaterial 'danger' of a new war but of the real and actual threat of a new war in general, and of a war against the USSR in particular....

The fact that the initiative in this matter of creating a united imperialist front against the USSR has been assumed by the British bourgeoisie and its general staff, the Conservative Party, should not come as any surprise to us....

The British Conservative government struck its first open blow in Peking with the raid on the Soviet Embassy....

This blow, as we know, failed.

The second blow was struck in London, by the raid on Arcos and the severance of relations with the USSR....

This blow, as we also know, failed.

The third open blow was delivered in Warsaw, by the instigation of the assassination of Voikov. Voikov's assassination, organised by agents of the Conservative Party, was intended by its authors to play a role similar to that of the Sarajevo assassination by embroiling the USSR in an armed conflict with Poland.

This blow also seems to have failed....

The task is to strengthen the defensive capacity of our country, to expand our national economy, to improve our industry – both war and non-war – to enhance the vigilance of the workers, peasants and Red Army men of our country....

The task is to strengthen our rear and cleanse it of dross, not hesitating to mete out punishment to ... terrorists ... who set fire to our mills and factories, for it is impossible to defend our country in the absence of a strong revolutionary rear.

(Source: J.V. Stalin, *Works. Volume 9*, 1954, pp. 328, 330, 331–332, 335)

Some indication of direct Soviet investment in defence, even during the First Five Year Plan, the least obviously defence-oriented of the three plans prior to the Great Patriotic War, is provided in Table 1.1. The production of tanks continued to receive high priority, the development of Soviet tank production by 1934 being the subject of Document 4:

DOCUMENT 4: *Basic indicators of the development of base motor-mechanization {of the Red Army} for the period of time from XVI–XVII Party congresses: From materials of Gosplan USSR, 11 January 1934*

The qualitative development and quantitative distribution of technical weapons resources has decisive significance in operational-tactical forms for the conduct of war, the driving force of which is the motor....

Bourgeois military specialists and the military headquarters of the capitalist states consider that the modern army should have in the region of 10,000 tanks, 200,000 automobiles and 30,000 tractors in service....

Up until 1929 a few tens of tanks, captured by the Red Army from the Whites ... were those sole examples, on which our Red Army learned.

Difficulty in the organisation of the production of tanks consisted of the fact, that up until 1928–1929 we did not have an automobile nor tractor industry, nor the corresponding technical cadres.

With the aim of establishing the production of tanks, examples were purchased abroad and from 1929/30 modern tank types were introduced into production.... Dynamics in the growth of production of significant types:

	1929/30	1930	1931	1932	1933
Tankettes T-27 and T-37	–	–	365	1,593	1,072
Tanks T-18 and T-26	170	239	535	1,361	1,405
Tanks T-24 and BT	1	–	28	393	1,005
Tank T-35	–	–	–	–	1
Artillery tractors	–	–	–	–	173
Tracked tractors	491	280	614	464	451

(Source: A.F. Kiselev and E.M. Shchagin, 1996, pp. 413–414)

Industrialization continued to be closely linked to the defence of the Soviet Union throughout the 1930s, providing a sense of urgency that would otherwise have been difficult to create. The Soviet regime, whilst advancing the revolution as Stalin and much of the Party saw it, was also rectifying weaknesses in the defence capabilities of the Soviet Union, heir to the Russian Empire:

Table 1.1 Soviet orders for and production of key armaments 1929/30–1930/31

Product	1929/30			1930/31		
	Plan	Actual	% plan	Plan	Actual	% plan
Artillery pieces	999	952	95.2	3,577	1,911	53.4
Artillery shells (1,000s)	2,365	790	33.4	1,690	751	44.4
Rifles (1,000s)	150	126	84.0	305	174	57.0
Machine guns (1,000s)	26.5	9.6	36.2	49.5	40.9	82.6
Cartridges (millions)	251	235	93.6	410	234	57.0
Aircraft	1,232	899	72.9	2,024	860	42.4
Tanks	340	170	50.0	1,288	740	57.4

Source: N.S. Simonov, *Voenno-promishlennii kompleks SSSR v 1920–1950-e godi: tempi ekonomicheskogo rosta, struktura, organizatsiia proizvodstva i upravlenie* (Moscow: ROSSPEN, 1996), p. 84.

> DOCUMENT 5: *The Tasks of Business Executives. Speech delivered at the First All-Union Congress of Leading Personnel of Socialist Industry, 4 February 1931*
>
> One feature of the history of Old Russia was the continual beatings she suffered because of her backwardness. She was beaten by the Mongol Khans. She was beaten by the Turkish beys. She was beaten by the Swedish feudal lords. She was beaten by the Polish and Lithuanian gentry. She was beaten by the British and French capitalists. She was beaten by the Japanese barons. All beat her – because of her backwardness: because of her military backwardness, cultural backwardness, political backwardness, industrial backwardness, agricultural backwardness. They beat her because it was profitable and could be done with impunity.... Such is the law of exploiters.... You are backward, you are weak – therefore you are wrong; hence you can be beaten and enslaved. You are mighty – therefore you are right; hence we must be wary of you.
>
> That is why we must no longer lag behind....
>
> We are fifty to a hundred years behind the advanced countries. We must make good this distance in ten years. Either we do it, or they crush us.
>
> (Source: J.V. Stalin, *Works. Volume 13*, 1954, pp. 31, 40–41)

Given the apparent urgency of the situation, longer-term defence concerns such as the location of strategic industries had to be balanced not only with shorter-term needs for equipment, but also the need for short-term achievements for political purposes. The latter meant, for instance, that strategically vulnerable concentrations of defence industrial capacity in the west, particularly in Leningrad, could not be simply and cheaply transferred to more secure locations.[5] Whilst the Soviet Union might have been able to afford to build the Baltic–White Sea Canal, the subject of Document 7, the construction of which had been long discussed under Tsarist rule, cost and the time for construction as a political rather than strategic issue were major factors in what was actually constructed and in what time. The canal, as finally constructed, was certainly not of the size and quality of construction that naval commanders had in mind.

Whilst the Soviet Union would officially continue to seek to foster revolution in the capitalist world through the Communist International or Comintern, given her military weakness this activity could not, however, be allowed to be sufficient to provoke capitalist powers into military activity against a Soviet Union far from prepared for war. Almost as importantly, such activity could not be sufficiently threatening to the West to hinder trade and the Soviet Union's acquisition of Western technology necessary for industrialization and the defence sector. Diplomatic relations with Britain, broken off in 1927 as a result of the Arcos crisis, were re-established in 1929 when a Labour minority government came to power, even if the resulting 'thaw' was short-lived. However, in addition to Soviet subversion, or at least fears of it, Tsarist debt continued to be a stumbling block in both British and French relations with the Soviet Union, or perhaps an excuse for preventing improved relations to be applied by the anti-communist right when

Soviet attempts to settle the issue did not meet expectations. The Soviet Union, more needing of the West than vice versa, continued to pursue improved ties behind the scenes, whilst the intensity of anti-Western rhetoric increased within the Soviet Union. Nonetheless, that continued references to 'capitalist encirclement' were clearly principally intended for domestic consumption is illustrated by the fact that during the show trials of the late 1920s and early 1930s, the Soviet Union was careful not to sentence foreign nationals accused of orchestrating the wrecking of Soviet industry as severely as her own. For instance, the Metro-Vickers Trial of April 1933 involved the accusation of 'espionage, bribery and wrecking' against six British engineers of Metropolitan Vickers Electrical Company on contract to the Soviet Union, the first charge having some foundation, if broadly defined. Two of the accused were sentenced to two- and three-year imprisonments respectively, although they actually only served two months as a result of subsequent diplomatic activity.[6] The Metro-Vickers affair was a serious threat to both diplomatic and economic Anglo-Soviet relations, resulting in short-term sanctions by the British, to which the Soviet Union responded. Nonetheless, Metro-Vickers understandably continued to obtain contracts with the Soviet Union given the priority accorded to the acquisition of foreign expertise and technology by the Soviet leadership.

The capitalist military threat, for planning purposes at this point still led nominally by a Britain largely unaware that its intentions were quite so aggressive, was characterized for the purposes of Soviet military-economic planning in a memo of early 1930 by N. Snitko to his superior, the Chairman of the Defence Sector of Gosplan, the body responsible for Soviet economic planning. Three future international scenarios in which the Soviet Union would have to fight Western capitalist powers were considered possible:

DOCUMENT 6: *To the Chairman of the Defence Sector of Gosplan. Report on the character of future war and the tasks of the defence sector. N. Snitko, 4/IV-1930*

Political Situation
Variation in the political context of future war between the USSR and the encircling capitalist powers is likely only in the detail, with basically only three significantly different variants possible:

The first, where the imperialists, having agreed some sort of temporary compromise amongst themselves, organise an attack on the USSR with the aim of deciding by force of arms the basic contradiction of the modern world order – the co-existence of two fundamentally opposed economic systems....

The second, where the imperialists start a new world war amongst themselves. We may end up being dragged in to such a struggle either on the side of one of the coalitions, or, the most likely for us, as a third warring party, having both of the hostile coalitions fighting amongst themselves as opponents....

The third, is where the objective pace of developing relations between the USSR and the external capitalist economic world ends up in a situation where the further

> development of socialist society demands the expansion of its international reach.... The adequate development of the revolutionary movement in capitalist society, a sufficiently strong economic and political base and purely military preparation might place before us the question of a move towards a military offensive against capitalism in order to further world revolution.
>
> (Source: O.N. Ken, 2002, pp. 365–366)

The first scenario was the situation that the Soviet Union claimed was threatening in the late 1920s and early 1930s, requiring the strengthening of Soviet armed forces as a matter of some urgency. Whilst the British-led threat did not materialize in any tangible form, Japan was identified as a concrete threat in the Far East in the early 1930s, particularly after her invasion of Manchuria in 1931. However, the threat to Soviet security from Japan was not a major identifiable factor driving Soviet rearmament in general, although it was a factor stimulating Soviet naval development, including such major projects as the opening of the Northern Sea Route from the European north to the Far East.

Even with Adolf Hitler's coming to power in Germany in 1933, it was, according to the Russian historian Ken, not until the mid-1930s that Soviet defence planning at the highest levels was focused on a specific threat, that emerging from Nazi Germany, and to a lesser extent Japan, rather than an abstract 'capitalist' threat involving many possible combinations of powers but usually including Poland and Britain.[7]

Perhaps the most prominent single capital project of the First Five-Year Plan, with defence significance, was the Baltic–White Sea Canal. Whilst justifications for its construction in the Soviet press were largely economic, in private the Baltic–White Sea Canal had military strategic benefits, which had been identified by Tsarist planners. These benefits were identified in materials of the Council of People's Commissars when the construction of the canal was being planned:

> DOCUMENT 7: *Preparatory Materials of the Council of People's Commissars of the USSR, 'Towards a justification for the construction* [obosnovaniiu sooruzheniia] *of the Baltic–White Sea Canal', no later than May 1930*
>
> I. Composition [*sostav*] and purpose of the waterway
> The route of the Baltic–White Sea Waterway: Port of Leningrad, River Neva, Lake Ladoga, River Svir', Lake Onega and the Onega–White Sea Canal, breaking through to the White Sea at Soroka Bay.
> Overall length of the waterway 906 km.
> The Baltic-White Sea Waterway ... is designed for the passage of ocean-going, lake and river vessels, with a maximum draught of 5.5 m (18 feet).
> The creation of this waterway provides:
>
> II. In military-strategic terms:
> The solution of a range of issues in the defence of the coastline from the Finnish border up to the coastline of Siberia accessible by sea, including the White Sea.

> The defence of the fishing industry in coastal waters and coastal commerce between points along the coastline and river shipping routes into the heart of the country. This task is to be achieved in the Northern Theatre, primarily through the ability to transfer submarines and surface torpedo craft and cruisers from the Baltic to the White Sea.
>
> The potential for our naval forces to operate on enemy lines of maritime communication ... in the North Sea and eastern portion of the Atlantic Ocean.
>
> The maintenance of our lines of communication with the outside world. Since the Baltic and Black Seas are easily blockaded, free access to the ocean via the north would acquire particularly great significance in wartime.
> ...
>
> (Source: A.F. Kiselev and E.M. Shchagin, 1996, pp. 395–396)

The construction of the Baltic–White Sea Canal, for which planning was underway in 1930 and construction completed in 1933, was primarily aimed at security against Britain. Providing 'the solution of a range of issues in the defence of the coastline from the Finnish border up to the coastline of Siberia accessible by sea, including the White Sea', almost certainly bore in mind the British attack on the naval base at Kronstadt and occupation of Arkhangel'sk during the Russian Civil War. In considering 'the defence of the fishing industry in coastal waters and coastal commerce between points along the coastline and river shipping routes into the heart of the country', fishing disputes with Britain in the far north during the 1920s and British forays down the River Dvina during the Civil War were most probably at the forefront of the minds of Soviet planners.

The Baltic–White Sea Canal was, as the Five-Year Plans themselves, a major achievement, albeit one at the expense of many human lives as Gulag labour was used for much of the new construction. However, as the Five-Year Plans as a whole, success was not as significant as the propaganda suggested. The military utility of the canal was certainly not as great as the Soviet Navy had hoped, its limitations being noted by the British naval attaché in Moscow in early 1937:

> The direct transfer of the Baltic Fleet or part of its heavy forces from the Gulf of Finland to the northern open seas and *vice versa* would be of obvious strategic importance. The Kiel Canal can play the same role for Germany, ... but the White Sea Canal and its river system cannot do the same for the Soviet Union. ... Owing to ice conditions this route is not available in the winter months, and during the ice-free period the very maximum which the canal can safely transport is a large type submarine or destroyer. For a larger type, such as the flotilla-leader *Leningrad*, the locks may just have the requisite length and beam, but I doubt it; the question of draught, however, would be the real obstacle. The draught difficulty to some degree might be met in an emergency by the employment of some kind of floating dock specially constructed for the canal.[8]

National socialism and collective security

During the 1920s and early 1930s the Soviet Union had to some extent been a pariah state in Europe. She did not, for instance, participate in the League of Nations, forerunner of the United Nations and founded in 1919, and maintained closer links with other pariah powers than the 'victors' of the First World War. Hence through the Rapallo Treaty of 1922 the Soviet Union and Germany co-operated not only politically and economically but also militarily, sharing hostility to the Anglo-French alliance that had seen both stripped of territory, and hostility to Poland, the key beneficiary of their losses. The Soviet Union was also on sufficiently good terms with Mussolini's Italy to seek Italian assistance in the construction of a new generation of destroyers for Soviet naval forces in the early 1930s, developing relations in this sphere extending back to 1925 and culminating in the Italian construction of the flotilla-leader *Tashkent* for Soviet naval forces, handed over incomplete to the Soviet Union in 1939, and Italian assistance in the construction of Type 7-series destroyers.[9]

The rise of National Socialism in Germany prompted a reorientation of Soviet diplomatic activity towards what appeared to be conciliation with the non-fascist capitalist powers, with the Soviet Union joining the League of Nations in September 1934. At the same time the Soviet Union sought security agreements with those capitalist powers that themselves felt most threatened by the re-emergent German threat, namely France and the young Czechoslovakia, with whom the Soviet Union signed mutual-assistance pacts in 1935. Just how far these pacts were supposed to go was, however, a matter for disagreement. For the French, and indeed British, such agreements were part of the post-Versailles international system, the web of agreements and pacts that were supposed to limit German ambitions much more cheaply than the rearmament required to add credibility to substantial and hopefully unnecessary commitments, along the lines of which the Soviet Union was seeking. Differing views on the scope and purpose of such pacts, as well as the strength of anti-Soviet feeling in French conservative circles, influenced the time it took France and the Soviet Union to actually sign the mutual-assistance pact of May 1935, without many of the add-ons such as military assistance to the Red Army that had been discussed during negotiations. That the pact was signed at all had much to do with Hitler's words and actions making it increasingly difficult not to sign. The new French Foreign Minister Laval was certainly more interested in strengthening his hand in negotiations with Germany than an agreement with the Soviet Union that might lead to significant rearmament, military action and bloodshed.[10]

During the mid-1930s, whilst her rearmament progressed at an increasing pace, the Soviet Union has been seen by most Western, Soviet and post-Soviet Russian historians to have been genuinely seeking some sort of 'collective security' from a re-emergent Germany, be it as a short-term measure or otherwise. Key proponents of this line in one form or another in the West include A.J.P. Taylor, Jonathan Haslam, Geoffrey Roberts and, perhaps most vociferously by virtue of his contrasting of genuine Soviet efforts with British ideologically motivated intransigence, Michael Carley.[11] Through 'collective' efforts the further spread of fascism in Europe was to be prevented, and foreign Communist parties were instructed by the Soviet-led Comintern to work with the 'Social Democrats' in the European democracies in order to defeat the electoral threat from fascist parties, engaging in 'popular front' politics against the right. This can be contrasted with the situation in 1933 when Hitler came to power in Germany and when German Communist hostility towards the moderate socialists had been encouraged.

In the introduction to his 1995 *The Soviet Union and the Origins of the Second World War*, Geoffrey Roberts identifies a 'German' school of historians offering an opposing line to those identifying sincere Soviet attempts to secure 'collective security'.[12] These historians, the most prominent of whom is arguably Hochman, see the eventual Soviet signing of the Nazi–Soviet Pact in 1939 as the result of a pro-German orientation, designed in part to divide the capitalist West, continuing on from Rapallo despite the rise of Hitler and behind the smokescreen of the quest for 'collective security'. This line is, however, very much a product of the Cold War and receives even less support amongst academics today than it did in 1995, despite the publication in 1997 of the veteran exiled Soviet historian Alexander Nekrich's *Pariahs, Partners, Predators*, very much part of this school.[13] Although the 'German' school receives little support from established historians, it is widely accepted that, given the mutual suspicion between the Soviet Union and the capitalist powers, British, French and Soviet leaders understandably did not rule out some sort of 'coming to terms' with Nazi Germany if it was in their perceived interests, that is delaying or preventing war. Despite the input of ideologues on both sides, the leanings of diplomats towards one or the other alternative need not have been due to ideological disposition or some sort of grand scheme, but pragmatic assessment of the likelihood of peace and stability being preserved in Europe, something both the Soviet Union and the Anglo-French 'bloc' were seeking, at least in the short term.

Soviet pragmatism in the pursuit of short-term security, set in the broader ideological context of the inevitable clash between capitalism and communism, is emphasized by Pons in *Stalin and the Inevitable War 1936–1941*.[14] His work represents something of a compromise between the 'German' and 'collective security' schools that can be termed the 'realist' school, incorporating a range of compromise positions. Pons, however, places considerable emphasis on the longer-term expansionist dimension to Soviet foreign policy, a tendency motivated by a fusion of Communist ideology and the Soviet Union's pre-Versailles Tsarist heritage, something apparent in Document 5. Certainly, as Ferris notes, to talk of a 'realist' school that does not consider ideology is nonsense in most instances, given that very few statesmen are psychopaths genuinely intent on power for its own sake. As he goes on to note, the noun 'realism' has to be combined with an adjective, be it 'Marxist-Leninist', or indeed 'Stalinist' in the case of the Soviet Union under Stalin.[15] The diplomatic confusion and misunderstanding created in negotiations with Britain and France by the pragmatic Soviet advancement of foreign policy goals informed by the heady ideological brew of the Stalinist international outlook is highlighted by Neilson. Both Britain and France were committed to the post-Versailles order and had foreign policies that varied as a result of Western pluralism, a very different motor to their foreign policies from that of the Soviet Union, making understanding and agreement between them and the Soviet Union difficult at best.[16]

Despite genuine Soviet efforts to promote 'collective security', something not in conflict with the notion of 'inevitable war' if seen as a short-to-medium term measure, with the threat of military action against a non-compliant Germany being anathema to Britain and France, the Western powers were more inclined towards appeasement of German and indeed Italian ambitions. Many among British Conservatives and on the French right were ultimately as, if not more, fearful of Bolshevism as National Socialism, the apparent aims of which many in Britain at least sympathized with. German re-occupation of the Rhineland in March 1936 passed with barely a murmur from the British, taking place behind the smokescreen of the Italian invasion of Abyssinia in October 1935, itself only provoking half-hearted sanctions from the League of Nations. After the outbreak of the Spanish Civil War in July 1936, Britain and France proved willing to tolerate flagrant German and Italian intervention on the side of Franco in the Spanish Civil War, towards whom there was considerable sympathy on the right in Britain. Soviet unwillingness to wholeheartedly support the left in Spain was to a significant extent in order to prevent a rift with these powers, particularly France, which would threaten the alliances that were designed to protect the Soviet Union from German ambitions in the east and prevent the emergence of an alliance between fascist and other capitalist powers against the Soviet Union.

The value of the Soviet Union's mutual-assistance treaties would be put to the test in September 1938, when, following on from the Anschluß with Austria of March 1938, Hitler sought the Sudeten border region of the young Czechoslovakia at the conference table in Munich, to which the Soviet Union was not invited. The Soviet Union had also not been invited to participate fully in other key international conferences of the 1930s, for instance the London Naval Conference of December 1935–March 1936. Whether this was because the Soviet Union was not taken seriously as a major European and particularly naval power or because she remained a political pariah to European conservatives is, from a Soviet perspective and in the context of the current discussion, less important than the fact that the Soviet leadership once again could claim to have been sidelined by Britain and France. The Soviet Union was understandably increasingly sceptical of the scope for Anglo-French commitment to a tripartite stand against German ambitions.

The Munich crisis and the Nazi–Soviet Pact

British and French appeasement of Hitler at Munich led not only to German acquisition of the Sudetenland but also the remainder of Czechoslovakia in March 1939, including her substantial arms industry. Prime Minister Chamberlain's vacillation in taking action could not help maintain Soviet confidence in an effective Anglo-French and Soviet alliance emerging against Hitler's ambitions. The Soviet Union could, with good reason, suspect that Hitler's attentions were being directed eastwards and towards her borders. Nonetheless, the Soviet Union was herself less than enthusiastic about intervention, and certainly unilaterally. Whilst Soviet forces in Western border regions were mobilized during the Munich crisis, there is little evidence they were being readied for offensive action of any sort. According to Steiner, even if the Czechoslovaks had made a stand, significant Soviet support could not have been relied upon on the ground, with which Ragsdale agrees, although, as he notes, serious preparations seem to have been made to provide air support to Czechoslovakia in late September.[17]

It remains unclear what degree of Western support would have been required for the Soviet Union to commit to military action, significant stumbling blocks being Soviet relations with Poland and Rumania. Any attack on Germany on the ground would have had to have been through a hostile Poland and Rumania; the former would not countenance the transit of Soviet forces through its territory lest they remain there indefinitely – the Soviet invasion of Poland of 1920 was still a recent event. Poland also had designs on Czechoslovak territory. Rumania's position was less obvious, but her poor transport network made her less desirable as a transit link to Czechoslovakia anyway. The Soviet Union had not worked hard in the longer term on trying to improve relations with either the Poles or Rumanians, whom her regional policy was geared to undermine, giving some credibility to Hochman's argument that the Soviet Union shares at least some responsibility for the failure of 'collective security' leading up to the German occupation of Czechoslovakia.

A second issue restraining the Soviet Union from action against Germany in late 1938 or indeed early 1939 was the fact that the Red Army was in a state of turmoil, undergoing a massive enlargement after having suffered the loss of experienced cadres during the Great Purges of 1936–38. Some indication of the damage done to the Soviet armed forces during the Great Purges and towards the Axis invasion of the Soviet Union is provided in Table 1.2, detailing damage done to upper command elements.

The damage caused by the Great Purges to the Soviet armed forces was a significant factor in low estimations of Soviet military capabilities by the

Table 1.2 The destruction of the upper echelons of the RKKA in 1937–41

Category	Number serving in 1936	Shot	Died in captivity	Suicide	Returned from captivity alive	% of those serving in 1936 killed
Marshals of the Soviet Union	5	2	1	–	–	60
Army commanders (1st and 2nd Rank)	15	19	–	–	1	133
Flag Officer of the Fleet (1st and 2nd Rank)	4	5	–	–	–	125
Corps commanders	62	58	4	2	5	112.6
Flag Officer (1st Rank)	6	5	–	–	1	100
Divisional commanders	201	122	9	–	22	76
Brigade commanders	474	201	15	1	30	52.1
Total	767	412	29	3	59	65.6

Source: O.F. Suvenirov, *Tragediia RKKA 1937–1938* (Moscow: Terra, 1998), p. 315.

Western powers at the time of the Munich crisis, being an additional reason or justification for dismissing the value of Soviet participation in any deterrent activity against Germany. The Great Purges were most probably launched in 1936–38, as the Russian historian Khlevniuk argues, as a result of the international situation.[18] Whilst identification of internal opposition was nothing new, dealing with it was now more urgent with war looming, during which such elements might destabilize the Soviet rear and threaten Stalin's position.

For the Soviet Union, particularly after Munich, it was crucial to buy time to prepare for an inevitable clash with Nazi Germany. British and French guarantees to Poland of March and indeed Rumania of April 1939 were understandably seen as of little significance to Soviet defence given Anglo-French inactivity over Czechoslovakia, and in part because Poland was seen as a potential German ally and hostile to the Soviet Union. At the same time, Britain and France were justifiably seen as unenthusiastic about reaching agreement with the Soviet Union on dealing with the German threat during negotiations in the spring and summer of 1939. It is in the context of diplomatic failure at the time of the Munich crisis of 1938, a centralization of control over foreign policy and British and French lack of enthusiasm for agreement with the Soviet Union that the removal of the pro-Western Commissar for Foreign Affairs, Litvinov, in May 1939 should be seen. His replacement by Molotov might have signalled to Germany that the Soviet Union was more receptive to new proposals to pursuit of 'collective security' with Britain and France, but did not mean a fundamental shift in policy and rule out agreement with Britain and France.[19]

Whilst the British had been dismissive of Soviet overtures in the spring of 1939, they became more willing to enter into negotiations as the threat of war became more serious during the summer. However, the issue of the transit of Soviet troops through Poland or indeed Rumania remained, and which the British and French were reticent to sanction without Polish and Rumanian agreement. Voroshilov, the Soviet Commissar for War, would subsequently lay the blame for the failure to halt Nazi aggression with Czechoslovakia with the British, French and Poles, stating in an interview at the end of August 1939, that:

> The Soviet military mission thought that the USSR, having no common frontier with the aggressor, could come to the help of France, England or Poland only if its troops were allowed to pass through Polish territory, for there is no other way to come into contact with the troops of the aggressor.[20]

Although it is completely obvious that this attitude was correct, the French and British military missions did not agree with the Soviet mission in this, while the Polish government openly stated that it did not need and would not accept military aid from the USSR. This circumstance made military co-operation between the USSR and these countries impossible.

At the same time it was apparent to Soviet negotiators that the British and French were still not in any hurry to reach agreement. As Taylor noted in his 1961 *The Origins of the Second World War*:

> The diplomatic exchange shows that delays came from the West and the Soviet government answered with almost breathtaking speed. The British made their first tentative suggestion on 15 April; the Soviet counter-proposal came two days later, on 17 April. The British took three weeks before designing an answer on 9 May; the Soviet delay was then five days.... Thereafter the pace quickened. The British tried again in five days' time; the Soviet answer came within twenty-four hours.... If dates mean anything, the British were spinning things out, the Russians were anxious to conclude. There is other evidence that the British treated negotiations in a casual way, more to placate public opinion than to achieve anything.[21]

At the same time Soviet negotiators noted that the British and French had no grand strategic plan for war against Germany, not surprising given that British and French intentions were to take measures to avoid war well in advance and to prevent the need for anything more than the most abstract planning for it. Both were rearming, but deterrence was the principal purpose of such efforts. The 'Maginot' mentality that indeed dominated during the 'Phoney War' of late 1939 and early 1940 would, it apparently seemed to Soviet observers, be likely to prevent significant Anglo-French moves against Germany even in the event of war. For a Soviet Union not deemed prepared for the inevitable war either by foreign observers or internally, a remaining option was to come to terms with Germany.

The Nazi–Soviet or Molotov–Ribbentrop Pact of August 1939 would result in the two powers dismembering Poland, the Soviet Union providing Germany with significant raw materials and even with very limited assistance in the war against Britain and France in order to shift German attentions to the West and away from the Soviet Union.[22] The second possible international scenario identified by Soviet planners in 1930 was 'where the imperialists start a new world war amongst themselves', a situation Stalin was now very much encouraging.[23] At the same time as directing German attention to the West, against whom she would most probably become embroiled in a protracted war, the Soviet Union would be free to expand her borders in what was deemed by the pact and subsequent additions as her sphere of influence.

The purpose of this expansion was subsequently argued by Soviet historians to be the provision of a defensive buffer zone between Germany and Soviet territory of 1939.[24] This argument was certainly consistent with Stalin's constant harking back to the Civil War in discussions on contemporary defence matters.[25] It does seem that the intention of negotiations with Finland prior to the Soviet invasion of November 1939 was to prevent her being the eventual launchpad for German invasion, with the Soviet regime being only too aware of the historical precedent for this to occur after the landing of German troops in Finland in February 1918 and threat to Petrograd had hastened the signing of the Treaty of Brest-Litovsk:

DOCUMENT 8: *To the Finnish government, from the government of the USSR, 14 October 1939*

In the negotiations with Finland, the Soviet Union is primarily concerned with the settling of two questions:

Securing the safety of Leningrad;

Becoming satisfied that Finland will have firm, friendly relations with the Soviet Union.

Both points are essential for the purpose of preserving the integrity of the Soviet Union against external hostile aggression....

In order to fulfil this duty it is necessary:

To make it possible to block the opening of the Gulf of Finland by means of artillery fire from both coasts of the Gulf of Finland ...;

To make it possible to prevent the access of the enemy to those islands in the Gulf of Finland which are situated west and north-west of the entrance to Leningrad;

To have the Finnish frontier on the Isthmus of Karelia, a frontier which is currently at a distance of 32 kilometres from Leningrad – i.e. within the range of shots from a long-distance gun – moved somewhat further northwards and westwards.

The question of the Ribachii and Srednii Peninsulas is a special case, where the frontier is unskilfully and artificially drawn and has to be adjusted in accordance with the annexed map....

[To be achieved by:]

> Leasing to the Soviet Union for a period of thirty years the port of Hango....
> Granting to the naval forces of the Soviet Union the right of using Lappohja Bay as an anchorage.
> Ceding to the Soviet Union, in exchange for other territories, the following territories: The islands,... part of the Isthmus of Karelia from the village of Lippola to the southern border of the town of Koivisto, and the western parts of the Ribachii and Srednii Peninsulas – in total 2,761 square kilometres, in accordance with the annexed map.
> In exchange for the territories mentioned in paragraph 3, the Soviet Union cedes to the Republic of Finland Soviet territory of the districts of Repola and Porajärvi to the extent of 5,529 square kilometres, in accordance with the annexed map.
>
> (Source: A.F. Kiselev and E.M. Shchagin, 1996, pp. 483–484)

The occupations of Latvia, Lithuania and Estonia during the summer of 1940 were similarly justified by Soviet security concerns, an argument perhaps given more credibility by the success of German operations in France.

However, the Soviet Union was not beyond opportunistic expansion, an accusation appropriately applied to the Soviet acquisition of Bessarabia and northern Bukovina from Rumania in June 1940. Indeed, the same might be said of evidence of Soviet intentions in late 1939 to prosecute the war against Finland to the point that Finland could be brought under Soviet control, perhaps in a similar manner to the Soviet takeovers in the Baltic Republics. The Soviet Union had most certainly not given up on the idea of spreading 'revolution' across Europe through force of arms – a task likely to be easier if the capitalist powers were fighting or had fought amongst themselves. Indeed, the third scenario identified in the planning memo of 1930 was for a situation where there was the prospect of the Soviet Union pursuing the never-forgotten international 'revolution', from a position of relative strength, where

> the adequate development of the revolutionary movement in capitalist society, a sufficiently strong economic and political base and purely military preparation might place before us the question of a move towards a military offensive against capitalism in order to further world revolution.[26]

Guide to further reading

Foreign relations

M.J. Carley, 'Behind Stalin's Moustache: Pragmatism in Early Soviet Foreign Policy, 1917–1941', *Diplomacy and Statecraft*, Volume 12, Number 3 (September 2001), pp. 159–174.

J. Haslam, *The Soviet Union and the Struggle for Collective Security in Europe, 1933–39* (London: Macmillan Press Ltd, 1984).

J. Hochman, *The Soviet Union and the Failure of Collective Security, 1934–1938* (Ithaca, NY: Cornell University Press, 1984).

Silvio Pons, *Stalin and the Inevitable War 1936–1941* (London: Frank Cass, 2002).
Hugh Ragsdale, *The Soviets, the Munich Crisis, and the Coming of World War II* (New York: Cambridge University Press, 2004).
G. Roberts, *The Soviet Union and the Origins of the Second World War: Russo-German Relations and the Road to War, 1933–1941* (London: Macmillan Press Ltd, 1995).
Zara Steiner, 'The Soviet Commissariat of Foreign Affairs and the Czechoslovakian Crisis in 1938: New Material from the Soviet Archives', *Historical Journal*, Volume 42, Number 3 (1999), pp. 751–779.

Military-industrial development and planning

Gunnar Åselius, 'The Naval Theaters in Soviet Grand Strategy during the Interwar Period', *JSMS*, Volume 13, Number 1 (March 2000), pp. 68–89.
Mark Harrison, *Soviet Planning in Peace and War 1938–1945* (Cambridge: Cambridge University Press, 1985).
Alexander Hill, 'Russian and Soviet Naval Power in the Arctic from the XVI Century to the Beginning of the Great Patriotic War', *JSMS*, Volume 20, Number 3 (July–September 2007), pp. 359–392.
L. Samuelson, 'Mikhail Tukhachevsky and War-Economic Planning: Reconsiderations on the Pre-War Soviet Military Build-Up', *JSMS*, Volume 9, Number 4 (December 1996), pp. 804–847.
L. Samuelson, *Plans for Stalin's War Machine – Tukhachevskii and Military Economic Planning 1925–1941* (Basingstoke: Palgrave, 2000).
N.S. Simonov, ' "Strengthen the Defence of the Land of the Soviets": The 1927 "War Alarm" and its Consequences', *Europe–Asia Studies*, Volume 48, Number 8 (1996), pp. 1355–1364.
David Stone, *Hammer and Rifle – The Militarization of the SU 1926–1933* (Lawrence, KS: University Press of Kansas, 2000).
David Stone, 'The First Five-Year Plan and the Geography of the Soviet Defence Industry', *Europe–Asia Studies*, Volume 57, Number 7 (2005), pp. 1047–1063.

The Red Army

Mary R. Habeck, *Storm of Steel: The Development of Armor Doctrine in Germany and the Soviet Union, 1919–1939* (Ithaca, NY: Cornell University Press, 2003).
Mark von Hagen, *Soldiers in the Proletarian Dictatorship: The Red Army and the Soviet Socialist State, 1917–1930* (Ithaca, NY: Cornell University Press, 1990).
Roger Reese, *Stalin's Reluctant Soldiers: A Social History of the Red Army, 1925–1941* (Lawrence, KS: University Press of Kansas, 1996).

The great purges and the Soviet armed forces

Gunnar Åselius, *The Rise and Fall of the Soviet Navy in the Baltic, 1921–1941* (London: Frank Cass, 2005).
O. Khlevniuk, 'The Objectives of the Great Terror, 1937–38', in D.L. Hoffmann (ed.), *Stalinism: The Essential Readings* (Malden, MA.: Blackwell Publishing, 2003) and in J. Cooper, M. Perrie and E.A. Rees (eds), *Soviet History 1917–1953: Essays in Honour of R.W. Davies* (New York: St Martin's Press, 1995).
V.S. Mil'bach, 'Repression in the 57th Special Corps (Mongolian People's Republic)', *JSMS*, Volume 15, Number 1 (March 2002), pp. 91–122.
V.S. Mil'bach, 'Repression in the Red Army in the Far East, 1936–1939', *JSMS*, Volume 16, Number 4 (December 2003), pp. 58–130.
V.S. Mil'bach, 'Political Repression of the Pacific Ocean Fleet Commanders and Chiefs in 1936–1939', *JSMS*, Volume 21, Number 1 (January–March 2008), pp. 53–112.
Roger Reese, *Stalin's Reluctant Soldiers: A Social History of the Red Army, 1925–1941* (Lawrence, KS: University Press of Kansas, 1996), Chapter 5.

2 The Icebreaker controversy and Soviet intentions in 1941[1]

During the second half of 1940 and early 1941, with Nazi Germany at the height of its power, the Soviet Union was in the middle of the third, and the most obviously defence-oriented, Five-Year Plan, due to be completed in 1942. The Second Five-Year Plan had seen considerable investment in defence; figures for the production of weapons and weapons systems for 1937 and 1938 are provided in Table 2.1 which can be compared to figures in Table 1.1 for 1929/30 and 1930/31 at the beginning of Chapter 1. Continued increases in production of key weapons systems such as tanks were achieved in 1939 and 1940, for which figures are provided in Table 2.2.

The immediate likelihood of the Soviet Union taking pre-emptive offensive action against Nazi Germany or more broadly against capitalist Europe was made less likely than it otherwise might have been after the poor performance of the Red Army during the Soviet invasion of Eastern Poland in September 1939, and the subsequent invasion of Finland in November 1939, during which the Red Army had suffered horrendous losses against a poorly equipped, albeit in Karelia, well-fortified Finnish opponent. Table 2.3 gives details of Soviet losses during the war with Finland from 30 November to 13 March 1940.

Table 2.1 Soviet orders for and production of key armaments 1937–38

Product	1937			1938		
	Plan	Actual	% plan	Plan	Actual	% plan
Artillery pieces	6,417	5,443	84.8	13,813	12,687	91.8
Artillery shells (1,000s)	8,855	4,924	55.6	16,065	12,426	77.3
Rifles (1,000s)	650	567	87.2	1,155	1,171	101.3
Machine guns	76,182	74,657	78.9	126,799	112,010	88.3
Cartridges (millions)	1,285	1,015	78.9	2,500	1,848	73.9
Aircraft	4,896	4,435	90.6	7,500	5,469	72.9
Tanks	2,030	1,559	76.8	2,375	2,271	95.6

Source: N.S. Simonov, *Voenno-promishlennii kompleks SSSR v 1920–1950-e godi*, p. 112.

Table 2.2 Soviet orders for and production of key armaments 1939–40

Product	1939			1940		
	Plan	Actual	% plan	Plan	Actual	% plan
Artillery pieces	19,620	16,459	83.8	8,266	13,724	166.0
Artillery shells (1,000s)	25,095	18,099	72.1	22,195	14,921	67.2
Rifles (1,000s)	1,920	1,497	77.9	1,986	1,461	73.5
Machine guns	115,881	96,433	83.2	46,000	No data	No data
Cartridges (millions)	2,160	2,194	101.5	3,143	2,820	89.7
Aircraft	9,091	10,758	118.3	13,864	10,565	76.2
Tanks	3,278	2,986	91.1	3,370	2,790	82.7

Source: N.S. Simonov, *Voenno-promishlennii kompleks SSSR v 1920–1950-e godi*, p. 129.

Table 2.3 Soviet irrecoverable losses in the Russo-Finnish War

Category	Commanders	NCOs	Ranks	Rank unknown	Total
Killed or died during evacuation	6,000	9,611	54,215	1,388	72,214
Died in hospital of wounds or disease	802	1,436	12,185	1,869	16,292
Missing in action	1,010	2,998	33,827	1,534	39,369
Total	7,812	14,045	100,227	4,791	126,875

Source: G.F. Krivosheev (ed.), *Soviet Casualties and Combat Losses in the Twentieth Century* (London: Greenhill Books, 1997), p. 77.

Such dismal Soviet performance during the initial stages of her invasion of Finland, bringing the Soviet Union the diplomatic embarrassment of expulsion from the League of Nations for her aggression, encouraged the German development of plans for the invasion of the Soviet Union in the summer of 1941. Whilst Anglo-French intervention in Finland did not materialize before the Finns had sued for peace with the Soviet Union in March 1940 and Germany had subsequently invaded Norway in April, preliminary British and French planning for such an operation was carried out, with the landing of French mountain or Polish troops at Petsamo being discussed.[2] Had such an operation taken place, it would have further complicated the diplomatic and strategic situation in Europe, with the prospect of the Nazi–Soviet Pact leading to joint military activities by the Soviet Union and Germany against Britain and France!

Red Army failings in Poland and Finland came under considerable scrutiny in the Soviet Union. One ramification of this Soviet military experience was to strengthen the position of what could now be called the officer corps vis-à-vis the ranks. Soviet ranks, such as brigade commander [*kombrig*] gave way to traditional officer's titles. There was also a move away from dual command in the Red Army, where the decisions of military officers were subject to political scrutiny from commissars, something bad for officer morale, given that officers were deemed the specialists in military affairs, and unhelpful in their fostering of authority in a unit. On 12 August 1940 dual command, having been reintroduced in 1937, gave way once more to unitary command:

DOCUMENT 9: *On the Reinforcing of Unitary Command in the Red Army and Navy. Decree of the Presidium of the Supreme Soviet of the USSR, 12 August 1940*

As a result of the institute of commissars having already fulfilled its basic purposes, that is the command cadres of the Red Army and Navy have in the last few years been strengthened, and at the same time with the aims of bringing about full unitary command and the future raising of the authority of the commander — the fully empowered leader of forces, carrying in the same way full responsibility for political work in units — the Presidium of the Supreme Soviet of the USSR decrees:

Rescind 'The situation regarding military commissars of the Workers' and Peasants' Red Army', ratified by the Central Executive Committee and Council of Peoples' Commissars of the USSR of 15 August 1937 No. 105/1387.

Bring in to units (corps, divisions, brigades),... ships,... military-educational institutions and establishments of the Red Army and Navy the institute of deputy commanders (heads) of political departments.

Require military soviets of military districts, *fronts* and armies to carry out the daily and active supervision of political work in corps, divisions and brigades.

Chairman of the Presidium of the Supreme Soviet of the USSR, M. Kalinin
Secretary of the Presidium of the Supreme Soviet of the USSR, A. Gorkin
Moscow, the Kremlin, 12 August 1940.

(Source: *KPSS o Vooruzhennikh Silakh Sovetskogo Soiuza*, 1981, pp. 289–290)

Whilst steps were being taken to improve the authority of officers, Soviet military experience in the war against Finland and the war in the West had to be analysed and conclusions applied to the development of Soviet armed forces. This experience was the subject of a conference of the upper elements of the leadership of the Red Army in December 1940. Summing up at the end of the conference, Marshal of the Soviet Union Timoshenko pointed out some of the key conclusions drawn:

DOCUMENT 10: *Closing speech of Marshal of the Soviet Union S.K. Timoshenko at a conference of the upper elements of the leadership of the Red Army, no later than 31 December 1940*

Experience of the most recent wars and especially the Western-European war of 1939–1940 shows that in the sphere of military art substantial shifts are taking place.
...

> The principal conclusion to be drawn is:
> The high speed of an operation is the decisive condition for the success of the operation.
> The high speed of an operation is provided for by the mass use of motorized units and aviation, used to strike the initial blow and for the uninterrupted deep development of the strike.
> The decisive impact of aviation is achieved not through raids deep in the rear, but in co-operation in the actions of forces on the battlefield, at divisional and army level.
> ...
> The experience of war shows, that contemporary defence cannot be limited to a single tactical zone of resistance, and that against new deep methods of breakthrough second and perhaps third operational echelons, made up of operational reserves, special anti-tank units and other means are required, operating from prepared rear-area defensive anti-tank zones or defensive positions.
> ...
> The fullest expression of the character of contemporary defence is found within the bounds of army-level defensive operations.
> ...
> The contemporary [offensive] operation most fully develops at *front* level.
> It is conducted with the strength of a number of armies in co-ordination with mobile groups, with strong close air support, and in specific circumstances naval forces.
> ...
> The most important task of the command and headquarters of armies and *fronts* is the creation of overwhelming superiority of force on the main axis of attack....
> The breaching of enemy lines has raised the question of the co-ordination of infantry, aviation, armour and artillery....
> [Timoshenko went on to highlight the weakness of Soviet training, a major stumbling block in increasing the effectives of Soviet forces:]
> War against the White Finns revealed the ruinous state of our system of military training.... Our commanders and headquarters ... were unable to genuinely command.
> ...
> We have to openly and honestly admit, that work to reorganise the training system ... demands a considerable period of time and persistent efforts.
> (Source: *RA T.12 (1)*, 1993, pp. 338, 340–341, 343, 349, 359, 363)

Such conclusions fed in to reorganization, rearmament and training that were far from complete in the summer of 1941. Soviet performance against Japan at Khalkin-Gol in Manchuria in August 1939 had, however, been more encouraging; along with their commitments in China, it encouraged the Japanese decision to restrict their ambitions in the region, culminating in the Soviet–Japanese non-aggression treaty of April 1941.

By mid-June 1941 the Red Army was, at least superficially on paper, an impressive force. Prior to the German attack a considerable proportion of its forces were massed on the Soviet–German border, with a second echelon moving into position, for what reason is not entirely clear. With the focus of

Soviet military doctrine by this stage focused very much on the offensive and her eastern front ostensibly a little more secure than it had been at the beginning of the year, it is easy to see how it could be suggested that the Soviet Union was massing forces for an attack, be it aimed at pre-empting the now-delayed German invasion of the Soviet Union or part of longer-term preparations for the third pre-war scenario mentioned above.

The argument that the Soviet Union was intending to attack Germany in July 1941, as presented by the Soviet defector writing under the pseudonym Viktor Suvorov in the mid-1980s, started a significant debate on Soviet intentions in 1941 and beyond in Germany and the Soviet successor states, particularly Russia, which only later received significant attention in the Anglo-Saxon world. According to Suvorov, in his first article on the subject in 1985, a TASS report of 13 June 1941, which sought to dispel rumours of an imminent German attack on the Soviet Union, was a desperate attempt to cover Soviet preparations for military action against Germany in July, for which Soviet forces were moving into position and which was in full accordance with the offensive thrust of Soviet military doctrine.[3] His subsequent work, largely only available in Russian, has to a large extent been geared to elaborating on this thesis.[4] Suvorov has at times presented interesting though poorly thought out or linked snippets of information suggesting that the Soviet Union had been engaged in longer-term preparation for this invasion of Europe during the 1930s, culminating, in his view, in moves in the summer of 1941. Extracts from the TASS report of 13 June are provided below:

DOCUMENT 11: *TASS communiqué – Soviet denial of reported disagreements between the USSR and Germany, 13 June 1941, published in* Izvestia, *14 June 1941*

Even before the arrival of Sir Stafford Cripps, English ambassador to the USSR, in London, and especially after his arrival, rumours began to appear in the English and foreign press more broadly about the 'proximity of war between the Soviet Union and Germany'....

Although these rumours are obviously absurd, responsible circles in Moscow have all the same considered it necessary in view of the constant repetition of these propaganda rumours spread by forces hostile to the Soviet Union and Germany, forces interested in the further expansion and spreading of the war, to authorize TASS to state that they are clumsy fabrications.

TASS states that:

...

2. According to Soviet data, Germany, like the USSR, is also strictly observing the stipulations of the Soviet-German non-aggression pact, and therefore, in the opinion of Soviet circles, rumours of Germany's intention to break the pact and open an attack on the USSR are devoid of all foundation; the recent transfer of German troops, freed from operations in the Balkans, to the eastern and north-eastern regions of Germany is, it must be assumed, connected with other reasons which have no bearing on Soviet-German relations;

3. The USSR, consistently with its policy of peace, has observed and intends to observe the provisions of the Soviet-German non-aggression pact, and therefore rumours that the USSR is preparing for war with Germany are lies and provocations;

4. The sole purpose of the summer call-up of Red Army reserves and forthcoming exercises is in the training of the reserves and the testing of the railway system which, as is known, takes place each year.

(Source: V.P. Naumov, 1998, p. 361)

Suvorov's argument had considerable appeal to revisionist historians in post-Soviet Russia, who were more than willing to adopt an argument running counter to the Soviet image of the Soviet Union desperately seeking to preserve peace. It also appealed to right-wing German historians such as Joachim Hoffmann, who could present the German invasion of the Soviet Union as a preventative strike.[5] Suvorov's argument was rapidly countered by much of the established Russian historical community, with the support of Western historians such as Gorodetsky on the diplomatic front and Glantz on military issues. Glantz showed in *Stumbling Colossus* that the Soviet Union was actually in no position to attack Germany in June 1941, with Soviet forces for instance lacking the logistical capabilities for offensive operations against German forces.[6]

Certainly, in late 1940, when the leadership elements of the Soviet armed forces were considering the war in the West to date, the Red Army was not deemed ready for offensive operations against a major European power. General K.A. Meretskov's opening paragraphs to his contribution to the conference of the upper elements of the leadership of the Red Army in December 1940, from which Document 12 is taken, stress the need to continue to improve the strength of the Soviet armed forces, albeit in the 'shortest possible time':

DOCUMENT 12: 'Results and tasks of military preparation of the ground forces, VVS and operational preparation of the officer corps': General K.A. Meretskov's introduction to a conference of the upper elements of the leadership of the Red Army, no later than 24 December 1940

1939 and 1940 have passed by leaving a complex international situation. The majority of peoples of the world have been dragged into a large-scale and difficult war by the imperialists. . . .

At the same time, . . . our great people, under the leadership of the great leader [*vozhd'*] Comrade Stalin, thanks to his wise strategy continue to remain outside the war and as before continue confidently towards their goal, improving their material condition and increasing the might of the armed forces of our country.

. . .

During the move westwards,[7] and in responding to provocation in the Far East and in Finland, the Red Army has gained considerable military experience of modern war. During the fighting in the Karelo-Finnish theatre. . .

> Alongside the successful fulfilment of broader tasks, in this war a number of inadequacies in organisational, operational-tactical and disciplinary questions emerged.
> ...
> Under the direction of the People's Commissar for Defence we must, in the shortest possible time, reorganise our army, and genuinely bring it to a high state of military readiness, to achieve a state of affairs whereby we are constantly ready at any time to set forth [*vistupit' v pokhod*] on the orders of the government.
>
> (Source: *RA T.12 (1)*, 1993, pp. 13–14, 29)

The Soviet Union was, however, gradually putting itself on what might be considered a war footing, a strong indicator of which was the decision to switch to an eight-hour working day, six-day working week in the summer of 1940, and strengthen labour discipline:

> **DOCUMENT 13:** *On the move to an eight-hour working day, seven-day working week and the forbidding of voluntary departure of workers and administrative staff from industrial concerns and administrative establishments*
>
> **Extract from the Decree of 25 June 1940**
> In accordance with the declaration of the All Union Central Council of Trade Unions, the Presidium of the Supreme Soviet of the USSR decrees:
> ...
> 2. To move over, in all state, co-operative and public concerns and administrative establishments, from a six-day working week to a seven-day week, considering the seventh day of the week – Sunday – a day off.
>
> (Source: *Sbornik zakonov SSSR v dvukh tomakh*, 1968, pp. 182–183)

Gabriel Gorodetsky's *Grand Delusion* is a direct response to the Suvorov thesis. Gorodetsky essentially reiterated the established Soviet line, with minor embellishments and additional supporting material, that the Soviet Union was desperate to ensure peace in the summer of 1941 without serious intention of anything more than a spoiling attack, without examining Soviet longer-term intentions, and in particular the ideological dimension to Soviet foreign policy and the notion of spreading revolution by force.[8] Perhaps the most useful product of Suvorov's work and the response from those such as Gorodetsky has been intensification of debate over Soviet intentions during the summer of 1941 and beyond, fuelled by sporadic new materials from Soviet archives, which has led to a much more nuanced picture of Soviet intentions emerging than that dominant in the mid-1980s and indeed portrayed by Gorodetsky.

First, it is apparent that the Soviet Union was preparing for war against Germany, even if not in July 1941, and that such a war, in line with Soviet doctrine, would involve initial offensive operations by Soviet forces. Second, it became apparent that the Soviet military leadership had, understandably, considered offensive operations against Germany in the summer of 1941, and the Soviet leadership had started to intensify propaganda efforts to prepare the Soviet population for war before switching abruptly back to a line of preserving peace with Germany at all costs, presumably in the face of the absence of the necessary military preparations.

Plans for operations against German forces massed on the Soviet border dated 15 May 1941 appeared in Russian publications after the collapse of the Soviet Union, as did the text of a speech made by Stalin to graduating officers on 5 May, during which he can reasonably be seen to have been preparing those present for war with Germany in the not-too-distant future.[9] A short extract from the speech of 5 May is followed by the bulk of the operational plan of 15 May:

DOCUMENT 14: *Third speech of I.V. Stalin to graduating officers, the Kremlin, Moscow, 5 May 1941*

The policy of peace is a good thing. We have up to now, up to this time, carried out a line – defence – up to the time when we have re-equipped our army, up until the time we have supplied the army with the modern means of battle. And now, when our army has been reconstructed, has been amply supplied [*nasitili*] with equipment for modern battle, when we have become stronger, now it is necessary to go from defence to offence [*ot oboroni k nastupleniiu*].

Defending our country, we must act offensively. From defence to go to a military doctrine of offensive actions. We must transform our training, our propaganda, our agitation, our press in an offensive spirit. The Red Army is a modern army and the modern army is an offensive army.

(Source: Jürgen Förster and Evan Mawdsley, 2004, pp. 101–102)

DOCUMENT 15: *Note by the People's Commissar of Defence of the USSR and head of the General Headquarters of the Red Army to the Chairman of the Council of People's Commissars of the USSR I.V. Stalin with considerations for a plan for the strategic deployment of the armed forces of the Soviet Union in the event of war with Germany and her allies. No earlier than 15 May 1941*

I provide for your consideration thoughts on a plan for the strategic deployment of the Armed Forces of the Soviet Union in the event of war with Germany and her allies.

I. At the current time Germany has, *according to the information provided by the Reconnaissance Board of the Red Army*, around 230 infantry, 22 armoured, 20 mechanized, 8 airborne and 4 cavalry divisions deployed, a total of around 284 divisions.

Of these, as of 15.5.1941, up to 86 infantry, 13 armoured, 12 motorized and 1 cavalry division, a total of up to 112 divisions, are concentrated on the borders of the Soviet Union.

It is supposed, that in terms of the current political situation, in the event of attack on the USSR Germany will be able to put up as many as 137 infantry, 19 armoured, 15 motorized, 4 cavalry and 5 airborne divisions against us, in all up to 180 divisions.

The remaining 104 divisions will be situated...

Most probably the principal strength of the German army in the form of 76 infantry, 11 armoured, 8 motorized, 2 cavalry and 5 airborne divisions, a total of up to 100 divisions, will be deployed to the south of Demblin for the striking of a blow on the axis Kovel' – Rovno – Kiev.

This blow, apparently, will be accompanied by a blow in the north from East Prussia on Vilnius and Riga, and at the same time short, concentric blows from the direction of Suvalki and Brest towards Volkovisk-Baranovichi.

In the south it figures that we can expect blows [by the Rumanian army, supported by German divisions, in the general direction of Zhmerinka, at the same time as those by the German army.

The possibility of a supporting blow by the Germans from behind the River San in the direction of L'vov cannot be ruled out.] *a) in the direction of Zhmerinka by the Rumanian army, supported by German divisions; b) in the direction of Munkakh, L'vov; c) Sanok, L'vov.*

The likely German allies can field the following against the USSR: Finland – up to 20 infantry divisions, Hungary – 15 infantry divisions, Rumania – up to 25 infantry divisions.

In all, Germany and her allies can deploy up to 240 divisions against the Soviet Union.

Bearing in mind, that at the current moment Germany holds her army in a fully mobilized state, with fully deployed rear-area services, she has the potential to anticipate our deployment and deliver a surprise blow.

In order to prevent this [and to destroy the German army], I consider it necessary, not under any circumstances, to allow the initiative to be gained by the German High Command, to pre-empt enemy deployment and to attack the German army at the point at which she is deploying, and prevent her having the time to organise a front and co-ordinate the different elements of her forces.

II. The first strategic aim for operations of forces of the Red Army is to be set as: the destruction of the principal forces of the German army deployed to the south of Demblin, with positions by day 30 of the operation along the front Ostrolenka, the River Narev, Lovich, Lodz, Kreitsburg, Oppeln, Olomoits. *The subsequent strategic aim is: advancing from the Katovitse region in a northerly or north-westerly direction to destroy major units of the Central and Northern wings of the German front and to seize the territories of former Poland and East Prussia.*

The most immediate task is to destroy the German army east of the River Vistula and on the Krakow axis, to emerge on the Rivers Narev and Vistula and seize the district of Katovitse, for which:

The principal blow by forces of the South-Western *Front* is to be struck in the direction of Krakow, Katovitse, cutting Germany off from her southern allies;

A supporting strike is to be made by the west wing of the Western *Front* in the direction of Sedlets, Demblin, with the aim of pinning down forces around Warsaw and co-ordinating with the South-Western *Front* in the defeat of enemy forces near Lublin;

To conduct an active defence against Finland, East Prussia, Hungary and Rumania and to be prepared to strike a blow against Rumania in favourable circumstances.

In such a manner the Red Army will commence offensive action along a front from Chizhov to Motovisko with a force of 152 divisions against 100 German divisions. On the remaining sections of the state border provision is to be made for active defence.

III. Stemming from the stated plan for strategic deployment the following deployment of the Armed Forces of the USSR is envisaged:

Ground forces of the Red Army consisting of: 198 rifle divisions, 61 armoured divisions, 31 mechanized division and 13 cavalry divisions (in total 303 divisions and artillery regiments of the High Command Reserve) are to be distributed in the following manner:

Principal forces consisting of 163 infantry, 58 armoured, 30 mechanized and 7 cavalry divisions (in total 258 divisions) and 53 artillery regiments of the High Command Reserve are to be in the West, of which making up the Northern, North-Western, Western and South-Western *Fronts* are 136 infantry divisions, 44 armoured divisions, 23 mechanized divisions and 7 cavalry divisions (in total 210 divisions) and 53 artillery regiments of the High Command Reserve; making up the High Command Reserve behind the South-Western and Western *Fronts* are 27 infantry, 14 armoured and 7 mechanized divisions (a total of 48 divisions);

The remaining strength, consisting of 35 infantry, 3 armoured, 1 mechanized and 6 cavalry divisions (in total 45 divisions) and 21 artillery regiments of the High Command Reserve are allocated for the defence of the Far Eastern, southern and northern borders of the USSR, of which: 22 infantry, 3 armoured, 1 mechanized and 1 cavalry division (in total 27 divisions) and 14 artillery regiments of the High Command Reserve are in the Far East and Trans-Baikal Military District.

– In Central Asia – 2 mountain-rifle and 3 cavalry divisions (a total of 5 divisions)
– In the Transcaucasus – 8 infantry and 2 cavalry divisions (a total of 10 divisions) and 2 artillery regiments of the High Command Reserve
– For the defence of the Black Sea coastline and the Northern Caucasus and Crimea – 2 rifle divisions
– On the White Sea coast – 1 rifle division.

...

2. The Air Forces of the Red Army made up of the currently available and combat-ready 97 fighter air regiments, 75 light bomber regiments, 11 close air support regiments, 29 long-range bomber regiments and 6 heavy bomber regiments (a total of 218 aviation regiments) are to be allocated according to the following:

a) The principal forces, consisting of 66 fighter air regiments, 64 light bomber regiments, 5 close support regiments, 25 long-range bomber regiments (in total 165 aviation regiments) are to be deployed in the west, of which:

– As part of the Northern, North Western, Western and South-Western *Fronts* – 63 fighter air regiments, 64 light bomber regiments, 5 close air support regiments, 11 long-range bomber regiments and one heavy bomber regiment;
– Making up the High Command Reserve behind the South-Western and Western *Fronts* are 14 long-range bomber regiments, 4 heavy bomber regiments, a total of 21 aviation regiments;

b) The remaining strength consisting of 51 fighter air regiments, 11 light bomber regiments, 6 close air support regiments, 4 long-range bomber regiments and 1 heavy bomber regiment – a total of 53 aviation regiments – are to be left over for the defence of the Far Eastern, southern and northern borders and the close air defence of Moscow, of which:

– to be in the Far East and the Trans-Baikal Military District – 14 fighter air regiments, 9 light bomber regiments, 5 close air support regiments, 4 long-range bomber regiments and 1 heavy bomber regiment, a total of 33 aviation regiments;
– in the Central Asian Military District – 1 fighter air regiment, 1 close air support regiment, a total of 2 aviation regiments;
– in the Transcaucasus Military District – 9 fighter air regiments, 2 light bomber regiments, a total of 11 aviation regiments;
– in the Arkhangel'sk Military District – 1 fighter air regiment.
For the defence of Moscow – 6 fighter air regiments.

...

In addition to the air forces mentioned, there are currently 52 fighter air regiments, 30 light bomber regiments, 4 close air support regiments, 7 long-range bomber regiments and 22 long-range escort [regiments], a total of 115 aviation regiments, in the process of forming and in no uncertain terms yet ready for combat, which can be expected to be in a full state of readiness by 1.1.42.

...

IV. Composition and tasks of *fronts* deployed in the west ...:
Northern *Front* (Leningrad Military District) – 3 armies, consisting of 15 rifle, 4 armoured and 2 motorized divisions, a total of 21 divisions, 18 aviation regiments and the Northern Naval Fleet, with the basic tasks of which being the defence of the city of Leningrad, the port of Murmansk, the Kirov Railway, and with the Baltic Naval Fleet to provide us with total supremacy on the waters of the Gulf of Finland. With this very aim in mind the transfer of the northern and north-western shores of the Estonian SSR to the Northern *Front* from the Pribaltic Special Military District is envisaged.

The boundary for the *front* on the left – Ostashkov, Ostrov, Viru, Vil'iandi, the Matasalu Inlet, and with the exception of the islands of Ezel' and Dago alone.

Front headquarters – Pargolovo.

North-Western *Front* (Pribaltic Special Military District) – 3 armies, consisting of 17 rifle divisions [(of which 6 national)], 4 armoured and 2 motorized divisions, a total of 23 divisions and 14 aviation regiments with the tasks: through stubborn defence to solidly cover the Riga and Vilensk axis, not allowing the enemy to break out of East Prussia; the defence of the western coastline and the islands of Ezel' and Dago, with the aim of preventing enemy landings.

Left border of the *front* – Polotsk, Oshmiani, Druskeniki, Margerabova, Lettsen. *Front* headquarters – Ponevezh.

Western *Front* (Western Special Military District) – 4 armies, consisting of 31 rifle, 8 armoured, 4 motorized and 2 cavalry divisions, a total of 45 divisions and 21 aviation regiments.

Tasks: the stubborn defence of the front Druskeniki-Ostrolenka, with the solid defence of the Lidsk and Belostok axis;

With the transition of the armies of the South-Western *Front* over to the offensive, with a blow by the left wing of the *front* in the directions of *Warsaw*, Sedlets, Radom, *to destroy the forces near Warsaw and the occupy Warsaw*, [in order to assist] *in co-ordination with* the South-Western *Front* to destroy the enemy in the Lublin-Radom region, *to move up to {viti na} the River Vistula and with mobile units to seize Radom* [and to facilitate this operation from the Warsaw and East Prussia direction].

Left border of the *front* – River Pripiat', Pinsk, Vlodava, Demblin, Radom.

Front headquarters – Baranovichi.

South-Western *Front* – 8 armies, consisting of 74 rifle, 28 armoured, 15 motorized and 5 cavalry divisions, a total of 122 divisions and 91 aviation regiments, with the most immediate tasks:

Concentric blows by the armies of the left flank of the *front* to encircle and destroy the key enemy concentration to the east of the River Vistula and in the Lublin area;

At the same time with a blow from the line Seniava, Peremishl', Liutoviska to destroy enemy forces on the Krakow and Sandomir-Keletsk axes and then seize the Krakow, Katovitse, Kel'tse districts bearing in mind in the future to attack from this area in a northerly or north-westerly direction in order to destroy the major force of the northern wing of the enemy front and the seizure of the territories of what was Poland and of Eastern Prussia;

To stubbornly defend the state border from Hungary and Rumania and be prepared for the striking of concentric blows against Rumania from the Chernovitsi and Kishinev regions, with the immediate aim of destroying the northern wing of the Rumanian army and ending up on the line of the Moldova River and Iassi.

In order to provide for the carrying out of the plan expounded above it is necessary to conduct the following activities in a timely manner, without which it will be impossible to strike a surprise blow against the enemy be it from the air or on the ground:

To conduct a concealed deployment of our forces under cover of the call up of reservists for training;

...

V. The concentration of High Command Reserves.

In the High Command Reserve there are to be 5 armies concentrated:

2 Armies, consisting of 9 rifle, 4 armoured and 2 motorized divisions, a total of 15 divisions, in the region of Viaz'ma, Sichevka, El'nia, Briansk, Sukhinichi;

One army, consisting of four rifle, two armoured and 2 motorized divisions, a total of 8 divisions, in the region of Vileika, Novogrudok, Minsk;

One army, consisting of 6 rifle, 4 armoured and two motorized divisions, a total of 12 divisions, in the region of Shepetovka, Proskurov, Berdichev and

One army, consisting of 8 rifle, two armoured and 2 motorized divisions, a total of 12 divisions, in the region of Belaia Tserkov', Zvenigorodka, Cherkassi.

VI. Concealment of concentration and deployment.

In order to cover ourselves against a possible sudden strike by the enemy, the concentration and deployment of our forces and preparation for them to attack must be covered, for which it is necessary to:

Organize the solid covering and defence of the state borders, utilizing for this all of the forces of the military districts along the border and almost all of the aviation allocation for deployment in the west;

To formulate a detailed plan for the air defence of the country and to bring AA resources to full readiness.

On these matters instructions have already been handed out, and the development of plans for the defence of the state border and AA will be fully complete by 01.06.1941.

...

At the same time it is necessary to take all the necessary measures to force through the construction and arming of the fortified districts, to start the construction of fortified districts on the border with Hungary during 1942, and in the same way to continue the construction of fortified districts along the old state border.

VII. Tasks for the Navy are to be set in accordance with my instructions as already confirmed by you.

VIII. The deployment of our forces and their operations are to be supplied with the available supply stocks as follows:

>Munitions – small calibre munitions for three weeks;
>Medium calibre munitions for a month;
>Heavy calibre munitions for a month;
>Mines for half a month;
>For AA fire –
>37 mm for 5 days;
>76 mm for one and a half months;
>85 mm for 5 days;
>Aviation munitions –
>High-explosive bombs – for a month;
>Armour-piercing bombs – for 10 days;
>'Bunker-busting' bombs – for 10 days;
>Fragmentation bombs – for a month;
>Incendiary bombs – for a month and a half;
>Fuel oils –
>Petrol B-78 for 10 days;
>Petrol B-74 for a month;
>Petrol B-70 for two and a half months;
>Automobile petrol for one and a half months;
>Diesel fuel for a month.

Reserves of fuel allocated to western military districts are stored 'in depth' in the necessary quantities (due to the lack of storage capacity on their territories) in internal military districts.

IX. I request:

Confirm receipt of the plan for the strategic deployment of the Armed Forces of the USSR and plan for projected military operations in the event of war with Germany;

In good time authorize the required conduct of concealed mobilization and hidden concentration of, in the first instance, all armies of the High Command Reserve and aviation;

Demand of the People's Commissariat for Communications full and timely fulfilment of railway construction according to the plan for 1941 and especially on the L'vov axis;

Require industrial concerns to fulfil plans for the production of material components for tanks and aircraft, and similarly for the production and provision of munitions and fuels strictly within the allotted timeframes.

...

People's Commissar for Defence of the USSR
Marshal of the Soviet Union – S. Timoshenko
Head of the General Headquarters of the Red Army
General of the Army – G. Zhukov

[Note: Text assumed to have been added by G.K. Zhukov appears in italics, that assumed to have been deleted by him is inside square brackets.]

(Source: V.P. Naumov, kn.2, 1998, pp. 215–220. See also I.A. Gor'kov, 1995, pp. 303–309)

At the same time, Nevezhin presents evidence of a planned, if abortive, shift in Soviet propaganda towards an anti-German stance compared to the placatory line taken as a result of the Nazi–Soviet Pact.[10] What is not apparent, as Mawdsley discusses, is the extent to which these developments were geared towards Soviet action within weeks or months, the latter placing the May plan more in line with a gradual Soviet mobilization of forces, including the transfer of units from the Far East, taking place before and after 15 May.[11] What is certain is that Red Army mobilization was by May or June 1941 a long way from the ambitious targets set in the 1941 general mobilization plan for the Red Army that appeared in February 1941, superseding a general mobilization plan of November 1937. The 1941 plan, or MP-41, called for a Red Army of 300 divisions, provided with the equipment indicated in Table 2.4 by 1 January 1942, compared to that available on 1 January 1941.

Whilst our picture of Soviet intelligence prior to mid-May does not suggest that the Soviet Union was convinced of the imminence of the German attack, a factor no doubt assisted by the delay in Operation 'Barbarossa' from mid-May to June, at least some in the Soviet Union had sufficiently good intelligence from a variety of sources to be convinced by mid-June 1941 at least that a German attack was imminent. Some examples of intelligence on the German military build-up and information on incursions into Soviet airspace by German aircraft are provided in the following three extracts:

> DOCUMENT 16: *From information of the Deputy People's Commissar of Internal Affairs of the Ukrainian SSR regarding German military activities and incidents on the border, 6 June 1941*
>
> According to observations of the 91st Rava-Russkii Border Detachment, in the border zone the appearance of large tank formations of the German army is coming to an end.
>
> 16 medium tanks passed in the direction of Plazuv. From Tomasheva to Belz up to a company of motorcyclists arrived, half a squadron of cavalry and up to two regiments of infantry.
>
> 5 June 1941, between 2:00 and 6:00 up to 100 tankettes and a significant number of medium tanks were on their way from Plazuv in the direction of Narol'. During the day the movement of tanks continues in isolated groups.
>
> ...
>
> Border incursion by a German aircraft
> 5 June 1941 at 11:43 on the sector of 93rd Leskovkii Border Detachment in the region of the village of Pavlokom at a height of 4,000 metres a single-engined German aircraft crossed the border.
> Penetrating our territory from between 3 and 8 km ...
> The aircraft was not shot at.
> Engagement [*obstrel*] of aircraft
> 5 June 1941 in the region of Dubov our single-engined reconnaissance aircraft, flying along the border at a height of 2,500 metres, was shot at by machine gun fire from the Rumanian side....

Deputy People's Commissar of Internal Affairs Ukrainian SSR, Colonel Strokhach.

(Source: V.P. Eroshin *et al.*, 1995, pp. 209–211)

DOCUMENT 17: *From communication of the NKVD SSSR No. 1996/B to TsK VKP (b) and SNK SSSR regarding breaches of the state border of the USSR from the German side from November 1940 to 10 June 1941, 12 June 1941*

In the recent past since October 1940 ... from the German side 185 aircraft have breached the border of the Soviet Union. During the last month and a half breaches of our border by German aircraft have become particularly frequent. During May and 10 days of June 1941 91 German aircraft have breached the border of the USSR.

Penetrations of the border of the Soviet Union by German aircraft have do not have the character of chance occurrences, confirmed by their direction and deep flights over our territory. In a number of instances German aircraft flew over our territory to a depth of 100 and more kilometres, and especially in the direction of districts in which defensive works are being erected, and over points where there are large garrisons of the Red Army.

...

Recently there have been a number of instances in which agents of German reconnaissance organs, equipped with portable two-way radios, arms and grenades, have been detained.

People's Commissar of Internal Affairs, Beria.

(Source: V.P. Eroshin *et al.*, 1995, pp. 220–221)

DOCUMENT 18: *From communication of the NKVD USSR to TsK VKP (b) and SNK USSR regarding breaches of the Soviet border by foreign aircraft from 10 to 19 June 1941, 20 June 1941*

Regarding breaches of the border of the Soviet Union by foreign aircraft the NKVD of the USSR informs, that from 10 to 19 June of the current year inclusive 86 instances of breaches of the border by foreign aircraft have been determined by detachments of the NKVD. Of these: from the Finnish side – 9 instances, from the German side – 63 instances, from the Hungarian side – 2 instances, from the Rumanian side – 12 instances ...

Deputy People's Commissar for Internal Affairs of the USSR, Maslennikov.

(Source: V.P. Eroshin *et al.*, 1995, pp. 269–270)

That a German or Axis attack was imminent was not, however, a conclusion reached by Stalin.[12] The fact that an impending short-term intensification of defensive measures was not taken (or at best half-heartedly and covertly) was no doubt because, from Stalin's perspective, if the Soviet Union was not in a position to go on the offensive because her armed forces were simply not ready, then she would have to seek to buy as much time as possible from the Nazi–Soviet Pact. On Stalin's insistence the Soviet Union would do all that was possible not to provoke Germany into striking first, something she was, according to the official Soviet line, not intending to do anyway.

The Nazi–Soviet Pact, in embroiling Germany in a war in the West, was no doubt intended by Stalin and the Soviet leadership to buy more time than the less than two years it had done by the summer of 1941. Whilst France had been defeated more rapidly than expected by most observers, Britain remained in the war and was, by mid-1941, starting to receive significant US support through Lend-Lease. In the early summer there were British warnings of German intention to invade the Soviet Union, which, despite corroboration by other sources, were not taken seriously by a Stalin seeing them as an attempt to provoke the Soviet Union into joining the war before she was ready, and thus ignored. Stalin, it is widely assumed, sought to convince himself that Germany would not intentionally make the mistake of the First World War of fighting on two fronts. This belief was reinforced by German talk of an invasion of Britain, and despite fears of a British 'coming to terms' with Germany, particularly after Hess, Hitler's second-in-command in the Nazi Party, had made his unauthorized flight to Britain in May 1941. The Soviet response to intensified insecurity was to increase the flow of resources to Germany, provided under the umbrella of the Nazi–Soviet Pact. With the war against Britain continuing, Germany was seen by the Soviet Union as desperately short of the strategic resources being provided to them, and presumably would not be so foolish as to throw away the opportunity to continue to receive them in the context of the drawbacks of a two-front war. Soviet deliveries continued to roll across the Soviet–German border right up to the invasion, for which the Soviet Union was not receiving what she had been promised in return. Up until the point on 22 June 1941 that it was clear that German operations were not mere 'provocation', Stalin remained unwilling to allow subordinates to take reasonable defensive measures in case they should provoke Germany or provide justification for German attack. Such concerns were present even in orders of 21 June 1941, not sent out to units until after midnight, and not to be received by many units before the German attack struck.

Guide to further reading

The Red Army on the eve of war and the Suvorov debate

N.E. Eliseeva and David Glantz, 'Plans for the Development of the Worker's and Peasants Red Army (RKKA) on the Eve of War', *JSMS*, Volume 8, Number 2 (June 1995), pp. 356–365.

David Glantz, *Stumbling Colossus: The Red Army on the Eve of War* (Lawrence, KS: University Press of Kansas, 1998).

G. Gorodetsky, *Grand Delusion. Stalin and the German Invasion of Russia* (New Haven, CT: Yale University Press, 1999).

J. Hoffmann, 'The Red Army until the Beginning of the German-Soviet War', in H. Boog, J. Forster, J. Hoffmann, E. Klink, R.-D. Muller, G.R. Ueberschar and E. Osers (eds),

Table 2.4 Red Army equipment as of 1 January 1941 and as expected by 1 January 1942, according to the 1941 general mobilization plan (MP-41) of (no later than) 12 February 1941

Item	Number required	Available on 1.1.1941	Expected from industry during 1941	Planned availability on 1.1.1942
Rifles (standard)	4,421,000	6,176,000	325,000	6,501,000
Heavy tanks (KV, T-35)	3,907	299 (of which 35 T-35)	900	1,199
Medium tanks (T-34, T-28)	12,843	562 (of which 447 T-28)	2,500	3,062
GAZ lorries	197,781	96,144	19,400	115,544
Battalion-level radio set 16-PK-RSB	33,813	20,814	5,020	25,834
Company-level radio set RRU, RBS	24,425	13,016	9,000	22,016
Motor-fuel/petrol tankers	34,165	9,156	1,250	10,406

Source: V.P. Naumov (ed.), *1941 god: V 2 kn. Kn.1* (Moscow: Mezhdunarodnii fond 'Demokratiia', 1998), pp. 617–624.

Germany and the Second World War. Volume IV. The Attack on the Soviet Union (Oxford: Clarendon Press, 1998), pp. 72–93.

Evan Mawdsley, 'Crossing the Rubicon: Soviet Plans for Offensive War in 1940–1941', *International History Review*, Volume 25, Number 4 (2003), pp. 818–865.

Silvio Pons, *Stalin and the Inevitable War 1936–1941* (London: Frank Cass, 2002).

C. Roberts, 'Planning for War: The Red Army and the Catastrophe of 1941', *Europe–Asia Studies*, Volume 47, Number 8 (1995), pp. 1293–1326.

V. Suvorov (pseud.), 'Who was Planning to Attack Whom in June 1941, Hitler or Stalin?', *Journal of the Royal United Services Institute for Defence Studies*, Volume 130, Number 2 (1985), pp. 50–55.

T.J. Uldricks, 'The Icebreaker Controversy: Did Stalin Plan to Attack Hitler?', *Slavic Review*, Volume 58, Number 3 (1999), pp. 626–643.

The Red Army against Japan, Poland and Finland 1939–1940

Alexander O. Chubaryan and Harold Shukman (eds), *Stalin and the Soviet-Finnish War 1939–1940* (London: Frank Cass, 2002).

Alvin D. Coox, *Nomohan: Japan Against Russia, 1939* (Stanford, CA: Stanford University Press, 1990).

Carl van Dyke, *The Soviet Invasion of Finland 1939–1940* (London: Frank Cass, 1997).

M.I. Lukinov, 'Notes on the Polish Campaign (1939) and the War with Finland (1939–1940)', *JSMS*, Volume 14, Number 3 (September 2001), pp. 120–149.

3 Barbarossa

Whilst Stalin could take much of the credit for the extent to which the Soviet Union was strategically prepared for war, his desire to avoid provoking Germany at almost any cost would nonetheless cost the Red Army dearly in the first days of Operation 'Barbarossa' – the German-led invasion of the Soviet Union. Only at 12:30 Moscow time on 22 June would the Red Army be ordered to ready itself for attack – insufficient time for many units to receive the order before they were hit only hours later.

DOCUMENT 19: Directive {Number 1} of the People's Commissar of Defence S.K. Timoshenko and Head of the General Headquarters Zhukov to commanders of border districts on the bringing of forces to a state of readiness due to the possibility of attack by Fascist Germany on the USSR, 21 June 1941

1. During 22–23 June 1941 there is the possibility of surprise attack by the Germans on the fronts of the LVO [Leningrad-], PribOVO [Pribaltic Special], ZapOVO [Western Special-], KOVO [Kiev Special-] and OdVO [Odessa] [Military Districts]. An attack might start with provocative activities.
2. The task of our forces is not to give in to any sort of provocative activities, which might lead to major complications. At the same time forces of the Leningrad, Pribaltic, Western, Kiev and Odessa Military Districts are to be at full battle readiness in order to meet the possible surprise blow by the Germans or their allies.

I order:

a) During the night of 22 June 1941 to covertly man firepoints of the fortified districts on the state border;
b) Before dawn on the 22 June 1941 to disperse all aviation, including military, on field aerodromes, and to carefully camouflage it;
c) To bring all units to battle readiness. Forces are to be held dispersed and camouflaged.
d) To bring anti-aircraft to battle readiness without additional personnel. To make all preparations in blacked-out towns and installations;
e) No other actions are to be taken without special authorisation.

Timoshenko
Zhukov

(Source: V.P. Eroshin *et al.*, 1995, p. 298)

The German attack began in earnest at 3:00 a.m. when the first German bombers struck. The navy was in a slightly better position to meet the German invasion than the Red Army, although it would not be the initial focus of significant German air activity. People's Commissar for the Navy Kuznetsov had ordered the navy over to Operational Readiness Number 1 (combat readiness) at 23:50, with communication with naval assets being more effective than with ground units, in part given their concentration in ports. Kuznetsov's initial order, simply ordering the military soviets of the fleets and flotillas that they 'Without delay go over to Operational Readiness Number 1', was elaborated on in a follow-up directive of 01:12, issued in the light of Document 19, calling for such measures to be carefully concealed to avoid being provocative.

DOCUMENT 20: *Directive to the military soviets of the KBF, SF, ChF and the commanders of the Pinsk and Danube Flotillas on the possibility of surprise attack by the Germans*

22 June 1941 01:12

During 22.6–23.6 there is the possibility of surprise attack by the Germans. The German attack might start with provocative actions. Our task is not to respond to any provocative actions that might lead to major complications. At the same time fleets and flotillas are to be at full combat readiness to meet a possible surprise attack by the Germans or their allies.

I order that, having gone over to Operational Readiness Number 1, that this increase in readiness be carefully concealed. The conduct of reconnaissance in foreign territorial waters is categorically forbidden. No other measures are to be taken without special permission.
Kuznetsov.

(Source: *RA T.21 (10)*, 1996, p. 12)

As the first German air attacks hit Soviet airfields during the early hours of 22 June, German artillery opened up on Soviet border positions. As dawn broke, heavier air strikes hit a total of 66 Soviet airfields in border regions; during the morning Soviet forces lost more than 1,200 aircraft.[1] By the time there could not be the slightest doubt that German operations were merely some sort of provocation, on the evening of 22 June Stalin and Timoshenko issued Directive Number 3 for a counter-offensive against the invading forces, adding flesh to a somewhat vaguer Directive Number 2 that had been issued early that morning. Both are provided below.

DOCUMENT 21: *Directive Number 2 to the military soviets of the Leningrad-, Pribaltic-Special-, Western-Special, Kiev-Special-, Odessa-Military Districts, VMF, on the German surprise attack and the military objectives of the armed forces*

No. 2 22.6.41 07:15

On the 22nd June 1941 at 4:00 in the morning, without cause, German aircraft attacked our aerodromes and towns along the western border and subjected them to bombing.

At the same time in a number of places German forces opened up artillery fire and crossed our border.

Due to this unprecedentedly brazen attack by Germany on the Soviet Union, I order:

1. Forces to pounce on [*obrushit'sia*] enemy forces with all strength and resources and destroy them in those districts, where they have crossed the Soviet border.
   In the future, without special authorization, ground forces are not to cross the border.
2. Reconnaissance and fighting aircraft are to establish locations of the concentration of enemy aviation and concentrations of his ground forces.

With heavy blows bomber and ground-attack aircraft are to destroy aircraft on enemy airfields and to bomb the principal concentrations of ground forces. Air strikes are to be conducted into German territory to a depth of 100–150 km.

Königsberg and Memel are to be bombed.

Overflights of Finnish and Rumanian territory are not to be made without special authorization.

Timoshenko, Malenkov, Zhukov

(Source: I.A. Gor'kov, 2002, pp. 491–492)

DOCUMENT 22: Directive Number 3 to the military soviets of the North-Western, Western, South-Western and Southern Fronts[2]

No. 3, Moscow, 22.6.41, map 1 000 0000

1. Having struck his principal blow from the Suvalki forward positions ... during 22.6, having suffered heavy losses, the enemy has achieved limited successes....
   On the remaining sections of the state border with Germany and along the whole state border with Rumania enemy attacks have been repulsed with heavy losses for him.
2. Immediate tasks for forces for 23–24.6 are:

   a) With concentrated focused blows forces of the North-Western and Western *Fronts* are to encircle and destroy the Suvalki concentration of the enemy and by the end of 24.6 have gained the Suvalki region.
   b) With powerful concentrated blows mechanized corps and all aviation of the South-Western *Front* and other forces of the 4th and 6th Armies are to encircle and destroy the enemy concentration attacking in the direction of Vladimir-Volinsk, Brodi. By the end of 24.6 the Lublin region is to be captured.

...

Timoshenko, Malenkov, Zhukov

(Source: I.A. Gor'kov, 2002, pp. 493–494)

The same evening it was left to Molotov to announce to the Soviet people:

> DOCUMENT 23: *Extract from a broadcast speech by Chairman of the Council of People's Commissars and People's Commissar for Foreign Affairs Molotov on the German invasion of the Soviet Union, 22 June 1941*
>
> Citizens of the Soviet Union!
>
> The Soviet government and its head Comrade Stalin have given me the task of making the following announcement:
>
> Today at four in the morning, without any claims having been presented to the Soviet Union, without a declaration of war, German troops attacked our country....
>
> This unheard of attack on our country was perpetrated despite the fact that a treaty of non-aggression had been signed between the USSR and Germany and that the Soviet Government has most conscientiously abided by all provisions of that treaty.
>
> (Source: V.P. Eroshin *et al.*, 2000, p. 14)

The Soviet leadership was quick to start to shift the country on to a wartime footing, an initial element of which was the provision for military rule in prefrontal areas outlined in Document 24:

> DOCUMENT 24: *From the decree of the Presidium of the Supreme Soviet of the USSR on the state of war, 22 June 1941*
>
> 1. Military rule [*voennoe polozhenie*], in accordance with article 49 paragraph P of the Constitution of the Soviet Union, is declared in specific areas or across the USSR in the interests of the defence of the USSR and for the provision of social order and state security.
> 2. In areas in which military rule has been declared all functions of state power in the sphere of defence, provision of social order and state security are in the hands of the military soviets of *fronts*, armies and military districts, and where there are not military soviets, the upper command of military formations.
> 3. In areas in which military rule is declared, the military authorities (p. 2) have the power to:
>   a) ... mobilize civilians for labour service for the construction of defensive works, the defence of transport arteries, other construction, means of communication, power stations, the electricity grid and other important objects, for participation in the struggle against fire, epidemics and natural disasters;
>   b) Establish obligations for the billeting of military units and institutions;
>   c) ...;
>   d) Commandeer transport resources and other such items for the needs of the defence from state, social and co-operative concerns and organizations, and from individuals;
>   e) ... enforce curfews, limit traffic movement, and where necessary search and arrest suspicious individuals;
>   f) Regulate trade and the work of trading organizations (markets, shops, warehouses ...), communal enterprises (saunas, laundries, hairdressers and so forth), and also establish norms for the distribution of foodstuffs and other goods to the population;

g) Prohibit entrance to and exit from areas declared under military rule;

h) To subject to administrative exile beyond the boundaries of areas defined to be under military rule ... those declared socially dangerous due to their criminal activities or links with criminal circles.

...

5. All local organs of state power ... are required to render full co-operation with the military authorities in the utilization of power and resources of a given area for the defensive needs of the country and the provision of social order and security.

6. For not submitting to the instructions and orders of the military authorities, and similarly for the committing of crimes in the area concerned, guilty parties face criminal prosecution....

7. ... all crimes directed against defence, social order and state security are to be handed over for consideration by military tribunals....[3]

Additionally, the military authorities are given powers to transfer cases of speculation, malicious hooliganism and other crimes for which provision is made in the criminal codes of union republics to military tribunals, should they see it as necessary.

(Source: *KPSS o vooruzhennikh silakh Sovetskogo Soiuza*, 1981, pp. 291–293)

The military soviets to which the document refers were military-political organizations down to *front* level, consisting of representatives of both military decision makers, i.e. military officers, and their political overseers, be they from GlavPU RKKA or the Party machinery, reflecting the importance of political supervision of military decision making during wartime, something that would increase dramatically as the situation at the *front* deteriorated.[4]

On 23 June, the day that Document 24 was actually published, the *Stavka* GK or Headquarters of the High Command (sometimes translated as Main Command Headquarters) was created to direct the Soviet military effort, with a number of civilian 'advisers' attached:

DOCUMENT 25: *On the joint decree of the SNK SSSR and TsK VKP (b) on the creation of a Headquarters of the High Command, 23.6.1941*

To military soviets of *fronts*, military districts and the VMF

The government of the USSR has decreed that a Headquarters of the High Command of the armed forces of the USSR is to be created, made up of the following comrades: People's Commissar for Defence of the USSR Marshal of the Soviet Union Timoshenko (Chairman), Head of the General Headquarters of the Red Army General of the Army Zhukov, Stalin, Molotov, Marshal of the Soviet Union Voroshilov, Marshal of the Soviet Union Budennii and People's Commissar for the Navy Kuznetsov.

Attached to the Headquarters an institute of permanent advisers is to be organized, consisting of Marshal of the Soviet Union Kulik, Marshal of the Soviet Union Shaposhnikov, Meretskov, Head of the VVS KA Zhigarev, Vatunin, Head of the PVO Voronov, Mikoian, Kaganovich, Beria, Voznesenskii, Zhdanov, Malenkov, and Mekhlis.

(Source: I.A. Gor'kov, 2002, p. 494)

Despite the creation of such a command, its key members were, as Mawdsley notes, actually dispersed overseeing *front*-level operations – Timoshenko and Shaposhnikov with the Western *Front*, Zhukov with the South-Western *Front*, and his deputy, Vatunin, with the North-Western *Front*.[5]

The attentions of key civilian members and advisers would soon be drawn away to what was effectively a war cabinet, the State Defence Committee, formed on 30 June 1941, with Stalin at its head as chairman:

DOCUMENT 26: *Decree of the Presidium of the Supreme Soviet of the USSR, TsK VKP (b) and* Sovnarkom *SSSR, 30 June 1941*

In view of the emerging state of emergency and in the interests of the rapid mobilization of all of the strengths of the peoples of the USSR for the repulsing of the enemy which has perfidiously attacked our Motherland, the Presidium of the Supreme Soviet of the USSR,... has recognized the necessity for:

1. The creation of a State Defence Committee made up of:

   Comrade Stalin, I.V. (Chairman)
   Comrade Molotov, V.M. (Deputy-Chairman)
   Comrade Voroshilov, K.E.
   Comrade Malenkov, G.M.
   Comrade Beria, L.P.
2. All powers of the state are concentrated in the hands of the State Defence Committee.
3. All citizens and all Party, state, *Komsomol* and military organs are required unquestioningly to carry out the decisions and decrees of the State Committee for Defence.

(Source: I.A. Gor'kov, 2002, p. 495)

On 10 July, ten days after the formation of the Headquarters of the High Command (*Stavka* GK), it was reorganized as the Headquarters of the Supreme Command (*Stavka* VK), to be reorganized again for the final time for the duration of the war on 8 August as the Headquarters of the Supreme High Command (*Stavka* VGK), with Stalin as self-appointed Supreme High Commander of the Soviet armed forces at its head.[6]

The fact that Stalin did not chair the Headquarters of the High Command of 23 June and did not make the address to the Soviet people on the evening of 22 June helped to create the myth that, shocked by the German invasion he had done so much to try to forestall, Stalin had lost control of the reins of power during the first two weeks of the war. This myth has subsequently been shown to be at best only partially true. Up to 28 June, as Stalin's appointment diary shows, Stalin was busy meeting key military, Party, government and security-services personnel. Some idea of the institutional affiliations of visitors to Stalin during the first days of the war is provided after their names and visiting times in Document 27:

DOCUMENT 27: Extracts from the appointments journals of Stalin's Kremlin office

22 June

Molotov	05:45–12:05	(NKO/MID)
Beria	05:45–09:20	(NKVD)
Timoshenko	05:45–08:30	(NKO)
Mekhlis	05:45–08:30	(GlavPU KA)
Zhukov	05:45–08:30	(GSh KA)
Malenkov	07:30–09:20	(VKP(b))
Mikoian	07:55–09:30	(SNK)
Kaganovich	08:00–09:35	(NKPS)
Voroshilov	08:00–10:15	(SNK)
Vishinskii	07:30–10:30	(MID)
Kuznetsov	08:15–08:30	(Either NK VMF or VKP(b))
Dmitrov	08:40–10:40	(Comintern)
Manuil'skii	08:40–10:40	(Comintern)
Kuznetsov	09:40–10:20	
Mikoian	09:50–10:30	
Molotov	12:55–16:45	
Voroshilov	11:40–12:05	
Beria	11:30–12:00	
Malenkov	11:30–12:00	
Voroshilov	12:30–16:45	
Mikoian	12:30–14:30	
Vishinskii	13:05–15:25	
Shaposhnikov	13:15–16:00	(NKO)
Timoshenko	14:00–16:00	
Zhukov	14:00–16:00	
Vatunin	14:00–16:00	(GSh KA)
Kuznetsov	15:20–15:45	(VMF?)
Kulik	15:30–16:00	(NKO)
Beria	16:25–16:45	

23 June

Molotov	03:20–06:25	(*Stavka* GK)
Voroshilov	03:25–06:25	(*Stavka* GK)
Beria	16:25–16:45	(*Stavka* GK)
Timoshenko	03:25–06:10	(*Stavka* GK)
Vatunin	03:30–06:10	
Kuznetsov	03:30–05:25	
Kaganovich	04:30–05:20	
Zhigarev	04:35–06:10	(VVS KA)
Timoshenko	18:50–20:45	
Merkulov	19:10–19:25	(NKVD)
Voroshilov	20:00–01:25	
Voznesenskii	20:00–21:25	(SNK)
Mekhlis	20:55–22:40	
Kaganovich	23:15–01:10	

Vatunin	23:55–00:55	
Timoshenko	23:55–00:55	
Kuznetsov	23:55–00:55	
Beria	00:00–01:25	
Vlasik	00:50–00:55	(Stalin's personal bodyguard – Okhr. IVS)
28 June		
Molotov	19:35–00:50	
Malenkov	19:35–23:10	
Budennii	19:35–19:50	(*Stavka* GK)
Merkulov	19:45–20:05	
Bulganin	20:15–20:20	(SNK)
Zhigarev	20:20–22:10	
Petrov	20:20–22:10	(Artillery construction)
Bulganin	20:40–20:45	
Timoshenko	21:30–23:10	
Zhukov	21:30–23:10	
Golikov	21:30–22:55	(GSh KA)
Kuznetsov	21:50–23:10	
Kabanov	22:00–22:10	(NK Electricity Production)
Stefanovskii	22:00–22:10	(Test pilot)
Suprun	22:00–22:10	(Test pilot)
Beria	22:40–00:50	
Ustinov	22:55–23:10	(NK Munitions)
Iakovlev	22:55–23:10	(GAU NKO)
Shcherbakov	22:10–23:30	(Sovinformburo)
Mikoian	23:30–00:50	
Merkulov	24:00–00:15	

(Source: I.A. Gor'kov, 2002, pp. 223–224, 228)

On 29–30 June, no such official meetings took place, at least not in Stalin's Kremlin office. Despite the blow no doubt felt by the fall of Minsk on 28 June, it seems that Stalin did not finally withdraw in despair to his *dacha* outside Moscow until the evening of Sunday 29 June, after communications had been lost with the Western *Front*, followed by a 'stormy' meeting of political and military leaders that took place in the People's Commissariat of Defence, during which, according to A.I. Mikoian, Deputy Chairman of the Council of People's Commissars and frequent participant in meetings with Stalin during the first days of the war, Zhukov purportedly sobbed.

DOCUMENT 28: *Extract from the memoirs of A.I. Mikoian on Stalin's leadership at the end of June 1941*

On the seventh day of the war, 28 June, fascist forces seized Minsk. Communications with the Belorussian Military District were cut.
    On the evening of 29 June Molotov, Malenkov, Beria and I gathered in Stalin's

Kremlin office. Detailed information on the situation in Belorussia had, at that time, not come in. We were aware only that there were no communications with forces of the Belorussian *Front*.

Stalin phoned the People's Commissar for Defence Timoshenko. But he could add nothing more on the situation on the western axis.

Alarmed by the way things had gone, Stalin suggested that we all head for the People's Commissariat for Defence and get to grips with the situation there.

At the commissariat were Timoshenko, Zhukov and Vatunin. Stalin conducted himself calmly, asking where the command for the Belorussian Military District was and what sort of communications there were with it.

Zhukov reported, that communications had been lost and they had been unable to restore them all day.

After that Stalin asked different questions: why had they allowed the German breakthrough, what measures had been taken for the restoration of communications, and so forth.

Zhukov replied on what measures had been taken, that people had been sent, but how long it would take to reestablish communications nobody could say.

They talked for around half an hour, relatively calmly. Then Stalin blew up: what sort of General Headquarters had they, what sort of Chief of Staff – that could lose control in such a way and not maintain communications with the troops....

Zhukov was of course no less worried than Stalin by the state of affairs, and Stalin's outburst was for him offensive. So this brave man burst into sobs [*razridalsia*] like an old woman and ran out into a different room. Molotov followed after him. We were all in a demoralized state. In about ten minutes Molotov brought in a superficially calm Zhukov, but his eyes were still moist. It was agreed that to communicate with the Belorussian Military District Kulik would go (this was suggested by Stalin).... Stalin was very depressed. As he left the People's Commissariat, he said the following phrase: 'Lenin left us with a great legacy, but we his beneficiaries, have ...'. We were shocked by this utterance. Did it follow, that we had lost everything for good? We considered, that he had said this for effect.

The following day, around four o'clock, Voznesenskii was with me in my office. Suddenly there was a call from Molotov requesting that we call in on him.

We went. Malenkov, Voroshilov and Beria were already with Molotov. We caught their conversation. Beria said, that it is necessary to form a State Defence Committee.. .. Voznesenskii and I agreed. It was agreed that Stalin be appointed head of the State Defence Committee.... We decided to go to him. He was at the nearby *dacha*.

It was in truth Molotov, who said that Stalin was in such a state of mental and physical exhaustion, that he wasn't interested in anything, had lost the initiative, and is in a bad way....

We arrived at Stalin's *dacha*. We found him in a small dining room sitting in an armchair. He looked at us questioningly and asked, 'Why have you come?' His demeanor was calm, but in a way strange, and his question was no less so. You see, as a matter of fact, he should have summoned us.

Molotov said, on behalf of all of us, that we have to concentrate power in order that things could be sorted out quickly, in order that the country be put on its feet. At the head of such an organization should be Stalin.

Stalin looked surprised but did not offer any opposition. 'OK', he said.

(Source: V.P. Naumov, kn.2, 1998, pp. 497–498)

On 3 July an apparently reinvigorated Stalin would address the Soviet people by radio:

> DOCUMENT 29: *Stalin's speech on the German invasion of the Soviet Union (radio address, Moscow, July 3, 1941)*
>
> Comrades! Citizens! Brothers and Sisters! Men of our army and navy! I am addressing you my friends!
>
> The perfidious military attack on our fatherland, begun on June 22 by Hitler's Germany, is continuing.
>
> In spite of the heroic resistance of the Red Army, and although the enemy's finest divisions and finest air force units have already been smashed and have met their doom on the field of battle, the enemy continues to push forward, hurling fresh forces into the attack.
>
> ...
>
> A grave danger hangs over our country.
>
> ...
>
> All our work must be immediately reconstructed on a war footing, everything must be subordinated to the interests of the front and the task of organizing the destruction of the enemy.
>
> ...
>
> The peoples of the Soviet Union must rise against the enemy and defend their rights and their land. The Red Army, Red Navy, and all citizens of the Soviet Union must defend every inch of Soviet soil, must fight to the last drop of blood for our towns and villages, must display the daring initiative and intelligence that are inherent in our people.
>
> We must organize all-round assistance to the Red Army....
>
> We must strengthen the Red Army's rear, subordinating all our work to this cause.
>
> ...
>
> We must wage a ruthless fight against all disorganizers of the rear, deserters, panic-mongers, rumour-mongers, we must exterminate spies and enemy parachutists.
>
> ...
>
> The collective farmer must drive off their cattle and turn over their grain to the safe keeping of the state authorities for transportation to the rear. All valuable property which cannot be withdrawn, must be destroyed without fail.
>
> In areas occupied by the enemy, guerrilla [partisan] units,... must be formed, diversionist groups must be organized to combat the enemy troops, to foment guerrilla warfare everywhere, to blow up bridges and roads, damage telephone and telegraph lines.... In the occupied regions conditions must be made unbearable for the enemy and all his accomplices. They must be hounded and annihilated at every step, and all their measures frustrated.
>
> This war with Nazi Germany cannot be considered an ordinary war. It is not only a war between two armies, it is also a great war of the Soviet people against the German fascist forces.
>
> ...
>
> In this war of liberation we shall not be alone. In this great war we shall have loyal allies in the peoples of Europe and America....
>
> In this connection the historic utterance[s] of the British Prime Minister Churchill regarding aid to the Soviet Union and the declaration of the United States government

signifying its readiness to render aid to our country,... can only evoke a feeling of gratitude in the hearts of the peoples of the Soviet Union....

Comrades, our forces are numberless....

The working people of Moscow and Leningrad have already commenced to form vast popular levies in support of the Red Army. Such popular levies must be raised in every city which is in danger of enemy invasion, all working people must be roused to defend our freedom, our honour, our country – in our patriotic war against German fascism.

In order to ensure the rapid mobilization of all forces of the peoples of the USSR and to repulse the enemy who treacherously attacked our country, a State Defence Committee has been formed in whose hands the entire power of the state has been vested.

(Source: Joseph Stalin, 1944, pp. 9–16)

Of note in the above speech is Stalin's referring to his audience as 'brothers and sisters' – a departure from pre-war norms and a move away from Communist terms and rhetoric in Soviet propaganda during the war, being replaced, particularly as many non-Russian Soviet republics in European Russia were under German occupation, by Russian nationalism. Also of note is Stalin's call for the population to take up arms against the invader on occupied territory, echoing calls to local Party leaders made on 29 June in Document 37. Finally Stalin mentions the raising of 'popular levies' or militia units [*narodnoe opolchenie*]. Such inadequately trained and equipped units would be thrown before German forces as they advanced on Leningrad and Moscow, suffering horrendous losses for little military gain.

Whilst forces of the German Army Group Centre had seized Minsk, the threat to the Ukrainian capital was also becoming stark, although on the Kiev axis German forces faced vigorous if unsustained counter-attacks by Soviet mechanized forces in the Dubno, Brodi, Lutsk and Rovno regions between 23 and 29 June. These Soviet counter-attacks were to a large extent unsuccessful because Soviet forces, typically short on fuel, were committed piecemeal. There is only partial truth to suggestions made by Konstantin Rokossovskii, then commanding 9th Mechanized Corps which counter-attacked near Novgorod-Volinsk, that 'German tank and motorized formations advancing on Kiev were provided with equipment that had far superior qualities to our outdated T-26 and BT-series tanks', although German forces were indeed assisted by 'a huge numerical superiority in tanks' and 'widespread use of aviation, which bombed our columns unhindered, especially there were the enemy struck'.[7] However, the superiority in tank strength was very much local[8] and despite the dearth of radios for Red Army tanks the T-26s and BT-series tanks could, if used effectively, have been a match for the PzKpfw IIs, IIIs and 38(t)s that were the backbone of German forces. German air superiority was, however, unquestionable, and certainly should have been mitigated by the appearance of more, albeit often outdated, Soviet aircraft over the battlefield, more of which could and indeed should have survived the initial German aerial onslaught if they had been dispersed on the basis of pre-war intelligence.

Rokossovskii's 9th Mechanized Corps was, as he notes, hopelessly under-strength on the eve of war with no more than a third of list strength in terms of armour and with its motorized infantry lacking transport – most Soviet units were in the process of reorganization and re-equipping. The 15th Mechanized Corps also in the south was in better shape, with more than two-thirds list strength, including 64-KV series and 71 T-34 tanks – vehicles that, even when deployed piecemeal, proved difficult to destroy.[9] On 23 June T-34s of 15th Mechanized Corps had caused the German 197th Infantry Division some concern, but were not deployed in sufficient strength or with sufficient support to overcome German anti-tank defences.[10]

Despite Soviet counter-attacks on the German flanks that slowed the German advance on Kiev, by early July the military situation seemed very much favourable to Germany, prompting German General Franz Halder, head of OKH, to comment in his diary entry for 3 July that, given the destruction of such substantial Soviet forces west of the Dvina and Dnepr Rivers, 'it is probably no overstatement to say that the Russian campaign has been won in the space of two weeks'.[11] By 9 July German forces of Army Groups Centre and North were making good progress towards Moscow and Leningrad respectively, even if progress in the south was somewhat slower, as illustrated in Figure 3.1.

Certainly at this stage of the war the destruction of enemy forces was more important than the conquest of territory, and Soviet mechanized forces deployed in the border regions been decimated. Soviet air forces had been similarly weakened, with German close-support aircraft able to rove fairly freely looking for targets little concerned by Soviet fighters. Taking the example of the South-Western *Front*, facing 1st Panzer Group: on the eve of war the Kiev Special Military District (which would become the South-Western *Front* on the outbreak of war) had 1,238 fighter aircraft available, of which 356 were modern types, namely Yak-1, MiG-1, MiG-3, LaGG-3, and a total of 1,913 aircraft including light and medium bombers, ground attack (65 Il-2) and reconnaissance aircraft. In addition, long-range bombers of 2 DBAK (Long-range Bombing Aviation Corps) and 18 DBAD (Long-range Bombing Aviation Division) under central control (DB-3, Il-4, TB-3 and 9 TB-7) were based in the military district at Kursk and Skomorokhi respectively, brining total aircraft available to 2,333. Only 1,683 aircrews were available for those aircraft under military district control, of which, whilst 92 per cent were considered fit for daytime flying in simple meteorological conditions, only 30 per cent were considered trained for complex daylight conditions, and 21.3 per cent for simple night flying.[12] On 11 July the aircraft shown in Table 3.1 were available or potentially available for operations.

Despite a lack of air cover, poor intelligence, command and control and other such deficiencies in Soviet organization during the summer battles of 1941, many Soviet units fought bravely, inflicting casualties on German

Figure 3.1 Changes in the frontline from the start of Operation 'Barbarossa' to the eve of the Soviet counter-offensive below Moscow, 22 June to early December 1941.

Key:

1. Murmansk
2. Arkhangel'sk
3. Tikhvin
4. Tallin
5. Novgorod
6. Pskov
7. Staraia Russa
8. Kalinin
9. Smolensk
10. Viaz'ma
11. El'nia
12. Briansk
13. Tula
14. Voronezh
15. Stalingrad
16. Khar'kov
17. Sevastopol'
18. Odessa
19. Brest
20. Warsaw
21. Kuibishev

forces that would have a cumulative impact. Perhaps the best-known example of protracted Soviet resistance in the first weeks of Barbarossa was the defence of the Brest Fortress, pockets in which continued to hold out until late July, despite being well behind German lines. Nonetheless, the resistance of many Soviet units was not so stubborn, understandable given they were without air cover, often encircled, low on supplies, with poor command and control over subordinate units and limited intelligence, and consequently unaware that the German noose around them was more permeable that it might have seemed.

In order to increase discipline in the armed forces, within weeks of the start of the war the Soviet leadership reintroduced dual command, returning to the situation that had first existed during the Russian Civil War and more recently between 1937 and 1940.

Table 3.1 Airpower of the South-Western *Front* as of 11 July 1941

Total aircraft for the South-Western Front

Type	Serviceable	Unserviceable	Total
SB	14	24	38
Ar-2	2	2	4
Pe-2	6	6	12
Yak-4	5	5	10
MiG-3	10	3	13
I-153	66	20	86
I-16	105	26	131
I-15	9	4	13
Yak-2	2	2	4
Yak-1	14	8	22
Il-2	10	10	20
Su-2	6	21	27
Totals	249	131	380

Source: *SBD 38*, pp. 7–8.

DOCUMENT 30: Decree of the Presidium of the Supreme Soviet of the USSR on the reorganization of organs of political propaganda and the introduction of the institute of military commissars in the Workers' and Peasants' Red Army, 16 July 1941

The war has increased the volume of political work in our army and demanded that political workers do not limit their work to propaganda, but in the same manner take upon themselves the responsibility for military work at the front as well.

From a different angle the war has increased the complexity of the work of the regiment and division and demands that the commander of the regiment and division be provided with full assistance from the direction of political workers not only in the sphere of political work, but also in the military sphere.

All of these new responsibilities in the work of political workers associated with the shift from peacetime to wartime demand that the role and responsibility of political workers be raised to a similar level to that at which it stood during the Civil War against the foreign military interventionists.

In accordance with this ... the Presidium of the Supreme Soviet decrees:

...

2. To introduce in all regiments and divisions, headquarters, military-educational institutions and establishments of the Red Army the institute of military commissars, and in companies, batteries and squadrons the institute of political supervisors [*politruki*].

(Source: O.A. Rzheshevskii, 1990, p. 421)

Further details of the role of the commissar were provided in the same issue of the journal *Red Army Propagandist* in which the above decree was published.

> DOCUMENT 31: *The position of military commissars in the Worker's and Peasant's Red Army (July 1941)*
>
> Confirmed by the Presidium of the Supreme Soviet of the USSR
>
> ...
>
> 2. The military commissar is the representative of the Party and government in the Red Army and along with the commander carries full responsibility for the carrying out of a military task by a unit, for its resilience in battle and its unwavering readiness to fight to the last drop of blood with the enemies of our Motherland and with honour to defend every last inch of Soviet ground.
> 3. The military commissar is the moral leader of his unit (formation), the first line of defence of its material and spiritual interests. 'If a commander is the head [*glava*] of the regiment, then the commissar of a regiment should be the father and soul of his regiment' (Stalin).
>
> ...
>
> 8. The military commissar must ... carry out a merciless struggle with cowards, panic mongers and deserters, spreading revolutionary order and military discipline with a firm hand. Coordinating his activities with the organs of the 3rd Board of the Ministry of Defence, the military commissar is obliged to nip any sign of treason in the bud.
> 9. The military commissar directs the activities of the political organs, and in the same way the Party and *Komsomol* organizations of military units.
>
> ...
>
> 11. All orders for a regiment, division, board or institution are signed jointly by the commander and military commissar.
>
> (Source: *KPSS o vooruzhennikh silakh Sovetskogo Soiuza*, 1981, pp. 305–306)

Also of significance for the political supervision of the armed forces was the transfer of counter-intelligence in the armed forces and under the 3rd Board of the Ministry of Defence mentioned in point 8 of Document 31 back to the NKVD after a brief period of control by the People's Commissariat for Defence.

> DOCUMENT 32: *Decree of the State Committee of Defence No. 187ss on the re-establishment of organs of the 3rd Board of the NKO SSSR as special sections of the NKVD SSSR, 17 July 1941*
>
> 1. To reestablish organs of the 3rd Board in both the field army and military districts (from departments in divisions and higher) as special sections, and the 3rd Board as the Board of Special Sections.
> 2. At the same time to subordinate the Board of Special Sections and special sections to the People's Commissariat for Internal Affairs, and the representative of the special section in a regiment and special section in a division to subordinate to the appropriate commissar of a regiment or division.
> 3. The principal task of special sections during war is to be considered the decisive struggle with espionage and treachery in units of the Red Army and the liquidation of desertion directly in the prefrontal zone.
> 4. To give special sections the power to arrest deserters, and where necessary to shoot them on the spot.

5. To require the NKVD to provide the special sections with the necessary armed detachments from NKVD forces.
6. To require heads of rear area security to have direct communication with the special sections and to render then full support.

Chairman of the State Defence Committee, Stalin

(Source: V.P. Eroshin *et al.*, 2000, pp. 337–338)

The security services would be responsible for enforcing Order Number 270 of the Headquarters of the Supreme High Command of 16 August 1941 on the armed forces, which made surrender tantamount to treason.

DOCUMENT 33: *Order of the Headquarters of the Supreme High Command of the Red Army Number 270, 16 August 1941*

Not only our friends, but also our enemies are forced to recognize that in our war of liberation with the German-Fascist conquerors, units of the Red Army, the majority by a huge margin, their commanders and commissars, are conducting themselves irreproachably, bravely, and at times heroically. Even those units of our army which are by chance separated from the army and fall in to encirclement preserve the spirit of perseverance and bravery and do not surrender, trying to inflict even greater harm on the enemy and to break out of encirclement.

...

But we cannot hide the fact that recently there have been a number of disgraceful instances of surrender to the enemy. Individual generals have exhibited a poor example to our forces.

...

Is it possible to tolerate cowards in the ranks of the Red Army, deserting to the enemy and giving themselves up, or the sort of leaders of limited spirit, who in the event of the first glitch at the front tear off signs of rank and desert to the rear? No, it is not! If we give freedom to these cowards and deserters, in a short time they will demoralize our army and ruin our Motherland. Cowards and deserters have to be destroyed.

...

I order:

1. That commanders and political workers who tear off indicators of rank and desert in battle to the rear or give themselves up to the enemy are to be considered malicious deserters, the families of whom are subject to arrest as the family of a deserter who has broken their oath and betrayed the Motherland.

    All commanders and commissars of higher rank are required to shoot such deserters from command-level ranks on the spot.
2. Encircled units and formations are to selflessly fight until the last possible moment, taking care of equipment,... breaking through to their own lines from the enemy rear, bringing defeat to the fascist dogs.

...

This order is to be read out to all companies, troops, batteries, squadrons, commands and headquarters.

Headquarters of the Supreme High Command of the Red Army:
Chairman of the State Defence Committee, I. Stalin.

(Source: O.A. Rzheshevskii, 1990, pp. 423–424)

A rise in cases of self-mutilation in order to avoid the horrors of combat presumably led to the following additional crime for which the special sections could mete out punishment, including summary execution:

DOCUMENT 34: *Decree of the State Defence Committee No. 377 ss, 2 August 1941, Moscow, Kremlin*

NKVD Query

Special sections are permitted to arrest, and in necessary instances shoot on the spot in the same manner as deserters, individuals who bring self-inflicted wounds upon themselves.
Chairman of the State Defence Committee, I. Stalin.

(Source: RGASPI f.644.o.1.d.5. l.176)

The stoicism of troops facing the Axis and particularly German advance would be encouraged not only by the influence of commissars on commanders but also by the use of blocking detachments of NKVD troops behind the front lines to prevent the unauthorized withdrawal of Red Army units, as suggested by the requirement for NKVD troops for special sections in Document 32 above. With the route to the rear blocked, courage in the face of the enemy, or at least some relief from the tensions of the front line, would be provided by the regulation vodka ration:

DOCUMENT 35: *Decree of the State Defence Committee Number 562/ss 'On the introduction of vodka to the supplies of the active Red Army', 22 August 1941*

From 1 September 1941 the provision of 100 grammes a day of 40 percent proof vodka per individual Red Army soldier and commander of forces in the front line of the active army is to be introduced.
Chairman of the State Defence Committee, Stalin

(Source: A.F. Kiselev and E.M. Shchagin, 1996, p. 519)

As the Soviet leadership sought to stiffen the resolve of waverers in the front line through fear or with vodka, many Soviet units fought on with tenacity, even if with dwindling resources. Not only had the Soviet armed forces lost huge numbers of men and vast quantities of materials at the borders, but the Soviet capacity to replace the latter in particular was deteriorating in the short term at least. From 24 June the Soviet leadership was making preparations for the evacuation of plant and materials from the enemy advance, starting with the creation of a Council for Evacuation:

> **DOCUMENT 36:** *From the decree of TsK VKP (b) and SNK SSSR on the creation of a Council for Evacuation, 24 June 1941*
>
> For the direction of the evacuation of population, institutions, military and other goods, the equipment of industrial concerns and other valuables the Central Committee of the Communist Party and Council of People's Commissars of the USSR decrees:
>
> 1. To establish a Council for Evacuation....
> 2. To require the Council to start work immediately.
> 3. To establish that the decisions of the Council for Evacuation are to be signed by its chairman and are compulsory.
>
> (Source: V.P. Eroshin *et al.*, 2000, p. 62)

That which could not be relocated would be destroyed, as outlined in the key joint directive by the Council of People's Commissars and the Central Committee of the Party of 29 June 1941,[13] in which it was stated that:

> **DOCUMENT 37:** *To Party and Soviet organizations of prefrontal regions, 29 June 1941*
>
> 4. In the event of the forced retreat of Red Army units it is necessary to remove railway rolling stock, not to leave the enemy a single steam engine, not a single wagon, not to leave the enemy a single kilogram of grain, not a litre of fuel. Kolkhoz peasants should drive away livestock, give grain over to the protection of state organs for removal to the rear. All valuable resources, including precious metals, bread and fuel, which cannot be taken away, should of course be destroyed.
>
> (Source: *KPSS o Vooruzhennikh Silakh Sovetskogo Soiuza*, 1981, p. 298)

Whilst some resources were inevitably lost to Axis forces, and much was destroyed which was earmarked for evacuation, Soviet achievements in relocating whole factories from European Russia to, in many instances, the eastern side of the Ural mountains were considerable. However, such factories would not be in operation for a number of months.[14]

At this point the Soviet Union had already requested a range of war materials from the Anglo-Saxon powers, the terms under which they would be provided being established during the first weeks of the war. Whilst the issue of Allied aid to the Soviet Union will be examined in Chapter 8, at this point it is worth noting that such aid would only start to play a significant role in the fighting by the Battle for Moscow in late November and early December 1941.

In the meantime, Soviet forces would have to manage with their own resources, with tanks of any sort, and particularly modern tanks, being one commodity in increasingly short supply as Soviet units were overrun and many tanks were either destroyed by their crews or captured by Axis forces. During the summer and autumn tanks were increasingly concentrated in battalion- and brigade-sized units for allocation by a Stalin attempting to micromanage many aspects of the fighting at the front. Justification for breaking up large armoured formations, initially reducing corps to divisions, was provided in a directive of the Headquarters of the Supreme Command of 15 July 1941.

DOCUMENT 38: *Directive of the Headquarters of the Supreme Command to commanders of the forces of fronts, armies and military districts, 15 July 1941*

The experience of three weeks of war with German fascism allows us to come to a number of conclusions, of critical importance from the point of view of the successful conduct of operations by the Red Army and the improvement of its organization.

Firstly: The experience of war has shown, that our mechanized corps, as far too massive amalgamations, are not very mobile, nimble and suitable for maneuver, not including the fact that they are vulnerable targets for enemy aviation. The Headquarters considers it necessary, at the first available opportunity ... to disband the mechanized corps, dividing them up into separate tank divisions, subordinate to army commanders, and motorized divisions to be reformed as standard rifle divisions with tanks....

Secondly: Experience of war has shown, that an excess of large and cumbersome armies with a large number of divisions significantly complicates the organization of battle and the direction of forces in combat, especially when one keeps in mind the youth and limited experience of our headquarters and commanders. The Headquarters considers that it is necessary to gradually ... prepare for a move to a system of small armies with five or a maximum of six divisions without corps-level command and direct subordination of divisions to the army command.

Thirdly: Experience has shown that rifle divisions have difficulty in countering the activities of enemy armoured units in not having perhaps a small number of tanks at their disposal. There is no doubt that our rifle divisions would fight better ... if they had at their disposal perhaps a company of medium or even light tanks. The Headquarters considers it necessary where possible to attach at least a company of medium or light tanks and where possible a platoon of KV (three tanks) to our rifle divisions.

Fourthly: Our forces have to some extent underestimated the significance of cavalry. In current circumstances at the front, where the enemy rear is extended for hundreds of kilometers in forested regions and completely unprotected against major raids from our lines, raids by Red cavalry ... could play a decisive role in the task of disorganizing command and control and the supply of German forces.... It follows that gradually, ... existing cavalry corps and divisions should be reformed into light cavalry divisions of a raiding type, with three thousand men in each....

Fifth: The experience of war has shown, that our aviation units, corps and multi-regiment divisions, and regiments consisting of sixty aircraft, are very clumsy, cumbersome and unsuited to a war of maneuver, not mentioning that the cumbersomeness of units inhibits the dispersal of aircraft on airfields and makes it easier for the enemy to destroy them on the ground. VVS experience of the last few days has shown, that regiments of 30 aircraft and divisions of two regiments without corps-level units is the best form of organization for aviation.... The Headquarters considers it necessary to gradually move to organizing aviation regiments with 30 aircraft (three squadrons), and aviation divisions with two such regiments, without corps-level units.

...

Headquarters of the Supreme Command

(Source: V.P. Naumov (ed.), kn.2, 1998, pp. 471–472)

Despite horrendous Soviet losses, Soviet counter-attacks against the advancing German forces were causing damage to the German spearheads. One of the most prominent examples of these counter-attacks during the summer of 1941 in the Soviet historiography is that which took place between 12 and 14 August to the east of Staraia Russa, during which the 11th and 34th Armies of the North-Western *Front* attacked forces of the German 16th Army as the 48th Army held defensive positions to the north near Shimsk to the west of Lake Il'men'. Whilst such counter-attacks suggested a relative cohesion to Soviet forces that had not existed only weeks before and slowed down German forces, as well as whittling away hard to replace strength, the costs of operations in the area were sizeable for Soviet forces. For instance, as of 1 September 1941, after German forces had broken through defensive positions on 16 August forcing the 48th Army back on Chudovo and Kolpino, the 48th Army was down to the strength (with official strength for such units as of 22 June 1941 in brackets) shown in Document 39.

DOCUMENT 39: *Report of the head of the Political Board of the Leningrad* Front *to the command of the North-Western* Front, *1 September 1941*

Incorporated into the 48th Army, subordinated to the Leningrad Front, are: 1st Mountain-Rifle Brigade, 21st Tank Division and 128th and 311th Rifle Divisions. However the serious misfortunes which befell the Army in the fighting for Novgorod and in the Liuban' region have led to the loss of the bulk of its personnel and almost all its equipment. On 1 September units of the Army had the following at their disposal:

Personnel

	Unit	Command	Political	Other officers	NCOs	Ranks	Total
1	128th Rifle Division	71	39	75	99	472	756 (14,448)
2	1st Mountain Rifle Brigade	69	16	83	113	797	1,078
3	311th Rifle Division	141	58	128	333	2,314	2,973
4	21st Tank Division – All command			119	101	811	1,031 (10,419)

continued

Armaments

	Unit	Rifles	Automatic rifles	HMGs	LMGs	Artillery and mortars
1	128th Rifle Division	475 (10,240)	29	2 (174)	1 (392)	45 mm AT – 2 Mortars – 16
2	1st Mountain Rifle Brigade	601	–	6	5	76 mm artillery – 2 122 mm howitzers – 3
3	311th Rifle Division	2,842	2	12	13	
4	21st Rifle [sic] Division	350	–	–	7	
	Total	4,268	31	20	26	Guns – 7 Mortars – 16

Munitions

	Unit	Rifle cartridges	Shells	Grenades	Mines
1	128th Rifle Division	62,000	–	20	Sufficient
2	1st Mountain Rifle Brigade	30,000	–	–	Not counted
3	311th Rifle Division	4,000,000	45 mm – 2,000	–	–
4	21st Rifle [sic] Division	53,000	–	–	–
	Total	4,145,000	2,000	20	–

Transport resources

	Unit	Horses	Light vehicles	Lorries	Special	Tractors	Motorcycles
1	128th Rifle Division	–	2	65 (657 – auto-mobiles + tractors)	4	–	–
2	1st Mountain Rifle Brigade	122	4	76	2	–	–
3	311th Rifle Division	730 (3,039)	5	136	2	2	2
4	21st Tank Division	–	1	40 (1,444 auto-mobiles + tractors)	–	5	–
	Total	852	12	317	8	7	2

Radio sets

Unit	Radio 4-A/rsb	5-AK/rb	6-PK
1 128th Rifle Division	1	2	–
2 1st Mountain Rifle Brigade	–	–	–
3 311th Rifle Division	7	–	–
4 21st Tank Division	–	2	5
Total	8	4	5

(Source: N.L. Volkovskii (ed.), 2004, pp. 175–176. List strengths for 22 June 1941 from K.A. Kalashnikov et al., 2003, p. 62)

Limited communications resources hampered Soviet command and control, although it gave German intelligence fewer sources of information on Soviet activities than they might otherwise have had, particularly where, at the beginning of the war, Soviet radio procedures had on numerous occasions been sloppy.[15] On 14 September 1941 the 48th Army was disbanded and the remnants used in the formation of the 54th Army.[16] It can be assumed that the 21st Tank Division had lost all of its tanks,[17] with trained tank crews subsequently being thrown into battle as infantry by many *fronts*.

DOCUMENT 40: *To commanders of the forces of* fronts *on the rules regarding the use of tank crews, temporarily without vehicles, 10 July 1941*

1. According to reports from *fronts*, the General Headquarters has become aware that the crews of armoured units, temporarily without tanks, have been used in the building of non-armoured units, which squander a well-trained contingent of tank crews without absolute necessity. This has especially been the case on the North-Western *Front*.
2. The People's Commissar of Defence ordered:
    a) That all tank crews be urgently removed from infantry and other units and be concentrated in *front* reserves and replacement units, carrying out in the process General Staff directive Number 946/org of 6.07.1941.

...

Sokolovskii.

(Source: *RA T.23 (12–1).*, 1998, p. 72)

The Soviet desperation to halt advancing German forces is indicated by the mobilization of poorly trained militia units for the defence of Moscow and Leningrad, mentioned by Stalin in Document 29 above. Such units were mobilized from Moscow according to State Defence Committee decree number 10 of 4 July 1941:

> DOCUMENT 41: *On the voluntary mobilization of workers of Moscow and the Moscow Region to militia divisions, from GOKO Decree Number 10 of 4 July 1941*
>
> In accordance with the desire expressed by workers and the suggestions of Soviet, Party, union and *Komsomol* organizations of Moscow and the Moscow Region the State Defence Committee decrees:
>
> To mobilize 200,000 people from Moscow and 70,000 from the Moscow Region to the militia divisions.
>
> The mobilization of workers, administrative personnel and students of Moscow and the creation of 25 divisions is to be conducted on district by district principles.
>
> In the first instance the formation of seven divisions is to be carried out by 7 July.
>
> The mobilized divisions are to receive a number and the name of the district, for instance 1st Sokolnicheskii District Division.
>
> ...
>
> The mobilization and barracking of units of the militia is to be conducted using the building resources of the district soviets (schools, clubs and other buildings), with the exception of buildings allocated as hospitals.
>
> ...
>
> The Headquarters of the Moscow Military Region is to supply units with arms, munitions and necessary items.
>
> ...
>
> During the full period of mobilization in units of the militia the following maintenance payments are to be preserved: for workers – to the sum of average wages, for administrative personnel the sum of their salary, for students the sum of their grants, and for the families of kolkhoz peasants financial assistance is to be determined according to the Decree of the Presidium of the Supreme Soviet SSSR 'On methods for the determination of payments to the families of military personnel of the ranks and NCOs during wartime' of 26.VI 1941.
>
> In the event of the disablement or the death of the mobilized the mobilized and his family have the right to receive a pension on a par with someone called up into the Red Army.
>
> (Source: *KPSS o vooruzhennikh silakh Sovetskogo Soiuza*, 1981, pp. 302–303)

Such poorly equipped and trained divisions of the *opolcheniia* were massacred by German units before both Moscow and Leningrad, buying little time at horrendous cost.

By the beginning of July German forces threatened both Moscow and Leningrad, the noose around the latter threatening with the help of the Finns to the north, although in the far south relatively organized resistance had slowed the German advance more significantly.

The construction of the Mozhaisk line to defend Moscow was ordered on 16 July 1941, with the construction of the Luga line to defend the approaches to Leningrad the subject of an order of 5 July (Document 97 in Chapter 7). The Mozhaisk line was to be manned primarily by the militia divisions and NKVD troops.

DOCUMENT 42: *Decree of the State Defence Committee No. 172 ss concerning the Mozhaisk defence line, 16 July 1941*

1. The addition of ten militia divisions to the list of those armed is to be given priority and they are to be fully equipped [*obmundirovat'*].
2. These divisions are to be divided into two armies of five divisions and Comrade Artem'ev [Commander of the Moscow Military District] is to be delegated to put forward candidates for the posts of commanders of armies and chiefs of staff.
3. The aim of these divisions is the defence of Moscow on the Mozhaisk line, their disposition along the Mozhaisk line.
4. ...
5. Making up the Mozhaisk defence line, in addition to ten militia divisions there will be a further five divisions of the NKVD....
6. To permit Comrade Artem'ev to take 200 85 mm AA guns from the Moscow PVO and organize them into ten light artillery anti-tank regiments (with five batteries in every regiment).
7. For each army of the Mozhaisk line (three armies in total) to organize one regiment of army artillery per army, for example of 122 mm howitzers, 152 mm guns or howitzers and 203 mm howitzers, and to also use naval artillery for this purpose....
8. The organization of the Mozhaisk line and its artillery provision is to be organized within a five-day period, that is by 21 July of this year.
9. To permit the command of the MVO to form ten militia battalions of 500 men for the reinforcement of militia divisions.

Chairman of the State Defence Committee, I. Stalin

(Source: V.P. Eroshin *et al.*, 2000, pp. 335–336)

Despite hastily prepared defences and the throwing in to the battle of militia divisions in addition to newly created Red Army units, German forces captured both Narva and Novgorod on the road to Leningrad on 17 August 1941; the capture of Schlissel'berg on 8 September signalling the start of the blockade, the subject of Chapter 7. The German encirclement of Leningrad had required armoured forces from Army Group Centre advancing on Moscow, which had also been redirected from the Moscow axis to encircle substantial Soviet forces near Kiev and secure the 'breadbasket' of the Ukraine for Germany. Whilst this redirection of forces from the end of July weakened German moves towards Moscow, Soviet resistance near Smolensk was also intense, with German forces under Guderian subsequently not having the resources to hold on to the bridgehead over the River Desna 75 miles south-east of Smolensk, against which the Red Army was able to concentrate significant resources.

DOCUMENT 43: *To the Head of Artillery of the Red Army on departure to the El'nia area, 1 August 1941*

The People's Commissar [of Defence] has ordered you to leave for El'nia now and assist locally in the organization of the destruction of the enemy near El'nia with artillery fire, mortar fire,... bearing in mind the need to destroy the enemy within the next 1–2 days. The People's Commissar sees this matter as being of particularly great significance.

...

Zhukov

(Source: *RA T.23 (12–1)*, 1998, p. 107)

DOCUMENT 44: *Military Situation Report of the Commander of forces of the Reserve* Front *to the Supreme High Command on the conduct of operations in the El'nia region, 21 August 1941 04:45*

Up to 20.8.1941 units of the 24th Army of the Reserve *Front* in the El'nia region have not succeeded in fully encircling and destroying the German units.

19.8 in the region of Gur'evo, Sadki the enemy brought in as an addition the 137th Infantry Division, previously in position before 43rd Army.

In the region of Klemiatino, Grichano the enemy brought in a new unit, the number of which has not been ascertained.

For the last ten days of operations I personally have been with all divisions and locally established the conditions in which the fighting was taking place and how units were conducting themselves.

Soldiers and their commanders hold themselves and the majority in good order. They are not afraid of losses and have already learnt the technical and tactical dimension to the destruction of enemy forces, but units are under strength and worn down from enemy attacks and fire, which recently has not ceased at night.

Given the existing lack of strength of our units to conclusively encircle and destroy 4–5 German infantry divisions is not possible.

The continuation of the battle with current forces will result in the terminal loss of fighting capability of the units in action.

We now have to reinforce units to at least 60% strength, bring in more munitions, allow troops a short breathing space, thoroughly establish the location of enemy weak spots, after which vigorously attacking.

I request your permission to:

...

4) Start the attack with fresh troops from the morning of 25.8.

...

Zhukov.

(Source: *RA T.16 (5–1)*, 1998, pp. 363–364)

The eventual destruction of the German bridgehead near El'nia was portrayed as a significant Soviet victory by Soviet leaders:

DOCUMENT 45: *Order of the military soviet of the Reserve* Front *to the troops due to the expected victory near El'nia, Novo-Aleksandrovskoe, 7 September 1941*

Comrade Red Army men, commanders, commissars, political workers and all of the command personnel of the *front*!

After persistent and bitter fighting by the courageous units of our 24th Army a significant victory is expected. In the El'nia region a crushing blow has been struck against German forces. The broken enemy, having suffered huge losses, bleeding to death, is retreating in disarray.

The High Command of the German Army saw the El'nia region as being of great significance as a very advantageous position for further advance. The Fascist command strove to hold the El'nia region in its hands regardless of the cost, not regretting the loss of the lives of thousands of its soldiers and officers.

...

Comrade Red Army men, commanders, commissars, political workers! The military soviet of the *front* congratulates you on your brilliant victory.

...

Commander of forces of the *front*, General of the Army, Zhukov
Member of the military soviet, Kruglov

(Source: O.A. Rzheshevskii, 1990, p. 425)

However, even this relatively minor success came at considerable cost:

DOCUMENT 46: *Headquarters of the Supreme High Command directive Number 001805 to the Western* Front *commander concerning a transition to the defence, 0335 hours, 10 September 1941*

The prolonged offensive by Western *Front* forces on the well-dug-in enemy has led to heavy losses. The enemy has withdrawn to prepared defensive positions and our units are being forced to gnaw through them.

The *Stavka* orders that you cease further attacks on the enemy....
B. Shaposhnikov

(Source: David Glantz, 'Forgotten Battles of the German-Soviet War (1941–1945), Part II', 2000, pp. 209–210)

DOCUMENT 47: *Headquarters of the Supreme High Command directive Number 001941 to the Reserve* Front *commander concerning shortcomings in the organization of the offensive, 0600 hours, 13 September 1941*

The recent 24th and 43rd Armies' offensive did not provide completely positive results and led only to excessive losses both in personnel and in equipment.

The main reasons for the lack of success were the absence of the required attack grouping in the armies, the attempt to attack along the entire *front*, and the insufficiently strong, overly short, and disgracefully organized aviation and artillery preparation for the infantry and tank attacks.

...

> B. Shaposhnikov
> (Source: David Glantz, 'Forgotten Battles of the German-Soviet War (1941–1945), Part II',
> 2000, p. 210)

Even Zhukov, organizer of the attack, was not beyond criticism, although with so few successes and with huge losses without success, the costs of this victory would to a large extent be ignored.

Soviet operations near Kiev were less successful, with authorization to withdraw coming too late to save the bulk of Soviet forces in the region, as German forces tightened the noose at Lokhvitsa, 125 miles behind Kiev, on 15 September 1941. Soviet losses near Kiev were staggering. According to Krivosheev, the 'Kiev Strategic Defensive' Operation from 7 July to 26 September saw the Soviet South-Western *Front* lose 531,471 troops as irrecoverable losses, out of a total of 627,000. German forces claimed to have captured 665,000 prisoners in the region.[18]

Nonetheless, German leaders were shocked by the Soviet ability to continue to throw new units in to the fighting, bringing about the gradual realization that, for many, the war in the East would not be over before the winter. Despite German losses and logistical difficulties in the vast expanses of what was only the European part of the Soviet Union, the renewed advance on Moscow, Operation 'Typhoon', started on 2 October 1941; Operation 'Typhoon' proper being preceded by diversionary operations in the south on 30 September, the official start of the defensive phase of the Battle of Moscow in Soviet sources.

Guide to further reading

H. Boog, J. Forster, J. Hoffmann, E. Klink, R.-D. Muller, G.R. Ueberschar and E. Osers (eds), *Germany and the Second World War. Volume IV. The Attack on the Soviet Union* (Oxford: Clarendon Press, 1998).

Charles Burdick and Hans-Adolf Jacobsen (eds), *The Halder War Diary, 1939–1942* (Novato, CA: Presidio, 1988).

'Collection of Combat Documents of the Great Patriotic War, Volume 34: Part IV, Operations of the North-Western Front, 15–23 June 1941', *JSMS*, Volume 4, Number 4 (December 1991), pp. 674–737.

'Combat Documents of the Soviet North-Western Front 24 June – 1 July 1941', *JSMS*, Volume 5, Number 1 (January 1992), pp. 115–157.

'Combat Documents of the Soviet North-Western Front Armies 21 June – 1 July 1941', *JSMS*, Volume 5, Number 2 (June 1992), pp. 267–299.

David Glantz, 'A Collection of Combat Documents Covering the First Three Days of the Great Patriotic War', *JSMS*, Volume 4, Number 1 (January 1991), pp. 150–190.

David Glantz, 'A Collection of Combat Documents Covering Soviet Western Front Operations: 24–30 June 1941', *JSMS*, Volume 4, Number 2 (June 1991), pp. 327–385.

David Glantz, 'Combat Documents of Soviet Western Front Armies 22–30 June 1941', *JSMS*, Volume 4, Number 3 (September 1991), pp. 513–534.

David Glantz (ed.), *The Initial Period on the Eastern Front 22 June-August 1941* (London: Frank Cass, 1993).

David Glantz, *Stumbling Colossus: The Red Army on the Eve of World War* (Lawrence, KS: University of Kansas Press, 1998).

David Glantz, 'Forgotten Battles of the German-Soviet War (1941–1945), Part I' ['The Red Army's July Counterstrokes'], *JSMS*, Volume 12, Number 4 (December 1999), pp. 149–197.

David Glantz, 'Forgotten Battles of the German-Soviet War (1941–1945), Part II' ['The August Counterstrokes'], *JSMS*, Volume 13, Number 1 (March 2000), pp. 172–237.

Curzio Malaparte, *The Volga Rises in Europe* (Edinburgh: Berlinn Limited, 2000).

4   The Battle of Moscow

With the redeployment of German armoured forces after the Kiev encirclement and from the Leningrad axis, 2nd Panzer Group resumed its advance eastwards on 30 September 1941 in preparation for the start of the principal thrusts towards Moscow by 3rd and 4th Panzer Groups – Operation 'Typhoon', commencing 2 October.

Within days 3rd and 4th Panzer Groups had encircled the bulk of Soviet forces defending Moscow to the west. The principal pocket of Soviet forces, containing the bulk of 19th, 20th, 24th and 32nd Armies, was that to the west of Viaz'ma, created on 7 October when forces of 3rd and 4th Panzer Groups linked up. German forces claimed to have captured 660,000 Soviet POWs. The second pocket was created south of Briansk, trapping the Soviet 3rd and 13th Armies, and netting the Germans another 100,000 Soviet POWs.

On 5 October, a German column was spotted about 90 miles east of the 'Typhoon' start line, and about one-third of the way from the line to Moscow. The Mozhaisk defensive line, 120 miles behind existing Soviet positions, the construction of which had been ordered in July, was hastily readied to halt the German advance on the capital.

Whilst on many occasions German troops faced stubborn resistance, the NKVD found numerous instances of desertion.

DOCUMENT 48: *To the People's Commissar of Internal Affairs SSSR General Commissar of State Security Comrade Beria, {October} 1941*

For information
From the start of the war up to 10 October of this year special sections of the NKVD and blocking detachments of the NKVD for rear area security have held 657,364 servicemen separated from their units and running away from the front.

Of these, 249,969 people have been held by operational screens of the special sections and 407,395 by blocking detachments of NKVD rear-area security forces.

Of those held, 25,878 were arrested, the remaining 632,486 formed in to units and sent back to the front.

Amongst those arrested by the special sections:

Spies	1,505
Saboteurs	308
Traitors	2,621
Cowards and panicmongers	2,643
Deserters	8,772
Those spreading provocational rumours	3,987
Self-inflicted wounds	671
Others	4,371
Total	24,878

By order of the special sections and according to sentences of military tribunals 10,201 people have been shot....

By *front*, these figures can be divided up as follows:

Leningrad [*Front*]	Arrested	1,044
	Shot	854 ...
Karelian	Arrested	468
	Shot	263 ...
Northern	Arrested	1,683
	Shot	933 ...
North-Western	Arrested	1,600
	Shot	730
Western	Arrested	4,013
	Shot	2,136 ...
South-Western	Arrested	3,249
	Shot	868 ...
Southern	Arrested	3,599
	Shot	919 ...
Briansk	Arrested	799
	Shot	389 ...
Central	Arrested	686
	Shot	346 ...
Reserve Army	Arrested	2,516
	Shot	894 ...

Deputy head of the Board of Special Sections of the NKVD SSSR
Commissar of State Security 3rd Class, Mil'shtein

(Source: A.A. Pechenkin, 2000, pp. 37–38)

In the face of the loss of regular forces defending Moscow in the encirclements near Viaz'ma and Briansk at the beginning of the month, on 13 October the Mozhaisk defence line was manned by the following:

> DOCUMENT 49: *To the Head of the Headquarters of the Western* Front *on the composition of forces on the Mozhaisk defensive line, 13 October 1941*
>
> In accordance with the report of the headquarters of the Moscow Reserve *Front* I can provide you with a list of units and formations of the Mozhaisk defence line.
>
> 1. On the Volokolamsk axis ...: Divisional School, 316th Rifle Division; military school of the Supreme Soviet of the RSFSR with 302nd Machine-Gun Battalion; 316th Rifle Division with 1/108th Reserve Rifle Regiment; 41st Independent Anti-Aircraft Division (two batteries); 584th Artillery Regiment Anti-Tank, a tank company, two mortar companies, an independent artillery division, a sapper company of the Moscow Military Engineering Academy, a division of 'RS' [Katiushas].
> 2. On the Mozhaisk axis ...: 230th Reserve Regiment (without one battalion); 32nd Rifle Division; a composite battalion of the Military-Political Academy; 305th Machine-Gun Battalion; 1st and 2/27th Reserve Rifle Regiment; 3/230th Reserve Training Rifle Regiment; a cavalry regiment; 121st, 367th, 408th, 421st Artillery Regiments Anti-Tank; two mortar companies; a tank company; 59th Independent Anti-Aircraft Division (2 batteries); 467th Independent Sapper Battalion; 2 divisions 'RS'; 20th Tank Brigade.
> 3. On the Maloiaroslavets axis ...: 312th Rifle Division with 108th reserve Rifle Regiment; Podol'sk Infantry Academy; Podol'sk Artillery Academy; 517th Howitzer Regiment of the High Command Reserve; a tank company; 5 mortar companies; 31 Independent Artillery Division; 222nd, 395th, 382nd, 452nd Artillery Regiments Anti-Tank; two divisions 'RS'; 538th Sapper Battalion; a sapper company of the Moscow Military-Engineering Academy.
>
> Sharokhin.
>
> (Source: *RA T.23 (12–1)*, 1998, p. 210)

Despite the first snow, followed by rain, and the increasingly heavy going as the *rasputitsa* [time without rain] set in, and despite the ferocity of albeit limited Soviet counter-attacks, the Mozhaisk line was effectively breached on 14 October when German forces took Kalinin; Soviet defences now increasingly being focused on a line only 40 miles from the centre of Moscow.[1]

The breaching of the Mozhaisk line and evacuation of Moscow beginning on 15 October saw panic hit the city, with a state of siege being announced on 20 October 1941:

> DOCUMENT 50: *Decree of the State Defence Committee 'on the evacuation of the capital of the USSR, Moscow'*
>
> No. 801
> 15.X.41
>
> Given the unfavourable situation in the region of the Mozhaisk defence line the State Defence Committee decrees:
>
> 1. Make Comrade Molotov responsible for the announcement to foreign missions that they must have evacuated to Kuibishev TODAY [*chtobi oni segodnia zhe evakuirovalis'*]. ...

2. To evacuate the Presidium of the Supreme Soviet, and also the Government headed by the Vice-Chairman of the Council of People's Commissars Comrade Molotov TODAY (Comrade Stalin will evacuate tomorrow or later, depending on the situation).
3. Without delay evacuate organs of the Ministry of Defence to Kuibishev, and the core of the General Headquarters staff [*Genstab*] to Arzamas.
4. In the event of the appearance of enemy forces at the gates of Moscow to require the NKVD, that is Comrades Beria and Shcherbakov, to carry out the demolition of industrial concerns, supply dumps and institutions which cannot be evacuated and also the electrical equipment for the metro (with the exclusion of water pipes and sewers).

Chairman of the State Defence Committee, I. Stalin

(Source: I.A. Gor'kov, 2002, p. 506)

DOCUMENT 51: Decree of the State Defence Committee on the declaration of a state of siege in Moscow, 19 October 1941

With the aim of ... strengthening the rear of the armed forces defending Moscow and in the interests of the prevention of the disruptive activities of enemy spies, saboteurs and other agents of German fascism the State Defence Committee decrees:

1. From 20 October to introduce in Moscow and attached districts a state of siege.
2. To forbid any movement of the streets ... from 12 o'clock at night to five o'clock in the morning, with the exception of transport and persons with special passes from the Commandant for Moscow....
3. That responsibility for the preservation of strict order in the city and suburban districts be passed to the Commandant of Moscow General-Major Comrade Sinilov, for which the commandant will have at his disposal the internal security forces of the NKVD, the militia [police] and volunteer worker detachments.
4. Those disturbing the peace should be quickly ... handed over to the courts of the Military Tribunals, and provocateurs, spies and other such agents of the enemy engaged in the disruption of order should be shot on the spot.

...

Chairman of the State Defence Committee, I. Stalin

(Source: O.A. Rzheshevskii, 1990, p. 427)

Whilst Soviet Party and government organizations were partly relocated to Kuibishev, the fact that actually Stalin remained in the capital helped limit any panic. The stabilization of the situation was assisted by the free reign given to the NKVD.

As the evacuation of Moscow was being ordered, desperate and relatively unco-ordinated Soviet counter-attacks continued to sap German strength, with particularly desperate measures being taken on the Moscow axis, where tank brigades, supported by the new Katiusha rocket launchers of 'RS', were thrown against the German spearheads:

> DOCUMENT 52: *Directive of the command of forces of the Western Front to commanders of the 16, 5 and 43 Armies on the destruction of armoured groups of the enemy, breaking through towards Moscow, 15 October 1941*
>
> According to reconnaissance reports, enemy armoured groups up to the end of 15.10 have made it as far as: 1st group – Turginovo – up to 50 tanks; 2nd group – Lotoshino, Osheikino – up to 100 tanks; 3rd group – Makarovo, Karacharovo – up to 100 tanks; 4th group – Borovsk region – up to 50 tanks with infantry; El'nia, Borodino – up to 40 tanks. All of these armoured groups, are apparently well aware of the weakpoints in our defences and have the task, avoiding fortified areas, of breaking through to Moscow.
>
> I order:
>
> 1. Preparation for the interception of these enemy armoured groups with the aim of destroying them, with:
>   a) 21st Tank Brigade to be given the task of conducting thorough reconnaissance of the nature of the region and dispositions of the Turginovo group of tanks and, attacking from different directions, to destroy it;
>   b) 22nd Tank Brigade, strengthened by no less than an anti-tank regiment, and with a division of RS, to be given the task of organizing an anti-tank ambush in depth, in the region of Teriaevo, Suvorovo, firing upon them from ambush positions before counterattacking and destroying them;
>   c) 20th Tank Brigade to move out before dawn on 16.10 to the Vasiukovo area, strengthened with no less than an anti-tank regiment and an RS division, with the task of firing on the enemy Makarovo group from ambush positions and destroying it;
>   18th and 19th Tank Brigades are to be left directly behind the infantry on the section Borodino, Znamenskoe;
>   d) 9th Tank Brigade, reinforced with an anti-tank regiment, is to move to the line Mitenino, Mitiaevo with the task of, from ambush positions, of firing upon the enemy tank group. In the region of Ermolino a tank battalion of the motor rifle brigade, situated in Vorob'i, is to have the same task.
>   17th Tank Brigade is to be in 43rd Army command's reserve for action principally in support of the left wing of the Maloiaroslavets Fortified District.
>
> Aviation will support our tank ambushes, in the main on request of army commanders. Identification of our tanks will be with a series of red flares and as backup, red markers on the ground on the left hand side of our tanks. Acknowledge receipt and implementation.
> Zhukov
> Bulganin
> Sokolovskii
>
> (Source: O.A. Rzheshevskii, 1990, p. 426)

Whilst in mid-October relatively few Soviet units stood between German forces and Moscow, German strength had been whittled down by more than three months of fighting and Soviet forces kept finding sufficient strength to prevent German forces making the final lunge forward to Moscow. German forces destroyed division upon division of the Red Army, but the Soviet replacement rate, even if the size and quality of divisions fell, was well above German expectations. As Glantz and House note, by 1 December 1941 the Soviet Union had deployed a further 97 existing divisions to the zone of operations over those deployed there at the start of the war, as well as having created an additional 194 divisions and 84 brigades from the mobilization base. The Soviet Union had in fact created twice as many divisions as German pre-war expectations – approximately 600 compared to an expected force of about 300.[2]

Glantz's characterization of the resulting situation is apt:

> By late October the Wehrmacht and the Red Army resembled two punch-drunk boxers, staying precariously on their feet but rapidly losing the power to hurt each other. Like prizefighters with swollen eyes, they were unable to see their opponents with sufficient clarity to judge their relative endurance.[3]

Both Soviet and German forces were suffering from a shortage in tanks. As the *Soviet Military Encyclopedia* notes, under the heading 'Tank Forces', where in mid-July the division was to become the largest armoured unit in the Red Army (see Document 38, Chapter 3), by the onset of winter scarce tanks were being parcelled out in brigades and increasingly battalions:

DOCUMENT 53: *Extract from the* Soviet Military Encyclopedia *on tank forces*

From the beginning of the Great Patriotic War Soviet auto-armour forces conducted military operations in exceptionally difficult circumstances. In the western border military regions there were only 1,475 new tanks (T-34 and KV); all of the remainder were outdated types. In addition, at that time Soviet armoured forces were a state of re-organisation and rearmament. Large scale losses of tanks at the beginning of the war and the necessity for their rapid replacement led to reduction in the size of the tank park of the field army. Already soon after the start of the war mechanized corps and the tank divisions which made them up were disbanded. The basic organizational unit in the auto-armour forces became the independent tank brigade and independent tank battalion. On 1 December 1941 there were 68 independent tank brigades and 37 independent tank battalions in the Soviet army.

(Source: *SVE* 7, p. 670)

These tank brigades and battalions were parcelled out by the centre along key axes, with the bulk of Soviet armoured strength being concentrated before Moscow. According to Rotmistrov, at the end of November 1941 there were only 670 Soviet tanks for the *fronts* before Moscow, that is, the recently formed Kalinin, and Western and South-Western *Fronts*, of which

Table 4.1 German tank and other armoured vehicle losses on the Eastern Front, June–November 1941 (initial force level 3,648)

	June	July	August	September	October	November	Total
PzKpfw I	34	146	171	7	18	33	409
PzKpfw II	11	112	104	32	65	30	354
PzKpfw III	21	155	74	104	77	116	547
PzKpfw 38(t)	33	182	183	62	85	149	694
PzKpfw IV	15	109	68	23	55	38	308
Assault gun	3	11	26	12	23	10	85
ACV	1	17	12	17	14	6	67
Total	118	732	638	257	337	382	2,464
Resulting force level	3,530	2,889	2,262	2,044	2,480*	2,177	1,803

Source: Rolf-Dieter Müller, 'The Failure of the Economic "Blitzkrieg Strategy"', in H. Boog et al., *Germany and the Second World War, Volume IV*, pp. 1120–1121 and 1129.

Note
* Including the addition of c.450 vehicles of 2nd and 5th Panzer Divisions from reserves.

only 205 were heavy or medium types. Most of this tank strength was concentrated with the Western *Front*, with the Kalinin *Front* having only two tank battalions (67 tanks) and the South-Western two tank brigades (30 tanks).[4] Alternative figures suggest that of 667 tanks with front-line units of the Kalinin, Western and right wing of the South-Western *Fronts* as of 1 December 1941, 607 were with the Western *Front*, of which 205 were KV series and T-34s, with the Kalinin *Front* and the right wing of the South-Western *Front* having 17 and 43 tanks respectively, none of which were apparently KV series or T-34s.[5] Either set of figures is a significant improvement on the 141 heavy and medium tanks available to the Western, Reserve and Briansk *Fronts* before Moscow as of 1 October 1941.[6]

Whilst Soviet armoured strength was increasing before Moscow, including more capable medium and heavy tanks, despite the boost provided to German armoured strength by the deployment of 2nd and 5th Panzer Divisions from reserves in October, German strength was waning. Table 4.1 gives some indication of the deterioration of German tank strength between June and November 1941.

As German forces pushed on towards Moscow, the twenty-fourth anniversary of the October[7] Revolution, which had brought the Bolsheviks to power, approached. On the eve of the anniversary Stalin gave a speech, safe below the ground in one of the showpiece stations of the Moscow Metro, extracts of which are provided below:

DOCUMENT 54: *Speech on the eve of the 24th anniversary of the October Revolution (speech delivered at a meeting of the Moscow Soviet, 6 November 1941)*

I already stated in one of my speeches at the beginning of the war that the war had created a serious danger for our country....

Today, as a result of four months of war, I must emphasize that this danger – far from diminishing – has on the contrary increased. The enemy has captured the greater part of the Ukraine, Belorussia, Moldavia and Estonia, and a number of other regions, has penetrated the Donbas, is looming like a black cloud over Leningrad, and is menacing our glorious capital, Moscow.

...

In four months of war we [have] lost 350,000 killed, 378,000 missing, and have 1,020,000 wounded men. In the same period the enemy lost over 4,500,000 killed, wounded and prisoners. There can be no doubt that as a result of four months of war, Germany, whose manpower reserves are already becoming exhausted, has been considerably more weakened by the war than the Soviet Union, whose reserves are only now unfolding to their full extent.

...

The defence of Leningrad and Moscow, where our divisions recently annihilated some three dozen professional German divisions, shows that the new Soviet men ... are being and already have been forged in the fire of the Patriotic War and tomorrow will be the terror of the German army.

...

> Wherein lie the reasons for the temporary military setbacks of the Red Army?
> One of the reasons for the setbacks of the Red Army consists in the absence of a second front in Europe against the German-fascist troops.
> ...
> The Hitlerite party and Hitlerite command ... call for the annihilation of the great Russian nation, the nation of Plekhanov and Lenin, Belinskii and Chernishevskii, Pushkin and Tolstoi, Glinka and Tschaikovskii, Gorki and Chekhov, Sechenov and Pavlov, Repin and Surikov, Suvorov and Kutuzov!
> The German invaders want a war of extermination against the peoples of the USSR. Well, if the Germans want a war of extermination, they shall have it.
> ...
> It is a fact that Great Britain, the United States, and the Soviet Union have united into a single camp which has set itself the task of crushing the Hitler imperialists and their armies of conquest....
> The recent three-power conference in Moscow with the participation of the representative of Great Britain, Mr Beaverbrook, and of the representative of the United States, Mr Harriman, decided systematically to assist our country with tanks and aircraft. As is known, we have already begun to receive shipments of tanks and planes on the basis of this decision.
> Still earlier Great Britain ensured to our country of such needed materials as aluminium, lead, tin, nickel and rubber.
> If to this is added the fact that recently the United States decided to grant a billion dollar loan to the Soviet Union...
> ...
> Our whole country and all peoples of the USSR should organize into a single war camp which together with our army and navy would wage a great liberation war for the honor and freedom of our country, for routing the German armies.
> ...
> Long live our Red Army and Navy!
> Long live our glorious country!
> Our cause is just; victory will be ours!
>
> (Source: Joseph Stalin, 1944, pp. 17–32)

There are a number of valuable points that can be made with reference to this speech. First, figures for Soviet and German casualties are symptomatic of the unrealistic thrust of Soviet propaganda during the first months of the war, a common theme in which was an absurdly distorted portrayal of events at the front that can only have increased mistrust of the regime. Propaganda would, however, increasingly focus on patriotic themes and on the cruelty of the enemy, often without reference to socialism or communism. This shift is apparent in this speech, where Stalin lists revolutionary figures such as Plekhanov, Chernishevskii and Lenin alongside both Soviet and non-Soviet writers such as Gorki and Chekhov, painters and musicians, and pre-revolutionary military heroes such as Suvorov and Kutuzov, harking back to the Patriotic War of 1812. With many non-Russian republics under German occupation the patriotic focus is clearly on Russian nationalism. This particular speech is also one of the few in which Stalin lavishes praise on assistance from his new-found Allies, despite noting the absence of a 'Second Front' against Germany in the West. This is arguably indicative of the extent to which the Soviet Union needed Allied assistance – the first British tanks, as noted below, arriving in time to participate in the Battle for Moscow.

The stalled German assault of Moscow resumed in earnest in mid-November, although clearly with inadequate resources, assisted, however (initially at least), by the fact that increasingly freezing temperatures brought the *rasputitsa* to an end. On 17 November 1941 the *Stavka* or Headquarters of the Supreme High Command issued its 'scorched earth' order in an attempt to deny Axis forces shelter from the elements as the winter set in.

DOCUMENT 55: *Order of the Headquarters of the Supreme High Command Number 0428, 17 November 1941*

I order:

1. That all populated areas in the German rear be utterly destroyed and burned for a distance of 40–60 km in depth from the front and 20–30 km to the left and right of roads. For the destruction of population centres within the radius concerned aviation is to be committed immediately, along with the widespread employment of artillery and mortar fire, teams of scouts, ski troops, and suitably prepared [partisan] diversion groups, equipped with Molotov cocktails, grenades and explosives.

...

3. In the event of having to withdraw on a particular portion of the front our forces are to take the Soviet population with them and must destroy, without exception, all population centres, so that the enemy cannot make use of them.

...

Headquarters of the Supreme High Command.
Supreme Commander, I. Stalin

(Source: P.N. Knishevskii *et al.*, 1992, p. 211)

Population centres were also the focus of a General Headquarters order of 24 November 1941 on the failure of the Red Army to fully utilize them, when of tactical or operational significance, in defence – a failing not typically associated with the Red Army given the subsequent stubborn defence of Stalingrad.

DOCUMENT 56: *To military soviets of* fronts *and armies on the defence of population centres*, *24 November 1941*

Fighting on all *fronts* has shown, that up till now the military soviets of *fronts* and armies and the commanders of formations have given little attention to the adaptation of towns and population centres for stubborn defence. Often population centres and towns are easily captured by the enemy without significant losses.

> Towns which have been adapted demand considerable expenditure of military strength and resources by the enemy....
>
> In order to destroy more enemy strength and resources the following are to be carried out:
>
> 1. All population centres with operational or tactical significance in the wider defensive system are to be prepared for defence, incorporating anti-tank and anti-personnel obstacles in them.
> 2. The defence of population centres should in the first instance be based around artillery and anti-tank guns....
> 3. Every street should be barricaded....
> 4. Barricades should be created using local resources.... Obstructions can be created by destroying buildings after evacuating civilians from them first....
> 5. In preparing buildings for defence, widespread use should be made of attics and balconies with openings on to the street, basement windows, sewers and communications passages for town utilities.
> 6. Fighting for population centres should be stubborn, fighting for every street, for every building, in order to destroy the maximum enemy human and other resources.
> 7. In finally giving up a population centre to the enemy all utilities and essential services to sustain life are to be destroyed ...
>
> B. Shaposhnikov
> F. Bokov
>
> (Source: *RA T.23 (12–1)*, 1998, pp. 252–253)

Certainly, as the Red Army sought to deal with superior German command and control and operational and tactical effectiveness, particularly in terms of armoured forces, better use of urban areas to slow the German advance on key axes might have been militarily effective, although the cost to the civilian populations of such a policy, as the example of Stalingrad would illustrate, was exceedingly high.

Had German officers had a more accurate picture of Soviet reserves in early November, and had they been able to get the decision past Hitler, however unlikely that might seem with the benefit of hindsight, the decision might and perhaps should have been taken to consolidate existing positions with a view to resuming the offensive the following year. The advance was nonetheless resumed. Whilst the Soviet General Headquarters was encouraging commanders to make use of urban areas for defence, as they approached Moscow German military leaders were certainly aware, as in the case of Leningrad a few weeks earlier, of the need for infantry resources in fighting for such cities that they did not possess.

German forces were not only overextended before Moscow, but also to the south, where the Axis advance was actually halted first, with Soviet forces of the South-Western *napravlenie* and Southern *Front* being able to report on 29 November that:

DOCUMENT 57: *Report of the military soviets of the South-Western* napravlenie *and Southern* Front *to the Supreme High Command on the defeat of the enemy Kleist battle-group and the course of fighting for the liberation of Rostov-on-Don, 29 November 1941*

Armies of the Southern *Front* had broken through defensive positions of the enemy with their left wing on the southern bank of the River Tuzlov ... by the morning of 29.11, and applied heavy pressure on him in a southerly direction [towards Rostov]. The Novocherkassk group of 9th Army seized the Shchepkin district with a decisive advance and with its 66th and 68th Cavalry Divisions broke in to the north-eastern suburbs of Rostov.

Elements of 56th Army continued to engage in street fighting in the southern and south-western extremities of Rostov....

From the morning of 29.11 the VVS of the Southern *Front* conducted active operations.... As a result of these actions the resistance by the Kleist battle-group was broken, and it began a retreat from Rostov to the west in disarray.

...
Timoshenko
Khrushchev

(Source: O.A. Rzheshevskii, 1990, p. 428)

Field Marshal von Rundstedt, commanding the German Army Group South, was to resign over Hitler's unwillingness to support a timely withdrawal to positions 30 km west of Rostov.[8]

On the Moscow axis it was soon apparent to Soviet leaders that as the German drive on Moscow resumed the threat from 3rd Panzer Group along the highway between Moscow and Kalinin was the most serious, with fierce fighting taking place near the Moscow–Volga Canal, over which German troops gained a bridgehead. To the south, the town of Tula was of considerable significance to the defence of Moscow. The defence of Tula by 50th Army saw German troops of 2nd Panzer Group attempting to encircle the town with dwindling mechanized forces, whilst 4th Panzer Group attacked eastwards towards the city, clearly running out of steam north-west of Naro-Fominsk during the first days of December, where Soviet tanks were able to push the weak German spearhead back.

DOCUMENT 58: *Report to the head of the operational department of the headquarters of the Western* Front *from the head of the Auto-Armour Board of the Western* Front, *31 January 1942, No. 61*

... – 'The activity of tanks on the front of 33rd Army'
1. The tank battle below Iushkovo 2–3 December 1941.

At approaching 12 hours and 30 minutes on 2 December 1941 forward units of the enemy passed through Iushkovo and occupied Petrovskoe and Burtsevo.... At about that time 136th Independent Tank Battalion, consisting of 22 tanks, approached Alabino, the remaining tanks being left, as a result of technical failures, at different points along the road between Moscow and Alabino. Ten tanks from this battalion were separated off for action with the left flank of the Army with 113th and 110th Rifle Divisions. The remaining tanks were sent to Petrovskoe.

At 1300 hours the tank battalion was met with artillery, mortar and tank fire from Petrovskoe, and with two tanks knocked out, pulled back.... Only medium and light tanks took part in the first attempt to capture Petrovskoe, the super-light tanks [*malie*] still remained in Alabino.

At 1400 hours the commander of the battalion was given the order to immediately attack the enemy in Petrovskoe.... The battalion knocked two [enemy] tanks out straight away and 2 [were] burnt out, and occupied the south-eastern outskirts of Petrovskoe. Further, meeting heavy anti-tank fire from Iushkovo and south-west of Petrovskoe, the battalion could not move forward. Using sub-machine gunners the enemy work their way around the left flank of 136th Independent Tank Battalion.... In order to counteract the enemy four super-light tanks were sent to the northern edge of the forest (200 m south-east of Petrovskoe), which halted the forward movement of the enemy in that direction.

The battalion was forced to spend the evening and night defending Petrovskoe with limited infantry support....

The commander of 136th ITB was ordered to position his tanks during the night, such that they covered each other with machine gun fire, and in addition, would not remain in one place, but would constantly change positions....

Towards the morning of 3 December units began to concentrate [in the area]. 18th Rifle Brigade and 23rd and 24th Ski Battalions arrived, with 140th Independent Tank Battalion approaching.

The commanders decision was as follows:

The tank group consisting of 136th and 140th Tank Battalions and 23rd and 24th Ski Battalions was, with the ski battalions concentrated in the forest south-west of Mamir' and tank battalions from Petrovskoe, to advance concentrically on Iushkovo, capture it and then, pursuing the enemy in the direction of Goloven'ka, Tashirovo, restore the army's position [i.e. eliminate the German penetration].

Approaching 1200 hours on 3 December 140th [Tank] Battalion had already arrived and concentrated at start positions in the forest 200 m east of the platform [halt] Alabino. The concentration of the infantry was delayed.... The possibility of enemy penetration from Burtsevo to Mamir' was countered by the positioning of four tanks of 136th TB in ambush positions [*v zasade*] in the forest on either side of the road 600m east of Burtsevo.

...

At the allotted time the infantry did not attack. The tank battalions acted alone [Note – with limited infantry riding on tanks].

...

At 1620 hours 136th ITB moved out to the northern edge of Iushkovo.... The enemy at speed fled from Iushkovo to the west, leaving behind four artillery pieces, rifles and other trophies. It was already getting dark. The battalion was in need of fuel, food for personnel, ammunition....

140th ITB broke through to the western spur of Petrovskoe, destroying a number of enemy firepoints, after which with tank-borne infantry it attacked the western spur of Petrovskoe and the forest to the north-west, ejecting the remains of the enemy from there and destroying two anti-tank guns....

Enemy tanks near Iushkovo, totaling 12, were active on 3 December only against 136th ITB, after having lost four not entering into open combat again, but firing sta-

> tionary from the edge of the forest south-west of Iushkovo, where they maintained until 1600 hours on 3 December, after which with the coming darkness departed to the heights 210.8 and behind the River Nara.
>
> Tank losses in the battle for Iushkovo and Petrovskoe were: four tanks knocked-out (three repaired) and one got stuck in a hole. The tanks attacked without the expectation of infantry, utilizing the reduced morale of the enemy after two salvoes of RS.
>
> (Source: V.M. Safir, 1997, pp. 84–91)

Soviet tank strength at the start of the battle was a total of 68 tanks for 5th Tank Brigade and 136th and 140th Independent Tank Battalions and 31 tanks for 20th Tank Brigade, a total of 99.[9]

In true Soviet Five-Year Plan style, Zhukov and Bulganin would report to the Supreme High Command that forces of the Western *Front* alone had inflicted terrible, almost fantastic casualties on German forces:

> DOCUMENT 59: *Report of the Command of Forces of the Western* Front *to the Supreme High Command on results of military activities for the period from 16 November to 10 December 1941, 12 December 1941*
>
> From 16.11.41 German forces, deploying 13 panzer, 33 infantry and five motorized divisions against the Western *Front*, started a second general offensive against Moscow.
> ...
> Up to 6.12 forces of the *front* engaged in a stubborn defensive battle, holding off the advance of the flanking shock groups of the enemy and repelling the supporting blows in the direction of Istrinsk, Zvenogorsk and Naro-Fominsk.
>
> During these battles the enemy suffered substantial losses. From 16.11. to 6.12. according to incomplete figures, and not including the activities of air forces, the following were destroyed and captured by our forces: 777 tanks, 534 motor vehicles, 178 artillery pieces, 119 mortars, 224 heavy machine guns and 55,170 enemy troops lost.
> ...
> Zhukov
> Bulganin
>
> (Source: O.A. Rzheshevskii, 1990, p. 431)

In the north, south and centre German forces were halted, and on 5 and 6 December Soviet forces went over to the counter-attack with the start of the 'Moscow Strategic Offensive' Operation. In late November forces were already being assembled for a counter-attack on the Moscow axis, in this instance from behind the South-Western *Front*:

> DOCUMENT 60: *To the head of the Political Board of 20th Army and command of 61st Army on the redeployment of 20th Army to Moscow, 28 November 1941*
>
> In accordance with the decision of the *Stavka* 20th Army is being redeployed to Moscow.
>
> 1. Brigades that have not already detrained are to be redirected to Moscow whilst on the move.
> 2. Having already detrained, 17th, 18th and 84th Brigades and 23rd and 24th Ski Battalions ... are to be sent to Moscow.
>   ...
>   a) 17th and 18th Brigades and 23rd and 24th Ski Battalions are to load in the region of Ranenburg Station.... Start of loading 20:00 29.11. Station for detraining – Moscow.
>   b) ...
>   c) 84th Brigade is to be sent ... to Riazhsk. Station for loading – Riazhsk, station for unloading – Moscow.
>   ...
>
> Deputy-head of the General Headquarters, Vasilevskii
>
> (Source: *RA T.23 (12–1)*, 1998, p. 255)

> DOCUMENT 61: *Letter of the commander of forces of the Western* Front *on the plan for a counter-attack by the* front, *30 November 1941*
>
> To the deputy-head of the General Headquarters, General-Lieutenant Comrade Vasilevskii, 30 November 1941
>
> I ask you as a matter of urgency to inform the People's Commissar for Defence Comrade Stalin of the plan for a counterattack by the Western *Front* and to issue the necessary directive, in order that we can undertake the operation, otherwise preparations might be delayed.
> Zhukov
>
> (Source: O.A. Rzheshevskii, 1990, p. 428)

With the Soviet resource situation continuing to improve as the Germans were suffering horrendous losses that they were clearly not able to replace, the Soviet counter-offensive was launched on 5–6 December by a Stalin increasingly confident that the tide of the war had turned, with 20th Army participating in offensive operations in the Klin-Solnechnogorsk region.

One aspect of the defence of and counter-offensive before Moscow that has remained largely hidden in the historiography is the contribution of Allied, in particular British, aid to the Soviet defence of Moscow. The 136th Independent Tank Battalion, playing a significant role in the elimination of the German Naro-Fominsk penetration as described above, was at least in part equipped with British Matilda tanks, at a time when there was a desperate shortage of Soviet medium and heavy tanks.

Whilst the Soviet capital was defended with Soviet lives and in the main with Soviet equipment, the desperate Soviet resource situation at the time meant that relatively small quantities of Allied aid were of greater significance than Soviet authors suggested – if Allied aid was even mentioned by Soviet authors it was suggested that Allied aid was arriving in such limited quantities at this stage of the war as to be dismissible. Certainly, when Allied, and in particular British, deliveries of key weapons systems for the war as a whole are compared to Soviet production for the same period they can understandably be viewed as being of little significance. If Soviet production of tanks and self-propelled guns is taken as 110,340 for the whole war,[10] then 4,542 tanks supplied by Britain might seem trivial.[11] However, Soviet production of principal types of tanks and self-propelled guns (T-34, KV series and light tanks) was in the region of only 4,649 for the second half of 1941.[12]

Given the quality of the latest model Soviet tanks, namely the T-34 and KV-1, Soviet authors could be particularly disparaging about Allied deliveries of tanks early in the war on qualitative as well as quantitative grounds. Under the provisions of the First Lend-Lease or Moscow Protocol, Britain supplied Matilda (Mk II) and Valentine tanks to the Soviet Union. However, whilst these models were inferior to the T-34, it worth noting that Soviet production of the T-34 (and to a lesser extent the KV series), was only just getting seriously underway in 1942,[13] hence the relative inferiority of British tanks to the Soviet armoured pool as a whole was less during this period than it would be only a few months later after the First Moscow Protocol period to the end of June 1942. It is also worth noting that Soviet production was well below plan targets. Production of the T-34 at Factory Number 112, the conversion of which from producing submarines to tanks was ordered on 1 July 1941, according to a GKO order of 9 July 1941 was supposed to rise from ten units in August 1941 to 250 by December, a total of 710 units over five months.[14] The reality was, in itself, a significant achievement given the conversion of this factory from the series production of submarines to armoured vehicles, the production of 173 units to the end of 1941.[15] Production targets continued to be unrealistic into 1942, with Factory Number 112 having targets to produce a total of 1,240 units during June–September 1942 alone, while actual production was 2,584 for 1942 as a whole.[16] From 22 June to 31 December 1941, according to Krivosheev, only 3,200 medium and heavy tanks were delivered to the Red Army, figures including 'Lend-Lease' equipment starting to filter through.[17] Simonov gives production of the T-34 and KV series for the second half of 1941 as 2,819 units, with Suprun noting 361 heavy and medium British 'Lend-Lease' tanks having reached the Red Army by this point, giving a grand total of 3,180.[18]

The Matilda and Valentine had two-pounder main armaments increasingly only satisfactory for light tanks, the absence of a high-explosive capability being a significant drawback that prompted Soviet attempts to up-gun both, the Matilda with a 76mm gun.[19] Nonetheless, the armour of the Matilda and Valentine tanks put them firmly in the heavy and medium categories, respectively. Yet, even excluding the issue of main armament, both the Matilda and the Valentine required modification for service in Russian conditions.[20] Whilst in British service in North Africa both faced contemporary German tanks, in Soviet service they were, apparently, more and more frequently used in defensive operations or for infantry support in conjunction with Soviet tanks.[21] This was certainly a realistic limitation from the second half of 1942 onwards, but prior to this, Soviet stocks of medium and heavy tanks did not always permit the relegation of British tanks to supporting roles.

Whilst the Soviet Union had developed tanks that were far superior to those in service in Britain and the United States, and indeed of such effectiveness to drive Germany to produce the over-complicated Panther in response to the T-34 and KV-1, not only did it not have the planned quantities of these types, but was barely able to maintain force levels in the face of horrendous losses. According to Krivosheev, the Soviet Union lost a staggering 20,500 tanks between 22 June and 31 December 1941, of which 3,200 were either heavy or medium, with an initial stock of such types of 1,400. Only 5,600 tanks were received during the same period, of which, as noted above, only 3,200 were medium or heavy tanks, including imports.[22] By the end of 1941, Britain had delivered 466 tanks out of 750 promised, of which 259 were Valentines and 187 Matildas, the remainder apparently Tetrarch. Of these, 216 Valentines and 145 Matildas had been supplied to the Red Army.[23] With total Red Army tank stocks, as of 31 December, consequently being in the region of 7,700 according to Krivosheev (or 6,347 on 1 December according to Suprun), of which only 1,400 were medium or heavy models, then British deliveries to date represented in the region of only 6.5 per cent of total Red Army tank strength, but over 33 per cent of medium and heavy tanks, with British vehicles actually in Red Army hands representing about 25 per cent of medium and heavy tanks in service.[24]

Given disruption to Soviet production and high losses, the Soviet Union was understandably concerned to put British and US armour into action as soon as possible, quickly attempting to amend any serious defects. A good indication of Soviet efforts to this end can be gained from the service diary of N.I. Biriukov, Military Commissar of the Main Auto-Armour Board of the Red Army from 10 August 1941. According to Biriukov's notes, the first 20 British Valentine tanks arrived at the tank training school in Kazan' on 28 October 1941, at which point a further 120 were unloading at Arkhangel'sk.[25] Courses for the preparation of Soviet crews for Valentines and Matildas had started during November whilst the first tanks, with British assistance, were being assembled from their in-transit states and undergoing testing by Soviet specialists.[26]

According to the British Military Mission in Moscow, by 9 December 1941 about 90 British tanks had been in action with Soviet forces.[27] On 20

November 1941 Biriukov reported that the Soviet armoured units (shown in Table 4.2) were equipped with British-supplied tanks.

Of the units in Table 4.2, the British Military Mission was referring to 146th Tank Brigade and 131st, 136th and 138th Independent Tank Battalions. The first of these units to have been in action seems to have been 138th Independent Tank Battalion, which, as part of 30th Army of the Western *Front* along with 24th and 145th Tank Brigades and 126th Independent Tank Battalion, was involved in stemming the advance of German units in the region of the Volga Reservoir to the north of Moscow in late November. The exploits of 136th Independent Tank Battalion have already been mentioned and at least in part described, and 131st Independent Tank Battalion was in action with the Western *Front* from early December with 50th Army to the east of Tula to the south of Moscow, with 146th Tank Brigade also seeing action with 16th Army the Western *Front* from early December in the region of Kriukovo to the immediate west of the Soviet capital.[28] It is reasonable to suggest that British-supplied tanks constituted in the region of 30–40 per cent of the heavy and medium tank strength of Soviet forces before Moscow at the beginning of December 1941, and that they made up a significant proportion of such vehicles available as reinforcements at this critical juncture.

What had started as a Soviet counter-offensive to remove the threat from Moscow soon developed into a counter-offensive across the whole front, with Soviet forces lacking the concentration and logistical support in the face of stubborn German resistance on key lines of communication to unhinge the German defences. Operations to the south of Moscow near Orel, as described and analysed by David Glantz, are a case in point. The 'Oboian'–Kursk (Belgorod) 'Offensive' of 3–26 January 1942, 'Orel–Bolkhov Offensive' Operation of

Table 4.2 Soviet armoured units equipped with British-supplied tanks, 20 November 1941

Name of unit	'Matilda' Mk-II	'Valentine' Mk-III	Armoured transporters (carriers)
146th Tank Brigade – 139th Tank Battalion		21	10
146th Tank Brigade – 137th Tank Battalion		21	
145th Tank Battalion			10
138th Tank Battalion	15	6	
136th Tank Battalion	3	9	
131st Tank Battalion		21	
132nd Tank Battalion	2	19	

Source: Biriukov, *Tanki – frontu!*, p. 57.

7 January–18 February and the 'Bolkhov Offensive' Operation of 24 March–3 April 1942 saw Soviet forces stabbing away at German defences with inadequate resources. In the latter two operations the Briansk *Front* squandered more than 60,000 men killed, missing and wounded for only limited gains.[29]

The fact that the Soviet counter-offensive dragged on towards spring, leading to a significant loss of resources with little prospect of major progress, was certainly indicative of a lack of realism on the part of Stalin and much of the military leadership, not only on the extent to which the *Wehrmacht* had been bled dry by operations during 1941, but also of the capabilities of the Red Army. Not only did Stalin's insistence on offensive operations across a broad front dilute Soviet strength, but also Soviet forces were not yet as capable as their German counterparts in combined-arms warfare, and in particular in support of armoured forces.

DOCUMENT 62: *Order of the Headquarters of the Supreme High Command Number 57 of 22 January 1942 on the use of tank units and formations in battle*

The experience of war has shown, that there are still a range of failings in the battlefield use of tank forces, as a result of which our units lose large numbers of tanks and personnel.

...

1. Up to now co-operation between infantry and tank formations and units is poorly organised with infantry commanders failing to establish concrete objectives and hastily doing so; the infantry lagging behind in the attack and not reinforcing advance positions captured by the tanks; in defence infantry not covering tanks in defensive positions; and in retreat even failing to warn commanders of tank units of the changed situation and throwing tanks into the arms of fate.
2. Tank attacks are not supported by our artillery, and artillery does not accompany the tanks, as a result of which fighting vehicles are lost to enemy anti-tank artillery.
3. Field commanders are extremely hasty in the deployment of tank units, throwing them into action in packets as they arrive, not setting aside time for the conduct of even the most elementary reconnaissance of the area and enemy positions.

...

I. Stalin
A. Vasilevskii

(Source: *SBD* 5, pp. 28–29)

Failings were not only with the infantry and artillery, as forces of the Western *Front* were told:

DOCUMENT 63: *Order to forces of the Western* Front, *19 February 1942 – On the battlefield use of and preservation of tanks in units of the Western* Front

Forces of the *front* are suffering large and unjustified losses....

Commanders of tank units introduce brigades into battle without the appropriate technical preparation, without having reconnoitred the terrain, without preparation of the means of recovering tanks, attempting to reach objectives using only tanks, without infantry. The provision of sapper, infantry and artillery ... support is poor.

Tank crews themselves, having been given objectives, attempt to reach them without the appropriate skills, in a straightforward manner, and most frequently attacking frontally. Tankers do not study terrain for concealed approaches to enemy positions and dead ground, as a result of this irresponsibility they suffer high casualties....

Tank losses on the Western *Front* are:

1st Guards Tank Brigade received 95 tanks	On 15.2. it had 28 tanks.
17th Tank Brigade received 72 tanks	On 15.2. it had 30 tanks.
20th Tank Brigade received 77 tanks	On 15.2. it had 18 tanks.
5th Tank Brigade received 89 tanks	On 15.2. it had 9 tanks.
18th Tank Brigade received 70 tanks	On 15.2. it had 15 tanks.
32nd Tank Brigade received 53 tanks	On 15.2. it had 9 tanks.
2nd Guards Tank Brigade received 79 tanks	On 15.2. it had 16 tanks.
146th Tank Brigade received 128 tanks	On 15.2. it had 12 tanks.
68th Tank Brigade received 46 tanks	On 15.2. it had 16 tanks.

With units and with repair bases there are 264 tanks out of action.

Up to this point there are still 322 tanks out of action which have not been recovered from the battlefield.

I order:

1. That military soviets discuss measures for the preservation of material assets and personnel of tank units.
2. That the reasons for losses suffered are analysed.
3. That every instance of tank losses is investigated and reported within 48 hours to the military soviet of the *front*.

Zhukov

(Source: P.N. Knishevskii *et al.*, 1992, pp. 241–242)

Certainly the relative absence of radio sets hampered Soviet command, control and co-operation between different arms,[30] and when available they were used without due regard for the fact that radio communications could be intercepted by the enemy, despite orders to prevent this.[31] In this instance, 2nd Shock Army[32] will be used as an example:

DOCUMENT 64: *To the head of the Headquarters of the Volkhov* Front *on the forbidding of open conversations using technical means of communication, 26 March 1942*

According to reports in the hands of the General Headquarters of the Red Army, within 2nd Shock Army there have been recent instances of the conduct of open conversations by telegraph and telephone on secret matters of an operational nature.

15.3.1942 General-Lieutenant Klikov passed orders to Colonel Amtiufeev, commander of the 327th Rifle Division, openly by telephone.[33]

11.3.1942 The army command and commanders of headquarters revealed operational preparations in open conversation.

It is demanded that all commanders follow NKO Order Number 0243 and General Headquarters Directive Number 10102.

...

Tikhimirov
Rizhkov

(Source: *RA T.23 (12–2)*, 1999, pp. 67–68)

Such factors, combined with a lack of imagination on the part of many commanders, contributed to a squandering of lives that even the Red Army could not sustain indefinitely.

DOCUMENT 65: *Directive Number 3750 of the military soviet of the Western* Front, *30 March 1942*

To all commanders and commissars of divisions and brigades.

The Headquarters of the Supreme High Command and the military soviet of the *front* receive numerous letters from Red Army men, commanders, and political workers that bear witness to the criminally negligent attitude of commanders of all levels to the preservation of Red Army men of the infantry.

In letters and discussions hundreds of instances are provided where commanders of units and formations wipe out hundreds and thousands of people in attacks on intact defences and intact machine guns, on unsuppressed firepoints during poorly prepared attacks.

...

I demand:

1. That every instance of atypical infantry losses be investigated within 24 hours,... informing a senior headquarters of the results. Commanders that criminally throw units against unsuppressed enemy firesystems are to be held responsible and demoted.

2. Before an infantry attack enemy firesystems should be suppressed and neutralized, for which every commander organizing an attack should have a carefully formulated plan for the destruction of the enemy through fire and assault. Such a plan should be confirmed by a senior commander....
3. Personal explanation should be attached to reports on losses, explaining who is responsible for atypical losses, what measures have been taken against the guilty party so that it doesn't happen again.

Commander of the Western *Front*
Zhukov

(Source: P.N. Knishevskii *et al.*, 1992, pp. 228–229)

It should not, however, be forgotten that, at tactical and operational levels, whilst the Red Army remained a relatively blunt instrument compared to the *Wehrmacht* in late 1941 and into 1942, the more capable survivors of the debacles of the summer and autumn of 1941 were rapidly learning the art of modern warfare or losing favour with a Supreme Commander increasingly more interested in results than political cronyism. Whilst, with the exception of communications and fighter aircraft, it is difficult to argue that there was a meaningful technological gap between German and Soviet forces during 1941 – and there was frequently local numerical parity, even in tanks – the human factor, both in terms of the effectiveness of the individual as part of the whole and of units and formations, was an area of Soviet weakness. Low military effectiveness hit morale, and low morale hit military effectiveness. In early 1942, with the next generation of Soviet fighter aircraft entering service, with the T-34 tank available in increasing numbers and with Allied aid starting to alleviate communications deficiencies, Germany was losing any sort of meaningful technological edge, and the overall numerical balance at the front was starting to shift noticeably in Soviet favour. Only in the exploitation of these resources was the Red Army still inferior to the *Wehrmacht*, but from Stalin down during 1942 the Red Army would make major advances in closing the gap with the *Wehrmacht* in this regard as well.

Guide to further reading

John Barber, 'The Moscow Crisis of October 1941', in J. Cooper, M. Perrie and E.A. Rees (eds), *Soviet History 1917–1953* (New York: St Martin's Press, 1995), pp. 201–218.
H. Boog, J. Forster, J. Hoffmann, E. Klink, R.-D. Muller, G.R. Ueberschar and E. Osers (eds), *Germany and the Second World War. Volume IV. The Attack on the Soviet Union* (Oxford: Clarendon Press, 1998).
Roderick Braithwaite, *Moscow 1941: A City and its People at War* (New York: Vintage Books, 2006) and other editions.
Charles Burdick and Hans-Adolf Jacobsen (eds), *The Halder War Diary, 1939–1942* (Novato, CA: Presidio, 1988).
David Glantz, 'Forgotten Battles of the German-Soviet War (1941–1945), Part 3: The

Winter Campaign (5 December 1941-April 1942): The Moscow Counteroffensive', *JSMS*, Volume 13, Number 2 (June 2000), pp. 139–185.

David Glantz, 'Forgotten Battles of the German-Soviet War (1941–1945), Part 4: The Winter Campaign (5 December 1941-April 1942): The Demiansk Counteroffensive', *JSMS*, Volume 13, Number 3 (September 2000), pp. 145–164.

David Glantz, 'Forgotten Battles of the German-Soviet War (1941–1945), Part 6: The Winter Campaign (5 December 1941-April 1942): The Crimean Counteroffensive and Reflections', *JSMS*, Volume 14, Number 1 (January 2001), pp. 121–170.

Alexander Hill, 'British "Lend-Lease" Tanks and the Battle for Moscow, November-December 1941 – A Research Note', *JSMS*, Volume 19, Number 2 (June 2006), pp. 289–294.

Geoffrey Hosking, 'The Second World War and Soviet National Consciousness', *Past and Present*, Volume 175, Number 1 (2002), pp. 162–187.

Klaus Reinhardt, 'The Turning Point', in J. Erickson and D. Dilks (eds), *Barbarossa – The Axis and the Allies* (Edinburgh: Edinburgh University Press, 1994), pp. 207–224.

5 The tide turns
The Battle for Stalingrad

Whilst Soviet forces had held off the *Wehrmacht* before Moscow, Stalin's overambitious winter offensive did not reap the rewards that he had expected. The Soviet winter offensive, which according to the Soviet literature took place from December 1941 to April 1942, had run out of steam by March, with German forces still clinging tenaciously to a number of forward positions projecting towards the Soviet capital, including those in and around Rzhev and Viaz'ma. A resource situation shifting by many measures, including tank strength, in Soviet favour at the end of 1941 and during the first weeks of 1942 had been squandered in operations along the whole front. Soviet losses were heavy, as indicated in Table 5.1.

The Soviet Union's manpower resources may have seemed limitless to the Soviet leadership in the autumn and winter of 1941 (compared to the dearth of tanks and aircraft), but by the summer of 1942, as the resource situation improved, naval forces, largely immobilized in the Black Sea and Baltic, along with the NKVD forces, were directed to contribute troops to the Red Army.

Table 5.1 Soviet losses during offensive operations November 1941–April 1942

Operation	When	Troops committed	Irrecoverable losses	Sick and wounded
'Tikhvin Strategic Offensive'	10 November–30 December 1941	192,950	17,924	30,997
'Rostov Strategic Offensive'	17 November–2 December 1941	349,000	15,264	17,847
'Moscow Strategic Offensive'	5 December–7 January 1942	1,021,700	139,586	231,369
'Kerch'–Feodosiia Amphibious'	25 December–2 January 1941	82,500	32,453	9,482
'Rzhev–Viaz'ma Strategic Offensive'	8 January–20 April 1942	1,059,200	272,320	504,569

Source: Krivosheev *et al.*, *Soviet Casualties and Combat Losses*, pp. 119–123.

DOCUMENT 66: *Decree of the State Defence Committee on the manning of the field army, GKO Number 2100ss, 26 July 1942*

The State Defence Committee DECREES:

1. That the NKO (Comrade Shchadenko) be required, through cutbacks in and the reorganization of rear-area units and the substitution of those in auxiliary positions with military personnel unfit for combat as a result of wounds and women, to find 400,000 men by 1 September 1942 for combat units.
2. To cut the strength of the Navy to 450,000 men and require the People's Commissar of the Navy, Comrade Kuznetsov, through those freed up by the cuts to transfer 100,000 men in the ranks and NCOs who have received training and are fit for front-line service to the field army by 25 August.
3. To require that from 10 August 1942 the NKO (Comrade Shchadenko) call up all of those born in 1924, and, regardless of their place of work and position, send them to:
   a) Military academies and reserve units – 450,000 men
   b) To the Navy – 100,000 men
   c) To forces of the NKVD – 75,000 men
   d) To forces of the Transcaucasian *Front* – 25,000 men
4. In exchange for the call up of those born in 1924 to free up the equivalent number of men from the Navy,... from the NKVD,... from the Transcaucasian *Front*,... a total of 200,000 men of the ranks and NCOs who have received training and are fit for front-line service, and hand them over for the manning of the field army by 1 September 1942.
5. To require military soviets of *fronts* and armies to hand over those called up from the prefrontal zone and born in 1924, by 10 August, for study in military academies and specialist reserve units (artillery, armour, communications etc) and reserve rifle brigades....
6. To require the People's Commissariats to hand over to the army, by 20 August:
   a) 100,000 men in manual and administrative positions protected from call up of age up to 35 years (Attachment 1: Breakdown for unprotecting positions by ministry);
   b) 50,000 men of call-up age and fit for service of age up to 45 years from those provided to ministries for the workers colonies (Attachment 2: Breakdown of call up by ministry);
7. To require the NKVD (Comrade Beria) to transfer 35,000 men of call-up age and fit for service and of up to 40 years old to the army from those in reserved positions in the militia [police], camps, correctional-labour colonies and institutions of the NKVD.
8. To require the NKVD USSR (Comrade Beria) and the Procurator of the Union SSR (Comrade Bochkov) to review cases of inmates of correctional-labour camps and colonies of the NKVD of men up to 40 years of age and able to undertake military service and sentenced for domestic and property crime, with the aim of urgent release and the transfer of 30,000 men to the army.

   The NKVD of the USSR (Comrade Beria) is to hand over and NKO (Comrade Shchadenko) to call up 15,000 labour exiles of up to 35 years old and fit for service to the ranks of the army.

...

Chairman of the State Defence Committee
I. Stalin

(Source: I.A. Gor'kov, 2002, pp. 514–516)

The mobilization of women for military service had begun on the second day of the war with the call up of medical workers; a total of 41,224 of whom were mobilized during the war. Women were also employed from the first months of the war as radio operators, with approximately 10,000 young male volunteer 'radio enthusiasts' and the same number of young women being sought from the ranks of the *Komsomol* in a GKO decree of 19 August 1941. Young women were also sought during 1941 as drivers, with 14,430 women being sought as drivers in a decree of the end of August 1941 alone. A GKO decree of 18 April 1942 sought 40,000 young women for rear-area work in the VVS of the Red Army.[1]

Also, as in Britain, as the war progressed, Soviet women would be mobilized for increasingly combat-oriented tasks such as in the AA system. From the spring of 1942 young women would be employed, on a volunteer basis, for example in the manning of observation posts, anti-aircraft batteries and other such tasks, although in the Soviet case women could easily find themselves, particularly at this stage of the war, closer to the front line than intended. The fulfilment of such tasks by women was predicted to allow the release of enough men for 12 rifle divisions:[2]

DOCUMENT 67: *State Defence Committee. Decree No. GOKO-1488ss of 25 March 1942....*
On the mobilization of young women [devushek] – *from the* Komsomol [komsomolok] *to units of the PVO*

With the aim of a more coherent use of trained contingents and for the strengthening of the field army with them the State Defence Committee decrees:

1. That in the air-defence forces of the territory of the country 100,000 Red Army men be replaced by women in the following positions: telephonists, radio operators, anti-aircraft battery instrument operators, AA-gun spotters and observation post personnel, some of the personnel of searchlight units, anti-aircraft machine gun and barrage balloon crews, and also as various specialists in service units.
2. That the TsK VLKSM be required to mobilize 100,000 young women of the *Komsomol* of ages 19–25 by 10 April 1942, of whom 40% should have full secondary education and the remainder with education to no less than 5–7 grade....
3. That mobilized young women of the *Komsomol* be dispatched as replacements for Red Army personnel in the home air-defence forces:
    a) To the anti-aircraft artillery – 45,000
    b) To anti-aircraft machine-gun units – 3,000
    c) To searchlight units – 7,000
    d) To barrage balloon units – 5,000
    e) To observation posts – 40,000

...

Chairman of the State Defence Committee, I. Stalin.

(Source: Online. Available www.soldat.ru/doc/gko/scans/1488-01-1.jpg and 1488-02-1.jpg)

More limited in terms of numbers, and where the Soviet case differed from other powers, was the deployment of a small number of women as front-line pilots and snipers. The 588th Air Regiment (Night Light-bomber Air Regiment) joined the field army in May 1942, to be followed by 587th Air Regiment in January 1943, both of which were led and made up of female pilots. Courses for female snipers from the end of 1942 led to the creation of a Central School for the Preparation of Female Snipers, which sent 1,061 snipers and 407 instructors to the front.[3] In fact, a volunteer rifle brigade was formed, 'as a means of coming to terms with the wishes of women to defend their socialist Motherland bearing arms', largely made up of female personnel, according to a GKO decree of 3 November 1942.[4]

Another way of sparing manpower was to replace full rifle divisions on quiet sectors of the front with reduced-strength but high firepower units:

DOCUMENT 68: *State Defence Committee. Decree No. GOKO-1619ss of 18 April 1942.... On the formation of units for fortified districts*

The State Defence Committee decrees:

1. That the following be formed for fortified districts:
    a) 100 independent machine gun-artillery battalions ... of 667 men in each;
    b) 15 independent trench-mortar companies ... of 127 men in each;
    c) 15 independent communications companies ... of 188 men in each;
    d) 15 headquarters units for fortified districts ... with 93 men in each;

...

Chairman of the State Defence Committee, I. Stalin
  (Source: Online. Available www.soldat.ru/doc/gko/scans/1619-01-1.jpg and 1619-02-1.jpg)

It was not, however, only manpower resources that were in increasingly short supply. Horses and other transport resources were required not only to keep the Red Army moving and supplied, but also by industry and agriculture. For the State Defence Committee the latter could to a large extent make do, with requests for transport going out to rear areas that simply demanded specific numbers of horses and vehicles for the Red Army.

DOCUMENT 69: *State Defence Committee. Decree No. GOKO-1914ss of 18 June 1942.... On the mobilization of horses, auto- and horse-drawn transport for rifle divisions of the Reserve Army ..., the State Defence Committee decrees:*

1. That the SNK of union and autonomous republics, *oblast'* and *krai*-level executive committees mobilize the following before 10 July of this year:
    a) 45,000 artillery and cart horses ... and 6,000 carts ...;
    b) 3,000 lorries, 1,000 functioning light trucks and 3,000 immobile lorries....
2. ...
3. That the head of GABTU (Comrade Fedorenko) set aside 1,200 tractors for the

> artillery regiments of the above divisions for artillery towing and spare parts and tires for the repair of 3,000 immobile lorries by 15 July of this year.
>
> ...
>
> Chairman of the State Defence Committee, I. Stalin
>
> (Source: Online. Available www.soldat.ru/doc/gko/scans/1614-01-1.jpg)

Whilst manpower and indeed horses and other means of transport were becoming resources requiring a little more care in their deployment than had been the case during 1941 (although as regards manpower and, to a much lesser extent, horses, unimaginative and costly frontal assaults, even with dramatic artillery and armoured support, would take place throughout the war), at least Soviet troops also had more and more effective weapons to fight with, as quarterly figures for the production of the T-34 tank 1941–42 (with alternative annual figures in brackets) illustrate in Table 5.2.

During the Soviet winter counter-offensive of 1941–42, Soviet armoured resources had still been parcelled out in battalion- or brigade-sized formations in support of operations along the whole front, but were not effectively co-ordinated with other arms. Against weak German spearheads before Moscow as in Document 58 in Chapter 4, poorly supported Soviet tank units could make some headway, but as German defences crystallized they were vulnerable to piecemeal destruction. After the destruction of Soviet formations of the summer and autumn of 1941, it would take time for the Red Army, with a vast number of conscripts and rapidly promoted officers, to recover and surpass even the experience in combined arms operations that existed in June 1941. In the below note of 8 April 1942, the *Stavka* once again (see Documents 62 and 63, Chapter 4) reminded heads of the headquarters of *fronts* of the necessity for the support of tanks with other arms, although it should be noted that by the spring of 1942 Soviet offensive operations did not have the resources they had enjoyed a couple of months before:

Table 5.2 Soviet T-34 production 1941–42

	1941	*1942*
First quarter	1,110	1,606
Second quarter		2,654
Third quarter	1,121	3,946
Fourth quarter	765	4,325
Total (Simonov)	2,996 (3,014)	12,531 (12,527)

Sources: M. Harrison, *Soviet Planning in Peace and War 1938–1945* (Cambridge: Cambridge University Press, 1985), p. 251 and Simonov, *Voenno-promishlennii kompleks SSSR*, p. 163.

> DOCUMENT 70: *To heads of the headquarters of* fronts *on inadequacies in the battlefield use of tank forces and measures for their elimination, 8 April 1942*
>
> Order of the Headquarters of the Supreme High Command of 22 January 1942 No. 57 'On the use of tank units and formations in battle' pointed out a range of major inadequacies in the use of tank forces in battle with the utmost clarity.
> This order demands of commanders organizing offensive operations the close co-ordination of tanks with infantry, artillery and aviation, to make use of tanks *en masse* and not to allow the introduction of tanks into battle without thorough reconnaissance.
> ... As before there are instances of the use of isolated tanks in battle, with poorly organized co-ordination between infantry, artillery and tanks and the absence of careful reconnaissance of enemy positions.... As a result of the incorrect use of tank forces they suffer huge and unfounded losses of personnel and equipment, and don't have that military effect which they could if they were used properly.
> ...
> It is necessary:
>
> 1. By order of military soviets of *fronts* and armies to conduct a thorough investigation of all factors in the incorrect use of tank units and the leaving behind of tanks on enemy territory. Individuals guilty of these are to bear responsibility [*privlekat' k otvetstvennosti*].
> 2. ...
> 3. You are asked to report on measures taken in carrying out Order of the High Command Number 57.
>
> Vasilevskii
> Bokov
>
> (Source: *RA T.23 (12–2)*, 1999, p. 78)

Whilst the Soviet Union lacked the armoured personnel carriers with which German Panzergrenadier units and increasingly US infantry were equipped (although they received significant numbers through Lend-Lease as the war continued), and which facilitated the support of tanks by infantry, the Soviet Union did receive lorries in large numbers from the United States, though certainly not enough for the mechanization of most rifle divisions during 1942. Close support could be provided by SMG companies and other infantry riding on tanks and disembarking at an opportune moment, although casualties were particularly heavy. At the same time, the chassis of outdated light tanks could be used as the basis for self-propelled guns for the support of both infantry and armour, the SU-76 coming into large-scale use in 1943, to be followed by heavier and better-protected assault guns and tank destroyers as the war progressed.

For the purposes of deep offensive operations, the increasing number of tanks available as 1942 progressed would allow their concentration in tank and later mechanized corps, with supporting arms, combined into tank and mechanized armies, the equivalent of a German Panzer corps of the beginning of the war. The *Soviet Military Encyclopedia* has the following to say about tank armies formed and operating during 1942:

> DOCUMENT 71: *Extract from the* Soviet Military Encyclopedia *on the deployment of tank armies*
>
> Tank army (TA), an operational formation of land forces, tasked during the years of the Second World War with the solution of operational tasks both independently and in co-ordination with other units and formations of a *front* (army group). In the Soviet armed forces the first two tank armies (3rd and 5th) were formed in May–June 1942... . An order of the People's Commissar for Defence determined the following exemplary makeup of a tank army: 3 tank corps, an independent tank brigade, 1–2 rifle divisions and a range of other units.... In November 1942 during the counteroffensive near Stalingrad 5th TA had 2 tank and 1 cavalry corps, an independent tank brigade and 6 rifle divisions.
>
> The initial conception of the tank army was that they should independently break through enemy defences using the strength of their rifle divisions and develop the success of the offensive using tank corps at operational depth.
>
> (Source: *SVE* 7, p. 660)

Whilst Soviet military theory was developing rapidly to the realities of modern warfare after the debacles of the summer and autumn of 1941, the effective translation of theory into practice would take considerable bloodshed and the weeding out of less able commanders during the spring and summer of 1942.

As the 1942 spring thaw, or *rasputitsa*, came, both sides took stock and prepared for summer offensive operations. The Soviet expectation for the summer was that the Axis would attempt to succeed in the task in which they had failed in late 1941, that is the capture of Moscow, and Soviet forces were deployed in strength to meet this threat. This appraisal of the situation was fuelled by an elaborate German deception operation, codenamed 'Kremlin'. At the same time as covering Moscow, as Mawdsley notes, Stalin was keen to preserve the initiative even before any major summer efforts, with the spring seeing local Soviet offensive operations from the continued and poorly co-ordinated efforts to relieve the siege of Leningrad in the north (covered in Chapter 7), to the continued throwing in of resources onto the Kerch' bridgehead in the Crimea. Both would end in disaster.

Most significant in terms of forces committed was the Soviet attempt to expand and secure the Barvenkovo or Izium salient in the Ukraine through operations northwards by forces from the salient and westwards by forces to the east of the city of Khar'kov, the seizure of which was the focus of the operation. Soviet operations starting on 12 May made less rapid progress than had been hoped in covering the 25 miles to Khar'kov on the east–west axis and 35 miles along the north–south one. On 17 May German forces launched a pre-prepared plan for the elimination of the Barvenkovo salient, which by the end of the month saw the destruction of 18–20 Soviet divisions unable to extract themselves in time, including the strike force assembled to attack Khar'kov from the south, all of which transpired despite German forces lacking local numerical superiority.

Soviet losses were also heavy when German forces overran the poorly fortified Kerch' bridgehead on the Crimea that had been retaken by Soviet forces in December 1941 (after having been lost in November) and reinforced between January and May 1942 to a strength of 21 divisions with 350 tanks, and overrun in German operations that lasted only a couple of weeks, launched on 8 May and concluded by 20 May. In just two weeks Soviet forces had lost 162,000 personnel.

With the destruction of the Soviet Kerch' bridgehead and the disbanding of the Crimean *Front*, the now somewhat isolated fortress city of Sevastopol' defended by the Coastal [*Primorskaia*] Army could be besieged, being taken after intense fighting at the beginning of July, with German forces taking another 90,000 prisoners; a total of about 150,000 Soviet personnel were lost during the nine-month siege.[5]

Although the Axis offensive in the south that took German forces to the gates of Stalingrad and the Caucasus mountains understandably dominates the historiography of the war in the east during 1942, Soviet operations would continue across the whole front throughout the year. Dealing with the German advance on the Caucasus and Stalingrad was in response to the German activity, but Soviet offensive operations had been planned against the German Army Group Centre for the summer on the Rzhev–Viaz'ma salient, then resumed in November, before German forces eventually abandoned it in early 1943, along with any hope of seizing Moscow. Fighting continued with considerable intensity below Leningrad into the summer of 1942, with Soviet attempts to lift the siege being resumed in January 1943. To the south, Soviet forces attempted to destroy the Demiansk salient, to which German forces had clung during the winter of 1941–42, with offensive operations in late 1942. The salient was not destroyed, being abandoned by the Germans in early 1943.[6]

Only in the far north were things relatively quiet: Soviet offensive operations during the winter of 1941–42 to deal with limited German incursions from Norway had become bogged down like those across the front, in a context where both sides found it difficult to concentrate and sustain large forces given the few road and rail routes for supply and severe weather conditions. However, even here German air and naval forces based in Norway fought to destroy Allied shipping carrying aid to the Soviet Union via the ports of Murmansk and Arkhangel'sk, with the destruction of the convoy PQ-17 in July 1942 being a major blow to deliveries for months afterwards and to British prestige.[7]

Despite plans to finally capture Leningrad in the summer of 1942, the German focus for the summer campaigning season was primarily on the securing of Caucasian oil, with any development having the potential for Axis troops to threaten the Allies in Africa and the Middle East from both east and west, cutting the increasingly important route for aid to the Soviet Union through Iran and possibly even bringing Turkey into the war on the side of the Axis. Operations specifically towards Stalingrad were initially about securing the rear and flanks of forces to the south.

Operation *'Blau'* was launched on 28 June 1942, the first stage of which was for the Soviet side the 'Voronezh-Voroshilovgrad Defensive' Operation, lasting from 28 June to 24 July, the end of which almost coincided with Hitler's Directive Number 45 of 23 July, Document 72 below.

DOCUMENT 72: *Führer Headquarters, 23 July 1942. Directive Number 45 for the continuation of Operation 'Braunschweig' {the Caucasus offensive}*

I. In a campaign that has lasted little more than three weeks, the broad objectives that I outlined for the southern flank of the Eastern Front have been largely achieved. Only weak enemy forces from the Timoshenko Army Group have succeeded in avoiding encirclement and reaching the far bank of the Don....

A further concentration of enemy forces is taking place in the Stalingrad area, which the enemy will probably defend tenaciously.

II. Aims of future operations.

A. Army.

1. The next task of Army Group A is to encircle enemy forces which have escaped across the Don in the area south and south-west of Rostov, and destroy them....
2. After the destruction of enemy forces south of the Don, the most important task of Army Group A will be to occupy the entire eastern coastline of the Black Sea, thereby eliminating the Black Sea ports and the enemy Black Sea Fleet....
3. At the same time a force composed chiefly of fast-moving formations will give flank cover in the east and capture the Groznii area....
4. The task of Army Group B is, as previously laid down, to develop the Don defences and, by a thrust forward to Stalingrad, to smash the enemy forces concentrated there, to occupy the town, and to block off the land bridge between the Don and the Volga and communication along the Don.

    Closely connected with this, fast-moving forces will advance along the Volga with the task of thrusting through to Astrakhan and blocking the main course of Volga in the same way....

(Source: *Hitlers Weisungen für die Kriegsführung, 1939–1945*, 1965, pp. 227–229)

With the centre of gravity of Soviet forces further to the north, Axis forces had advanced rapidly in the south as Soviet forces fell back, often in disarray. For the Soviet side, the next phase of Operation *'Blau'*, only later *'Braunschweig'*, would last from 25 July until 18 November, and would be known as the 'Stalingrad Defensive' Operation. After the fall of Rostov, still relatively light Soviet forces in the south fell back towards Stalingrad and the Volga in the face of Army Group B, which had, along with Army Group A advancing to the south, been formed from Army Group South on 9 July.

Army Group A would make rapid progress until a combination of the Caucasus Mountains, deteriorating weather and extended supply lines would halt the advance well short of the oilfields, before most of the Army Group made its escape in early 1943 when its position became untenable due to events to the north near Stalingrad.[8]

The Soviet 62nd Army had been ordered to occupy defensive positions on the Don bend before Stalingrad on 11 July.

DOCUMENT 73: *To the command of the 62nd Army on the occupation of the Stalingrad defensive line, 11 July 1942, 00 h. 20 min.*

The Headquarters of the Supreme High Command orders:

1. That rifle divisions of the army occupying outlying areas around Stalingrad [*obvod*] and situated in the Stalingrad district rapidly be moved to occupy the Stalingrad defensive line, prepared along the line Karazhenskii (on the Don, 18 km SW of Serafimovich), Evstratovskii, Kalmikov, Slepikhin, Surovikino Station, Farm Number 2, ... Suvorovskii Station.
2. The transfer of divisions is to start no later than 11.7.1942....

The line is to be occupied by three divisions by the morning of 12.7 and the remainder are to follow during 13 and 14 July.
...
On the authorization of the Headquarters of the Supreme High Command
Head of the General Headquarters A. Vasilevskii.

(Source: *RA T.23 (12–2)*, 1999, p. 229)

At this point, the defence was not based on nor planned to be based on the city itself, as indicated by the fact that the city's civilians were not evacuated in time. Indeed, whilst 62nd Army became known for its defence of the city itself, much of its summer strength would be encircled by German forces away from the city.

The crumbling of Soviet resistance before Stalingrad had forced Stalin to reiterate his famous Order Number 270 of 16 August 1941 (Document 33, Chapter 3) in slightly modified form as Order Number 227 of 28 July 1942, which became known as 'Not a Step Back' (Document 74), hardly suggesting that German forces were being lured into some sort of trap with Stalingrad as the bait.

DOCUMENT 74: *Order of the People's Commissar of Defence of the USSR Number 227, 28 July 1942, Moscow*

The enemy is throwing ever increasing forces at the front, and, not taking due consideration of the huge losses he has suffered, he thrusts himself forward, tearing into the depths of the Soviet Union, capturing new districts, ravaging and laying waste to our towns and villages, raping, robbing and killing the Soviet population. The struggle is taking place in the region of Voronezh, on the Don, in the south at the gates of the Northern Caucasus. The German occupiers are breaking through in the direction of Stalingrad, towards the Volga, and hope, at any cost, to capture the Kuban' and the Northern Caucasus with their wealth in oil and bread. The enemy has already captured Voroshilovgrad, Starobel'sk, Rossosh', Kupiansk, Valuiki, Novocherkassk, Rostov-on-Don, and half of Voronezh. Elements of the Southern *Front*, following the lead of panic-mongers, gave up Rostov and Novocherkassk without putting up serious resistance and without orders from Moscow, drenching their banners in shame.

...

Certain unintelligent people at the front comfort themselves with talk that we can retreat to the east even further, because we have a huge territory, vast quantities of land, a large population, and we will always have surplus bread. With this they hope to justify their shameful conduct at the front. But such conversations are deceitful and false through and through, of benefit only to our enemies.

Every commander, Red Army soldier and political worker should understand, that our resources are not without limits. The territory of the Soviet State is not desert, but people – workers, peasants, the intelligencia, our fathers, mothers, wives, brothers and children. The territory of the Soviet Union, which has been seized and is in the process of being seized by the enemy is bread and other foodstuffs for the army and the rear; metals and fuel for industry; mills and factories, which are supplying the army with arms and munitions; and railway lines.... We have already lost more than 70 million of our population, more than 800 million puds of bread per annum and more than 10 million tons of metal per year. We now no longer have superiority over the Germans in terms of population reserves, nor in reserves of bread. To retreat further means to ruin oneself together with our Motherland....

From this it follows, that it is time to put an end to the retreat.

Not a step back! Such should now be our principle call.

We must stubbornly defend every position, every metre of Soviet territory to the last drop of blood, cling to every last scrap of Soviet soil and hold our ground until the all other possibilities have been exhausted [*do poslednei vozmozhnosti*].

Our Motherland is living through difficult days. We must halt, and then repulse and shatter the enemy....

Can we survive this blow, and then repel the enemy to the west? Yes, we can....

What exactly are we lacking?

We are lacking order and discipline in our companies, battalions, regiments, divisions, tank units and squadrons. This is what at the moment is our main inadequacy. We have to restore strict order and iron discipline in our army if we hope to save the situation and hold on to the Motherland.

It is no longer acceptable to tolerate commanders, commissars, political workers, units and formations which on their own initiative give up fighting positions. It is no longer acceptable when commanders, commissars and political workers allow a few panicmongers to determine the situation on the field of battle, and that they draw others to retreat and open up the front to the enemy.

Panicmongers and cowards should be wiped out on the spot.

...

Commanders of companies, battalions, regiments, divisions and their equivalent commissars, who retreat from fighting positions without higher orders, are traitors to the Motherland....

After their winter retreat under pressure from the Red Army, when discipline had been shattered, in order to reassert this discipline the Germans took a number of severe measures, leading to far from negative results. They formed more than 100 punishment companies from soldiers who had been found guilty of breaching discipline.... They formed in addition a further dozen punishment battalions out of commanders.... It now transpires, that German forces have excellent discipline, despite the fact that they don't have the superior moral aim of defending their motherland....

Does it not follow that we should learn from our enemies in this regard ...?

I consider, that it follows.

The Supreme High Command of the Red Army orders:

1. That military soviets of *fronts* and above all the commands of *fronts*:
    a) Completely liquidate the idea amongst forces of retreat and with an iron fist suppress propaganda that we apparently can and should retreat even further to the east ...;
    b) Without discussion remove commanders of armies from their posts who tolerate unauthorized withdrawals,... without order from *front* command, and dispatch them to the High Command in order that they be brought to trial by military tribunal;
    c) Form within the boundaries of a *front* from one to three (depending on the situation) punishment battalions (of 800 men each) are to be formed, to which middle-ranking and senior commanders are to be sent and the corresponding political workers of all types of unit who are guilty of breaching discipline either through cowardice or a lack of resolve, and placed on the most difficult sectors of the front, so that they might pay back the Motherland in blood for their crimes against her.
2. That military soviets of armies and above all commanders of armies:
    a) ... remove commanders and commissars of corps and divisions from their posts who tolerate unauthorized withdrawals of forces from the positions they occupy without the order of the army command, and dispatch them to the military soviet of the *front* for trial by military tribunal;
    b) Form within the boundaries of an army three–five well-armed blocking detachments (with up to 200 men in each) and place them directly in the rear of irresolute divisions and require, that in the event of panic and retreat without order of units of the division that they shoot panicmongers and cowards on the spot and in doing so assist honest troops of the division in fulfilling their duty to the Motherland;
    c) Form within the boundaries of an army from five to ten (depending on circumstances) punishment companies (with from 150 to 200 men in each) and send rank and file Red Army men and NCOs....
3. That commanders and commissars of corps and divisions:
    a) ... remove commanders of regiments and battalions....
    b) Render all possible assistance and support to the blocking detachments of the army in maintaining order and discipline in units.

This order is to be read out to all companies....

People's Commissar of Defence

I. Stalin

(Source: O.A. Rzheshevskii, 1990, pp. 435–436)

Blocking detachments, the work of which was handled by much smaller military police units in other armies, were therefore formed specifically in response to Order Number 227 on the Stalingrad and Don Fronts. These units seem to have been kept busy during the late summer and autumn, as Document 75 suggests:

DOCUMENT 75: *Note of the OO NKVD STF to UOO NKVD USSR on the activities of blocking detachments of the Stalingrad and Don* Fronts *{no earlier than 15 October}* 1942

In accordance with Order Number 227 of the NKO in active units of the Red Army 193 blocking detachments have been formed as of 15 October 1942. 16 of these have been formed in units of the Stalingrad *Front* and 25 of the Don, a total of 41 units, which are subordinated to the NKVD special sections of armies.

Blocking detachments have, from their formation (from 1 August to 15 October of the current year) detained 140,755 service personnel running away from the front lines.

Amongst those detained: 3,980 were have been arrested, 1,189 shot, 2,776 sent to punishment companies, 185 to punishment battalions, with 131,094 returned to their units and or higher echelon units.

The bulk of detentions and arrests have been conducted by blocking detachments of the Don and Stalingrad *Fronts*.

On the Don *Front* 36,109 persons were detained, 736 persons arrested, 433 persons shot, 1,056 sent to punishment companies, 33 sent to punishment battalions, and 32,933 were returned to their units or to higher echelon units.

On the Stalingrad *Front* 15,649 persons were detained, 244 persons arrested, 278 persons shot, 218 persons sent to punishment companies, 42 persons to punishment battalions, and 14,833 returned to their units or higher echelon units.

It is worth noting that blocking detachments, and especially detachments of the Stalingrad and Don *Fronts* (subordinate to NKVD special sections of armies) during a period of brutal fighting with the enemy played a valuable [*polozhitel'nuiu*] role in the business of bringing order to units and the prevention of the disorganized retreat from the positions they were occupying, and the return of a significant number of service personnel to the front line.

(Source: *Stalingradskaia epopeia*, 2000, p. 222)

By the beginning of September, German forces were rapidly approaching the city after the destruction of much of 62nd Army in forward positions on the Don bend. The situation provoked the following telegram from Stalin to Zhukov, now Deputy Commander-in-Chief with responsibility for the south:

DOCUMENT 76: *Telegram of the Supreme High Commander to the representative of the Supreme High Command on the rendering of assistance to Stalingrad. To General of the Army Comrade Zhukov.* 3 September 1942, 22:30

The situation with Stalingrad has deteriorated. The enemy is now only three versts[9] from Stalingrad. They might take Stalingrad today or tomorrow if the northern group of forces does not render immediate assistance.

> You are to demand of the commanders of forces situated to the north and northwest of Stalingrad to make haste in striking the enemy and to come to the aid of Stalingraders.
>
> Any sort of delay is forbidden. Delay is now tantamount to a crime. All aviation is to be thrown in to aid Stalingrad. In Stalingrad itself little aviation remains.
>
> Receipt and the taking of appropriate measures are to be communicated without delay.
>
> I. Stalin
>
> (Source: O.A. Rzheshevskii, 1990, p. 436)

With the throwing in of *Stavka* reserves, Soviet resistance would solidify along the Volga as intense resistance in the city of Stalingrad itself sucked German units into what would be a seemingly bottomless pit for German resources. During the second half of September and throughout October, German forces sought to clear Stalingrad of the defending 62nd and 64th Armies. Stalingrad's three key factories, the Red October steel works, Stalingrad Tractor Factory and Barricade Ordnance Factory became battlegrounds.

Only on 14 October 1942, after much of the city was in German hands, were orders were issued by the Supreme High Command making it plain that the defence of built-up areas in and around Stalingrad was to be given a high priority, particularly the fortification of the remaining Soviet positions in the city of Stalingrad.

> DOCUMENT 77: *Extracts from the Directive of the Headquarters of the Supreme High Command No. 170,655 of 14 October 1942 on measures for the defence of Stalingrad. To the Commander of the Stalingrad* Front, *Comrade Eremenko*
>
> 4. Immediately to start the construction of no less than three defensive military belts, one after the other, and prepare all centres of population in the defensive belt and along all lines for defence.
>
>   All towns and major population centres regardless of their distance from the defence lines are to be readied for defence. The principal focus is to be on those parts of Stalingrad still in our hands, with every house, every street and every district becoming a fortress. In addition, the most decisive measures are to be taken to clear the enemy from those areas of the city which he occupies and in addition to securely fortify that recaptured behind you.
>
> ...
>
> 5. In preparing population centres for defence to supervise the following:
>   a) Every population centre, system of defensive positions and barrier on the approaches to and in the centre itself is to be transformed in to a fortress, capable of halting the movement of the enemy through it, and capable of independently conducting defence for a sustained period, even if fully encircled ...
>
> (Source: *SBD 5*, pp. 15–16)

During the first half of October, German forces gained control of much of the northern industrial district of the city, with the situation apparently becoming increasingly desperate for the defenders but with German forces being eaten up division by division, like their Soviet counterparts, in the heavy street fighting. As of 15 October at 20:00, the NKVD would report on the deteriorating situation around the Stalingrad Tractor Factory in the north of the city:

> DOCUMENT 78: *Telegraph UNKVD S{talingrad}0 to the NKVD USSR on the situation in Stalingrad, 16 October 1942. To Comrade Beria*
>
> I am informing you of the situation in Stalingrad as of 15.X.1942 at 20:00. During this 24-hour period the situation in the district of the tractor factory has deteriorated sharply. The enemy has gone over to the offensive in the district of the Stalingrad Tractor Factory and occupied the mining [*gornii*] and southern settlements and the territory of the factory.
>
> Fighting continues along the banks of the Volga. Enemy aviation has without pause bombed ... our troops, the crossings over and both banks of the Volga.
>
> ...
> Voronin
>
> (Source: *Stalingradskaia epopeia*, 2000, p. 228)

The next day, on 16 November, on behalf of the Headquarters of the Supreme High Command, Vasilevskii would make threatening noises regarding the apparent giving up of the Stalingrad Tractor Factory district of the city, unaware of the cost of such success for German forces:

> DOCUMENT 79: *To the command of the 62nd Army regarding a report on the reasons for the giving up of the Stalingrad Tractor Factory {STZ}, 16 October 1942, 16:30*
>
> For a report to the *Stavka* you are to without delay report on the reasons for such a rapid relinquishing control of the district of the STZ, on the situation in the city at the time of receipt of this instruction and on your future intentions.
> On behalf of the Headquarters of the Supreme High Command, Vasilevskii
>
> (Source: *RA T.23 (12–2)*, 1999, p. 372)

However, whilst German forces continued to make gains, the steam was rapidly running out of the German push through the city as reserves were bled dry, with the Soviet counter-offensive outside the city looming on the horizon.

As late as 5 July, the Soviet High Command had perhaps still seen Operation '*Blau*' as the first stage of an attack on the Soviet capital.[10] From August, the Soviet leadership had started to fully appreciate the potential significance of operations in the south relative to those closer to Moscow, and to allocate resources accordingly.

During the summer, as Zhukov acknowledges, a counter-offensive on the scale of that which took place from November near Stalingrad was not being planned:

DOCUMENT 80: *Extracts from the memoirs of Georgii Zhukov on the Soviet counter-offensive near Stalingrad*

There are suggestions, that the first notions of a future offensive operation were developed in the High Command apparently still during August 1942....

But these were not suggestions of a future counteroffensive operation, but merely a plan for a counterblow with the aim of holding the enemy before Stalingrad. Nobody in the High Command was thinking of anything more, because at the time we did not have either the strength or the resources for more.

[On 13 November the counteroffensive, as prepared by the *Stavka*, was presented to Stalin by Zhukov and Vasilevskii:]

Having completed preparation of the plans for the forces of the Stalingrad *Front* on 12 November, A.M. Vasilevskii and I phoned I.V. Stalin and said, that we need to personally inform him of a number of issues associated with the forthcoming operations.

On the morning of 13 November we were with I.V. Stalin. He was in a good frame of mind and in detail questioned us on the state of affairs near Stalingrad and on the progress of preparation for the counteroffensive.

...

The Supreme Commander listened to us intently. Because he did not rush to smoke his pipe, stroked his moustache and did not once interrupt our report, it was obvious, that he was pleased. The conduct of such a massive counteroffensive signified, that the initiative was passing to Soviet forces.

...

Whilst we were making our report, members of the State Defence Committee and and number of the members of the Politburo were gathering in the office. We had to repeat the basic points, which we reported in their absence.

After a brief discussion of the plan for the counteroffensive it was agreed upon in full.

Vasilevskii and I brought it to the attention of the Supreme Commander that the German High Command would be forced to transfer units of their forces from different regions, and in part from the Viaz'ma region, in support of their forces in the south, once a serious situation had developed in the Stalingrad region and in the North Caucasus.

So that this did not take place, it was necessary to quickly prepare and conduct offensive operations in the region north of Viaz'ma, in the first instance to destroy the Germans in the Rhzev salient. For this operation we suggested drawing on forces of the Kalinin and Western *Fronts*.

That would be good – said Stalin. But which of you will take care of it?

Alexander Mikhailovich [Vasilevskii] and I had agreed in advance on our suggestion on this point, and therefore I said:

– The Stalingrad operation is in all senses already prepared. Vasilevskii can take the co-ordination of the activities of our forces in the Stalingrad region, and I can take preparation for the offensives of the Kalinin and Western *Fronts*.

(Source: G.K. Zhukov, 1995, pp. 337 and 346–348)

Whilst operations around Stalingrad had certainly gained considerable significance, it is questionable, as Mawdsley notes, whether operations below Moscow were deemed at the time to be in support of 'Uranus' at all or were, in fact, seen as significant in themselves as a means for the Soviet Union to seize the initiative in the centre, rather than simply responding to the Axis attack in the south. The November offensive in the Viaz'ma region, Operation 'Mars', will be discussed below, but it is only with the failure of 'Mars' that the successful Stalingrad offensive would become the apparent focus of Soviet efforts in late 1942, with failed operations below Moscow being all but ignored in the Soviet historiography.

The Soviet counter-offensive against German forces at Stalingrad, Operation 'Uranus', began on 19 November 1942, with the front line situated as illustrated in Figure 5.1. Soviet mechanized forces of the South-Western *Front* to the north-west of the city made rapid headway against poorly equipped German allies, in the first instance Rumanians, defending the

Figure 5.1 Changes in the frontline from the Soviet 'Moscow Strategic Offensive' Operation to the eve of the 'Stalingrad Strategic Offensive' Operation, early December 1941 to mid November 1942.

Key:

1. Murmansk
2. Arkhangel'sk
3. Tikhvin
4. Novgorod
5. Pskov
6. Kalinin
7. Ivanovo
8. Kazan'
9. Rzhev
10. Viaz'ma
11. Smolensk
12. Kuibishev
13. El'nia
14. Briansk
15. Tula
16. Orel
17. Voronezh
18. Khar'kov
19. Warsaw
20. Brest
21. Odessa
22. Sevastopol'
23. Kerch'
24. Rostov-on-Don
25. Maikop
26. Groznii

overexposed flanks of Axis forces. On 20 November a second thrust was launched by the Stalingrad *Front* to the south of the city, with the two pincers of the encirclement meeting up near Kalach on the Middle Don River on 24 November, leaving German forces at Stalingrad encircled.

With Hitler having ordered German forces to stand fast, and after a relief attempt had been launched, Soviet forces would expand upon the existing inner layer of the encirclement during Operation 'Little Saturn', a scaled-down version of Operation 'Saturn' that had been planned to turn the Stalingrad encirclement and destruction of Army Group B into the destruction of all German forces in the south, cutting off Army Group A at Rostov. German attempts to relieve Stalingrad contributed to the impracticability of 'Saturn', as indeed did the ten weeks it took for the Red Army to reduce the Stalingrad pocket. Whilst Glantz is correct in suggesting that in 1942–43, as in 1941–42, 'the Red Army had repeatedly attempted to do too much too rapidly', at least the decision to downscale 'Saturn' from an attempt to seize Rostov and destroy Army Group A to a counter-attack against Manstein's attempt to relieve Stalingrad was, as Mawdsley suggests, 'symptomatic of a genuinely greater command flexibility and of the maturity of the *Stavka*'s system'. On 2 February 1943 the elimination of the pocket was complete, two days after the German commander, the recently promoted Field Marshal von Paulus, had surrendered.[11]

On 2 February 1942 the *Stavka* representative on the Don *Front*, charged with reducing the German pocket, and the commander of the *front*, Colonel-General Rokossovskii, would report to Stalin:

DOCUMENT 81: *Combat report of the Headquarters of the Supreme High Command representative and commander of the Don* Front *on the liquidation of the encircled enemy forces in the Stalingrad region, 2 February 1943, 18 h. 30 min.*

In carrying out your orders, at 16:00 on 2.2.1943 forces of the Don *Front* completed the defeat and destruction of the encircled Stalingrad grouping of enemy forces.

Completely destroyed and in part captured were: 11th Infantry Corps, 8th Infantry Corps, 14th Panzer Corps, 51st Infantry Corps, 4th Infantry Corps, 48th Panzer Corps, made up of 22 divisions: 44th, 71st, 76th, 79th, 94th, 100th Light Divisions; 113th, 376th, 295th, 297th, 305th, 371st, 384th, 389th Infantry Divisions; 14th, 16th, and 24th German Panzer Divisions; 1st Cavalry and 20th Infantry Rumanian Divisions.

...

More than 91,000 prisoners were taken, of whom more than 2,500 were officers and 24 generals....

As a result of the total destruction of encircled enemy forces military operations in the city of and region surrounding Stalingrad have ceased.

...

Representative of the Headquarters of the Supreme High Command, Marshal of Artillery Voronov

Commander of forces of the Don *Front*, Colonel-General Rokossovskii

...

(Source: O.A. Rzheshevskii, 1990, pp. 440–441)

The blow to German prestige for the loss of the bulk of 6th Army and elements of 4th Panzer Army was immense, as indeed were losses in addition to those captured in the city itself at the time of the final surrender. The German 6th Army alone had suffered 147,000 killed and 91,000 taken prisoner.[12]

The Stalingrad counter-offensive was undoubtedly a success, and indeed a turning point in the war in the sense that Axis forces would penetrate no further into the Soviet Union.

Returning to the issue of Soviet military organization and the tank armies considered at the beginning of this chapter, it is worth noting that whilst their contribution to the encirclement of German forces at Stalingrad was significant, they had not matured, in part for material reasons, into the tools for the deep-bound or encircling sweeps that Soviet forces would be able to make later in the war. As the *Soviet Military Encyclopedia* notes, continuing its discussion of the development of tank armies from Document 71:

> The experience of tank armies during the winter of 1942/43 showed, that the incorporation into them of both rifle and tank formations, possessing differing capacities for maneuverability, critically complicated the military use of such armies and the command of forces, particularly at operational depth.[13]

Put simply, the tanks easily outran their infantry support. Only with the greater availability of mechanized corps, the first of which was formed in September 1942 and which became a constituent part of tank armies, would Soviet infantry, with supporting arms, be able to keep up with the armour and strike at 'operational depth' into the enemy rear, providing a penetration for general [*obshchevoiskovie*] armies to exploit,[14] as described in an NKO order on the use of tank and mechanized units of 16 October 1942, which provides a useful summary of Soviet armoured doctrine at this stage of the war:

DOCUMENT 82: *Order on the battlefield use of tank and mechanized units and formations, Number 325, 16 October 1942*

The conduct of the war with the German fascists has shown that in the case of the use of tank units we still show significant weaknesses....

The battlefield use of tank regiments, brigades and corps

1. Independent tank regiments and brigades are used for the strengthening of the infantry on the principal axis and operate in close co-operation with them as tanks providing direct infantry support.
2. Tanks operating together with the infantry have the principal task of the destruction of enemy infantry and should not be broken away from the infantry by more than 200–400 m.

   ...

5. In the case of the appearance of enemy tanks on the battlefield the bulk of the fighting with them should be undertaken by artillery.[15] Tanks should engage enemy

tanks only in the case of an obvious superiority in strength and in the case of an advantageous situation.
6. [Close air support]
7. [Use of speed, maneuver, cover and flanking and rear attacks]
8. Independent tank regiments and tank brigades are a resource for deployment by army commanders to be provided to rifle divisions for their reinforcement.
9. Independent regiments of assault tanks [*tanki proriva*], equipped with heavy tanks, are provided to the troops as a resource for strengthening them for the breakthrough of enemy defences in close co-operation with the infantry and artillery. After having carried out their task of breaking through fortified lines heavy tanks are to be concentrated at rally points and to prepare for the rebuttal of enemy counterattacks.
10. In defensive fighting tank regiments and brigades ... are to be used as a resource for the delivery of counterattacks against enemy units breaking into the defensive depth. In certain instances tanks can be dug in as immobile firepoints....
11. Tanks corps are subordinate to the commanders of *fronts* or armies and are used on the principal axis of attack as an echelon for the exploitation of success in the defeat and destruction of enemy infantry.

    In offensive operations tank corps carry out the task of delivering a massive blow with the aim of breaking up and encircling the principal grouping of enemy forces and its destruction in co-operation with aviation and other ground forces of the *front*.

    A corps should not become entangled in tank battles with enemy tanks if there is not an obvious superiority over the enemy. In the case of engagement with large enemy tank units the corps should separate off anti-tank units and a portion of tanks,... and the corps should use its principal strength, covered by these resources, to move round and hit the enemy infantry with the aim of separating them from the enemy tanks and paralyzing the activities of the enemy tanks....
12. In defensive operations by the *front* or army a tank corps ... is used as a powerful resource in the counterattack from depth and is to be deployed in the rear areas of the army beyond the reach of enemy artillery (20–25 km).
13. [Choice of suitable terrain and reconnaissance of this terrain for operations by a tank corps]
14. In all types of action for a tank corps the decisive element is surprise. Surprise is achieved through camouflage and deception [*maskirovka*], the extent to which the location for deployment and redeployment is concealed, the use of night marches and cover for concentration from the air.

The battlefield use of mechanized brigades and mechanized corps
1. The independent mechanized brigade is a tactical formation and is used by the army command as a mobile reserve.
2. In the attack ... mechanized brigades carry out the task of seizing and holding key objectives until the arrival of remaining forces.
    ... strengthening existing success.
    ... protecting the flanks of advancing units.
3. In the pursuit of a retreating enemy a mechanized brigade seizes river crossings, defiles, key road junctions ... and co-operates in the encirclement and destruction of the enemy.
4. In an army defensive operation a mechanized brigade is used for counterattack against enemy breakthroughs.

5. In mobile defence a mechanized brigade carries out the task of active defence along a broad front and facilities the regrouping of units of the army.
6. The fundamentals of the activities of a mechanized brigade should be established as – a high level of maneouver, courage, decisiveness and persistence in the pursuit of objectives set for it.
   Using its high level of mobility, a mechanized brigade should seek out enemy weak points and inflict short, sharp blows on him.
7. A mechanized corps is a resource for the commander of a *front* or army and is used on the principal axis as an echelon for development of successes of our forces and the pursuit of the enemy.
   The breaking up of a mechanized corps and subordination of individual brigades to commanders of rifle divisions should not occur.
8. In the development of success in an offensive operation a mechanized corps, as a concentrated force of motorized infantry, tanks and supporting units, breaks forward, and is able to achieve offensive goals independently against an enemy who has failed to fortify himself.
9. The use of a mechanized corps as an echelon for the development of a breakthrough should only take place after the penetration of the principal enemy defensive belt by general formations and where infantry have reached the area in which enemy artillery positions are located.
   In special circumstances, in which the enemy defence is poorly provided for, a mechanized corps can independently carry out the task of breaking through the enemy front and the destruction of the enemy to the full depth of his defences. In these instances a mechanized corps must be reinforced with indirect artillery support, air support and where possible assault tanks.

...

People's Commissar of Defence USSR, I. Stalin

(Source: *RA T.13 (2–2)*, 1997, pp. 333–337.)

With the rise in the number of tanks being produced by Soviet industry, the increase in trained cadres and increased experience of large tank and mechanized formations, the conditions emerged for the formation of 'single-type' [*odnorodnii sostav*] tank armies with motorized infantry, assisted by the increasing availability of Lend-Lease supplied lorries. Their formation started in January 1943, when in GKO Order Number 2791, from which Document 82 below is taken, the formation of ten such armies was ordered by June 1943. Single-type TAs usually consisted of two tank and one mechanized corps, and independent tank and one to two self-propelled artillery brigades, a range of artillery, AA guns, engineers and other units. On paper they had about 800 tanks and SPs and up to 750 artillery pieces, mortars and *Katiusha* rocket launchers.[16]

> DOCUMENT 83: State Defence Committee. Decree GOKO No. 2791ss of 28 January 1943..
> .. On the formation of ten tank armies
>
> During February–June 1943 ten tank armies are to be formed....
> In a tank army there are to be 430 'T-34' and 210 'T-70', a total of 640 tanks.
> ...
> The Head of the Genshtab of the Red Army and *front* commanders are to provide ... 25,500 men from the fortifed districts by 10 February for personnel for the tank and mechanized corps.
> ...
> Attachment No. 1....
> Inventory of formations and units making up a tank army
>
> | | Titles of units and formations | | Number in army | Personnel list strength |
> |---|---|---|---|---|
> | I. Fighting units | | | | |
> | 1 | Tank army headquarters | ... | 1 | 284 |
> | 2 | Tank corps | ... | 2 | 19,334 |
> | 3 | Mechanized corps | ... | 1 | 15,740 |
> | 4 | Motorcycle regiment | ... | 1 | 1,485 |
> | 5 | Anti-aircraft division | ... | 2 | 1,345 |
> | 6 | Tank-destroyer regiment | ... | 1 | 518 |
> | 7 | Howitzer regiment | ... | 1 | 1,025 |
> | 8 | Guards mortar regiment | ... | 1 | 808 |
> | 9 | Aviation-communication regiment U-2 | ... | 1 | 158 |
> | Total | | | | 40,697 |
> | II. Supporting units | | | | |
> | 1 | Communications regiment | ... | 1 | 575 |
> | 2 | Engineers battalion | ... | 1 | 531 |
> | 3 | Automobile regiment | ... | 1 | 2,145 |
> | 4 | Repair and maintenance battalion (one tank and one automobile) | ... | 2 | 532 |
> | Total | | | | 3,783 |
> | ... | | | | |
> | Total in army | | | | 46,121 |
>
> (Source: Online. Available www.soldat.ru/doc/gko/scans/2791-01-1.jpg, 2791-03-1.jpg, 2791-06-1.jpg, 2791-07-1.jpg, 2791-08-1.jpg)

Such units, backed up by an increasingly mobile supply system, would increase the extent to which Soviet forces could break through the German defence in depth that focused on key communications arteries and that had prevented Soviet exploitation of initial breakthroughs during the winter of 1941–42.

The success of the Stalingrad operation was considerably greater, despite the impracticability of the broader encirclement of Operation 'Saturn', than the other large-scale Soviet operation of the period Operation 'Mars' (and proposed follow-on Operation 'Jupiter'). Operation 'Mars' or the 'Rzhev-Sichevka' Operation was also launched in November 1942 but against the German Army Group Centre, in the first instance aiming at the destruction of 9th Army near Rzhev. As Glantz notes, the notion in Zhukov's memoirs that the 'Rzhev-Sichevka' Operation, as in Document 80, was devised merely in order to pin German troops in the region seems to have been developed after the failure of Operation 'Mars' and success of 'Saturn'. Glantz notes many factors going against Zhukov's claim, perhaps the most significant being the resources lavished on 'Mars' that exceeded those provided for Saturn, and included more than 2,352 tanks and almost 10,000 guns and mortars.[17]

After the start date for 'Mars' had been delayed from 12 October and in the light of encouraging news from the south, Soviet forces of the Kalinin and Western *Fronts* struck German forces in the Rzhev salient on 25 November. Weather suited to the defence hampered Soviet artillery preparations and the operation suffered from poor concentration and co-ordination of forces. Struggling through deep snow, the Soviet advance became increasingly bogged down as casualties mounted. By the end of the operation on 20 December 1942, Soviet forces in the region had suffered 'catastrophic losses' for little gain – with personnel losses of more than 100,000 killed and missing and the loss of more than 1,600 tanks.[18] Such losses certainly contributed to the relative quiet of the region for months afterwards.

Despite the failure of Operation 'Mars', Stalin, Zhukov and other Soviet commanders involved could bask in the success of Operation 'Saturn' and the destruction of the German 6th Army in and around Stalingrad. Patriotism, broadly defined, along with fear of the NKVD and the Germans, no doubt contributed to Soviet victory at Stalingrad and associated operations, but these factors would have been insufficient without a resource balance shifting in Soviet favour. Whilst Soviet manpower resources were increasingly a limiting factor, in terms of tanks and artillery the fact that the Red Army could launch 'Mars' and 'Saturn' at the same time with such resources committed was indicative of the growing Soviet superiority in tanks and artillery in particular. At the same time, the Soviet military leadership was becoming increasingly experienced in large-scale operations in increasing depth (experience including failures such as 'Mars'), the sustaining of which from the railheads was increasingly assisted by the thousands of lorries provided by the Allies. The growing confidence of Soviet military leaders in their abilities was shared by Stalin, who went as far as to allow the disbanding of dual command (see Document 30, Chapter 3) in October 1942:

> DOCUMENT 84: *On the establishment of full unitary command and the abolition of the institute of commissars in the Red Army. Decree of the Presidium of the Supreme Soviet of the USSR, 9 October 1942*
>
> The system of military commissars established in the Red Army during the years of the Civil War emerged on the basis of a certain lack of trust towards command cadres, to the ranks of which old-school military specialists were attracted, who did not then believe in the permanence of Soviet power and were even alien to it. During the years of the Civil War military commissars played a decisive role in the task of strengthening the Red Army and the selection of commanders, in their political educations and in the instilling of military discipline.
>
> ...
>
> The Great Patriotic War with the German occupiers has tempered our command cadres, pushing forward a deep layer of new and talented commanders, experienced in battle and to the very end true to their military responsibilities and the honour of command. In bitter fighting with the enemy Red Army commanders have shown their loyalty to our Motherland, and acquired significant experience of modern war, growing and becoming stronger in both military and political respects.
>
> ...
>
> Hence, it has become inevitable that the institute of commissars in the Red Army be disbanded and that unitary command be established, and responsibility for all aspects of work with troops become the responsibility of commanders.
>
> It therefore follows, that the Presidium of the Supreme Soviet decrees, that:
>
> 1. Full unitary command be established in the Red Army and that all aspects of military and political life of a unit, formation or institution of the Red Army become the sole responsibility of commanders ...
> 2. The institute of commissars be dissolved....
> 3. The institute of deputy commanders on political matters be introduced....
> 4. The transfer of the most militarily prepared military commissars and political workers, who have gained experience of modern war, to command responsibilities be improved.
> 5. Military ranks and insignia common to the Red Army as a whole be established for deputy commanders on political matters and other remaining political workers.
>
> Chairman of the Presidium of the Supreme Soviet of the USSR
> M. Kalinin
>
> (Source: *KPSS o Vooruzhennikh Silakh Sovetskogo Soiuza*, 1981, pp. 326–327)

Although the dissolution of the institute of commissars did not mean the end to political supervision of the Red Army, with the special sections of the NKVD continuing their work for the time being, the abolition of the institute of commissars was nonetheless a significant statement of confidence in the Red Army command, whose position and status continued to be strengthened during 1943, and in particular with the recognition of those in command positions from junior lieutenant to colonel as 'officers' rather than simply 'command elements'.[19] The Red Army paid back this confidence with the victory at Stalingrad, although given the strategic situation and resource balance it is arguable that the German offensive was misguided and doomed to failure in any reasonable scenario.

Germany and her Axis allies, it seemed, had been able to seize the initiative with an operation of potential strategic significance, but in reality had lost any significant chance to bring the war to a rapid close either at the gates of Moscow or even during the first weeks of 'Barbarossa', when Soviet resistance and the scale of Soviet reserves were revealed to be greater than the wildly optimistic assessments that had led to the invasion in the first place.

By the end of January 1943 Soviet forces had not only destroyed the German 6th Army at Stalingrad but the land blockade of Leningrad had also been lifted and a significant amount of additional Soviet territory liberated, as an increasingly confident Stalin could report in an order of the Supreme High Command of 25 January 1943:

DOCUMENT 85: *Order of the Supreme High Command to forces of the South-Western, Southern, Don, North-Caucasus, Voronezh, Kalinin, Volkhov and Leningrad Fronts, 25 January 1943*

As a result of offensive operations over the last two months the Red Army has penetrated the defence of the German-fascist forces along a wide front, shattered one hundred and two enemy divisions, seized more than 200 thousand prisoners, 13,000 pieces of heavy weaponry and many other pieces of equipment and moved forward up to 400 kilometres. Our forces have won a serious victory. The advance by our forces continues.

I congratulate our soldiers, commanders and political workers of the South-Western, Southern, Don,... *Fronts* for their victory over the German-fascist occupiers and their allies – the Rumanians, Italians and Hungarians[20] – at Stalingrad, on the Don, in the North Caucasus, below Voronezh, in the region near Velikie Luki and south of Lake Ladoga.

I declare my appreciation to our command and our valiant soldiers, that have destroyed the Hitlerite army on the road to Stalingrad, relieving the siege of Leningrad and liberating the towns of ... Nal'chik, Mineral'nie Vodi, Piatogorsk, Stavropol',... Rossosh',... Velikie Luki, Shlissel'berg, Voronezh and many other towns and population centres from the German occupiers.

Onward to the total defeat of the German occupiers and their driving out from the four corners of our Motherland!

The Supreme High Commander
I. Stalin
Moscow, the Kremlin, 25 January 1943.

(Source: *Prikazi Verkhovnogo Glavnokomanduiushchego v period Velikoi Otechestvennoi voini Sovetskogo Soiuza* (Moscow: Voenizdat, 1975), p. 13. Online. Available www.soldat.ru/doc/vgk/unnum1.html)

Stalin's praise might have been generous and sincere, but the cost had been high, and it would be more than two years before the suffering and bloodshed would come to an end.

Guide to further reading

A. Beevor, *Stalingrad* (New York: Viking, 1998) and other editions.

H. Boog, Werner Rahn, Reinhard Stumpf and Bernov Wegner, *Germany and the Second World War, Volume VI* (Oxford: Clarendon Press, 2001).

W. Craig, *Enemy at the Gates: The Battle for Stalingrad* (New York: Reader's Digest Press, 1973) and other editions.

David Glantz, 'The Khar'kov Operation, May 1942: From the Archives, Part I', *JSMS*, Volume 5, Number 3 (September 1992), pp. 451–493 and maps pp. 494–510.

David Glantz, *Kharkov 1942: Anatomy of a Military Disaster* (New York: Sarpendon, 1998) and other editions.

David Glantz, *Zhukhov's Greatest Defeat: The Red Army's Epic Disaster in Operation Mars, 1942* (Lawrence, KS: University Press of Kansas, 1999).

David Glantz, 'Forgotten Battles of the German-Soviet War (1941–1945), Part 7: The Summer Campaign (12 May–18 November 1942): Voronezh, July 1942', *JSMS*, Volume 14, Number 3 (September 2001), pp. 150–220.

David Glantz, 'The Red Army's Donbass Offensive (February-March 1943) Revisited: A Documentary Essay', *JSMS*, Volume 18, Number 3 (September 2005), pp. 369–503.

David Glantz, 'Prelude to German Operation Blau: Military Operations on Germany's Eastern Front, April-June 1942', *JSMS*, Volume 20, Number 2 (April–June 2007), pp. 171–234.

Joel S.A. Hayward, *Stopped at Stalingrad: The Luftwaffe and Hitler's Defeat in the East, 1942–1943* (Lawrence, KS: University Press of Kansas, 1998).

Geoffrey Roberts, *Victory at Stalingrad: The Battle that Changed History* (Harlow: Longman, 2002).

6 The Battle of Kursk and the race for the Dnepr

Despite widespread acceptance in both the former Soviet Union and the West that the battle for Stalingrad constituted the turning point in the war on the Eastern Front (which it indeed did in the sense that it marked the furthest penetration eastwards of Axis forces), the *Wehrmacht* was far from beaten in early 1943. Whilst the loss of 6th Army and elements of 4th Panzer Army at Stalingrad was a major material and psychological blow to the *Wehrmacht*, Army Group A had withdrawn from the North Caucasus and escaped the threat of being cut off from the main German force.

In February 1943, after the remnants of 6th Army had surrendered at Stalingrad, Soviet forces continued to advance westwards in the south and grand plans were being drawn up for the effective destructions of Army Groups Centre and North before the summer. Although Army Group Centre had survived the Soviet 'Mars' offensive in the Rzhev-Viaz'ma region in November 1942, with the Soviet advance to the south into the Kursk region, the flank of German forces in the Briansk-Orel region, covering the Rzhev-Viaz'ma salient from the south, was now threatened. Plans for the destruction of the bulk of Army Group Centre, and indeed North, were, however, forestalled by German withdrawals from the Rzhev-Viaz'ma and Demiansk salients respectively in February–March. The shortening of German lines greatly enhanced the defensive capabilities of both army groups.

In the south, however, the situation remained more fluid thanks to the collapse of Axis forces near Voronezh, allowing the capture of Kursk and Khar'kov by Soviet forces on 8 and 16 February 1943 respectively. Nonetheless, Soviet plans for a race to seize a bridgehead over the Dnepr River to the west, behind which it was assumed German forces would retreat, were curtailed by German counter-attacks that saw Khar'kov retaken by forces of the Waffen SS on 16 March and saw the rapid Soviet reinforcement of what was rapidly becoming the Kursk salient.[1]

Even without German counter-attacks, whether such ambitious Soviet offensive plans were feasible from a supply point of view against all but the most hopelessly optimistic assessments of enemy strength and intentions was also, however, debatable. Document 86 illustrates both the scale of the logistical effort to sustain Soviet offensive operations in this period and the extent to

118 *The Battle of Kursk and the race for the Dnepr*

which the supply situation would have been a limiting factor on proposed further Soviet offensive operations in the next few weeks, particularly in the face of the *rasputitsa*, even if winter weather caused its own problems. Petrol, required for lorries even if not Soviet tanks, was a particular problem.

> DOCUMENT 86: *Summary report on the work of the rear area of the South-Western* Front *in the period of the January–February 1943 offensive operation, 20 February 1943*
>
> I. Preparation for the operation:
> 1. In making up the South-Western *Front* the following formations were included:
> 6th Army, numbering 60,000 men
> 1st Guards Army numbering 76,000 men
> 3rd Guards Army numbering 78,000 men
> 5th Tank Army numbering 73,000 men
> Other *front* formations and units numbering 67,000 men
> ...
> 8. Supplies of material goods:
> ...
> Available supplies of basic supply items with the troops and in supply dumps of operational units as of 1 January 1943 can be characterized as follows [Figures for 1st and 3rd Guards Armies have not been included separately, but are included in *front* totals]:
> ...
>
> | Item | 6th Army | | 5th Tank Army | | Front supply dumps and in transit | Total for front |
> |---|---|---|---|---|---|---|
> | | With troops | Supply dumps | With troops | Supply dumps | | |
> | *Munitions (unit = boekomplekt or BK):* | | | | | | |
> | Small arms | 0.7 | 0.8 | 0.8 | 0.5 | 0.4 | 1.8 |
> | Artillery | 0.8 | 1.8 | 0.8 | 0.5 | 0.6 | 2.1 |
> | Mortars | 0.7 | 1.0 | 1.1 | 0.2 | 0.5 | 1.5 |
> | *Fuels and lubricants (unit = complete refuel):* | | | | | | |
> | Petrol KB-70 | 0.8 | 5.2 | 0.9 | 0.1 | 1.7 | 4.7 |
> | Petrol (lower octane) | 1.4 | 0.2 | 0.6 | 0.1 | 1.7 | 2.7 |
> | Diesel | 0.7 | 0.4 | 1.6 | 1.0 | 1.0 | 5.4 |
> | Lubricating oil | 0.9 | 3.5 | 1.1 | 0.7 | 4.8 | 11.6 |
> | *Food supplies (unit = daily ration):* | | | | | | |
> | Bread | 7.0 | 14.0 | 12.2 | 2.6 | 1.8 | 9.7 |
> | Grains | 9.0 | 9.0 | 10.5 | 7.0 | 11.5 | 24.5 |
> | Meat | 7.0 | 2.2 | 1.4 | 2.8 | 9.7 | 19.1 |
> | Fats | 2.0 | 8.0 | 6.7 | 0.3 | 14.4 | 26.0 |
> | Tobacco | 9.0 | 25.0 | 2.1 | 2.5 | 19.9 | 31.0 |
> | Fodder (grains) | 6.0 | 1.0 | 0.2 | 17.0 | 11.0 | 26.0 |
> | Fodder (bulking) | 27 | 60.0 | 0.2 | 1.5 | 6.8 | 33.7 |

Statistics by weight for operational units of supplies for 1 January 1943, in tonnes:

Item	6th Army	5th Tank Army	Other units attached to front	Front *total* (overall = 15,800 tonnes)
1 *boekomplekt*	2,609	3,441	–	11,777
1 refuel	508	547	637	2,718
1 daily ration	201	320	240	1,305

...

Taking into account using up 0.2 BK of munitions, 0.25 refuels, 1 daily ration of foodstuffs, that is 4,338 tonnes per day, then the *front* requires the following for supplying its forces:

a) Standard railway trucks – 270 or 45 trains.
b) GAZ lorries – 3,615 for supply over 100 km. The number of lorries in working order in army automobile battalions and in *front* reserves ... comes to 950 vehicles, that is 26% of requirement.

...

II. The conduct of operations

...

By 15 February forces of the South-Western *Front* had moved forward, compared to the frontline on 1 January 1943:

a) To the west 250 km as the crow flies;
b) To the south 70–80 km as the crow flies.

2. Difficulties in repairing railway bridges totally destroyed by the enemy ... meant that during January and the first ten days of February the Rear Area Board of the *front* was not able to move rear-area units and establishments to new locations nearer to the troops, that significantly extended the distances over which they had to be shipped [by road] and hampered the supply of the troops.

...

5. The distances over which supplies had to be shipped by road are characterized in the following figures:

	6th Army	5th Guards Tank Army
1. Distance from railhead bases to forward supply dumps	130	310
Distance from forward supply dumps to frontline troops	300	60
Total distance for road transport	430	370

6. Total *front* supplies of material resources in operational units of supply during the period of operations:

Item	Front *supply as a whole in operational units of supply*		
	On 1.1.1943	On 15.1.1943	On 1.2.1943
a) Munitions [selected items] Rifle cartridges	2.1	2.1	2.0
... 76 mm shells [all types, average]	2.25	1.9	1.9
152 mm shells	5.9	5.3	5.9
b) Fuel and lubricants			
KB-70	4.7	2.6	5.26
Other petrol	2.7	2.1	3.4
Diesel	5.5	5.4	7.7
Lubricants	11.6	12.5	7.5
c) Foodstuffs			
Bread	9.7	30.4	26.9
Grains	24.5	20.5	42.5
Meat	19.1	25.5	20.7
Fats	26.0	18.0	38.6
Tobacco	31.0	25.0	14.0
Fodder (grains)	26.0	48.5	47.0
Fodder (bulking)	37.7	34.6	30.6

...

7. Experience of military operations has shown, that the average daily use of material resources can be expressed as: Munitions – 1/8 *boekomplekt*; Fuels and lubricants – 1/4 refuel; Foodstuffs – 1 daily ration, which in terms of weight means an average daily demand of 3,464 tonnes.

...

Actual reserves of material resources:

Item	Front *total in operational units*		
	On 1 February	On 15 February	On 1 March
a) Munitions [selected items] Rifle cartridges	2.0	2.4	1.90
... 76 mm shells [all types, average]	1.9	1.8	1.45
152 mm shells	2.2	2.5	1.8
b) Fuel and lubricants			
B-70/KB-70	5.3	3.3	2.8
Other petrol	3.4	2.5	1.3
Diesel	7.7	6.4	10.0
Lubricants	7.5	6.4	2.8
c) Foodstuffs			
Bread	26.9	32.0	28.2
Grains	25.0	19.4	14.0
Meat	20.7	15.6	9.7
Fats	28.6	18.8	16.1
Tobacco	14.0	4.3	10.4
Fodder (grains)	47.0	55.0	38.0
Fodder (bulking)	30.6	32.2	19.2

...

7. Numbers, condition and the work of vehicular transport:

The number and condition of vehicles expressed in terms of GAZ-AA lorries can be characterized as follows:

As of	On the books	Under repair	Operative
Front *auto-transport*			
On 1 February 1943	2,999	658	2,341
On 1 March 1943	3,151	291	2,860
Army auto-transport			
On 1 February 1943	1,159	179	980
On 1 March 1943	940	142	798
(%)	100	15	85

Supplies shipped by road transport:

Item	January		February	
	Tonnes	% of total shipped	Tonnes	% of total shipped
Munitions	9,758	[43.8]	7,877	43.0
Foodstuffs	4,012	[18]	1,950	11.0
Fuels and lubricants	3,757	[16.9]	4,164	23.0
Clothing	164	0.7	1,266	6.5
Medical supplies	523	[2.4]	143	0.5
Trophy items	108	[0.5]	813	4.0
Grain and other freight	3,930	[17.7]	2,246	12.0
Total	[22,252]	100.0	18,459	100.0

Conclusions:

... up to 15 February 1943 forces of the *front* successfully advanced, ... 250 km to the west and 70–80 km to the south as the crow flies. This was at the same time as, due to the destruction of the railway bridge over the Don, with a width of 366 m, and a host of other severe difficulties in the repair of the railways, the rear-areas of the *front* and armies ... were unable to follow behind the frontline forces.... As a result the rear of the *front* was spread out over 400 km.

...

A particularly intense period for the work of auto-transport resources was during the last ten days of January and the first ten days of February. At that time with a depth for transshipment of 400 km, in order to provide the troops with 3,500 tonnes of supplies per day, and with a 4–6 day turnaround for vehicles, the *front* required a total of 11,500 GAZ lorries, but had – both *front* and army 3,000 ... – a shortfall of 8,500.

On 5 February 1943, after the rolling out of the railway bridge in the Liska region the *front* gained the possibility of relocating and re-siting railheads nearer to the troops. However, there was a second task making the work of rail transport more difficult – not reducing the rate at which supply and operational trains were moving through, whilst rapidly and directly moving rear-area supply dumps of the *front* and armies forward, totally up to 5,000 truckloads in volume.

... Assisting the supply of troops was:

...

b) A significant volume of trophy material captured from the enemy was related to the provisioning of troops – 6th Army was able for a month to almost completely provide the troops with foodstuffs from trophy supplies.

...

10. The mobile field group of forces of General-Lieutenant Comrade Popov, organized during the third ten-day period of January, was sufficiently well materially supplied.

The group was especially well supplied with foodstuffs, in the main either through local resources or captured stocks.

The supply of munitions occurred without interruption.... At the end of the operation the supply of the group with auto-fuel was however somewhat worse, the supply of which, especially in 3rd, 18th and 10th Tank Corps, as of 20.2.1943 did not exceed 0.5 of a refuel.

...

Head of the Headquarters of the Rear-area Board of the South-Western *Front*, Colonel Smirnov

...

(Source: *RA T.25 (14)*, 1998, pp. 354–370)

In early 1943, both militarily and logistically the Red Army had overextended itself as it had during the same period the previous year, to a large extent due to Stalin's optimism for the prospect of a German collapse and the relative capabilities of the Red Army. Nonetheless, the German position was, despite the operational-level success at Khar'kov, and with the subsequent front line at the end of March 1943 situated as in Figure 6.1, now very much worse in a strategic sense than it had been a year before, both on the Eastern Front and in the wider war. As Stalin noted in his May Day Order of the Day for 1943:

DOCUMENT 87: *Stalin's Order of the Day for 1 May 1943*

Order of the Day

Comrades, Red Army and Red Navy men, commanders and political workers, men and women partisans, working men and women, men and women peasants, people engaged in intellectual work; brothers and sisters who have temporarily fallen under the yoke of the German oppressors!...

The winter campaign has demonstrated that the offensive power of the Red Army has grown....

Even for a counter-offensive on a narrow sector of the front in the area of Khar'kov the Hitlerite command found itself compelled to transfer more than thirty fresh divisions from Europe. The Germans calculated on surrounding Soviet troops in the area of Khar'kov and arranging a 'German Stalingrad' for our troops. However, the attempt of the Hitlerite Command to take revenge for Stalingrad has collapsed.

Simultaneously the victorious troops of our Allies routed the Italo-German troops in the area of Libya and Tripolitania, cleared these areas of enemies and now continue to batter them in the area of Tunisia, while the valiant Anglo-American aviators strike shattering blows at the military and industrial centres of Germany and Italy, foreshadowing the formation of a second front in Europe against the Italo-German fascists.

(Source: Joseph Stalin, 1944, pp. 83–84)

Figure 6.1 Changes in the frontline from the eve of the 'Stalingrad Strategic Offensive' Operation of November 1942 to the end of 1943.

Key

1. Murmansk
2. Arkhangel'sk
3. Novgorod
4. Demiansk
5. Rzhev
6. Vitebsk
7. Smolensk
8. Orel
9. Kursk
10. Voronezh
11. Khar'kov
12. Korsun'-Shevchenkovskii
13. Kirovgrad
14. Odessa
15. Voroshilovgrad
16. Rostov-on-Don
17. Kerch'

Specifically on the Eastern Front, Axis forces were no longer in a position to seize the strategic initiative, as representative of the Headquarters of the Supreme High Command, Konstantinov, detailed in a report of 8 April 1943 concerned with future operations by Axis and Soviet forces during the remainder of 1943:

> DOCUMENT 88: *Report by the representative of the Stavka VGK to the Supreme High Commander on possible operations by the enemy and Soviet forces in the spring and summer of 1943, 8 April 1943*
>
> I hereby report my opinions on possible enemy operations in the spring and summer of 1943 and thoughts on our defensive fighting in the near future.
>
> 1. Having suffered heavy casualties in the winter campaign of 1942/43 the enemy, apparently, will be unable to form significant reserves before the spring in order to again advance with the aim of seizing the Caucasus and breaking through to the Volga with the aim of a wide sweep around Moscow.
>   Bearing in mind the absence of substantial reserves, during the spring and first half of the summer the enemy will be forced to conduct offensive operations on a

much narrower front and achieve goals in strict stages, with the basic aim of the campaign being the capture of Moscow.

Given the presence of the enemy grouping against our Central, Voronezh and South-Western *Fronts* at the present moment, I consider that the principal enemy offensive operation will be conducted against these three *fronts* with the aim of destroying our forces on this axis in order to gain freedom of maneuver around Moscow by the shortest route.

2. It is apparent that during the first stage, having amassed maximum strength, including up to 13–15 Panzer divisions, the enemy will strike a blow with heavy aviation support with its Orlov-Kromi group in order to maneuver around Kursk from the north-east and with the Belgorod-Khar'kov group from the south-east.

...

At the current time the enemy has up to 12 Panzer divisions before the Central and Voronezh *Fronts*, and, moving up 3–4 Panzer divisions from other sections of the front might be able to throw up to 15–16 Panzer divisions against our Kursk forces, with around 2,500 tanks.

...

Konstantinov

(Source: *RA T.15 (4 4)*, 1997, pp. 17–18)

German planning for operations against the Kursk salient was certainly delayed by the need for German forces to replenish their strength, with waiting for the end of the spring *rasputitsa* also certainly making sense for the attacker. Hitler's championing of the need to wait for new equipment to be available in quantity for the forthcoming offensive, and in particular the new Tiger tanks, also added to the delay, which saw Citadel put back from mid-April to mid-July 1943.[2]

Stalin and the Soviet leadership could be ever more confident that the focus of resources for the summer was on the correct region thanks to a range of increasingly high-quality intelligence on different levels, whether from Soviet agents in Europe and leaked or officially provided ULTRA intelligence from the British, down to reconnaissance reports from partisans, the VVS, RDF and the GRU. When the German attack came in July, Soviet forces of the Central and Voronezh *Fronts*, and indeed the South-Western *Front*, were well-prepared defensively for German operations either to pinch the Kursk salient off or indeed encircle it through a wider sweep from positions south of Khar'kov, with forces massed in depth for both defence and counter-attack. Tables 6.1 and 6.2 provide details of the force composition and echeloning of the Central *Front* of the Kursk salient prior to the German attack.

Soviet airpower had also recovered from its parlous condition during the first year of the war. In July 1943 the Central *Front* alone was supported by 16th Air Army, consisting of 6th Fighter-, 6th Mixed-, 3rd Bomber Corps, and three fighter divisions, two assault (ground-attack) divisions and one night-bomber division – by the beginning of combat operations a total of

Table 6.1 Composition of the Central *Front*, Kursk salient, July 1943 (prior to German attack)

Formations and units	Number in three echelons	Front *reserve*	Total
Rifle divisions	41	–	41
Rifle brigades	4	–	4
Motorized rifle brigades	–	2	2
Tank brigades	2	13	15
Separate tank regiments	15	–	15
RGK field artillery regiments	27	–	27
Self-propelled artillery regiments	6	–	6
High-powered artillery brigades	2	2	4
Gun artillery brigades	–	1	1
Anti-tank (tank-destroyer) artillery brigades	3	3	6
Separate anti-tank artillery regiments	6	4	10
Mortar brigades	–	1	1
Guards mortar brigades	3	–	3
Guards mortar regiments	9	–	9
Separate guards mortar battalions	1	–	1
Army mortar regiments	16	6	22
Anti-tank rifle battalions	5	–	5

Note
Front reserve: 2nd Tank Army and 9th and 19th Tank Corps.

455 fighters, 241 ground-attack aircraft, 260 day bombers, 74 night bombers.

According to Soviet sources, German strength opposite the Central *Front* as of 4 July 1943 consisted of 24 infantry divisions (of which four were engaged in anti-partisan operations), six Panzer divisions, one cavalry division (engaged in anti-partisan operations) and two Panzergrenadier divisions – a total of 267,000 men. In addition reinforcements included three heavy panzer battalions (3 × 50 PzKpfw VI Tiger) and one tank destroyer regiment (90 Ferdinand tank destroyers).[3]

The most recent Russian-language multi-volume history of the Great Patriotic War suggests that the balance of forces at the start of July 1943, excluding the Soviet strategic reserve, was as provided in Table 6.3.

In addition to forces of the Central and Voronezh *Fronts*, Soviet forces defending the Kursk salient were backed by strategic reserves of the Steppe *Front*, providing another 500,000 men, 1,400 tanks and self-propelled guns and 2,800 artillery pieces and mortars.[4]

After a false alarm of German offensive operations in May prompting spoiling air attacks by the VVS over a number of days from 6–8 May, it was only on 2 July that the *Stavka* could give Soviet forces warning of the actual German offensive, which began in earnest on 5 July after pre-emptive Soviet

Table 6.2 Distribution of forces of the Central *Front* to three defensive echelons prior to the German attack, Kursk salient, July 1943

Army	Front width (km)	First echelon	Second echelon	Third echelon
48th	40	3 rifle divisions	4 rifle divisions 3 tank regiments 1 anti-tank brigade	None
13th	32	4 rifle divisions 1 artillery penetration corps (2 artillery and 1 guards mortar division)	3 rifle divisions 3 tank regiments	5 rifle divisions 1 tank brigade 2 tank regiments
70th	62	4 rifle divisions 1 artillery division	4 rifle divisions 3 tank regiments 1 anti-tank brigade	None
65th	82	6 rifle divisions 1 rifle brigade	3 rifle divisions 4 tank regiments	None
60th	92	3 rifle divisions 2 rifle brigades	2 rifle divisions 1 rifle brigade 1 tank brigade 1 anti-tank brigade	None
Front total (738,000 men)	308	20 rifle divisions, 3 rifle brigades, 1 artillery preparation corps and 1 artillery division	15 rifle divisions, 1 rifle brigade, 1 tank brigade, 13 tank regiments, 3 anti-tank brigades	5 rifle divisions, 1 tank brigade, 2 tank regiments

Sources: Adapted from David M. Glantz and Harold S. Orenstein (trans. and eds.), *The Battle for Kursk 1943: The Soviet General Staff Study* (London: Frank Cass, 1999) pp. 11–14 and Krivosheev, *Soviet Casualties and Combat Losses*, p. 132.

Table 6.3 Balance of forces on the Kursk axis at the beginning of July 1943

	Central and Voronezh Fronts	9th Army and 2nd Army (Army Group Centre) and 4th Panzer Army and Battle Group Kempf (Army Group South)	Balance of forces
Personnel (000s)	1,336	900	1.4:1
Artillery pieces and mortars	19,100	c.10,000	1.9:1
Tanks and self-propelled guns	3,444 (including >900 light tanks)	2,733 (including 360 outdated models)	1.2:1
Aircraft	2,172 (excluding long-range and night bombers, bringing total to 2,900)	c.2,050	1:1 (1.4:1 including long-range and night bombers)

Source: *Velikaia Otechestvennaia voina. 1941–1945. Voenno-istoricheskie ocherki. Kniga vtoraia. Perelom* (Moscow: Nauka, 1998), p. 259.

artillery bombardment of German troop concentrations and Soviet air strikes on German airfields. It had been predicted that the strongest German thrust would come from the north, whereas in fact it was from the south, where German forces made strongest progress against the echeloned Soviet defences. In the north, where German forces penetrated at most 8–12 km into the Soviet defences, Soviet counter-attacks began on 6 July and had halted the German advance by 12 July.[5] In the south, Soviet counter-attacks ('active defence') would start in earnest on 8 July.

> DOCUMENT 89: *Report of the command of forces of the Voronezh Front to the Supreme High Commander on the military situation and thoughts on preparations for going over to the offensive, 8 July 1943, 15:40*
>
> As of the end of 7.7.1943 it has been established from POWs and documents that in the first echelon of the enemy before the Voronezh *Front* nine enemy Panzer divisions are attacking, namely the SS Panzer Corps – four Panzer divisions, 48th Panzer Corps – three Panzer divisions, and, in addition to these 3rd and 19th Panzer Divisions from the south.
>
> The principal thrust, by a force of no less than six Panzer divisions, is being struck along the Oboian' road.

In addition to the above, it has been established by aerial reconnaissance as of 18:00 that fresh enemy forces are approaching.

a) A column of up to 200 tanks and 700 vehicles from Akhtirka moving towards Orlovka.
b) A column of up to 150 tanks and 1,000 vehicles from the Khar'kov direction approaching Iakhontov.
c) A column of up to 400 vehicles and tanks from Murom approaching the Maslovaia landing stage.

We consider, that the enemy is at the current time bringing 11 Panzer divisions against the Voronezh *Front*, a total of more than 2,000 tanks, of which up to eight are operating on the Oboian' axis and up to three Panzer divisions against Shumilov.

Today the enemy is attacking, as before, with his principal thrust along the Oboian' road against Katukov.

Our counterattack started at 12:30....

(Source: *Bitva pod Kurskom*, 2006, p. 605)

Despite German forces suffering heavy losses on the Oboian' axis, they were nonetheless able to shift the principal thrust of the attack to the east towards the railway junction of Prokhorovka and penetrate further into the Soviet defences. The German thrust towards Prokhorovka would be met with reserves from the Steppe *Front*, the commitment of which started on 10 July.

DOCUMENT 90: *From a report by the senior officer of the General Headquarters attached to the Voronezh Front to the head of the General Headquarters on defensive operations of forces of the front from 4 to 23 July 1943, 23 August 1943*

The conduct of operations from 4 to 23 July 1943

...

Strengthening of the Oboian'-Kursk axis ... in the end forced the enemy by the evening of 10.7.1943 to no longer strike further blows in the Oboian' direction.

Not having achieved decisive success on the Oboain'-Kursk axis by the evening of 10.7.1943 the enemy had gone over to the defence and principal forces (... SS Panzer Corps and 17th Panzer Division) were sent to Prokhorovka, and 48th Panzer Corps was thrown in to the attack towards Ivnia and further to the west, attempting to turn our flank from the west and north-east.

On the Ivnia axis the enemy met the organized defences of 6th Guards Army, alongside which 184th, 219th and 309th Rifle Divisions of 40th Army and 204th Rifle Division of 38th Army had been brought in.

In addition in order to strengthen 6th Guards Army 5th Guards Tank Corps had been redirected, along with a number of anti-tank regiments and a regiment of RS.

Further attacks by the enemy in this axis were repulsed with heavy losses for him.

On the Prokhorovka axis during 11 July the enemy regrouped his forces with the aim, from the morning of 12 July, of decisively defeating our forces near Prokhorovka and striking towards Mar'ino and moving round Oboian' from the east and on to Kursk.

As a result of the decision of the Headquarters of the Supreme High Command two Armies were allotted to the Voronezh *Front* (5th Guards Tank and 5th Guards Armies) from the Steppe *Front*, which on 10 July started to redeploy to the battlefield.

(Source: *RA T.15 (4–4)*, 1997, pp. 375–383)

The subsequent mass engagement of armour in the Prokhorovka region constituted the largest such engagement of the Great Patriotic War and, indeed, in history. Whilst the German attack would be blunted, Soviet losses were heavy:

DOCUMENT 91: Report of the representative of the Stavka *VGK to the Supreme High Commander on military operations in the Prokhorovka region, 14 July 1943*

I yesterday personally witnessed a tank engagement to the south-west of Prokhorovka by our 18th and 29th Corps with more than 200 enemy tanks on the counterattack. Simultaneously hundreds of artillery pieces and all our available RS batteries participated in the battle. As a result the battlefield was littered within an hour with burning German and our own tanks.

Over two days of fighting 29th Tank Corps of Rotmistrov suffered 60% destroyed and damaged tanks and 18th Corps lost up to 30% of its tanks....
Vasilevskii

(Source: *RA T.15 (4–4)*, 1997, p. 53)

Whilst Prokhorovka was a Soviet victory in the sense that German forces did not succeed in reaching their objectives and German losses in the battle were far more of a blow to overall German capabilities than those of the Red Army, Soviet losses were certainly numerically greater; Soviet T-34 tanks were forced to rush headlong across open territory to close the range with the more powerfully gunned German Panther and Tiger tanks, although figures for actual losses on both sides vary wildly.[6]

On 12 July, as the battle at Prokhorovka raged, Soviet forces launched the first stage of their strategic offensive (Operation 'Kutuzov'), to the north of the Kursk salient against German forces in the Orel region – Orel falling on 5 August. More overwhelming given the fact that both the Central and Steppe *Fronts* involved had been heavily committed in operations near Kursk, was the Soviet launching of a second offensive to the south of the Kursk salient (Operation 'Rumiantsev'), starting on 3 August and developing as in Document 91:

> DOCUMENT 92: *Directive of the* Stavka *VGK Number 30160 to representatives of the* Stavka *{Zhukov and Vasilevskii} on tasks for and the co-ordination of the activities of* fronts *during the 'Belgorod-Khar'kov' and 'Donbass' Offensive Operations, 6 August 1943*
>
> The plan presented by Comrade Iur'ev for the conduct of Operation 'Rumiantsev' is confirmed by the Headquarters of the Supreme High Commander, which at the same time orders:
>
> 1. That Gagen's 57th Army be transferred to forces of the Steppe *Front* from the South-Western *Front* from 24:00 hours on 8 August with the task of striking around Khar'kov from the south in co-operation with the main force of the Steppe *Front* in the seizure of Khar'kov....
> 2. The principal task of the South-Western *Front* is to be the striking of the principal blow to the south in the general direction of Golaia Dolina, Krasnoarmeiskoe and in co-ordination with the Southern *Front* to destroy the enemy Donbass group of forces and to seize the Gorlovka, Stalino region.
> 3. The principal task of the Southern *Front* is to strike a principal blow in the general direction of Kuibishevo, Stalino, where it is to close with the shock group of the South-Western *Front*.
>   Preparations for the offensive of the South-Western and Southern *Fronts* are to be completed by 13–14.8.1943. The plan ... is to be submitted to Comrade Alexandrov by 10.8 for confirmation by the *Stavka*.
> 4. Responsibility for co-ordination of operations is to be placed on: Comrade Iur'ev between the Voronezh and Steppe *Fronts*, and on Comrade Alexandrov between the South-Western and Southern *Fronts*.
>
> ...
>
> I. Stalin
> A. Antonov
>
> (Source: *RA T.16 (5–3)*, 1999, p. 187.)

Despite German reserves having been drawn into the Donbass by a Soviet feint, and the growing mass of artillery support provided for the initial breakthrough, as to the north of Kursk Soviet commanders operating on the Khar'kov axis had to commit tank corps for the initial penetration of German defences. Despite desperate German counter-attacks, Khar'kov was in Soviet hands by 28 August.[7]

Document 92 is of interest in highlighting the role of *Stavka* representatives on the spot in co-ordinating increasingly complex combined-arms and deep-penetration operations by more than one Soviet *front* – more informally carrying out the function of the *napravlenie* commands introduced and disbanded in 1941 – that had formally brought more than one *front* under a single commander. As Shtemenko, Head of the Operations Department of the *Genshtab* from May 1943, suggests, some of the *front* commanders saw the presence of the *Stavka* representative as unnecessary interference, at least post-war, even if he at least goes on to suggest that, on balance, the

Stavka representatives served a valuable role. Similarly, *Genshtab* 'Officers of the General Staff' served important functions as emissaries lower down the chain of command in sharing hard-won experience with fresh units earlier in the war whilst keeping the *Stavka* informed of events at the front, a role of less importance as a greater number of *front* and army commanders and their staffs gained experience in the handling of the forces under their command.

Certainly by mid-1943 the *Genshtab* and *Stavka* of the Supreme High Command were working increasingly effectively in the broad planning and co-ordination of Soviet operations, the *Genshtab* playing a key role advising Stalin as Supreme Commander. Shtemenko suggested that it was about halfway through 1942 that 'the organizational forms of the General Staff fitted the nature of the work to be done', by which time 'rush jobs' in planning 'had become a thing of the past'.[8]

Whilst the Soviet leadership could be pleased with the progress of Soviet operations in the aftermath of the German Operation 'Citadel' against the Kursk salient, Soviet losses continued to be considerable against typically stubborn German resistance, as illustrated by Table 6.4 for the fighting up to late August 1943 in the immediate north and south of the Kursk salient.

In the aftermath of the operations shown in Table 6.4, and with the Soviet recapture of the Donbass, German thoughts, with Hitler's agreement, were on stabilizing the front along what would be termed the Panther Line: a defensive line running from Narva in the north all the way down to the Dnepr River for much of its length, with additional fortifications further south. On 15 September Hitler in fact agreed in principle to withdrawal behind the *Ostwall*, as yet existing in practice largely only given the fact that even without fortification of the west bank the Dnepr River was an imposing obstacle.

For the Soviet side, during continued bloody fighting in the Ukraine during August and early September 1943, the race was on to reach the Dnepr and throw bridgeheads over it before the German defence crystallized against what constituted a Soviet general offensive in the region, made up of a series of multi-*front* operations along the lines of the aftermath of the encirclement of German forces at Stalingrad.[9]

Rapid success, in terms of breaching the as-yet weak German *Ostwall*, was achieved in the far south, where Soviet forces were able to advance much further east without having to cross the Dnepr, in mid-October penetrating the *Ostwall* as it crossed the steppe between Zaporozh'e and Melitopol'. Soviet sources perhaps downplayed the superiority enjoyed in armour at the start of the operation, one Soviet source suggesting that 778 tanks and assault guns [*sturmovie orudii*] of the Southern *Front* faced 'up to 300' German equivalents, against which the German 6th Army could apparently field in the region of 65 tanks [*Kampfpanzer*] and 98 assault guns [*Sturmgeschütze*], figures perhaps not including lightly armoured tank destroyers [*Panzerjäger*]. The Southern *Front* (from 20 October 4th Ukrainian *Front*),

Table 6.4 Soviet strengths and irrecoverable losses for the 'Kursk Strategic-Defensive' Operation and subsequent offensives

Front	'Kursk Strategic-Defensive' Operation (5–23 July 1943)		'Orel Strategic-Offensive' Operation – 'Kutuzov' (12 July–18 August 1943)		'Belgorod-Khar'kov Strategic-Offensive Operation – 'Rumiantsev' (3–23 August 1943)	
	Strength	Irrecoverable losses	Strength	Irrecoverable losses	Strength	Irrecoverable losses
Central Front	738,000	15,336	645,300	47,771	–	–
Voronezh Front	534,700	27,542	–	–	739,400	48,339
Steppe Front	–	(09.07–23.07) 27,452	–	–	404,600	23,272
Western Front (left wing)	–	–	(12.07–18.08) 233,300	25,585	–	–
Briansk Front	–	–	409,000	39,173	–	–
Totals	1,282,700	70,330	1,387,600	112,529	1,144,000	71,611

Source: Krivosheev, *Soviet Casualties and Combat Losses*, pp. 132–134.

had soon bypassed the entrance to the Crimean Peninsula and advanced to eventually secure a bridgehead over the lower Dnepr where it enters the Black Sea by the end of November, forward Soviet KMGs advancing up to 250 km during a seven-day period.[10] The speed of the Soviet pursuit was, however, hampered by logistical problems in the face of the German 'scorched earth' policy. Similar problems were experienced to the north, for instance in providing fuel for forward units and given the fact that artillery units lagged far behind forward units in what was now the rainy season or *rasputitsa*, which prevented Soviet forces from seizing large bridgeheads over the Dnepr 'on the march' in late September and early October. Nonetheless, many footholds were seized on the western bank of the river, such as that obtained by elements of 13th Army of what was, at the time, the Voronezh *Front*, near the then relatively unknown town of Chernobyl:

DOCUMENT 93: *Summary report of the Head of Engineers of 13th Army to the Head of Engineers of the 1st Ukrainian* Front *on engineering support for the forcing of the Dnepr off the march by the army in September 1943, 21 November 1943*

Before approaching the Dnepr River forces of the army had forced the River Desna near Korop, the River Seim, the River Desna on the Chernigov sector, Morovsk....

Engineering reconnaissance established that the enemy had not constructed defensive positions on either the eastern or western bank of the Dnepr. Only on isolated sectors of the front line, near railway or wooden bridges, and similarly from settlements situated near the river, did the enemy subject us to machine gun fire. From the rear artillery and mortar fire targeted the river and the approaches to it.

All the bridges and barges had been destroyed. Many fishing boats had been disabled. There were relatively few in working order.

There was lumber for the construction of rafts in sufficient quantities.

The width of the Dnepr varied on different sectors from 190 to 350 m. The banks of the river sloped gently, were sandy, and covered in small bushes, allowing for good cover. Reconnaissance confirmed locations for crossing points and marked out the routes for columns to move up to them, which in future, after improvement and repair, would serve as permanent roads.

...

By 24:00 21.9.43 army forces of the left flank consisting of 17th Guards Rifle Corps and by 24:00 22.9.43 on the right flank, consisting of 15th Rifle Corps, reached the Dnepr. 28th Rifle Corps covered the right flank on the army from the north given the threat to the flank from enemy counterattack given that the army had moved forward deep into enemy territory.

...

At daybreak 22.9.43 units of 17th Guards Rifle Corps ... and at daybreak on 23.9.43 units of 15th Rifle Corps,... off the march and on a wide front, started to force the Dnepr.

By this time 25 rafts made of wood and barrels had been collected, 42 fishing boats, two barges and four A-3 assault boats. The overall capacity of these resources was 45.5 tonnes with two barges with a capacity of 85 tonnes.

...

The enemy put up heavy defensive fire,... but was forced out of these areas by units crossing to the north and south of them.

Forward units, with artillery support, successfully pushed inland to the west, widening the captured bridgehead. In order to allow the crossing of the main force and for the crossing of transport resources the construction of pontoon and wooden bridges started. [Army] river crossing resources that arrived on the scene were used for ferrying. By this time [27.9.43] all engineering units had arrived....

In total, in this period [27.9.43] there were 12 crossing points in operation.

The overall capacity for all the crossing points was 483 tonnes, including using army engineering resources – 356 tonnes, and resources found locally – 127 tonnes for a single crossing. These resources were capable of allowing in a single crossing, using all crossing points: personnel – 1,850 men, divisional artillery and vehicles – 85, anti-tank guns – 45, heavy machine guns – 185, carts – 72....

Head of Engineers of the forces of 13th Army, Colonel Kolesnikov

(Source: *SBD 30*, pp. 5–8)

One of these smaller bridgeheads to the north of Kiev proved to be particularly valuable, 5th Guards Tank Corps of the Voronezh, later 1st Ukrainian *Front*, covertly redeploying and being thrown across the Liutezh bridgehead on the junction of 38th and 60th Armies to the south of that seized by 13th Army. Despite inevitable losses as tanks sank in the soft ground of what was marshy terrain and hence relatively poorly defended by German forces, the bridgehead was consolidated and then expanded as 3rd Guards Tank Army and forces of 38th Army were thrown across the Dnepr, supported by the advance of 60th and 13th Armies to the north. Soviet forces broke out of the bridgehead on 3 November and had seized the Ukrainian capital, Kiev, by 6 November – the eve of the anniversary of the Russian Revolution.[11] The 3rd Guards Tank Army pressed forward, only to be halted by German counter-attacks, with German forces actually retaking Zhitomir and pushing Soviet forces back, but with Soviet troops nonetheless having held a huge bridgehead that could be exploited during the next wave of offensive operations beginning before the end of the year.

Meanwhile, to the south, a second large bridgehead over the Dnepr was being carved out by Soviet forces of the Steppe (2nd Ukrainian) and South-Western (3rd Ukrainian) *Fronts*, from Cherkassi in the north to Zaporozh'e in the south. Plans for the extension of small, existing bridgeheads and deep penetration to the west by forces of the Steppe *Front* are provided in Document 94:

DOCUMENT 94: *Plan of the Command of the Steppe* Front *of 1 October 1943 on the conduct of offensive operations including the forcing of the River Dnepr*

I. The immediate task of the Steppe *Front*: the destruction of the Kirovograd-Krivoi Rog grouping of enemy forces and entry in to the rear areas of the Dnepropetrovsk grouping.

II. Stages of the operation

First stage. Forcing of the Dnepr River.... Seizing and supporting a bridgehead on

> the right bank of the River Dnepr for the subsequent advance. Time allotted up to 5 October 1943.
>
> Second stage. Advance with the aim of destroying the enemy Kirovograd-Krivoi Rog grouping of forces and enter into the rear of the Dnepropetrovsk grouping. By 19–20 October to have reached the front line Bolshoi Viski, Ingulo-Kamenka, Shevchenkovo, Krivoi Rog.
>
> III. Grouping of Armies for the conduct of the operation and their compositions.
>
> 1. The thrust for the destruction of the Kirovograd grouping of the enemy is to be struck by four Armies. General direction of the blow: Znamenka, Kirovograd:
>   a) 52nd Army – five rifle divisions....
>   b) 4th Guards Army – six rifle divisions....
>   c) 5th Guards Army – seven rifle divisions and one artillery division....
>
>   Artillery grouping:
>   82 mm and 120 mm mortars – 424
>   Light artillery (excluding 45 mm) – 493
>   Heavy – 90
>   Total artillery pieces and mortars – 1,007
>   d) 53rd Army – seven rifle divisions....
>   Artillery grouping:
>   82 mm and 120 mm mortars – 463
>   Light artillery (excluding 45 mm) – 373
>   Heavy – 36
>   Total artillery pieces and mortars – 872
> 2. Blow in the general direction of Piatikhatka, Krivoi Rog, with the aim of entry into the rear areas of the Dnepropetrovsk grouping of enemy forces to be struck with three Armies.
>   a) 37th Army – eight rifle divisions....
>   b) 7th Guards Army – eight rifle divisions and one artillery division....
>   c) 57th Army – six rifle divisions....
> 4. Use of motor-mechanized formations.
>   1st and 7th Mechanized Corps are allocated for use in the frontal zone of 37th Army in the general direction of Annovka, in order to encircle Krivoi Rog from the west.
>   5th Tank Army will be used to encircle Kirovograd from the west.
>
> (Source: *SBD 24*, pp. 5–7)

The delayed Soviet advance in this sector was, however, halted short of its objectives by the end of December by the redeployment of German armoured forces from further south, as 40th and 17th Panzer Corps cut off and destroyed forward mechanized units of 5th Guards Tank Army advancing on Krivoi Rog, with forward elements of 7th Guards Army suffering a similar fate at Novgorodka in the face of forces of 40th and 3rd Panzer Corps.[12] Once again, however, Soviet forces held on to a huge bridgehead over the Dnepr, with the two key bridgeheads leaving German forces holding sections of the Dnepr north and south of Korsun' vulnerable to encirclement.

Little mention has been made of the Soviet Navy up to this point. That the Soviet Navy was certainly not a priority during the war is highlighted by the transfer of naval productive capacity from shipbuilding to tanks and other land-weapons systems, as in the case of the conversion of Factory Number 112 from submarine to tank production (see Chapters 4 and 8). As for existing capabilities, the bulk of the Baltic Fleet, the largest of the pre-war Soviet fleets, was bottled up for most of the war in Leningrad and at Kronstadt after the costly evacuation of forward-deployed units from Tallinn in the face of the German advance. Plans were made for its scuttling should the Germans have taken the city (see Chapter 7) and significant numbers of sailors transferred to the Red Army (see Document 66, Chapter 5). The second largest Soviet pre-war fleet was the Black Sea Fleet, which, although successfully supporting the 'Kerch'-Feodosiia' Operation from 25 December 1941 to 2 January 1942, suffered heavy losses in supporting and then evacuating personnel from both Odessa in 1941 and Sevastopol' during 1942 (see Chapter 5). Despite limited naval resources in the region, the Axis was able to dominate the Black Sea for much of the war through airpower. Even when German air superiority was challenged and subsequently lost, the Black Sea Fleet, as all Soviet fleets with the exception of the Northern Fleet, remained relatively inactive. Perhaps the best explanation for this inactivity, other than the relative backwardness of the Soviet Navy compared to other arms until Allied aid and accrued experience started to have an impact (see Chapter 8), was that warships were such large units to lose that few commanders were willing to fully exploit them after the horrendous losses of 1941 lest they fall foul of Stalin's wrath. This fear of losses applied even to the Northern Fleet during the 'Petsamo-Kirkenes' Operation of October 1944, even when it enjoyed overwhelming superiority over German forces in the region (see Chapter 10). A good illustration of the attitude towards naval forces of Stalin and other Soviet military leaders is provided in Document 95, concerned with the operations of the remnants of the Black Sea Fleet in October 1943. During the night of 6 October 1943 the Flotilla Leader *Khar'kov* and the destroyers *Besposhchadnii* and *Sposobnii* shelled the ports of Feodosiia and Yalta in the Crimea, still in Axis hands, and enemy shipping. Early in the morning, as the warships were making their way back to the Soviet port of Tuapse in the North Caucasus, with fighter cover, they were attacked by German JU-87 dive bombers, the end result being, after additional air attacks, the sinking of all three vessels with the loss of 780 lives.[13]

> DOCUMENT 95: *Directive of the Headquarters of the Supreme High Commander Number 30221 to the Black Sea Fleet and forces of the North-Caucasian Front, to the People's Commissar for the Navy on the co-ordination of the military activities of fleet and front, 11 October 1943*
>
> According to information received, operations of the Black Sea Fleet of 6 October that ended in failure, and with the unnecessary deaths of personnel and the loss of three major warships, were conducted without the knowledge of the command of the North-Caucasian *Front*, despite the fact that the Fleet was subordinated to him in an operational sense.
>
> The Headquarters of the Supreme High Command orders:
>
> 1. That the commander of the Black Sea Fleet agrees on all operations intended to be conducted with the commander of the North-Caucasus *Front* and that no operations be conducted without his agreement.
> 2. That the core forces of the Fleet be used to support the military operations of ground forces. Long-distance operations with significant surface forces are to be conducted only with the agreement of the Headquarters of the Supreme High Command.
> 3. That responsibility for the operational use of the Black Sea Fleet be given to the commander of the North-Caucasian *Front*.
>
> Headquarters of the Supreme High Commander
> I. Stalin
> A. Antonov
>
> (Source: *RA T.16 (5–3)*, 1999, p. 221.)

Consequently, whilst the Black Sea Fleet would support the landing of Soviet forces for a second time on the Kerch' Peninsula during the Kerch'-El'tingen landings of 21 October to 11 December 1943, German support of forces in the Crimea after it had been cut off from the main body of Axis forces and the eventual evacuation during 1944 would not be interdicted by Soviet surface forces. The Kerch'-El'tingen landings, whilst conducted only a short distance from Soviet bases across the Kerch' Straights on the Taman' Peninsula, nonetheless involved the landing of four rifle divisions, involving a total of 119 launches and 159 other support and transport vessels, 667 artillery pieces of more than 76 mm calibre and 90 RS launchers providing supporting fire, and covered and supported by more than 1,000 aircraft of the 4th Air Army.[14]

Just as naval forces were relatively little-used, so were other 'novelty' troops such as airborne forces. The limited impact of their use during the Moscow counter-offensive of 1941–42 did not stop their being used in the expansion of the Dnepr River crossing near Bukrin during the second half of October 1943, during which Soviet paratroops, much like their British counterparts would be just under a year later during Operation 'Market

Garden' in the Netherlands, were too widely dispersed during drops for rapid concentration where needed. Whilst elements of the more than two brigades were dropped behind Soviet lines, and others into the Dnepr, inadequate intelligence saw the remainder dropped in areas in which German armoured forces were deployed, namely 24th Panzer Corps, with 19th Panzer Division in position in the area before the first drops, with other elements of the corps in transit to the area. Many airborne troops ended up, as in the winter of 1941–42, dispersed in forested areas and engaging in partisan warfare. For Stalin this was the last point at which highly trained airborne forces would be used in any numbers during the war.[15]

At the end of 1943 the *Wehrmacht* was spent as an offensive military force able to conduct more than local counter-attacks in order to contain increasingly deep Soviet penetrations into German defences. Local Soviet numerical superiority was commonplace by this stage of the war, with the qualitative divide between the Red Army and the *Wehrmacht* of the first months of the war now no longer the norm. The limited number of elite German Panzer and Panzergrenadier divisions being transferred from one Soviet breakthrough to another represented an ever-smaller proportion of German forces. The apparently dramatic battlefield performances of these *Wehrmacht* and SS units was in reality exaggerated partly by the fact that the ostensibly larger Soviet units they destroyed or halted (that typically had smaller basic complements than their German equivalents anyway), were far more hopelessly under strength than they were. For example, 18th and 29th Tank Corps of 5th Guards Tank Army (2nd Ukrainian *Front*) operating on the Krivoi-Rog–Kirovograd axis, were, by 8 December 1943, down to 37 and 22 tanks and self-propelled guns compared to an authorized complement of 257.[16] Nonetheless, whilst German 'fire-brigade' units still achieved much in the aftermath of Operation 'Citadel' during the second half of 1943, they would prove increasingly inadequate during 1944.

Guide to further reading

H. Boog, Werner Rahn and Reinhard Stumpf, *Germany and the Second World War, Volume VI* (Oxford: Clarendon Press, 2001).

Anders Frankson and Niklas Zetterling, *Kursk 1943: A Statistical Analysis* (Abingdon: Frank Cass, 2004).

David Glantz, 'Soviet Operational Intelligence in the Kursk Operation, July 1943', *Intelligence and National Security*, Volume 5, Number 1 (1990), pp. 5–49.

David Glantz, 'The Defensive Battle for the Kursk Bridgehead, 5–15 July 1943', *JSMS*, Volume 6, Number 4 (December 1993), pp. 656–700.

David Glantz, 'The Battle of Kursk (Continued): Tank Forces in Defense of the Kursk Bridgehead', *JSMS*, Volume 7, Number 1 (January 1994), pp. 82–134.

David Glantz, 'Prelude to Kursk: Soviet Strategic Operations, February–March 1943', *JSMS*, Volume 8, Number 1 (January 1995), pp. 1–35.

David Glantz, 'The Red Army's Donbass Offensive (February–March 1943) Revisited: A Documentary Essay', *JSMS*, Volume 18, Number 3 (September 2005), pp. 369–503.

David Glantz and Jonathan House, *The Battle of Kursk* (Lawrence, KS: University Press of Kansas, 1999).

David Glantz and Harold Orenstein (trans. and eds.), *The Battle for Kursk, 1943: the Soviet General Staff Study* (London: Frank Cass, 2001).

Timothy Mulligan, 'Spies, Ciphers and 'Zitadelle': Intelligence and the Battle of Kursk, 1943', *Journal of Contemporary History*, Volume 22 (1987), pp. 235–260.

Steven H. Newton (trans. and ed.), *Kursk: The German View* (Cambridge, MA: Da Capo Press, 2002).

7 The siege of Leningrad

During Operation 'Barbarossa', the Axis invasion of the Soviet Union, the focus of the attention of the German Army Group North was the city of Leningrad, previously called St Petersburg and then Petrograd, the capital city of Russia until 1918 and birthplace of the Russian revolution. The Soviet government had long feared the threat to Leningrad from the north through Finland (see Document 8, Chapter 1), with a precedent having been set with the landing of German troops in Finland in February 1918. Similarly, with the advance from the south in early 1918, German forces had come within striking distance of the city from this direction as well. With the buffer zone of the Baltic Republics secured in the summer of 1940, Leningrad seemed much more secure from the south than it had with the prospect of foreign forces using them as a launchpad. However, by late June it was apparent that German progress to the south of the city was such that Leningrad was vulnerable from both Finland and the south. The first line of defence for Leningrad from the south would be the so-called Pskov–Ostrov Fortified Region:

DOCUMENT 96: *To the military soviets of the Leningrad Military District and North-Western* Front *on preparation of defensive positions along the line Pskov, Ostrov, Opochka, Sebezh, 29 June 1941*

The People's Commissar for Defence decrees:
1. To re-subordinate the Pskov-Ostrov Fortified District to the military soviet of the North-Western *Front*.
2. Using the resources of construction battalions, the Directorate of Field Construction [UPS], construction sites and the local population to build, in addition to the Fortified Districts fortified field positions on the line Pskov, Ostrov, Opochka, Sebezh. In the first instance anti-tank obstacles are to be constructed and all reinforced concrete positions of the Fortified Districts are to be brought to readiness.
3. ...
4. Time for preparation of the line is no later than 2.7.1941
5. ...
6. Work is to be organized such, that the line is in a state of permanent readiness.

N. Vatunin

(Source: *RA T.23 (12–1)*, 1998, p. 53)

However, as early as 4 July the Northern *Front* was being informed of the necessity for a defence line well behind the Pskov–Ostrov positions given the likelihood of imminent enemy breakthrough in the Pskov region, the new defence line to be along the line Kingisepp–Luga–Novgorod:

DOCUMENT 97: *Directive of the Main Command Headquarters to the military soviet of the Leningrad Military District on preparation of a defensive line on the approaches to the city of Leningrad, 5 July 1941*

For the covering of the city of Leningrad and principal axes from the south-west and south, that is – Gdov-Kingisepp-Leningrad; Luga-Leningrad; Novgorod-Leningrad; Vishnii Volochek-Leningrad, the construction of a defensive line along the front Kingisepp, Tolmachevo, Ogoreli, Babino, Kirishi and onwards along the western banks of the River Volkhov is required. A cut-off [*otsechnaia*] position [is to be prepared] along the Luga-Shimsk line.

The axes Gdov-Leningrad; Luga-Leningrad; Shimsk-Leningrad should be covered the most soundly.

...

[In] the first instance anti-tank obstacles should be constructed [with] the simultaneous construction of field positions.

...

The Leningrad Region Council of Worker's Deputies and the Leningrad Region Committee VKP(b) are to provide the labour, transport, machinery, tools and materials for the construction of the line from construction organizations and the local populations of the city of Leningrad and the Leningrad Region.

The construction of the line should start immediately. Construction is to be completed by 15 July 1941.
Zhukov

(Source: N.L. Volkovskii (ed.), 2004, pp. 10–11)

With the Germans having captured Pskov on 9 July and moving in the direction of Luga, and with increasingly heavy fighting between Finnish forces and 7th Army between Lake Ladoga and Onega, a unified command for the region, bringing together the North-Western and Northern *Fronts* and the Baltic and Northern Fleets, was introduced on 10 July. This *napravlenie* command was led by Voroshilov, a close crony of Stalin who owed his position more to political reliability than ability. In order to slow German forces on the key Luga axis, the Luga Operational Group had been formed by the Northern *Front* on 5 July and had been in action against German forces near the town on 12 July. Meanwhile, during early July the progress made by the German 18th Army through the Baltic Republics had been rapid, forcing the Soviet 8th Army back in relatively good order towards Leningrad. The 18th Army now added a western threat to the city, forcing the creation of the Narva Operational Group on 14 July, the same day that German forces crossed the Luga River south of Kingisepp. Whilst intense fighting continued near Luga and Kingisepp, Soviet forces (34th and

11th Armies) counter-attacked to the east of Staraia Russa on 12 August.[1] Whilst failing to halt the German advance, this attack at least sucked in German forces from the Moscow axis and was part of a crucial and gradual whittling down of German strength, although such incremental damage was less noticeable than the penetration of German forces to the north-west of Novgorod, prompting a blunt request from the *Stavka* to the North-Western *Front*:

> DOCUMENT 98: *To the command of forces of the North-Western* Front *regarding the holding of Novgorod, 16 August 1941*
>
> The town of Novgorod is not to be given up and is to be held to the last soldier.
> B. Shaposhnikov
>
> (Source: *RA T.23 (12–1)*, 1998, p. 123)

By 18 August, the spectre of the encirclement of Leningrad by 4th Panzer Group and 16th Army had reared its head; the High Command in Moscow was concerned that the North-Western *napravlenie*, still led by Stalin's crony Voroshilov, was doing little to prevent this:

> DOCUMENT 99: *Directive of the Supreme High Command Number 001029 to the military soviet of the North-Western* napravlenie *on measures for the prevention of the encirclement of Leningrad, 17 August 1941*
>
> The High Command considers the most dangerous direction of enemy attack to be the eastern axis Novgorod, Chudovo, Malaia Vishera and onwards across the River Volkhov. If the Germans are successful in this direction, then it will mean the envelopment of Leningrad from the east, the cutting of communications between Leningrad and Moscow and a critical situation for the Northern and North-Western *Fronts*. In this event it is likely that the Germans will unify their front with the front of the Finns in the area of Olontsa. It seems to us that the head of the North-Western *napravlenie* does not see this critical danger and therefore is not taking any sort of special measures for its liquidation.
>
> (Source: N.L. Volkovskii (ed.), 2004, p. 13)

However, on 20 August Chudovo still fell to German forces. On 23 August, the Northern *Front* became the Leningrad and Karelian *Fronts*, separating off the Finnish threat to the north-east of Leningrad from responsibilities for its immediate defence to the north and south, but no doubt adding further confusion to a chain of command that had been tinkered with far too often in recent weeks. Indeed, on 30 August the unwieldy North-Western *napravlenie* was to be disbanded, the day that German forces broke through the Neva River near Ivanovskoe and captured the key railway junction of Mga, severing the last rail connection between Leningrad and the remainder of Soviet

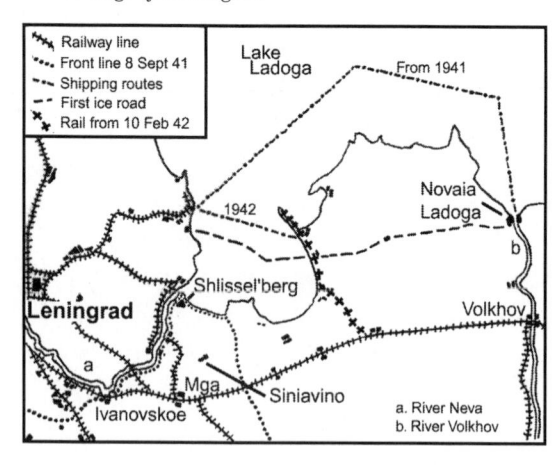

Figure 7.1 The Leningrad blockade and relief routes to the city from September 1941–January 1943.

territory. German forces reached Lake Ladoga on 8 September and captured Schlissel'berg, cutting off Leningrad's land communications in their entirety, as illustrated in Figure 7.1.

Soviet attempts by 54th Army to the east to de-blockade Leningrad from 10 September failed, with the German forces below Leningrad and the Oranienbaum pocket to the west of the city below Kronstadt, which had come into being on 16 September, going over to the defensive towards the end of the month, leaving Leningrad isolated.

After 5 September, Leningrad became a secondary concern to Moscow in German strategy, even if this would not be noticeable to Soviet leaders for some time.[2] The Leningrad leadership had been intensifying the construction of defences for the city from 3 September, with plans for the destruction of much of the city in the event of German capture, for which instructions were issued on 13 September, the same day that Zhukov took over command of the Leningrad *Front* from Voroshilov. The plan included the destruction of the Baltic Fleet:

DOCUMENT 100: *Report of the deputy People's Commissar of the Navy to the Supreme High Command on the plan for action in the event of the necessity to pull out of Leningrad (regarding ships and vessels), 13 September 1941*

I. General situation

1. In the event of having to pull out of Leningrad all ships of the navy and merchant fleet, as well as fisheries and technical vessels are to be blown up.
2. This destruction is to be conducted with the aim that:
   a) The enemy is not given the possibility of using them.
   b) To rule out the possibility that the enemy might sail freely in the Kronstadt-Leningrad region and make use of [waterways and port facilities].

3. The destruction is to be carried out with the greatest possible damage being inflicted for the longest possible period, that is objectives and ships are to be blown up and sunk.
4. Destruction is to be carried out according to a strictly sequential plan from the moment at which the High Command gives the signal.

II. Organization of preparations

1. Preparations for destruction and actual destruction is to be conducted by district:
   a) Kronstadt district (including Kronstadt itself, the military port of Oranienbaum ...);
   b) Leningrad port ...;
   c) The mouth of the River Neva ...;
   d) Shipyards (Factories Numbers 190, 189, 196, 194, 5, 205, 273 and 270).
2. All vessels face destruction regardless of ownership.
3. The destruction of shore facilities (cranes, berths, docks ...) is to be carried out by their respective institutions on the order of and according to the plan of the City Committee of the VKP(b).
4. Depending on the operational situation destruction and sinking might take place only in a district under direct threat of occupation by the enemy, in the event of which a variant of the plan is to be worked out for the withdrawal of ships from dangerous to less dangerous districts, and also the withdrawal of vessels from Leningrad to Kronstadt should they no longer be able to remain in the former.
5. All preparations for destruction are to be worked out by the Headquarters of the KBF together with the Headquarters for Maritime Defence of the city of Leningrad (clandestinely).

...

Deputy People's Commissar for the Navy, Admiral Isakov

(Source: V.P. Gusachenko *et al.*, 2000, pp. 88–90)

With Leningrad encircled and with the continued threat that German and Finnish forces might seize the city, on 20 September 1941 the State Defence Committee set up an air-bridge to bring military supplies into the city, without mention at this stage of evacuations on return flights.

DOCUMENT 101: *State Defence Committee. Decree No. GKO-692ss of 20 September 1941.... On the establishment of an aerial transport link with the city of Leningrad*

The State Defence Committee Decrees:

1. To give the Civilian Air Fleet responsibility for transport by air to Leningrad: of fuses, shells, cartridges, explosives, small arms, motors, communications equipment, optical equipment, parts in short supply for military vehicles and precious metals, and from Leningrad: tank guns F-32, radio sets, telegraph and telephone sets, electrical equipment for aircraft,... and parts in short supply for the M-8 and M-13.

   That Comrade Khrulev be given the power to decide upon the actual list and quantity of items to be delivered by air to and from Leningrad.

2. That the quantity of goods shipped be established up to 1 October 1941 as 100 tonnes and from 1 October 1941 as 150 tonnes per day, based on one return flight for all aircraft and a second return flight for half of the aircraft.
...
4. For the provision of this route with PS-84 aircraft the GUGVF is to set aside 50 aircraft....
5. From 22 September 1941 flights to Leningrad are to take place from Moscow airfields. From 25 September 1941 flights are to take place from the following home airfields:
Velikoe selo – 10 PS-84 aircraft
Bol'shoi Dvor – 10
Shibenets – 10
Podborov'e – 15
Khvoinaia – 10
Kashin – 10
...
6. ... The loading and unloading of aircraft at these airfields is to be the responsibility of the Main Board of the Rear of the Red Army.
7. ...
8. That commander of the VVS Comrade Zhigarev remove from the Reserve, Western and Leningrad *Fronts* up to 30 aircraft of types I-153 and I-16, and concentrate them by 23 September at the airfields at Kaivaks and Plekhanovo with the task of escorting these transport aircraft to Leningrad and back.
...
Chairman of the State Defence Committee, I. Stalin.
(Source: Online. Available www.soldat.ru/doc/gko/scans/0692-01-1.jpg and 0692-02-1.jpg)

Whilst German forces were able to seize Tikhvin on 9 November in an attempt to link up with the Finns and widen the encirclement to include the eastern shore of Lake Ladoga, they were dangerously overextended, with Soviet counter-attacks by 54th and 52nd Armies on both flanks. Whilst Tikhvin was recaptured by Soviet forces on 8 December, poorly co-ordinated Soviet attempts to de-blockade Leningrad during November failed.[3] Stalin was impatient for results, on 8 November pressing the new commander of the Leningrad *Front*, Khozin, for forces from Leningrad to cross the Neva and join up with units of 54th Army:

DOCUMENT 102: *Record of a conversation by direct line of the Supreme High Commander with the command of the Leningrad* Front, *8 November 1941*

Leningrad: On the line ZHDANOV, KHOZIN.
Moscow: On the line STALIN. We are very concerned by your sluggishness in the business of the conduct of the operation of which you are well aware.... If in the space of the next few days you do not break through to the east then you will destroy the Leningrad *Front* and the people of Leningrad. We are told, that after artillery preparation the infantry are indecisive in advancing. But you ought to know, that the infantry, without tanks, will not go....

> ZHDANOV: The advance of the infantry comes up against fairly solid defensive positions.... As regards tanks, then even with the measures we have taken, we have only succeeded in getting seven [tanks] ... across to the left bank, which were knocked out fairly quickly. As regards KV [tanks], then up to this point then it has not proved possible to get a single one across.... We are inhibited by the limited numbers of our forces. We are taking measure to reduce rear-area forces (artillery) by 8,000 men, communications troops by 5,000, anti-aircraft troops by 8,000 and sending them as infantrymen....
>
> STALIN: It is necessary to decide between captivity on the one hand, and the sacrificing of a number of divisions on the other. I repeat – make sacrifices and force a corridor through to the east, in order to save your *front* and Leningrad.... Take measures to get KV tanks across to the other side of the river.... Try to separate off groups of *jaegers* [*okhotnikov*], the bravest men, and make up one or two independent regiments of them. Explain the great significance of that feat which is demanded of them in order to force through a corridor....
>
> (Source: N.L. Volkovskii (ed.), 2004, pp. 61–63)

Three volunteer regiments supported by up to 40 tanks made it across the river to attack between 9 and 11 November but failed to make headway, whilst 54th Army's attentions were divided between the relief of Leningrad and the containment of the German thrust towards Volkhov. Whilst the Soviet winter counter-offensive would see the elimination of the German penetration in the Tikhvin direction, preventing German forces joining with the Finns in Karelia and sealing Leningrad off completely, the over-ambition of Soviet operations that sought the destruction of Army Group North meant that a resource balance shifting in Soviet favour was, as along the whole front, not effectively utilized. The relief of Leningrad, the expected by-product of broader Soviet operations, did not take place, nor would it for more than another year.

In the city, other than the prospect of the enemy capturing Leningrad, two concerns became the focus of government attention. First, the food situation could only deteriorate from the end of August, and with the deteriorating food situation and enemy threat there were concerns for social order. Norms for the distribution of bread to the population started to drop as winter approached, as Table 7.1 indicates, reaching a low of 250 g per day for workers, and only 125 g per day for other civilians.

The food situation was made significantly worse by the failure to protect existing resources from air attack, 8 September seeing the destruction of the antiquated Badaev warehouses, in the attack on which an estimated '3,000 tons of flour and about 2,500 tons of sugar' were lost, although during the worst months of the winter about 700 tons of 'blackened, dirty and scorched sugar' would be reclaimed and turned into 'candy'.[4]

With the German capture of the last railway link to the city at the end of August and the subsequent capture of Shlissel'berg, the principal means of bringing food and other supplies into the city was across Lake Ladoga,

Table 7.1 On the shipping of goods across Lake Ladoga. Report of the Headquarters of the Leningrad *Front* to the Headquarters of the Rear of the Red Army, 8 December 1941 – norms introduced for the supply of the population of Leningrad with bread per day during the initial period of the blockade

From what date norm introduced	Group of the population			
	Workers (grammes)	Administrative (grammes)	Dependant (grammes)	Children up to 12 years old (grammes)
18.7.41	800	600	400	400
2.9.41	600	400	300	300
12.9.41	500	300	230	200
2.10.41	400	200	200	200
13.11.41	300	150	150	150
20.11.41	250	125	125	125

Source: Volkovskii (ed.), *Blokada Leningrada v dokumentakh*, p. 669.

although the infrastructure for such convoy operations did not exist on either the eastern or western banks of the lake, and took time to develop. The seriousness of the situation prompted the temporary use of aircraft for bringing in supplies and further removal of 'valuable goods' from the city:[5]

> DOCUMENT 103: *Decree of the State Defence Committee No. 871ss on the allocation of aviation for the delivery of supplies to Leningrad, 9 November 1941*
>
> 1) The GUG VF (Comrade Kartushev) is required to allocate 24 'Douglas' transport aircraft in addition to the 26 already working on the Leningrad service starting on the morning of 10 November this year up to 14 November inclusive ..., in order that for the supply of foodstuffs to Leningrad and the removal of valuables 50 'Douglas' aircraft are working, with the condition that every aircraft does on average no less than one and a half round trips per day.
> 2) The VVS (Comrade Zhigarev) is to:
>   a) Allocate 10 TB-3 aircraft ..., with the condition that every aircraft does no less than a round trip per day;
>   b) Organise air cover by fighter aircraft, allocating an air regiment in addition to those already operating.
> 3. It is established that for the five-day plan for shipments to Leningrad no less than 200 tonnes per day of foodstuffs are to be delivered ...
>
> Chairman of the State Defence Committee
> I. Stalin
>
> (Source: N.L. Volkovskii (ed.), 2004, pp. 64–65)

The volume of materials that could be brought in was not only very limited, but German air superiority made such operations risky. Indeed, by mid-November supplies delivered by air had not even reached the quantities aimed for in Document 103 above.

> DOCUMENT 104: *Record of conversation between Molotov and the command of the Leningrad* Front
>
> 16 November 1941
>
> ...
>
> Gusev....
>
> 4. We are receiving foodstuffs in 'Douglases', however not in the quantities established by the GKO. We have yet to receive all the 'Douglases'. In order to increase the turn-around speed of the 'Douglases' and make no less than two flights per day we have decided to ship the foodstuffs in the 'Douglases' from Novaia Ladoga, that straight away increases the quantity and rate of delivery of provisions.
>
> (Source: N.L. Volkovskii (ed.), 2004, pp. 71–72).

The situation would be eased when Lake Ladoga had frozen and the subsequently legendary 'Ice Road', better known as the 'Road of Life', could be opened. As the lake froze, there would of course be a period when shipments either by boat or road were not possible, and the air bridge was the only source of new supplies. The decision to establish communications across the ice was taken by the military soviet of the Leningrad *Front* on 13 November. Towards the end of November, communications across the frozen lake were being established, with the first 60 lorries with supplies for the city crossing the ice on 22 November, establishing the viability of further exploitation of this link.

> DOCUMENT 105: *Decree of the military soviet of the Leningrad* Front *No. 00419*
>
> 24 November 1941
>
> 1. For the shipment of provisions, fuel and munitions to Leningrad and the evacuation of population and material items from Leningrad a front-line automobile road is to be constructed by 30 November on the route: Zebor'e Station, Serebrianskaia, Velikii Dvor, Lakhta, Nikul'skoe, Shan'govo, Eremina Gora, Novinka, Iamskoe, Korpino, Novaia Ladoga, Kobona, with an average turnaround at each end of 2,000 tonnes per day with the opening of a transshipment base at Zabor'e.
> 2. The construction of the road is to be the responsibility of a of the Leningrad *obkom* VKP (b) (Comrade Vorotov) with time for completion before 1 December 1941.
>
> ...
>
> 5. The Chairman of the Executive Committee (*Ispolkom*) of the Leningrad City Council of Worker's Deputies is to:
>   a) Mobilize 500 lorries of varied types from the civilian economy and one

hundred tankers (working) with drivers by 25 November for the period of the functioning of the road, and transfer them to the 17th Independent transport Brigade (OATB) for use on the road;
    b) Set aside in the charge of the commander of the road Comrade Shilov the necessary inventory and equipment [*iz rascheta*] for ten feeding points each with the capacity for 4,000 persons each, by 27 November 1941;
    c) Set aside in the charge of the independent transport brigade a one off allocation of 3,000 sets of rubber tires for the autopark of the road by 25 November.
6. The head of the Auto-Armour Board of the Leningrad *Front*, Colonel Dement'ev is to be allocated 1,000 lorries and 100 tankers with drivers from the army transport of the Leningrad *Front* by 26 November, to be handed over to the command of the 17 OATB for work on the road.

...

Commander of forces of the Leningrad *Front*
General-Lieutenant Khozin
Members of the military soviet of the *front*
Secretary of the TsK VKP(b) Zhdanov
Divisional Commissar Kuznetsov

(Source: N.L. Volkovskii (ed.), 2004, pp. 233–235)

The road across Ladoga, and indeed the air bridge, allowed the evacuation of some of Leningrad's population to the east:

DOCUMENT 106: *Report of the {Leningrad} City Evacuation Commission, 26 April 1942*

1. The evacuation of the population of Leningrad has had two phases:
a) The first period – evacuation before the blockade of the city;
b) The second – evacuation during the blockade.
2. Evacuation of the first period continued from 29.VI.1941 to 27.VIII.1941 and has two specific characteristics:
    a) The first – unwillingness to evacuate from the city;
    b) The second – a large number of children were evacuated from Leningrad to districts of Leningrad Region (easterly and south-easterly), meaning that 175,400 children were returned back to Leningrad.
3. During the period from 29.VI to 27.VIII.1941 from Leningrad the following were evacuated:
    a) 395,091 children, of whom 175,400 were returned to Leningrad, the result 395,091 – 175,400 = 219,691 people.
    b) Leningrad residents – 104,691 people;
    c) Workers and administrative personnel, evacuated with industrial concerns – 164,320 people.

Total: 488,703 people.
    In addition, during the same period 147,500 people were evacuated to Leningrad from the populations of the Estonian, Latvian, Lithuanian and Karelo-Finnish SSRs.

1. The second phase of the evacuation has had three stages:
    a) First stage – the evacuation by water across Lake Ladoga to Novaia Ladoga, and then by road transport to Volkhov Station;
    b) Second stage – evacuation by air transport;
    c) Third stage – evacuation by the ice road across Lake Ladoga.
    By water transport 33,479 people were evacuated.
       Of these 14,854 people were not from the Leningrad population.
    35,114 people were evacuated by air.
    16,956 of these were not from the Leningrad population.

From the end of December 1941 on foot or by motor transport outside that officially organized 36,118 people were evacuated.
(Population not from Leningrad)
From 22.I.1942 to 15.IV.1942 554,186 people were evacuated on the ice road, of whom:
1. 66,182 people were workers and administrative personnel.
2. 193,244 people were families of workers or administrative personnel.
3. 92,419 people were students of vocational colleges.
4. 37,877 were young specialists, students, professors, lecturers and research workers with families.
5. 4,442 people were pupils and teachers of (military) specialist schools.
6. 12,639 people were children from children's homes.
7. 7,343 people were invalids of the [Great] Patriotic War.
8. 8,135 people were population from the evacuation points of the city (previously evacuated to Leningrad from districts of the *oblast'*).
9. 35,713 were wounded Red Army personnel and commanders of the RKKA.
10. 1,150 people were prisoners.
11. 8,825 people were specialist contingent (administrative exile) from the city.
    30,489 people from the *oblast'*.
12. 27,274 people were *kolkhoz* peasants from the Karelian isthmus.

Total evacuated for the period from 29.VI.41 to 15.IV.42 1,295,100, of whom:
  a) 970,718 people were from the population of Leningrad
  b) 324,382 people were population of the Estonian, Latvian, Lithuanian and Karelo-Finnish SSR, previously evacuated to Leningrad, population from districts of Leningrad *oblast'* and wounded Red Army personnel and commanders.

...

Chairman of the Leningrad Evacuation Commission, Popkov
Members – Smirnov, Motilev, Lagunov, Vorotov

(Source: N.L. Volkovskii (ed.), 2004, pp. 692–696)

A significant number of those evacuated to the Soviet rear were Finns and 'Germans' moved for security reasons:

> DOCUMENT 107: *Report by the Leningrad NKVD on evacuations from Leningrad and outlying districts, 4 April 1942, No. 10448*
>
> To the People's Commissar of Internal Affairs ... Comrade Beria
>
> By decision of the military soviet of the Leningrad *Front* the NKVD board for Leningrad *oblast'* exiled 39,075 persons from the city and nearby districts from the second half of March, including:
>
> Compulsory evacuation [*evakuirovano v obiazatel'nom poriadke*] of Finns and Germans 35,162 people.
>
> Administrative exile [*Vislano v administrativnom poriadke*] of socially dangerous elements 13 people.
>
> All of this contingent were sent:
>
> To Krasnoiarskii *krai* – 26,283 people.
> To Irkutsk *oblast'* – 9,488 people.
> To Omsk *oblast'* – 3,304 people.
>
> Additionally, as a result of the exceptional significance of Kronstadt as a strongpoint and naval base on the approaches to Leningrad, 431 people were removed from Kronstadt, of whom:
>
> 67 people – anti-Soviet elements subject to administrative exile.
> 75 people – the product of the compulsory evacuation of Germans and Finns.
> 289 people – socially dangerous elements removed as part of the general evacuation.
> As they left Finns and Germans evacuated from prefrontal districts handed over livestock and dwellings to local Soviet organizations. According to incomplete figures the following were handed over:
>
> Cows – 1,020
> Horses – 134
> Small livestock – 92
> Dwellings – 7,540
>
> During the conduct of the exiling and evacuation there were no incidents and displays of anti-Soviet sentiment.
> Head of the Board of the NKVD for Leningrad *oblast'*
> Komissar for State Security 3rd Class
> (Kubatkin)
>
> (Source: N.A. Lomagin, 2004, p. 37)

Whilst Zhdanov reported to Malenkov on 25 December that the food situation had improved, such that 100 g could be added to the bread rations of workers and 75 g for the remainder, making 300 and 200 g respectively, such statements hid the absence of other foodstuffs and indeed the inability to deliver rations to all.[6] Food deliveries across Ladoga would, as Table 7.2 shows, consistently improve month by month in early 1942 before the thaw, assisted greatly by the reopening of the railway line through Tikhvin to Volkhov in January 1942 and the extension of the railway all the way to Ladoga during February, and the improvement of communications between the shore of the lake and the city.

Table 7.2 Goods shipped across the ice road from 24 November 1941 to 21 April 1942 (according to figures of the Leningrad *Front*) by month

Month	Quantity of goods per month in tonnes	Including		
		Foodstuffs and fodder	Munitions	Other goods
November–December 1941	16,499	15,125	713	661
January 1942	52,934	42,558	4,794	5,582
February	86,041	67,198	9,953	8,890
March	118,382	88,607	9,105	20,770
April	87,253	57,588	7,345	22,320
Total	301,109	270,976	31,910	58,223

Source: Volkovskii (ed.), *Blokada Leningrada v dokumentakh*, p. 670.

Although the tonnage being delivered to the city might have improved, according to the NKVD, whilst flour was delivered to the city during the first half of January, no other foodstuffs reached the city.[7] By this stage many were beyond relief and increased deliveries from the second half of January came too late for many; the number of deaths in the city rose from 4,162 in June 1941 to 52,881 in December, to 101,583 in January 1942 and 107,477 the following month, as shown in Table 7.3.

In addition to the increasing number of deaths brought about primarily by the shortage of food, additional casualties were caused by German bombing and shelling as shown in Table 7.4, which, in addition, disrupted the flow of supplies into the city.

Some appreciation of the horrors of life in the city during the winter of 1941–42 can be gained from the personal diaries of those that experienced the blockade, the example here being that of A.I. Vinokurov, a schoolteacher:

DOCUMENT 108: *Extracts from the diary of Aleksei Ivanovich Vinokurov, Leningrad, 2 January–1 February 1942*

January 1942
Thursday 2 January
Today, after a break of two days, they gave us electricity in our block for three hours. What an amazing thing electric light is!
...
Sunday 5 January
The water and drainage have not been working for a few days....

Monday 6 January

I found out about the death of S.N.F., the Physics teacher, today. The poor soul died of emaciation, leaving behind a wife bloated from hunger and three children, the fate of which is beyond doubt.

...

Monday 8 January

M.V.P., the teacher of Mathematics, died.

It is strange, but in the last few days news of death no longer disturbs as it did before. Death has become a day-to-day occurrence. We have got used to it. On the street just about every hundred metres or so there lies the body of someone who has either died or starvation or frozen to death. The public has got so used to this, that they walk by unconcerned. I met with the director of the school, A.V.U. He is bloated from hunger. I tried to convince him that it is better to be without possessions than dead.

...

Sunday 12 January

Every day there are fires. There is no water so nothing to put them out with....

Wednesday 15 January

Tomorrow I will go to school. I measured the distance from home to school on a map of the city ...; there and back is about 12 kilometres. It will be difficult to walk there and back in such freezing temperatures with such sustenance.

16 January

Classes started up again at school. The pupils understand all too well, that under current circumstances there cannot be serious classes, but according to old habits they continue to adhere to the crazy demands of GORONO [City Department of People's Education]. The temperature in classrooms does not get above 2–3 degrees C. Everyone sits there in hats and winter coats. It is natural, that the children are more concerned with the receipt of lunch in the school canteen, consisting of muddy water smelly of shit, masquerading as soup, and sweets, than classes.

Friday 17 January

I traveled to the [River] Neva for water....

18 January

I spent the whole day on the registration of ration cards.

19 January

My female neighbour, S.A.B., died. Mortality in the city has reached a massive scale. During the last week 12 people have died in our block and three have gone missing, probably having died somewhere on the street. Their relatives tried to find them but with no success. In our [communal] flat the number living here has decreased by half; two have been killed at the front, three have died of emaciation, and one is in the Red Army.

In some flats there is already nobody left.

20 January

...

It is difficult to understand for what purpose grocery shops open up daily. The shop assistants have absolutely nothing to do. For all of January the population has not received any sort of groceries other than bread....

The trams have not been running since the first days of December. The rails are not visible. They lie under a thick layer of snow....

Friday 23 January

> The frost has got more severe. The temperature has reached -30 C. Lessons in school have been cancelled. They essentially weren't taking place anyway. Only 5–6 people were in every class, the remainder going to school solely in order to receive soup and sweets.
> 24 January
> The bread ration has been raised. Workers will be given 400 g of bread each per day, white-collar workers 300 g each, and dependants and children 250 g each.
> 25 January
> On the streets there are long queues for bread....
> 26 January
> As before there are long queues for bread. One has to stand in line from 6–7 in the morning until the middle of the day in order to receive bread. To stake your claim on a place in line after 10 in the morning is meaningless, because by the evening the baker no longer has any bread.
> ...
> February 1942
> 1 February
> ...
> I am deathly tired today, barely being able to get myself back home under my own steam. Near the Petropavlovsk hospital I saw three naked corpses. They had fallen out of a vehicle – a lorry ..., and were lying on the street for the whole day (<u>nobody was interested in them). Only rarely would an inquisitive woman, halting for a minute and glancing at the blue-green bellies, express any sympathy for the victims of this silent, meaningless cruelty taking place before our very eyes.</u> [Underlined in the original by the NKVD investigator.]
>
> (Source: *Blokadnie dnevniki i dokumenti*, 2004, pp. 236–245)

Vinokurov's diary is available to us from the archives of the FSB, successor to the NKVD and KGB. Vinokurov was arrested on 12 February 1943 and subsequently charged with 'counterrevolutionary anti-Soviet agitation' and holding 'defeatist perspectives on the war', amongst other 'crimes' under Article 58 of the criminal code of the RSFSR, to be shot on 19 March 1943. He was rehabilitated in 1999, rehabilitation indicating that after review it was decided that he had been executed as a traitor without due foundation and for 'political' reasons. The usual paranoia of the NKVD had plenty of scope for finding 'traitors' during the blockade as the following statistics indicate, in addition to a desperate population being willing to risk life to acquire food and possibly therefore save it:

Table 7.3 On deaths and reasons for them for the second half of 1941 for 15 districts of Leningrad according to the city statistical board, 31 October 1942

Cause of death	July		August	September	October	November	December	
	Total deaths	Infants up to one year	Total deaths	Total deaths	Total deaths	Total deaths	Total deaths	Infants up to one year
Total deaths	4,162	1,211	5,357	6,808	7,353	11,085	52,881	5,959
Typhoid and paratyphoid	6	–	11	15	3	6	10	–
Typhus	–	–	–	–	–	1	–	–
Measles	14	2	35	53	369	481	467	112
Scarlet fever	6	2	8	12	20	13	21	1
Whooping cough	34	20	58	73	77	98	121	65
Diphtheria	24	4	33	56	86	65	86	14
Flu	7	–	7	11	41	72	276	27
Dysentery	40	11	204	190	195	124	359	108
Hemocolitis	26	7	38	57	36	45	69	14
Malaria	–	–	2	–	1	–	4	1
Tuberculosis (lungs)	404	12	364	382	466	535	1,572	1
Tuberculosis (other)	74	6	69	56	63	65	111	6
Croupos/lobar pneumonia	51	–	46	66	152	231	414	11
Other forms of pneumonia	358	222	336	565	1,098	1,836	4,528	2,392
Toxic dyspepsia	523	489	937	373	211	203	614	551
Acute gastro-enteritis (children under 3 years)	331	245	742	651	569	598	1,501	1,082
Acute gastro-enteritis (children of 3 years and older)	28	–	93	70	65	131	585	–

Source: Volkovskii (ed.), *Blokada Leningrada v dokumentakh*, pp. 700–701.

Table 7.4 From a report of the Leningrad PVO on the results of aerial attacks and artillery bombardment from 4 September 1941 to 1 March 1942, 11 March 1942. II. Number of artillery rounds and aerial bombs

	Artillery rounds	High-explosive bombs	Incendiary bombs
From 4–15.IX [1941]	550	418	11,509
From 16–30 IX	1,664	830	3 893
From 1–15 X	1,867	635	34,906
From 16–31 X	1,425	325	8,081
From 1–15 XI	2,256	603	5,962
From 16–31 XI	2,859	442	–
From 1–15 XII	1,180	224	1,779
From 16–31 XII	576	16	70
From 1–15.I.42	337	–	–
From 16–31.I	678	–	–
From 1–16.II	486	–	–
From 16–28.II	1 580	–	–
Total	16,158	3,493	66,200

III. ... Losses

	Wounded	Killed	Total
From 4–30.IX [1941]	5,886	1,302	7,188
From 1–15 X	2,226	584	2,810
From 15–31 X	1,004	224	1,228
From 1–15 XI	2,957	905	3,862
From 15–31 XI	1,940	825	2,765
From 1–15 XII	1,015	446	1,461
From 15–31 XII	515	197	712
From 1–15.I.42	27	83	110
From 16–31.I	288	34	322
From 1–15.II	72	25	97
From 16–28.II	95	36	131
Total	16,025	4,661	20,686

Source: Volkovskii (ed.), *Blokada Leningrada v dokumentakh*, pp. 680–685.

DOCUMENT 109: *From a report by the head of the UNKVD LO to A.A. Zhdanov on numbers arrested and the confiscation of weapons from them during the war, 2 April 1942*

The NKVD Board has arrested 7,942 people during the Patriotic War.
Amongst those arrested are:
276 Spies
1,327 Traitors to the Motherland
277 Terrorists
48 Saboteurs

146 Wreckers
224 Participants in opposition groups
During the period concerned 334 anti-Soviet groups were liquidated, during which 1,183 people were arrested.
 The militia [police] arrested 18,548 people.
 Arrests can be broken down by the nature of the crime:
  For theft of social property – 5,349 people
  Speculation – 959 people
  Banditry and brigandage – 1,684 people
  For other criminal offences – 10,556 people
  Criminal and bandit groups liquidated – 696
  Total arrests – 26,493 people
  After sentencing by military tribunals during this period 3,727 people were shot.
...
 Weapons seized from criminal elements and individuals, not having permission for them:
  Military rifles – 890
  Revolvers and pistols – 393
  Machine guns – 4
  Grenades – 27
  Hunting rifles – 11,172
  Small-calibre rifles – 2,954
  Cold weapons – 713
  Rifle and revolver cartridges – 26,676
  Head of the Board of the NKVD for the Leningrad Region
  Commissar for State Security 3rd Rank, P. Kubatkin
            (Source: N.L. Volkovskii (ed.), 2004, pp. 689–690)

Given the desperation of the food situation, it is perhaps not surprising that cannibalism reared its head in the city:

DOCUMENT 110: On cases of cannibalism. Extracts from reporting notes of the Military Procurator A.I. Panfilenko to A.A. Kuznetsov

In the special conditions created by the war with fascist Germany in which Leningrad finds itself, a new type of crime has emerged. All [murders] with the aim of eating the meat of the victim, given the special nature of the threat, qualify as banditry (Article 59-3 of the Criminal Code of the RSFSR).
...
 From the moment that such crimes appeared in the city of Leningrad, that is from the start of December 1941 to 15 February 1942 investigations by organs [of state security] led to the bringing to justice for these crimes of 26 people in December 1941, 366 in January 1942, and 494 for the first 15 days of February 1942.
...
 In isolated incidences, those committing these crimes not only ate the meat of corpses themselves but also sold the meat to others.
...

> Amongst those brought to justice ... there were specialists with higher education.
> ...
> Of 886 people brought to justice ..., only 2% had previous convictions.
> As of 20 February 1942 311 people were sentenced by military tribunals for the above crimes.
> Military Procurator for the city of Leningrad
> Brigade Military Lawyer, A. Panfilenko
>
> (Source: N.L. Volkovskii (ed.), 2004, pp. 679–680)

By November 1942, norms for bread rations had reached 400 g for workers, 300 for administrative personnel and 250 g for the remainder, but at the expense of other foodstuffs, and hardly enough to lift the mood in the city. By mid-June a pipe along the bottom of Ladoga laid as a result of a GKO decision in late April was supplying 300–400 tonnes of fuel a day to the city, and in September the city was receiving electricity from across the water.[8] The winter of 1942–43 would not be a repeat of 1941–42, but nor would it be a pleasant one by the standards 'enjoyed' by the remainder of the Soviet population.

There were further attempts to relieve the blockade during 1941, part of the Soviet front-wide counter-offensive of the winter of 1941–42. The ambitious Liuban' offensive by forces of the Volkhov *Front* and 54th Army of the Leningrad *Front*, stemming from a *Stavka* directive of 17 December 1941 to lift the siege of the city and destroy German forces below Leningrad, did not limit itself to creating some sort of corridor for the establishment of land communications with the city as the offensive of early 1943:

> DOCUMENT 111: *Directive of the* Stavka VGK *Number 005826 to the command of the* Volkhov Front *on the transition to a general offensive, 17 December 1941 20 h. 00 min.*
>
> The Headquarters of the Supreme High Command orders:
>
> 1. That forces of the Volkhov *Front* consisting of 4th, 59th, 2nd Shock and 52nd Armies go over to a general offensive, having the aim of destroying the enemy defending the western bank of the river Volkhov....
>
>   Further operations are to consist of an advance in a north-westerly direction, encircling the enemy defending below Leningrad, in co-ordination with forces of the Leningrad *Front*.
>
>   ...
>
> 5. 2nd Shock Army, consisting of 327th Rifle Division, 22nd, 24th, 25th, 3rd, 57th, 53rd, 58th, and 59th Rifle Brigades, six ski battalions, two independent tank battalions ... is to advance in the direction of Chashcha Station,... with a further blow towards Luga.
>
> ...
>
> I. Stalin, B. Shaposhnikov
>
> (Source: N.L. Volkovskii (ed.), 2004, pp. 79–80)

160 *The siege of Leningrad*

In seeking to destroy the 'Liuban'–Chudovo' concentration of German forces, the aim was nothing less than the effective destruction of the German 18th Army, and was representative of the unrealistic nature of Soviet operational planning during this period. Continued hounding by the *Stavka* pushed forces of the Volkhov *Front* to press on, despite the fact that any momentum and surprise had long gone:

DOCUMENT 112: *Directive of the* Stavka *VGK Number 170126 to the command of the* Volkhov Front *on the destruction of the Liuban'–Chudovo grouping of the enemy, 26 February 1942 02 h. 30 min.*

The Headquarters of the Supreme High Command does not oppose the suggested strengthening of the Liuban' and Chudovo groupings of 2nd Shock Army and 59th Army.

The *Stavka* however at the same time categorically demands that under no circumstances are offensive operations by 2nd Shock and 59th Army on the Liuban' and Chudovo axes to be discontinued in expectation of reinforcement, on the contrary, it is to be demanded of them that they have reached the Liuban'-Chudovo railway by March, so that after their reinforcement and no later than 5 March the Liuban'-Chudovo grouping of the enemy has been liquidated.
Headquarters of the Supreme High Command
I. Stalin
B. Shaposhnikov

(Source: N.L. Volkovskii (ed.), 2004, p. 92)

The 2nd Shock Army would eventually suffer the same fate as forces engaged in operations to seize Khar'kov to the south during the spring of 1942, much equipment and many personnel not escaping to Soviet lines after the German encirclement, including the commander of 2nd Shock, Lieutenant-General A.A. Vlasov, captured by German forces on 12 July,[9] the day before the *Stavka* request below:

DOCUMENT 113: *To the Head of the Headquarters of the Volkhov* Front *on measures for the clarification of the situation for forces of the 2nd Shock Army, 13 July 1942*

The exit [from encirclement] of groups of and individual soldiers of units of 2nd Shock Army still continues....

Nonetheless, the Headquarters of the Volkhov *Front* ... has not reported anything on the situation for units of 2nd Shock Army remaining in encirclement.

Take urgent action for the collection of materials from the questioning of those breaking out of encirclement, and through the personal questioning of commanders, and by 20.7.1942 present your conclusions on these materials.
Tikhimorov
Rizhkov

(Source: *RA T.23 (12–2)*, 1999, p. 238)

In mid-1942 a second, more realistic Soviet operation was launched to relieve the siege of Leningrad, the 'Siniavino' Operation, beginning in mid-August, which pre-empted and stalled the proposed German operation 'Northern Lights', an attempt to execute a close encirclement of the city from the east that would cut Leningrad off from her lifeline across Lake Ladoga. Whilst the Soviet operation for the relief of Leningrad sucked German troops intended to execute 'Northern Lights' into defensive operations, during which they suffered high casualties, and prevented operations for the proposed close encirclement to be launched, it nonetheless failed to break through heavily fortified German positions of the Shlissel'berg corridor below Lake Ladoga.

Only in January 1943 would the land blockade finally be lifted with Operation 'Spark' ['*Iskra*'], the objective of which was a repeat of the unsuccessful attempt to relieve the blockade of the summer of 1942. Operation 'Spark' started on 12 January 1943 and had led to a breakthrough of German positions below Lake Ladoga and the linking up of forces of the Leningrad and Volkhov *Fronts* by 18 January, allowing a railway line to be laid along the five to seven-mile wide corridor to the city, albeit one under constant German bombardment:[10]

DOCUMENT 114: *Letter of the military soviet of the Leningrad* Front *to the commander of the 63rd Guards Rifle Division on the military achievements of the division and with congratulations on its reorganization as a guards division, 21 January 1943*

The military soviet of the Leningrad *Front* warmly congratulates you and salutes you and all the personnel of the units entrusted to your command on the reorganization of your division as the 63rd Guards Rifle Division.

In bitter fighting to break the enemy blockade, units of your division in the first wave of the shock group of 67th Army, having overcome the River-Neva line broke through heavily fortified enemy positions, destroying the Mar'ino strongpoint and developing a thrust in the direction of Worker's Settlement Number 5, on the second day of fighting broke through to a depth of 7 km. Having cut off the Shlissel'berg enemy grouping and facilitating the development of the penetration of neighbouring divisions to Shlissel'berg, on 18 January units of your division were the first to join up with forces of the Volkhov *Front* and with those same forces played a leading role in the fighting for the breaking of the blockade of Leningrad.

...

Honour and glory to the commanders and guards, first to break through the enemy blockade of Leningrad!

...

Commander of the forces of the Leningrad *Front*, Colonel-General L. Govorov
Member of the military soviet of the *front*, Secretary TsK VKP(b) A. Zhdanov

...

(Source: N.L. Volkovskii (ed.), 2004, p. 337)

The complete relief of the blockade would have to wait another year.

Guide to further reading

J. Barber and A. Dzeniskevich (eds), *Life and Death in Besieged Leningrad, 1941–1944* (Basingstoke: Palgrave Macmillan, 2005).

R. Bidlack, 'The Political Mood in Leningrad during the First Year of the Soviet-German War', *Russian Review*, Volume 59, Number 1 (2000), pp. 96–113.

David M. Glantz, *The Battle for Leningrad, 1941–1944* (Lawrence, KS: University Press of Kansas, 2002).

Harrison E. Salisbury, *The 900 Days: The Siege of Leningrad* (New York and Evanston: Harper and Row, 1969) and many other editions.

C. Simmons and N. Perlina (eds), *Writing the Siege of Leningrad – Women's Diaries, Memoirs and Documentary Prose* (Pittsburgh, PA: University of Pittsburgh Press, 2005).

8 Lend-Lease aid, the Soviet economy and the Soviet Union at war

Given the legitimating role that eventual victory in the Great Patriotic War would play for the Soviet regime, and the terrible cost the Soviet population would pay for victory, it is understandable why the role of Allied aid in the Soviet war effort was played down in Soviet writing on the war, to the point that it was almost ignored. This is particularly understandable in the context of Cold War animosities. Aid, provided by the United States, Britain and the Commonwealth, was provided in the main without charge under the US Lend-Lease Act of March 1941 or its principles as described below and adopted by the British. Whilst the capitalist world could be accused of providing material assistance to the Soviet Union to save the lives of its own troops, it could not reasonably be accused of profiteering at Soviet expense. Military and associated aid, provided at Soviet request, was a stark reminder of the limitations of the Soviet system under Stalin and the debacle faced by the Soviet Union as a result of Soviet foreign and defence policy on the eve of war.

Despite considerable political and academic interest in 'Lend Lease' in the United States particularly during the Cold War, a lack of detailed information on the Soviet war effort in general and Soviet use of Allied aid in particular prevented Western authors from coming to a balanced assessment of the significance of Allied aid for the Soviet Union during the war. With not only Western but also most Soviet authors denied access to relevant archival materials, detailed analyses of the application of Allied aid were kept out of Soviet historical monographs. Analysis of the significance of Allied aid for the Soviet war effort in general works and even more focused journal articles often did not go further than the frequently cited claim, attributed to the wartime First Vice-Chairman of the Council of People's Commissars Voznesenskii, that Allied aid represented 'only 4 per cent' of Soviet production during the war.[1] The following extract is perhaps not typical of much work published in the 1970s and 1980s that follows the above characterization, but represents the most balanced Soviet appreciation of Lend-Lease aid. During Khrushchev's premiership and a brief period afterwards, that is, from at the earliest 1956 to the mid-1960s – a period known as the 'thaw' – historians were allowed much more leeway in what they wrote. The example here is from the six-volume 'official' history of the Great Patriotic War, the last volume of which was completed in 1965:

> DOCUMENT 115: *Extract from the concluding volume of the Khrushchev-era 'official' Soviet history of the Great Patriotic War on the significance of Lend-Lease aid for the Soviet war effort*
>
> Bourgeois propaganda of the post-war years spent not inconsiderable energy in order to convince the world that the growth of the material means [*osnashchennost'*] of the Red Army during the war was achieved to a large extent thanks to deliveries of weapons, technical equipment, and a variety of materials by the Allied countries – USA and Britain. Of course these deliveries were not inconsequential, especially the supply to troops and the rear of automotive transport, fuels and lubricants (from the USA and Britain 401,400 automobiles and 2,599,000 tons of oil products). But if speaking of the general increase in the armament of the Red Army, then the assistance of the Allies played, overall, an insignificant role.
>
> During the war years 489,900 artillery pieces of all calibres, 136,800 aircraft and 102,500 tanks and self-propelled guns were delivered by Soviet industry. From the USA and Britain during the same period 9,600 artillery pieces, 18,700 aircraft and 10,800 tanks were received.... In addition it was often the case that the Allies sent us already outdated examples of weapons. For instance tanks and a large proportion of the aircraft did not fully satisfy demands of weapons required by the character of military activity on the Soviet-German front.
>
> (Source: *Istoriiia Velikoi Otechestvennoi voini Sovetskogo Soiuza 1941–1945*, 1965, p. 48)

Photographs of Allied equipment in Soviet use were not intentionally published in Soviet works. Mention of Allied aid would creep into military memoirs, but only apparently on the understanding that the value of Allied equipment was denigrated or at least compared unfavourably to Soviet equivalents, to which there appear to have been few exceptions. The following example, concerned with the conversion of a Soviet unit to British-supplied Hurricane fighter aircraft in the summer of 1942, is not unusual. The author, Kaberov, using the device of fictitious dialogue, reports on the assessments of Soviet pilots on the aircraft concerned:

> Vladimir Konstantinovich brought the machine in to land.
> 'Thank you', he said, climbing out of the cockpit. 'Of course, it's not a Yak, but with the types of cannon that have now been fitted in to the Hurricane, I think it is possible to use it in aerial combat.'
> ... I thought that the name 'Hurricane' hardly matched the technical qualities of the machine....
> Yefimov, our Commissar, got it right: 'The aircraft is fine; it's metal, so it won't catch fire. You can shoot from it. But instead of manoeuvrability and speed – you'll have to use your Russian wits!'[2]

Whilst a considerable English-language literature emerged during the Cold War on the diplomatic dimensions to 'Lend-Lease' aid to the Soviet Union during the Great Patriotic War (of which key works appear in the section on further reading for this chapter), as a result of the lack of access to Soviet sources there is very little on the value of Allied aid to the Soviet war effort. There is certainly little that focuses on British aid alone, with the exception of Beaumont's *Comrades in Arms*. In more general Western literature, such as Overy's *Russia's War*, and indeed much post-Soviet work in Russian, including Sokolov's article translated into English in the *Journal of Slavic Military Studies*, both in the Further Reading section, it is often assumed that 'Lend-Lease' aid only became of significance to the Soviet war effort as deliveries increased from 1943 onwards, in particular in facilitating the forward movement of the Red Army with lorries and other transport resources. The value of arms provided by Britain and the United States, with the possible exception of aircraft, is often played down, and in particular the significance of the relatively small quantities being delivered during the period of the First Moscow Protocol (agreement), covering the period to 30 June 1942, the only period during which Britain bore the heavier burden in the provision of aid than the United States.

This chapter will examine the scale and importance of Lend-Lease aid for the Soviet war effort during three phases of the war: the first phase, up to November 1942, during which Germany was able to take the strategic initiative; a second phase from November 1942 to July 1943, during which the Axis could take the initiative only at an operational or at best operational-strategic level; and a third, from August 1943, during which the Soviet Union certainly held the strategic initiative against an Axis only able take the offensive at an operational level and even then in response to Soviet activity. These three phases coincide approximately with four different Allied aid protocols or agreements with the Soviet Union, covering the period up to June 1942 (the 1st (Moscow) Protocol); from July 1942 to June 1943 (the 2nd (Washington) Protocol); with the final two protocols from July 1943 to June 1944 and June 1944 to the end of the war (the 3rd and 4th London and Ottawa Protocols, respectively) being taken together.

Britain, the United States and aid to the Soviet Union

At the beginning of June 1941 Britain still stood alone against Nazi Germany. Whilst the level of participation of the United States short of war was, by this point, significant, the United States was far from prepared for intervention in Europe, even without war in the Pacific. At the beginning of September 1940, the 'destroyers for bases' agreement was finally signed by Britain and the United States, with Britain paying a high price for 50 badly needed World War I-vintage destroyers, exchanged for 99-year leases on bases in the Caribbean. Safe after his November 1940 presidential election victory, President Roosevelt could increasingly move to make commitments to assist the British (with whom relations were ever more tense as ad hoc agreements for the delivery of war materials on a 'cash-and-carry' basis led to the rapid loss of British assets worldwide) that were more substantial than the 'destroyers for bases' agreement. The US Lend-Lease Act or Public Law 11 came into force in March 1941, allowing the executive, for a two-year initial period, to authorize the manufacture or procurement of items for transfer to any nation whose defence was deemed vital to that of the United States. By this point Britain's gold reserves were depleted and a considerable proportion of her overseas assets had been sold off to pay for purchases from the United States. With Britain facing practical bankruptcy, war materials provided under the Lend-Lease Act were crucial in sustaining Britain's war effort. Materials provided by the United States to the United Kingdom were to be categorized as expended, returnable, military and non-military, with payment only to be required for the latter, be it in reverse 'Lend-Lease', the exchange of information or technology, or ultimately post-war settlement.[3]

The US political establishment was initially far more sensitive towards the issue of aid to the Soviet Union than to Britain, given the strength of anti-Soviet feeling brought about to a large extent by Soviet activities under the auspices of the Nazi–Soviet Pact of August 1939, including the occupation of the Baltic Republics. Attempts were made by those most critical of the Soviet Union to exclude her from future use of the Lend-Lease Act even before German troops crossed the Soviet frontier. Nonetheless, immediately after the German invasion of the Soviet Union and initial Soviet approaches to the United States, the US government thawed frozen Soviet assets totalling $40 million and opted not to apply the provisions of the Neutrality Act of November 1939 obstructing the sale of arms to her. This allowed the Soviet Union to purchase war materials from the United States subject to export permit. The first Soviet order was received by the United States on 30 June and a Soviet military mission arrived in the United States on 26 July 1941. Nonetheless, even if purchased and not under the Lend-Lease Act, opposition to assistance to the Soviet Union was significant, and in July 1941 Congress reviewed legislation introduced pre-emptively to exclude the Soviet Union from Lend-Lease and indeed ensure the application of the Neutrality Act to her. Given the Soviet Union's long-term shortage of hard currency and diminishing gold reserves, the amount of military aid that could be provided to the Soviet Union by the United States would be strictly limited unless it could be provided under the Lend-Lease Act. Such a move would require negotiation with the Britain, which in the short term at least would have to pass over some material originally destined for her.[4]

By late summer 1941, a considerable range of Soviet requests for aid had been received by both the British and Americans. As early as 29 June 1941, the Soviet Union had requested 3,000 modern fighter aircraft and 3,000 bombers from the British, as well as items such as ASDIC (sonar) sets and anti-aircraft guns. Also significant were Soviet requests for raw materials such as aluminium and rubber.[5] Only on 6 September would responses to Soviet requests for aid from the United Kingdom be formally considered to be on a 'Lend-Lease' basis, on which date Prime Minister Churchill's often-reproduced letter of 4 September was received by Moscow. In this letter, responding to Stalin's use of the word 'sell' with regard to UK fighter deliveries to the Soviet Union in his message to Churchill of 3 September, Churchill pointed out that 'any assistance we can give you would better be upon the same basis of comradeship as the American Lend-Lease Bill, of which no formal account is kept in money'. Up to this point all items or materials were apparently deemed to be either purchased on credit with the expectation of eventual payment, be this in gold or raw materials, or, in the instance of the first 200 Tomahawk fighters, a 'gift' from the United Kingdom.[6] Extracts from the two letters are reproduced as Documents 115 and 116 below:

DOCUMENT 116: *Personal Message from Stalin to Churchill, sent 3 September 1941*

Please accept my thanks for the promise to sell to the Soviet Union another 200 fighter aeroplanes in addition to the 200 fighters promised earlier. I have no doubt that Soviet pilots will succeed in mastering them and putting them to use.

I must say, however, that these aircraft, which it appears we shall not be able to use soon and not all at once,... cannot seriously change the situation on the Eastern Front.

...

I think the only way [to seriously change the situation] is to open a second front this year somewhere in the Balkans or in France,... and to supply the Soviet Union with 30,000 tons of aluminium by the beginning of October and a minimum monthly aid of 400 aeroplanes and 500 tanks (of small or medium size).

(Source: *Correspondence between the Chairman of the Council of Ministers of the USSR and the Presidents of the USA and Prime Ministers of Great Britain during the Great Patriotic War of 1941–1945*. Volume 1, 1957, pp. 27–28)

DOCUMENT 117: *Message from Churchill to Stalin, received 6 September 1941*

3. About supplies. We are well aware of the grievous losses which Russian industry has sustained, and every effort has been and will be made by us to help you.... For our part we are now prepared to send you, from British production, one-half of the monthly total for which you ask in aircraft and tanks. We hope the United States will supply the other half of your requirements.

...

6. In your first paragraph you used the word 'sell'. We had not viewed the matter in such terms and have never thought of payment. Any assistance we can give you would better be upon the same basis of comradeship as the American Lend-Lease Bill, of which no formal account is kept in money.

...

4 September 1941

(Source: *Correspondence* ... Volume 1, 1957, pp. 29–30)

Table 8.1 indicates the extent to which supplies received by the Soviet Union during the war were purchased, as during the first few weeks of the war for instance, or received through 'Lend-Lease' or the British and Commonwealth equivalent (described here for Britain and Canada as 'mutual aid').

Whilst Soviet requests for some items such as raw materials or naval supplies could be met immediately from British and Commonwealth stocks, the delivery of significant numbers of weapon systems such as tanks and aircraft was more complicated. British plans to equip her own forces were dependent on US supplies, and the addition of the Soviet Union into the equation required co-ordination between the two Anglo-Saxon powers prior to discussion with the Soviet Union.

Whilst the British government was relieved that the Soviet Union was now in the war and hopeful that she would remain so, members were also concerned that aid to Russia from the United States would not be to the detriment of British military priorities. This thought can only have been made all the more unpleasant by the fact that Britain had considered going to war against the Soviet Union in early 1940 in order to aid the Finns (see Chapter 2). Of particular concern were deliveries of aircraft, in particular medium and heavy bombers, which would be one of the few means for British forces to take offensive action against the Axis outside North Africa.

As a result of Anglo-American discussions prior to the October 1941 Moscow Conference, certain Soviet requests for aid had been turned down. At this point in the war, neither the British nor the Americans were willing to supply the eight destroyers requested by the Soviet Union,[7] nor indeed did it seem likely that the nine minesweeping trawlers requested could be supplied, although the United States was apparently 'looking into the possibility of production of the latter'. Nonetheless, the United States and Britain went to the negotiating table in Moscow willing to provide 400 aircraft and 500 tanks per month, the provision of which, if cuts to allocations to the British and US forces were not to be severe, would require significant increases in US output.[8] British estimates of her future loss of aircraft strength due, to a large extent, to deliveries to Russia stood at 13 per cent for medium and heavy bomber squadrons, 14 per cent for light bombers and 9 per cent for fighters.[9]

The Moscow Supply Conference between the Soviet Union, United States and Britain took place between 28 September and 1 October, and saw US commitments under the First Moscow Protocol covering the period to 30 June 1942 to supply 1,500,000 tons of supplies to the Soviet Union paid for, in part, by cash advances on gold deliveries and future supply of raw materials from the Soviet Union. Attempts in Congress to specifically exclude the Soviet Union from the second Lend-Lease appropriation failed, and on 28 October it was passed into law, with the President preserving the right to designate Lend-Lease countries. By this point, US neutrality was increasingly a myth, with US warships convoying non-US merchantmen as

Table 8.1 Import dynamics to the Soviet Union from 22 June 1941 to 1 July 1945 according to the People's Commissariat of Foreign Trade (thousands of rubles)

		1941–45	1941	1942	1943	1944	1945 (to 01.07)
		1,290,494.9	4,504.5	169,529.1	338,966.1	459,194.3	318,300.9
From the US	Total	968,053.0	1,133.7	120,789.3	273,642.2	319,311.1	253,176.7
	Lend-Lease	957,351.3	–	114,453.9	270,842.7	319,226.4	253,174.9
	Soviet account	10,701.7	1,133.7	6,335.4	2,799.5	84.7	1.8
From the UK	Total	200,416.3	3,370.8	48,739.8	58,856.3	651,154.8	24,294.6
	Mutual aid	187,625.5	3,370.8	48,621.9	52,762.9	58,567.8	24,294.6
	Credit	12,790.8	–	117.9	6,093.4	6,586.9	–
From Canada	Mutual aid	122,025.6	–	–	6,467.6	74,728.4	40,829.6

Source: RGAE f.413.o.9.d.548.l.189.

far as Iceland and with the US establishing a presence in Iran on the basis of a Presidential Directive of 13 September. On 7 November 1941 Roosevelt finally declared the defence of the Soviet Union essential to that of the United States, and incorporated the Soviet Union in the provisions Lend-Lease Act.[10] Nonetheless, even meeting commitments under the First Moscow Protocol to supply 1,500,000 tons of goods to the Soviet Union by 30 June 1942 was a challenge to the US administration as the industrial giant started to flex its muscles. This left the United Kingdom as an equal partner in the provision of aid to the Soviet Union for the period of the First Protocol, even if some weapons supplied by Britain to the Soviet Union were from British Lend-Lease allocations or previous direct purchases from the United States (a good example of US-manufactured equipment being supplied to the Soviet Union as British aid are the 200 Tomahawk fighters mentioned above).

In addition the British would play the dominant role in the delivery of aid during the First Protocol period. Where supply routes via Iran and Alaska would require development, materials were largely delivered to the Soviet ports of Arkhangel'sk and Murmansk via the increasingly perilous route round German-occupied Norway, from which German submarines, surface ships and aircraft could launch attacks on these 'northern' or 'Arctic' convoys.[11]

First Moscow Protocol commitments and aid

In terms of basic weapons systems, the United Kingdom and United States had committed in Moscow to supply the Soviet Union with 200 aircraft each per month until the end of June 1942, along with 250 tanks, giving totals of 3,600 and 4,500 respectively over a nine-month period. However, initial British deliveries of tanks would be 300 per month 'decreasing to 250 as American supplies increase'. For the aircraft, the commitment was to supply, in full, the quantity requested by the Soviet Union. However, the requested ratio of 300 light/medium bombers to 100 fighters would be replaced by 200 fighters per month from the United Kingdom and 100 of each from the United States in order to satisfy British demands to be able to preserve the expected rate of expansion of her bomber forces.[12] The relative significance of British deliveries would be increased temporarily during December 1941 by US reaction to the outbreak of war with Japan, as up to 17 December 1941 US supplies destined for the Soviet Union were unloaded from merchant vessels and provided to US forces:

DOCUMENT 118: *From a report of the People's Commissar for Foreign Trade of the USSR A.I. Mikoian to Stalin and Molotov on the fulfilment of responsibilities for the supply of weapons, equipment and war materials to the USSR for October–December 1941 following the three-power Moscow Conference, 9 January 1942*

British deliveries

... Assessing British deliveries as a whole,... recognition follows, that Great Britain is fulfilling her obligations more or less accurately and carefully, the same however cannot be said of the USA, on which, see below.

American deliveries

The requirements of the USA for monthly deliveries of aircraft total 600 for three months.

...

In the following clarification for monthly deliveries the Americans have given new figures for their aircraft deliveries, that is:

	October	November	December	Total
Total (aircraft)	128	107	160	395
Including:				
Fighters	93	107	100	300
Bombers	5	–	60	65
Reconnaissance	30	–	–	30

In fact only 204 have been shipped.
    These include:
        131 fighters.
        43 bombers.
        30 reconnaissance aircraft.
Of the 204 shipped aircraft:
        95 have arrived in the Soviet Union.
        106 are en route.
        Including 8 to arrive on 12.1.1942.
        3 loaded on transports but not yet sent.
Hence, unshipped aircraft ... total 396.

Such a large number of unshipped aircraft can be explained by the fact that, between 13 and 17 December the American government recalled almost all aircraft supplied from those situated in US ports at that time. This meant a total of 447 aircraft of 457 situated in ports. The large number of aircraft in US ports on 15 December 1941 that had yet to be dispatched was due to 152 Aerocobra fighters being sent to ports without propellers, armament or spares. In addition, for a long period the American government did not provide a sufficient number of transports and, in the end, recalled all of the aircraft to be sent. In doing this a portion of the aircraft were actually unloaded from transports....

In the same way the number of tanks to be supplied has fallen well short.

The USA ... was required to supply 750 tanks for a three-month period.

On 31 October the American government provided a new monthly figure for deliveries of tanks, that is: In October 166 tanks, in November 207 tanks, and in December 300 tanks, a total of 673 tanks.

172 *Lend-Lease aid and the Soviet economy*

> In reality only 182 have been supplied.
> Of these: Medium – 72 tanks.
>   Light – 110 tanks.
> Of these: Arrived in the Soviet Union – 27 tanks.
>   En route – 139 tanks.
>   In ports – 16 tanks.
> ...
> Overall US deliveries are being conducted most unsatisfactorily.
> ...
> A. Mikoian.
> (Source: G.N. Sevost'ianov, *Sovetsko-amerikanskie otnosheniia. 1939–1945*, 2004, p. 122)

As discussed briefly in Chapter 4 with reference to tanks, when Allied, in particular British, deliveries of key weapons systems for the war as a whole are compared to Soviet production for the same period they can understandably be viewed as being of little significance. However, as shown, during the Battle for Moscow in late 1941 the Soviet resource situation was so dire that relatively small inputs of tanks were of some significance. This situation would continue well into 1942. Tables 8.2 and 8.3 show tanks and aircraft delivered to the Soviet Union for 1941, with Soviet production figures for the same period, as well as force levels as of 22 June 1941, losses for the first six months of the war, and numbers available (including foreign supplies) on 1 January 1942.

A steady stream of British-supplied tanks continued to be provided to Soviet units during the spring and summer of 1942. From 10 May 1942 British tanks were being sent to reinforce the Briansk and Kalinin *Fronts* and South-Western *napravlenie*, with the South-Western *napravlenie* to receive 90 Matildas and 70 Valentines during May 1942.[13] According to Suprun, immediately prior to July 1942 and therefore at the end of the First Moscow Protocol period, the Red Army had 13,500 tanks in service, of which 2,200 or 16 per cent were imported, and of which over 50 per cent were British.[14] However, mechanical problems, in part due to Soviet unfamiliarity with this new, foreign equipment, kept in the region of 50 per cent of imported tanks out of service at any one time up to the end of 1942. Soviet sources did, however, note the general relative reliability of Leyland engines of Matildas compared to Soviet models.[15]

Whilst by late 1942 Soviet production lessened the significance of British tank supplies, aircraft deliveries, the importance of which arguably exceeded tanks during the First Moscow Protocol period, remained significant into 1943. Soviet combat aircraft production from the end of June 1941 to the end of June 1942 was in the region of the 16,468 aircraft given by Harrison.[16] By the end of June 1942 the UK had delivered 1,323 fighter aircraft, or about 8 per cent of Soviet production from the start of the war.[17] Given that Soviet combat-aircraft losses for this period at best approached domestic supply, and were particularly severe for the first six months of the

Table 8.2 Allied tank deliveries compared to supplies to the Red Army for the second half of 1941, force levels on 22 June 1941, losses to the end of 1941 and numbers available (including foreign supplies) on 1 January 1942

	Heavy	Medium	Light	Total
Number available 22.06.41	500	900	21,200	22,600
Received by Red Army 22.6–31.12.41 (inc. Allied)	1,000	2,200	2,400	5,600
Losses 22.6–31.12.41	900	2,300	17,300	20,500
Arrived from UK	187 (Matilda II)	259 (Valentine)	20 (Tetrarch – via Persian Gulf)	466
Arrived from US			27 (M3 Light)	27
Total arrived from Allies	187	259	47	493
Number available 01.01.42 (inc. Allied)	600	800	6,300	7,700

Sources: Krivosheev, *Soviet Casualties and Combat Losses*, p. 252; 'Iz spravki Narodnogo komissara vneshnei torgovli SSSR A.I. Mikoaina...', in Sevost'ianov (ed.), *Sovetsko-amerikanskie otnosheniia*, p. 193; Alexander Hill, 'British Lend-Lease Aid and the Soviet War Effort, June 1941–June 1942', *Journal of Military History*, Number 71 (July 2007), p. 788; Suprun, *Severnie konvoi*, p. 49; and TNA FO 371/29582 and FO 371/32859.

Table 8.3 Allied aircraft deliveries compared to Soviet supplies to the Soviet VVS for the second half of 1941, force levels on 22 June 1941, losses to the end of 1941 and numbers available (including foreign supplies) on 1 January 1942

	Fighters	Bombers	Total combat aircraft	Total aircraft
Number available 22.06.41	11,500	8,400	20,000	32,100
Received by VVS 22.6–31.12.41 (inc. Allied)	6,000	2,500	9,900	11,000
Losses 22.6–31.12.41	5,100	4,600	10,300	10,600
Arrived from UK	711 (484 Hurricane, 216 Tomahawk, 11 Aerocobra)	0	711	711
Arrived from US	(P-40)	5 (B-25) [extra to protocol]	>90	> = 95 + or inc. 5 O-52 [extra to protocol]
Total arrived from Allies	<806	5	>801	> = 806
Number available 01.01.42 (inc. Allied)	7,900	3,700	12,000	21,900

Sources: R.C. Lukas, *The Army Air Forces and the Soviet Union, 1941–1945* (Tallahassee, FL: Florida State University, 1970) pp. 29, 54, 61 and Appendix A; TNA FO 371/29582 and FO 371/32859; RGAE f.413.o.9.d.539.l.19, RGAE f.413.o.9.d.540.l.23; Krivosheev, *Soviet Casualties and Combat Losses*, p. 254; 'Iz spravki Narodnogo komissara vneshnei torgovli SSSR A.I. Mikoaina...', in Sevost'ianov (ed.), *Sovetsko-amerikanskie otnosheniia*, p. 192; and Suprun, *Severnie konvoi*, p. 49.

war, British deliveries alone were of some significance, especially when the particularly high Soviet losses of the first weeks of the war, depleting pre-war stocks, are taken into account. As early as 12 October 1941, 126th Fighter Air Regiment of the PVO was operating with Tomahawks, the first Soviet unit to be equipped with this aircraft.[18] PVO use of Allied aircraft during 1941–45 is indicated in Table 8.4. As with much Western equipment, the process of training, conducted by 27th Reserve Air Regiment that was formed in August 1941 for the task of conversion to Allied aircraft, was hampered by a lack of technical documentation, particularly in Russian.[19]

Tomahawks (P-40s) also served in late 1941 in defence of the '*Doroga zhizni*' or 'Road of Life' across the ice of Lake Ladoga to the besieged Leningrad:

Table 8.4 Aircraft in service with the Soviet PVO, 1942–45

Type of aircraft	Available on 1.1.42	1942 Total	1942 Written off	1943 Total	1943 Written off	1944 Total	1944 Written off	1945 Total	1945 Written off
I-153	264	143	52	39	15	17	17	–	–
I-16	411	333	131	131	69	97	94	3	1
MiG-3	351	409	192	215	215	83	83	–	–
LaGG-3	170	418	172	252	68	165	108	–	–
Yak-1	136	261	119	336	113	303	201	57	57
Yak-7	–	109	17	559	136	493	199	121	91
Yak-9	–	–	–	108	9	671	81	288	74
LaGG-5	–	–	–	343	104	608	159	876	49
LaGG-7	–	–	–	–	–	47	–	400	63
Hurricane	99	468	121	823	242	975	204	98	1
Tomahawk	39	56	15	43	11	31	4	760	42
Kittyhawk	–	98	56	383	62	910	90	27	–
P-39	–	12	3	65	10	597	110	844	11
Spitfire V	–	–	–	20	3	19	7	682	18
Spitfire IX	–	–	–	–	–	297	–	12	1
Kingcobra	–	–	–	–	–	5	–	825	7
								54	–
Total	1,470	2,307	879	3,317	1,057	5,318	1,357	5,047	415
Of which Lend-Lease	138	634	195	1,334	328	2033	415	3,204	79
% Lend-Lease	9.4	27.5	22.2	40.2	31.0	38.2	30.6	63.5	19.0

Source: I. Izotikov, 'Na kakikh samoletakh letal Pokrishkin, ili ne boites' britantsev, dari prinosiashchikh?', in *Vestnik protivovozdushnoi oboroni*, Number 4 (1991), p. 35

> DOCUMENT 119: *Order of the Commander of the VVS of the Leningrad Front to Air Forces, 8 December 1941*
>
> The task of covering the road transport route sustaining the Leningrad *Front* and the city of Lenin on the section mis Osinovets, Zabor'e Station is allocated to the VVS LF by the Military Soviet of the Leningrad *Front*. For the covering of this route 159th IAP 39th IAD, 13th IAP 13th AE VVS KBF are allocated.
> I order:
>
> 1. ...
> 2. 159th IAP consisting of 20 Tomahawk aircraft is to cover the road transport route on the section including Eremina Gora, including Zabor'e Station. Airfields as bases: Shugozero – 6 aircraft, Podborov'e – 14 aircraft.
> 3. Start for covering the route from 12 December 1941.
> ...
>
> Commander of the VVS of the Leningrad *Front*, General-lieutenant of Aviation, Novikov
> Military Commissar of the VVS of the *front*, Brigade Commissar Ivanov
> Head of the headquarters of the VVS of the *front*, General-Major of Aviation, Ribal'chenko
>
> (Source: N.L. Volkovskii (ed.), 2004, pp. 242–243)

Even without 154th Fighter Air Regiment, also equipped with P-40s and also committed to the defence of the ice road, the 20 Tomahawks of 159th Fighter Air Regiment represented, according to the Commander of the VVS for the Leningrad *Front* (later Marshal) Novikov, almost 14 per cent of the fighter strength of the *front* as of the end of November (20/143) and more than 11 per cent of the total air strength of the *front* (20/175) at the end of December 1941.[20]

Those aircraft types supplied by Britain either from domestic production or from British orders from the United States such as the Kittyhawk/Tomahawk and Hurricane were inferior to the latest marks of the German Bf109, and indeed in aspects of performance to the latest Soviet types. Britain was reticent to supply Spitfires to the Soviet Union given her own needs.[21] However, the Hurricane was, for instance, both rugged and tried and tested, superior to many Soviet pre-war designs still being operated on the periphery and arguably at least as useful at that point to many potentially superior Soviet designs such as the LaGG- and MiG-3s and developments that were suffering considerable teething troubles in early war production aircraft. Initial Soviet concerns focused on its armament and armour. Not only was the armour plating protecting the pilot seen as inadequate against medium-calibre ammunition at ranges of 50 to 200 m, but also the all-machine gun-armament was seen as weak. The latter was to prompt a Soviet programme of rearmament to two 20 mm cannon and two 12.7 mm heavy machine guns.[22] However, according to Soviet experts, 80 per cent of the specialist equipment of British aircraft such as the Hurricane, for example radio and navigational equipment, was of such value that it was recommended for manufacture by Soviet industry.[23]

Document 120 gives some indication of the range of supplies, including tanks and aircraft, as well as their destinations within the USSR, being supplied to the Soviet Union under the first aid protocol, in this case arriving with the convoy PQ-12 in March 1942:

DOCUMENT 120: *Secret. State Defence Committee. Decree No. GOKO 1497s of 26 March 1942, Moscow, Kremlin, concerned with the distribution of Allied aid arriving with convoy PQ-12*

To confirm the following plan for the distribution of armaments, equipment and materials arriving from abroad with the 12th convoy:

1. Aircraft

[Model]	[Total]	[Destination]	[Number]
Hurricane	136	VVS Karelian *Front*	60
		6th AK PVO (Moscow)	40
		22nd Reserve Air Regiment (Ivanovo)	36
Curtiss P-40E[24]	44	VVS Karelian *Front*	10
		27th Reserve Air Regiment (for the Leningrad *Front*)	20
		6th AK PVO (Moscow) for 126th Air Regiment	14
Aerocobra[25]	20	22nd Reserve Air Regiment (Ivanovo) for assembly	20
Cartridges		VVS Karelian *Front*	800,000
		Depot Number 50 (Bui)	4,900,000
		Depot Number 53 (Seima)	4,857,000
Merlin engines	4	VVS Karelian *Front*	2
		VVS VMF	2
Propellers	12	VVS Karelian *Front*	4
		Depot Number 28 (Iaroslavl')	8
Radiators	47 boxes	VVS Karelian *Front*	14
		Depot Number 28 (Iaroslavl')	33
Spares		VVS Karelian *Front*	30%
		Depot Number 28 (Iaroslavl')	70%

2. Tanks

Valentine[26]	43	For the formation of 170th, 59th, 201st, 177th, 103rd Tank Brigades
Matilda[27]	75	For the formation of 186th, 184th, 140th, 136th Tank Brigades
American M-3[28]	44	For the formation of 137th and 179th Tank Brigades
Bren Gun Carrier	53	For the equipping of tank brigades

178 *Lend-Lease aid and the Soviet economy*

Prime Movers with 3-ton crane and winch	6	GABTU for evacuation companies[29]	

Tanks are distributed equipped with arms and munitions.

...

4. Communications equipment

Radio sets Mk-111–18 (received earlier by the NK VMF)	300	NK VMF	200
		Main Board of Communications of the Red Army)	100
Telegraph cable (including 1,500 km arriving via Iran)	24,000 km	Karelian *Front*	2,500 km
		7th Independent Army	1,000 km

...

5. Automobiles

Lorries and spares for them (including 1,680 arriving via Iran)	3 374	For distribution according to Appendix 1	
Reconnaissance cars Bentam [sic][30]	128	For the equipping of tank brigades	80
		GUSKA for the fitting of radio sets and handing over to commanders of armies with a machine each	48

6. Naval weapons

Parts for ASDIC[31] sets	To the Communications Department of the Northern Fleet (for construction)
Station for the determination of the magnetic field of a ship	To the Northern Fleet for setting up at Poliarnoe[33]
...	...
Spares for trawlers[32]	Northern Fleet

...

7. Supply items for quartermasters

Boots	119,611 pairs	For the distribution by the Quartermaster General of the Red Army
Blankets	600 tons	As above
Knitted items	46 tons	As above
Red Cross items	128 tons	As above
Leather	243 tons	To the People's Commissariat of Light Industry

8. Metal-cutting tools – 312 items		
People's Commissariat for the Aviation Industry	In accordance with GOKO decrees Numbers 1283, 1038, 1039	239 items
...		
9. Various items of equipment		
People's Commissariat for the Aviation Industry	Presses (including for Factory Number 30 – 5 items)	14 items
...		
10. Metals		
Main Engineering Board of the Red Army	Barbed wire	2,314 tons
...		
People's Commissariat for the Aviation Industry	Duraluminum[34]	339 tons
...		
People's Commissariat for Foreign Trade...	Aluminium	2,991 tons[35]
...		
11. Petroleum products and chemicals		
...		
USG KA	Aviation lubricant	236 tonnes
...		
People's Commissariat for Munitions	Toluol[36]	1,965 tonnes
...		
People's Commissariat for the Aviation Industry	Perspex[37]	86 tonnes
12. Foodstuffs		
Board for Provisions of the Red Army	Sugar	429 tonnes
People's Commissariat of the Food Industry	Sugar Cocoa beans	628 tonnes 400 tonnes
Narkomzagu[38]	Wheat	1,530 tonnes

Chairman of the State Defence Committee, I. Stalin.

(Source: Alexander Hill, 'The Allocation of Allied "Lend-Lease" Aid ...', 2006, pp. 732–737)

Whilst the number of lorries delivered to the Soviet Union during the First Moscow Protocol was neither as significant relatively or absolutely as it would be during subsequent protocols,[39] even during the First Lend-Lease Protocol period lorries were a scarce resource carefully allocated by the centre, as the appendix on page 181 to the above decree suggests.

It is important to remember, especially given the historiography of 'Lend-Lease' in Soviet literature, that 'Lend-Lease' aid items were requested by the Soviet Union. Whilst models of weapons systems supplied might not always have been those desired, for example Hurricanes instead of Spitfires, nonetheless what was requested was subject to genuine need. In this context, raw materials not subject to any quality concerns (be they justifiable or not), such as aluminium and rubber requested from the Allies and supplied in significant quantities by Britain and the Commonwealth, should be seen as having been of significance. Some 18,000 tons of aluminium was promised by Britain during the First Moscow Protocol period, of which 14,147 tons had been supplied by the end of June 1942. Soviet production of aluminium was 67,600 tons for the whole of 1941, dropping to 51,700 tons for 1942 (see Table 8.7). During the same period, 34,856 tons of rubber was delivered, compared to 54,000 tons initially promised and revised down to 42,000 tons in the light of the war with Japan. Also worthy of note were medical supplies from the United Kingdom and India, although deliveries fell far short of Soviet demands.[41]

A range of items were delivered by Britain to the Soviet Union that, whilst the Soviet Union was able to produce, could not be produced in the desired quantities whether due to the loss of plant or the disruption caused by its evacuation, possibly in the context of limited initial capacity. An example of aid in this category is telecommunications equipment. A significant shortage of field telephone sets for the Red Army was highlighted in a GKO order of 20 July 1941. Whilst the People's Commissariat for Communications could be ordered to seize 20,000 standard sets from subscribers in order to free up field sets at supply dumps, hospitals, air defence sites and other rear-area objectives, such a solution was only a stop-gap. Production of field sets was ordered to be re-established at the Gor'kovsk Factory Number 197 of the People's Commissariat for Electrical Industry, in part because field telephone production was disrupted due to the evacuation of Factory Number 8 from Leningrad to Molotov, with production scheduled to be restored at this factory in September with a planned output for that month of 5,000 units.[42] Actual output for this factory for November was only 1,000 units, prompting fresh exhortations from GKO on 6 December 1941 to increase production; existing production at all factories being described as 'extremely unsatisfactory', with their directors being reminded of their 'personal responsibilities' for the fulfilment of these military orders.[43] In this context 'Lend-Lease' aid could, to some extent, make up for shortfalls in Soviet production. Whilst only 2,010 field telephones and 7,565 km of cable had been delivered through Arkhangel'sk by the end of navigation during 1941, these items were delivered outside the Moscow Protocol in response to urgent Soviet request. The Soviet Union had in fact asked for 6,000 field telephones per month at the end of September 1941.[44] Britain could offer only 2,000 immediately, with the promise of similar quantities in future months.[45] Whilst it was subsequently decided that the

DOCUMENT 121: Attachment Number 1 to GOKO Decree Number 1497s of 26 March 1942, concerned with the distribution of motor vehicles arriving with convoy PQ-12

Distribution of Automobiles

Type of unit and board	Total	Including 1.5 tonne Ford, Dodge, Chevrolet, Bedford	2.5 tonne Studebaker and International	3 tonne Bedford	For what purpose allotted
Arrived in Murmansk and southern ports					
1 Mortar units	703	441	—	262	For the installation of M-8 and M-13 [rockets] and the equipping of rockets regiments[40]
2 Tank brigades	1,150	990	160	—	For artillery, mobile kitchens and the equipping of tank brigades
3 Artillery units	421	—	421	—	For the towing of artillery and equipping of artillery regiments
4 Auto-battalions RVGK	250	250	—	—	For the equipping of battalions
5 GUVVS Red Army	400	400	—	—	For fuel lorries, mobile starters, mobile repair shops and oxygen stations
6 Main Board of Communications	200	200	—	—	For radio stations
7 GVKhU Red Army	150	150	—	—	For mobile dispensing stations, decontamination stations and other chemical-related machines
8 Main Artillery Board	100	100	—	—	For sound locators and AA gun directors...
Total	3,374	2,531	581	262	

(Source: Hill, "The Allocation of Allied "Lend-Lease" Aid ...', pp. 737–738)

United States would take over the whole order, nonetheless these 2,000 phones and an additional 2,000 were shipped by Britain by the end of the First Protocol period, along with 19,125 miles of cable and 400 switchboards.[46] During 1942, 23,311 field telephones would be delivered through Murmansk alone by the United States and Britain, along with more than 280,000 km of field-telephone cable.[47]

The Soviet Union experienced similar production and supply problems to those for land-line communications with radio sets, sustaining horrendous radio equipment losses during the retreat of the summer and autumn of 1941. According to Krivosheev, whilst 37,400 sets were available to the Red Army on 22 June 1941, by 31 December 1941 total stock was only 19,300 due to losses of 23,700 and new supplies totalling only 5,600 sets.[48] Whilst only 333 separately listed sets had been supplied by Britain through Arkhangel'sk by the end of navigation of 1941, British equipment such as tanks and aircraft was typically supplied with radio sets, contrary to the Soviet norm.[49]

The import of such items as metalworking machinery highlights the fact that 'Lend-Lease' aid items were at times a factor in increasing Soviet production or establishing the production of new items. With convoy PQ-12 alone, arriving in March 1942, 312 metal-cutting machine tools were delivered (see Document 120), in addition to a range of other items for Soviet industry such as machine presses and compressors. The principal recipient of the metal-cutting tools in this instance was the People's Commissariat for the Aviation Industry, receiving 239 tools. The number of machine tools delivered by Britain was, even in terms of Soviet wartime production, limited. Britain shipped 1,210 machine tools during the period of the First Protocol, compared to Soviet production (excluding presses) for 1941 of 44,510 and 1942 of 22,935.[50] However, the raw figures ignore the fact that the Soviet Union could request specific items that it may or may not have been able to produce for itself. Additionally, many of the British tools arrived in early 1942, during the first quarter of which Soviet production was, according to Suprun, only 2,994. The impact of relatively small numbers of machine tools ordered according to requirements should not, as Suprun goes on to suggest, be underestimated. For instance, the handing over of 40 imported machine tools to Aviation Factory Number 150 in July 1942 was apparently crucial in enabling the factory to reach projected capacity within two months.[51]

During the first Lend-Lease protocol period British supplies of basic weapons systems were significant when Soviet production was recovering from the loss and relocation of industrial capacity as a result of the Axis invasion. British aid would also go some way to compensating for unrealistic planning in the Soviet Union, both in topping up Soviet production and providing scarce resources on demand, even if with delay, which could, as in the case of machine tools, unclog bottlenecks and put unused capacity in the system to use. Perhaps also important, although difficult to assess, was the psychological impact of British readiness to support the Soviet Union for the Soviet population and indeed the leadership. Particularly early in the war, the Soviet population was reminded that it was not alone in the fight against Nazi Germany, but was now part of an alliance that would have seemed unthinkable only months before when there was the genuine prospect of the Soviet Union and Germany both being at war with Britain and France had the latter countries intervened in Finland. For the Soviet leadership, it was clearly comforting to be increasingly aware that, despite pre-war animosities, the West was willing to provide, with few questions asked and without financial recompense, not only equipment and raw materials, but also the latest technology. The praise that Stalin lavished on his allies in November 1941 would not be repeated later in the war:

DOCUMENT 122: *Extract from a speech made by Stalin on the eve of the twenty-fourth anniversary of the October Revolution, 6 November 1941*

The recent three-power conference in Moscow with the participation of the representative of Great Britain, Mr Beaverbrook, and of the representative of the United States, Mr Harriman, decided systematically to assist our country with tanks and aircraft. As is known, we already have begun to receive shipments of tanks and planes on the basis of this decision.

Still earlier, Great Britain ensured the supply to our country of such needed materials as aluminium, lead, tin, nickel, and rubber.

If to this is added the fact that recently the United States decided to grant a billion dollar loan to the Soviet Union, it can be confidently said that the coalition of the United States, Great Britain and the USSR is a real thing which is growing and which will continue to grow for the benefit of our common cause of liberation. Such are the factors determining the inevitable death of German fascist imperialism.

(Source: Joseph Stalin, 1944, pp. 30–31)

Before looking at aid delivered during the Second and Third Protocol periods, it is worth noting that high-technology items such as RADAR and ASDIC sets, in the development of which the Soviet Union lagged far behind Britain, the United States and Germany, were also being delivered to the Soviet Union during the First Protocol period, and assisted in the technological advancement of the Soviet Union as the war progressed. As an initial example of the sort of RADAR technology provided to the Soviet Union during the first year of the war, we will take British GL-2 sets. These sets were provided to the Soviet Union for the purpose of air defence. Whilst the effectiveness of such early 'gun-laying' radars was limited to giving accurate range and limited elevation data, their use by the sea gave increased effectiveness in determining elevation.[52] These sets were of sufficient perceived value to the Soviet Union to be the subject of a GKO order of 10 February 1942, requiring that Soviet industry copy the GL-2 set as the SON-2, importing key components and indeed allocating 100 metal-cutting machine tools from imported supplies for the establishment of production.⁵³ Six GL-2 or SON-2 sets arrived at Murmansk with the convoy PQ-13 in March 1942 with more following.⁵⁴

More significant were ASDIC and RADAR for naval use, examples of which arrived during the First Protocol period but took time to install on Soviet ships and for Soviet crews to master. Where basic weapons systems supplied by Britain were an important top-up to Soviet production during the First Protocol period, and could be deployed and used effectively by Soviet units in a short space of time as shown with tanks in Chapter 4, it can be argued that in additional to the supply of raw materials and machinery, British aid had the most significant impact (albeit not always immediately) in technological areas where British expertise and production were most advanced compared to the Soviet Union, generally on the periphery of the Soviet war effort.

The geographical area in which 'Lend-Lease' aid from Britain during the first year of the war can be argued to have had the most significant impact on the Soviet war effort was in the far north, and in particular for the Northern Fleet. Much of the material initially requested by the Soviet Union from Britain was naval, in the development and production of which Britain maintained a considerable technological lead in many spheres. The Soviet Union was also willing to cut the production of naval equipment at the beginning of the war and transfer capacity to other, more pressing needs on land, as in the case of Factory Number 112 switching capacity from the production of submarines to tanks (see Table 8.6 below). Whilst the historical and wartime neglect of naval forces made sense in the 1930s and during the summer and autumn of 1941 when the focus was on the Red Army, with German forces turned back before Moscow and with the significance of northern waters for the delivery of Allied aid and for Soviet internal communications naval forces had a role to play in the Soviet war effort. 'Lend-Lease' ships, aircraft and equipment, when combined with its own war and, to some extent, British experience, would go some way to make up for the relative Soviet neglect of naval forces since the October Revolution.

Lend-Lease aid during the second and third Lend-Lease protocols

From the second Lend-Lease protocol onwards, the Allies were able to exploit shipment routes to Iran and the Far East in addition to the perilous Arctic route. Weapons received by the USSR via the different routes are illustrated in Table 8.5.

Whilst, as Table 8.4 illustrates, Lend-Lease aircraft deliveries continued to be of significance to the Soviet Union after the period of the First Protocol, during the Second Protocol tank deliveries from Britain and the United States were of less importance to the Soviet war effort given the staggering increases in Soviet production achieved during 1942 and 1943. Production

Table 8.5 Weapons imports to the Soviet Union by route, 22 June 1941 to 1 July 1945 (000s tons)

Total		1941–45	1941	1942	1943	1944	1945
	Tonnage (000s tons) %	1,517.0 100	26.2	200.3	447.2	533.8	309.5
Via Soviet northern ports	Tonnage	600.2	26.2	168.0	114.9	188.7	102.5
	%	39.6	99.6	83.9	25.7	35.3	33.1
Via Soviet Baltic ports	Tonnage	0.1	–	–	–	–	0.1
	%	0.01	–	–	–	–	0.03
Via Soviet Far Eastern ports	Tonnage	284.9	–	5.2	75.9	69.0	134.8
	%	18.8	–	2.6	17.0	12.9	43.6
Via Soviet Arctic (Northern Sea Route)	Tonnage	38.79	–	1.0	18.7	18.4	0.6
	%	2.5	–	0.5	4.2	3.5	0.2
Via Black Sea ports	Tonnage	24.3	–	–	–	–	24.3
	%	1.6	–	–	–	–	7.8
Via Iran	Tonnage	511.0	0.1	18.8	222.1	233.6	36.4
	%	33.7	0.4	9.4	49.7	43.8	11.8
Under own power or by air	Tonnage	56.0	–	6.3	15.3	23.6	10.8
	%	3.7	–	3.1	3.3	4.4	3.5
Other	Tonnage	1.8	–	1.0	0.3	0.5	–
	%	0.1	–	0.5	0.1	0.1	–

Source: RGAE f.413.o.9.d.555.l.17.

Table 8.6 Soviet T-34 production, 1940–45

	1940	1941	1942	1943	1944
Total production	117	3,014	12,527	15,821	14,648
Factory Number 183 (Khar'kov)	117	1,560	–	–	–
Factory Number 183 (evacuated to N. Tagil)	–	–	5,684	7,466	6,583
Factory Number 174 (Omsk)	–	–	417	1,347	2,163
Factory Number 112 (Sormovo)	–	173	2,584	2,962	3,619
Kirov (Cheliabinsk)	–	–	1,055	3,594	445
UZTM (Sverdlovsk)	–	–	257	452	–
STZ (Stalingrad)	–	1,256	2,520	–	–

Source: Simonov, *Voenno-promishlennii kompleks SSSR*, pp. 163–164 (amended).

of the T-34 will serve as an example, as provided in Table 8.6. Such increases in production were, however, at the expense of other heavy industrial products, in particular lorries. Table 8.7 gives an indication of the cost to production in other areas of the Soviet economy of the German invasion and focus on the production of key weapons systems.

Particularly hard hit by the loss of labour, plant and indeed territory was Soviet agriculture. The Soviet Union lost the Ukrainian 'bread basket' for much of the war, with agriculture elsewhere being hit by the loss of adult male labour to the Red Army which was not replaced by the intensified use of remaining land through mechanization or greater use of fertilizers, for instance. Even horses for use in the fields were in high demand from the Red Army throughout the war (see Document 39, Chapter 3 and Document 69, Chapter 5), as motor and horse-drawn transport resources were required in the civilian economy to get produce to railheads and local population centres. Table 8.8 illustrates the agricultural crisis that hit the Soviet Union during the Great Patriotic War, just as it was starting to recover from the self-inflicted crisis of collectivization from the late 1920s.

Unsurprisingly, the Soviet Union introduced rationing in stages during 1941, which soon applied to the urban population across Soviet territory and the rural population with the exception of collective farmers. Official rations were not, however, always available, and many Soviet citizens not in the Red Army, key manual occupations or privileged white-collar positions did not receive minimum nutrition from their rations. Auxiliary farms, for instance belonging to factories, private allotments and purchases from *kolkhoz* markets at unregulated prices would save some, but starvation was a stark reality for many in the Soviet rear, and not just in besieged Leningrad. There was inevitably a thriving 'black' market.[55] Allied food aid undoubtedly made an important contribution to the Soviet war effort. The United States alone shipped more than 4.5 million tons of food to the Soviet Union during the war, with much provided in the form of concentrated (often dried) high-calorie foods. Such non-perishable foodstuffs, including tinned goods, were particularly valuable to the advancing Red Army from mid-1943 (the start of the Third Protocol) onwards.[56]

During 1941 and 1942, when Soviet units were on the defensive or falling back on railheads, the absence of local automotive transport production was perhaps not critical given the more pressing need for tanks and other weapons to stop the enemy, but by the time Soviet troops had gone over to the sustained offensive from mid-1943 transport resources were an issue of considerable operational significance. Without the means to keep advancing Soviet units supplied beyond railheads that were often considerable distances from mobile forces, and which in the face of German scorched-earth policy would take time to extend into formerly occupied territory, lorries gained great significance. Without motor vehicles, bounding Soviet deep-offensive operations would not have been possible, making it more likely that even the fairly immobile German infantry divisions of the latter half of the war could have pulled back to form successive defensive lines. The importance of imported motor vehicles for the Red Army vehicle park, as well as the overall increase in vehicles available and the extent to which motor vehicles were drained from the Soviet economy for the use of the Red Army, is apparent in Table 10.3.

Also of considerable significance in maintaining the momentum of the Soviet advance was, as indicated above, the ability to supply by rail as far as possible (see for example Document 143, Chapter 10). Soviet heavy industry had focused to such an extent on the production of armoured vehicles and weapons that the production of track and locomotives had been neglected, with much of the former destroyed where possible by the retreating Axis forces and where a significant quantity of rolling stock had either been captured or destroyed during the German advance. Table 8.9 below provides details of US Lend-Lease shipments for six key items for the war as a whole, including locomotives, compared to Soviet production for the period 1941–45, and in many ways illustrates both Soviet economic achievements despite the damage caused to her economy by the German invasion and the importance of Lend-Lease aid for the Soviet war effort.

It would be difficult and unconvincing to argue that 'Lend-Lease' aid 'saved' the Soviet Union from defeat in 1941 or, indeed, at any point during the war. Axis forces were halted before Moscow with Soviet blood, and to a large extent with Soviet-manufactured arms and equipment. Soviet troops continued to fight largely with Soviet-produced arms, even if they were increasingly frequently ferried into battle, resupplied and mounted on US-supplied lorries.

Lend-Lease aid provided during the period of the First Moscow Protocol certainly had a far more significant impact on the Soviet war effort and indeed on front-line capability both during and after the Battle for Moscow than the Soviet and indeed Western historiography would suggest. What is

Table 8.7 Soviet civilian industrial production of key products, 1940–45

Product	1940	1941	1942	1943	1944	1945
Crude Steel (000s tons)	18,317	17,893	8,070	8,475	10,887	12,252
Pig iron (000s tons)	14,902.3	13,815.6	4,779.1	5,591.1	7,296.4	8,802.7
Tubular steel (000s tons)	966.1	780.3	280.9	370.4	482	571.4
Rolled metal (000s tons)	13,113	12,588	5,415	5,675	7,278	8,485
Rails (000s tons)	1,360	874	112	115	129	308
Wire (000s tons)	680	649	210	191	224	350
Aluminium (000s tons)	60.1	67.6	51.7	62.2	82.7	86.7
Nickel (000s tons)	10.3	11.3	8.9	13.4	15.8	18.4
Coal (000s tons)	165,923	151,428	75,536	93,141	121,470	149,333
Oil (000s tons)	31,121	33,038	21,988	17,984	18,261	19,436
Petrol (000s tons)	4,435	4,306	2,537	2,782	3,792	3,159
Diesel fuel (000s tons)	629	936	209	478	535	518
Mineral fertiliser (000s tons)	3,237.7	2,674.4	364.4	539.3	775.6	1,121.2
Toluene (000s tons)	37.9	57.9	38.1	39.8	38.3	33.5
Lathes	58,437	44,510	22,935	23,281	34,049	38,419
Mainline steam locomotives	914	708	9	43	32	8
Mainline freight trucks	30,880	33,096	147	108	13	819
Lorries/buses	139,879	118,704	32,409	46,720	55,167	69,662
Cars	5,511	5,472	2,567	2,546	5,382	4,995
Caterpillar tractors	26,530	23,827	3,520	1,063	2,889	6,562
Wheeled tractors	5,119	0	0	0	265	1,166
Tractor ploughs	38,438	18,527	1,338	3,056	3,371	8,474
Horse ploughs	34,252	36,495	1,212	41,736	35,638	39,230
Tractor seed drills	21,426	13,173	0	0	504	1,578
Horse seed drills	10,927	15,591	33	151	1,648	3,289

Cranes	454	350	1	26	62	57
Elevators (loading)	513	268	12	11	9	44
Commercial timber (million cu. m.)	117.9	115.1	48.2	43.4	52.4	61.6
Leather footwear (000s pairs)	211,033	157,687	52,675	55,804	67,423	63,115
Granulated sugar (000s tons)	2,165	523	114	117	245	465
Refined sugar (000s tons)	628	638	14	28	25	54
Tinned goods (millions tins)	1,113	926	485	546	557	558
Flour (millions tons)	29	24	16	13	13	15

Source: Harrison, *Accounting for War*, pp. 195–197.

Table 8.8 Soviet agricultural production, 1940–45

Product	1940	1941	1942	1943	1944	1945
Grains (millions of tons)	95.5	55.9	29.7	29.4	49.1	47.2
Potatoes (millions of tons)	75.9	26.4	23.8	34.9	54.9	58.1
Other vegetables (millions of tons)	13.7	5.5	4.3	6.7	10.2	10.3
Sunflower seeds (000s tons)	2,636	909	283	784	1,042	843
Sugar beets (millions of tons)	18	1.9	2.1	1.3	4.1	5.5
Milk (millions of tons)	33.6	25.5	15.8	16.4	22	26.4
Meat (live weight) (000 tons)	7,502	7,044	3,405	3,288	3,632	4,690
Eggs (billions)	12.2	9.3	4.5	3.5	3.6	4.9

Source: Harrison, *Accounting for War*, p. 262.

perhaps of particular note is not only the speed with which Britain in particular was willing and able to provide aid to the Soviet Union after initial hesitation, but how quickly the Soviet Union was able to put foreign equipment to use.

During the second protocol the quantity of Allied aid being shipped to the Soviet Union increased significantly, as indeed did the number of routes via which it was delivered, and coincided with the period during which the Soviet Union was wresting the strategic initiative from the *Wehrmacht*. During this period the United States overtook the United Kingdom as the dominant provider of aid. Whilst the importance of Allied tanks declined compared to the first protocol, given the re-establishment of evacuated plant and then dramatic increase in Soviet production, the importance of Allied aircraft remained high and the delivery of Allied lorries started to have an impact on the mobility of the Red Army. Such vehicles, along with radio sets, had an increasingly significant impact on Soviet operational effectiveness and the command and control of Soviet forces.

During the third and fourth protocols, the import of weapons systems was far less important than the role of Lend-Lease supplies not only in maintaining the momentum of the Red Army advance through the provision of lorries and other transport resources, but also through the provision of non-perishable foods. Such foods for the Red Army to some extent released local stocks for civilian use. During the third and fourth protocols, Lend-Lease aid can be said to have allowed the Soviet Union to continue to focus on the production of key weapon systems without this focus leading to an economic imbalance that would have started to create bottlenecks or forced the re-allocation of valuable Soviet resources from the production of weapons systems.[57]

Table 8.9 Comparison between Soviet production and US Lend-Lease aid for key items, 1941–45

Item	Lend-Lease shipments 1941–45	Soviet production 1941–45
Tanks and self-propelled guns	1,683 light, 5,489 medium, 115 heavy, 1,807 'gun-motor carriages' = 9,094	104,477 (July 41–September 45)
Trucks	433,967, including 49,250 quarter-ton 4 × 4 Command (Jeep), 104,485 2.5 ton 6 × 6 Cargo Studebaker	322,662 (January 41–December 45)
Boots and shoes	302,445 pairs boots and 14,604,766 'shoes' (including 13,470,936 Russian Service) = 14,907,211	396,704 (January 41–December 45)
Steam locomotives	1,908, including 1,685 2–10–0 105-ton 60" gauge	800 (January 41–December 45)
Aircraft (military)	11,450, including 865 medium and 3,066 light bombers, 6,695 fighters and 739 transport aircraft (708 C-47)	117,591 (July 41–September 45)

Sources: Harrison, *Accounting for War*, pp. 180 and 195–198 and Office, Chief of Finance, War Department, *Lend-Lease Shipments. World War II* (Washington, DC: 31 December 1946).

Guide to further reading

J. Barber and M. Harrison, *The Soviet Home Front, 1941–1945* (London: Longman, 1991), chapters 7–11.

J. Beaumont, *Comrades in Arms: British Aid to Russia 1941–1945* (London: Davis-Poynter, 1980).

M. Harrison, 'Resource Mobilization for World War II: the USA, UK, USSR and Germany, 1938–1945', *Economic History Review*, Volume XLI, Number 2 (May 1988), pp. 171–192.

M. Harrison, *Accounting for War. Soviet Production, Employment and the Defence Burden, 1940–1945* (Cambridge: Cambridge University Press, 1996).

Alexander Hill, 'The Allocation of Allied "Lend-Lease" Aid to the Soviet Union arriving with Convoy PQ-12, March 1942 – A State Defense Committee Decree', *JSMS*, Volume 19, Number 4 (December 2006), pp. 733–734.

Alexander Hill, 'British Lend-Lease Aid and the Soviet War Effort, June 1941-June 1942', *Journal of Military History*, Volume 71, Number 3 (July 2007), pp. 773–808.

R.H. Jones, *The Roads to Russia: United States Lend-Lease to the Soviet Union* (Norman, OK: University of Oklahoma Press, 1969).

Richard C. Lukas, *Eagles East: The Army Air Force and the Soviet Union, 1941–1945* (Tallahassee, FL: Florida State University Press, 1970).

R. Munting, 'Soviet Food Supply and Allied Aid in the War, 1941–1945', *Soviet Studies*, Volume 36, Number 4 (1984), pp. 582–593.

Jacques Sapir, 'The Economics of War in the Soviet Union during World War II', in I. Kershaw and M. Lewin (eds), *Stalinism and Nazism: Dictatorships in Comparison* (Cambridge: Cambridge University Press, 1997), pp. 208–236.

B.V. Sokolov, 'The Role of Lend-Lease in Soviet Military Efforts, 1941–1945', *JSMS*, Volume 7, Number 3 (September 1994), pp. 567–586.

H.P. Van Tuyll, *Feeding the Bear: American Aid to the Soviet Union 1941–1945* (Westport, CT: Greenwood Press, 1989).

V.F. Vorsin, 'Motor Vehicle Transport Deliveries through "Lend-Lease"', *JSMS*, Volume 10, Number 2 (June 1997), pp. 153–175.

9 The Soviet Partisan Movement

From the first days of the Great Patriotic War, Stalin and the Soviet leadership sought to foster resistance to the Axis invasion not only at the front line but in Axis rear areas. Whilst the Soviet authorities could utilize the Russian tradition of partisan warfare on which they had drawn during the Civil War and intervention, with the shift in Soviet doctrine in the late 1930s towards a primacy of the offensive, preparations for partisan warfare on Soviet territory in the event of foreign invasion were curtailed. As Panteleimon Ponomarenko, wartime head of the partisan movement recalled:

> DOCUMENT 123: *Retrospective comments by Panteleimon Ponomarenko, wartime head of the partisan movement, on pre-war preparations for partisan warfare*
>
> Despite a rich tradition and experience of partisan warfare and underground activity in previous wars, we did not have a single academic work putting this experience in context. The preparations being carried out during peacetime for partisan warfare were cut short in the mid-1930s, and caches of weapons, supplies and technical equipment created for this end were liquidated. The reason for this was without a doubt the unrealistic thrust of our military doctrine, stating that if the imperialists unleash war against the Soviet Union, then it will only take place on enemy territory. Even if it wasn't accepted unconditionally by the military leadership in planning, this doctrine was nonetheless promoted in the press and in the speeches of prominent political and military figures, and supplanted the idea that war could be transferred to our territory.
>
> (Source: P.K. Ponomarenko, 1965, p. 34)

Most of those involved in such preparations seem to have perished during the Great Purges of 1936–38.[1]

As the scale of the Axis invasion of 22 June 1941 became apparent, the Soviet leadership sought to resurrect previous plans to hamper an enemy advance through partisan activity:

> DOCUMENT 124: *Directive of the SNK SSSR and TsK VKP (b) to Party organizations of the prefrontal zone on the decisive reorganization of all work onto a war footing, 29 June 1941*
>
> The *Sovnarkom* SSSR and TsK VKP (b) requires all Party, Soviet, union and *Komsomol* organizations to bring an end to placidity and a carefree attitude and mobilize all of our organizations and all the force of our people for the total defeat of the enemy....
> The *Sovnarkom* of the Union of SSR and TsK VKP (b) demands of you, that:
> ...
> 5. In districts occupied by the enemy you create partisan detachments and diversion groups for the struggle with units of the enemy army; for the stirring up of partisan war here, there and everywhere; for the destruction of bridges and roads; for the disruption of telephone and telegraph communications; the raizing of supply bases and so forth. In occupied areas intolerable conditions are to be created for the enemy and those locals assisting him....
> For the timely direction of all of these activities, underground cells and safe houses are to be created in every town, district centre, worker's settlement, at every railway station and on *sovkhozi* and *kolkhozi*, under the supervision of the First Secretaries of regional and district Party committees.
> ...
> Stalin ... Molotov....
>
> (Source: *RA T.20 (9)*, 1999, pp. 17–18)

More detailed instructions were provided on 18 July in a decree concerned specifically with partisan warfare:

> DOCUMENT 125: *Decree of the TsK VKP (b) on the organization of the struggle in the rear of German forces, 18 July 1941*
>
> In the struggle with Fascist Germany, which has seized part of Soviet territory, the struggle in the rear of the German army has acquired especially great significance....
> In order for this struggle in the rear of the German army to acquire the largest possible scale and greatest intensity it is necessary for the leaders of republican, regional and district Party and Soviet organizations to take on the organization of this undertaking on the ground themselves; personally organising work in the German-occupied districts, leading groups and units of self-motivated fighters who are already waging the struggle to disorganise enemy forces and for the destruction of those who have seized our territory. Meanwhile there have still been a number of certainly not isolated instances where the leaders of Party and Soviet organisations of the districts threatened by the German fascists have shamelessly left their posts and retreated deep into the rear to quiet locations, in the process becoming deserters and pitiful cowards. In the face of this heads of republican and regional organisations of the Party have not been taken energetic measures in a number of instances with these shameful facts.
> The TsK VKP (b) demands of all Party and Soviet organisations, and above all of their leaders, that they bring and end to this intolerable situation and warns, that our Party and government will not stop at less than the most severe measures in regard to such self-serving individuals and deserters, and expresses confidence that Party organi-

sations will take all measures for the purging of Party organisations of these degenerates....

In accordance with the above the TsK VKP (b) demands of the TsK of national Communist parties, regional and district Party committees of occupied areas and those threatened with occupation that they carry out the following:

1. Send the most reliable Party, Soviet and *Komsomol* leadership elements, and, at the same time, loyal non-Party comrades familiar with conditions in the district to which they are being sent, for the organisation of underground communist cells and the direction of the partisan movement and struggle to create diversions in districts occupied by the enemy. The assignment of workers to these districts should be thoroughly prepared for and well concealed, with this end in mind it following that every group (2–3-5 persons) that is sent should have a single point of contact, with groups sent not having contact between themselves.

2. In districts threatened with enemy occupation leaders of Party organisations should without delay organise underground cells....

For the facilitation of the wider development of the partisan movement in the enemy rear Party organisations should in all haste organise armed bands and diversion groups from amongst participants in the Civil War and from those comrades that have already proved themselves in the destruction battalions, in militia units and also from amongst the NKVD, NKGB and others. In these groups communists and *Komsomol* members not used for work in the underground cells should be inserted.

Partisan units and underground groups should be provided with weapons, munitions, money and valuables, with supplies being buried and hidden in appropriate locations in advance.

In the same way it is necessary to take care to organise communications between underground cells and partisan detachments and Soviet-held districts, for which they are to be supplied with radio equipment – couriers, codes and similar are to be used – and likewise provide for the distribution and printing of leaflets, slogans and newspapers in the field.

...

Central Committee of the All-Union Communist Party (Bolsheviks)

(Source: *RA T.20 (9)*, 1999, pp. 18–20)

As mentioned in point two, partisan units were to draw on the so-called 'destruction battalions' that had been charged with such activities as combating enemy agents parachuted into the Soviet rear. On 24 June 1941, the SNK SSSR had passed a special decree, ratified by the Politburo, 'On action to be taken in the struggle with enemy parachutists and saboteurs in the prefrontal zone', providing the foundation for an NKVD order of 25 June 1941.[2]

Important in fulfilling the requirements of the decree of 18 July was the streamlining of the Party hierarchy undertaken from 4 July 1941 in the Leningrad region with the establishment of *troiki* led by the first secretary of the *raikom* to take decisions on behalf of the local Party and state apparatus.[3] In the light of the decree of 18 July such *troiki* would be expected to remain on occupied territory and co-ordinate the fledgling partisan movement.

Although many Party personnel fled in the face of the German advance, or evacuated during the first weeks of the war prior to the order of 18 July,[4] after 18 July Party personnel, along with state and NKVD officials, were frequently formed into partisan units on the Soviet side of the front and sent back to the district from which they had retreated as partisans. For example, there is the case of the Sebezh partisan detachment. Prior to the occupation of Sebezh by German forces on 7 July 1941, members of the executive committee of the local district soviet, the district Party committee and local NKVD personnel retreated with the Red Army to Velikie Luki where a partisan detachment was formed from the 'Party-Soviet active' and on 11 August despatched back to Sebezh district.[5] This unit consisted of:

DOCUMENT 126: *Composition of the Sebezh partisan detachment, August 1941*

1.	Vinogradov	Head of the district office of the NKVD
2.	Krivonosov	Secretary of the district committee of the VKP(b)
3.	Petrov	Secretary of the district committee of the VKP(b)
4.	Kulesh	Secretary of the district committee of the VKP(b)
5.	Feschenko	Chairman of the district executive committee
6.	Petrov	Chairman of the Sebezh town council
7.	Morgo	Head of the district education office
8.	Stepashkin	Acting head of the district branch of the state procurement agency
9.	Sidorov	Chairman of the Sovinskii 'parish' council
10.	Tumashev	Chairman of the kolkhoz 'Comintern'
11.	Nikiforov	*Kolkhoz* chairman
12.	Mitinskaia	Head of the district health department
13.	Kuz'mina	District censor
14.	Grigor'ev	Driver for the district executive committee

(Source: 'Sekretariu Kalininskogo obkoma VKP(b) tov. Vorontsovu. Ot Sekretariu Sebezhskogo RK VKP (b) Petrova V.E.... 15 noiabria 1941 g., gor. Kashin. Dokladnaia zapiska', RGASPI f.69.o.1.d.347.l.25)

Some partisan detachments or diversion groups, sometimes called partisan-diversion groups, were formed primarily on the initiative of the NKVD. In fact, a directive of 29 July for the NKVD/NKGB of the Kalinin region had, in the light of the failure of many partisan detachments formed under Party auspices, suggested by implication that partisan detachment be formed solely from personnel from the destruction battalions, a responsibility of the NKVD, and from members of the NKVD and NKGB. Such detachments would, however, require the assistance of military formations for supply and equipment.[6] On 25 August 1941, NKVD operational groups tasked with dealing with the threat from enemy parachutists and other saboteurs in the Soviet rear, and established as a result of an NKVD order of 25 June 1941, were reorganized as more significant fourth departments in the hierarchy of republican and regional NKVD apparati, and sought to raise and dispatch NKVD partisan detachments to the enemy rear.⁷ An example of a detachment formed on the initiative of the NKVD is one formed on 4 September 1941 by the Kalinin region NKVD. This 24-strong 'partisan-diversion group' was, after due preparation, on 12 September despatched for operations in the enemy rear in the Idritsa area on the border with Belorussia.⁸

Meanwhile, whilst the Party and NKVD were taking measures for the establishment of a front in the enemy rear with varying degrees of co-operation between them depending on location, the Red Army through the military soviets was taking steps to establish a presence on enemy-occupied territory. The military soviets, re-established in 1937 at the beginning of the Purges, were a key vehicle for political influence over the Red Army, with, at *front* level for instance, both the civilian Party apparatus and political organs of the Red Army being represented. They were indeed useful organs for the co-ordination of different arms, for instance at *front* level formally bringing together *front* commanders, commanders of artillery and of the air armies, and hence had value in operational planning.⁹ Given both the political sensitivity of a partisan movement that gave its members unprecedented scope for independent action and hence required close political supervision, and political and military interests in its activities, the military soviets were, if they had the time after dealing with other concerns, the most suitable existing organs for directing partisan activity. Without sufficient time for dealing with detailed issues concerning the partisan movement, the military Soviets kept track of and facilitated partisan activity before their respective *fronts* and armies through subordinate organs. Initially of particular importance were the political boards of *fronts* and armies, under the Main Political Directorate headed until 1942 by Lev Mekhlis.

With the Party, NKVD and political administration of the Red Army all sponsoring partisan detachments, or, in some instances where they were well-trained and equipped, what might be described as 'special forces' units, it became increasingly apparent that command and control needed to be more unified, in particular for partisan units. Apparently moves had been taken within days of the German invasion to provide some sort of central direction to the organization and activities of partisan detachments. According to Ponomarenko, who at the end of May 1942 would become a key figure in the further development of the partisan movement, before the end of June 1941 the Central Committee of the Party had taken the decision to establish a special commission for the direction of underground activity on German-occupied territory. Ponomarenko was, it seems, to have been a member of this commission, along with Mekhlis. Of this Ponomarenko only apparently became aware after the war since no further action was taken.¹⁰ On 12 August 1941 General I.V. Boldin was apparently approached by Stalin with the suggestion that Boldin assume the position of head of a board for the direction of the partisan movement being set up in Moscow.¹¹ Other than being seen as politically reliable, Boldin had on 10 August 1941 just escaped with 1,650 men from 45 days on German-occupied territory following encirclement, which was no doubt an important factor in his being approached.[12] Boldin apparently turned down the position on the grounds that he ought to remain with the field army.[13] High-level consideration of the need for a central organization for the co-ordination of the partisan movement seems subsequently to have been postponed until the end of the year.[14]

During 1942 and into 1943 considerable progress was made in providing the Soviet partisan movement with a coherent and effective organizational structure to replace a situation where in many areas the Party, NKVD and Red Army were all involved in fostering partisan activity in the German rear. These organizations were engaged in the development of partisan units in the German rear at best without effective liaison with other organizations concerned, at worst in competition with each other. On 30 May 1942, a GKO order was given for the creation of a Central Headquarters of the Partisan Movement [*Tsentral'nii shtab partisanskogo dvizheniia*, or TsShPD], a body that would take overall responsibility for the partisan movement across the Soviet Union:

DOCUMENT 127: *GKO Decree Number 1837ss on the formation of a Central Headquarters of the Partisan Movement attached to the Headquarters of the Supreme High Command, 30 May 1942*

1. With the aim of unifying the direction of the partisan movement in the enemy rear for the further development of the movement a Central Headquarters of the Partisan Movement is to be created, attached to the Headquarters of the Supreme High Command.

...

3. In its practical activities in the direction of the partisan movement the Central Headquarters of the Partisan Movement should proceed from the assumption that the principal task of the partisan movement is the disorganisation of the enemy rear:
   a) The destruction of enemy lines of communication (the blowing up of bridges ...);
   b) The destruction of means of communication (telephone, telegraph, radio stations);
   c) The destruction of supply dumps ...;
   d) The attacking of headquarters and other such military objectives in the enemy rear;
   e) The destruction of material assets on enemy airfields;
   f) The informing of Red Army units of the location, strength and movement of enemy forces.
4. The staff of the Central Headquarters of the Partisan Movement is to consist of P.K. Ponomarenko (TsK VKP(b)) (in charge of the headquarters), V.T. Sergienko (NKVD), and T.F. Korneev (Reconnaissance Board of the NKO).

Chairman of the State Defence Committee
I. Stalin

(Source: *RA T.20 (9)*, 1999, pp. 114–115)

According to Ponomarenko, appointed head of the TsShPD, he had first actually been approached by Stalin regarding the creation of such a headquarters in November 1941. However, despite arrangements for the central training of radio operators and other preparatory work, 'without warning a decree ordering the curtailment of the organization of the headquarters was received'. According to Ponomarenko, the reason for this decree was 'a memorandum by Beria regarding the inexpediency of the creation of such a headquarters, since, in his opinion, he himself could provide leadership for the movement, without a specialist headquarters'.[15] No doubt Beria intended to use the Fourth Departments and special-section apparatus of the NKVD (OO/NKVD) as a vehicle for organization and control.[16] Certainly, with high expectations for the December 1941 Soviet counter-offensive, the need to further develop organs of the partisan movement could have been seen to have passed.[17]

The eventual creation of the Central Headquarters of the Partisan Movement in May 1942 would be followed in September 1942 by what can be deemed the basic Union-wide instructions for the conduct of partisan warfare for the remainder of the war:

DOCUMENT 128: *Order of the People's Commissar of Defence Number 00189 on the tasks of the partisan movement. 5 September 1942*

The history of war teaches us that victory over invaders is often achieved not only through the struggle of the regular army but simultaneously through a popular partisan movement....

That was how it was during the Patriotic War of 1812....

That was how it was during the [Russian] Civil War....

Currently,... the people's [*norodnoe*] partisan movement on our territory temporarily occupied by the German invaders is becoming one of the decisive factors in victory over the enemy.

...

It is necessary, above all, to achieve a state of affairs where the partisan movement has developed more broadly and deeper.... The partisan movement should become a genuine movement of the whole people [*vsenarodnoe*].

The basic tasks of partisan activity are: the destruction of the enemy rear....

At the current time the destruction of enemy supply lines is of considerable importance....

I order:

1. With the aim of disrupting movement by rail and the collapse of regular transportation in the enemy rear with all means available it is necessary to provoke railway accidents, blow up railway bridges, blow up and burn down station facilities, to blow up, set fire to and shoot up steam engines, wagons and cisterns at stations and on sidings....
2. The taking of all opportunities to destroy enemy garrisons, headquarters....
3. The destruction of supply dumps....
4. The destruction of telephone and telegraph lines....

5. The attacking of airfields and the destruction of aircraft....
6. The destruction of all kinds of economic commands, enemy foragers, commands and agents for the seizure of grain....
7. ...
8. Mercilessly kill or capture fascist political figures, generals, significant bureaucrats and traitors to the Motherland....
9. Partisan detachments and individual partisan are to conduct uninterrupted reconnaissance work in the interests of the Red Army:
   a) To carefully select persons capable of conducting covert reconnaissance work ...;
   b) Constantly keep track of the location and movement of enemy forces and supplies by rail and road ...;
   c) Establish the precise locations of enemy troops and headquarters ...;
   d) Reconnoitre enemy airfields and establish their locations, the number and types of aircraft....
   e) Organise the reconnaissance of towns and major population centres with the aim of establishing the number of troops in their garrisons,... anti-aircraft defences....
   f) To clarify where and what sort of defensive lines have already been constructed, their composition in an engineering sense, weapons, communications, whether they are garrisoned;
   g) To follow and precisely establish the results of bombing by our aviation;
   h) Take all opportunities to seize orders, reports, operational maps and other such enemy documents....
10. Leadership organs of the partisan movement and commanders and commissars of partisan units are, alongside their military functions, to foster and conduct political work amongst the population....

Through the combined activities of the Red Army and partisan movement the enemy will be destroyed.
People's Commissar for Defence
I. Stalin

(Source: 'Prikaz Narodnogo komissara oborони ot 5 sentiabria 1942 goda', 1975, pp. 61–65)

Soviet historical works on the partisan movement tended to be rather bombastic on the significance of the resultant and increasingly well-organized partisan movement for the Soviet war effort from 1942. This was unsurprising given the 'legitimacy' the Communist Party gained from the idea that even under conditions of German occupation the Party was able to gain the support of, and organize, the population against the invader. Soviet historians tended to emphasize a groundswell of popular pro-Soviet sentiment on German-occupied territory, making the partisan movement a genuinely popular mass movement, as well as emphasizing the role of the Communist Party in turning a willing population into an organization making a significant military contribution to the defeat of Nazi Germany. It was the six-volume Soviet 'official' history of the war published between 1961 and

1965 that really enshrined the notion of a Communist-led *vsenarodnoe* movement in the Soviet historiography of the war. In typically bombastic fashion, the second volume of *The History of the Great Patriotic War 1941–1945* states that the partisan movement was:

> A genuinely popular movement, a force founded on ... continuous communication between the Party and the people.... Gradually growing in strength, the partisan movement became one of the most important political and military-strategic factors contributing to the victory of the Soviet Union over fascist Germany.[18]

According to the Soviet historian of the partisan movement in the Leningrad region, Petrov, partisans of the Leningrad region alone killed 104,242 'Hitlerites', destroying 105 enemy aircraft, 327 tanks and 4,503 automobiles.[19] At the end of the war the Ukrainian Headquarters of the Partisan Movement would claim that, from the start of the Great Patriotic War until 1 September 1944, Ukrainian partisans killed or wounded 464,682 enemy soldiers and officers, police and Soviet traitors, 200,322 during train derailments, of which there were apparently 4,958, including 61 'armoured' trains. Ukrainian partisans also claimed to have destroyed or damaged 211 aircraft and 1,566 tanks and other armoured vehicles.[20]

These losses for the Axis war machine and benefits to the Red Army were, however, apparently achieved at a remarkably low cost by the standards of the slaughter at the front. In the case of the Leningrad region, according to Petrov 13,000 'Soviet patriots gave their lives in the struggle against the Hitlerite occupiers',[21] of whom, according to alternative figures, 4,326 were partisans identified as such by the Central Headquarters of the Partisan Movement and lost up to 15 February 1944,[22] out of a total of 39,905 total official participants in the Leningrad partisan movement from the start of the war.[23] As of 15 February 1944 the partisan movement as a whole, excluding the Ukraine, had apparently lost 30,047 killed and missing, out of a total of 208,206 official participants.[24] These figures, including Petrov's broader notion of 'Soviet patriots' as opposed to 'partisans', do not, however, fully account for civilian casualties of the partisan war.

Particularly during 1941, when the fledgling partisan movement was considerably less effective as a weapon of war than it would be by 1943, civilian casualties during anti-partisan operations indicate that German forces were at least over-zealous and often simply murderous in dealings with the civilian population under the guise of anti-partisan measures, as indicated in Table 9.1. However, as Petrov's figures above for losses of 'Soviet patriots' compared to official partisan losses for the Leningrad region at least suggest, many Soviet citizens were certainly killed, in addition to official partisan losses, who considered themselves or were at least considered by partisans as participants, even if non-combatant, in the partisan war.

Table 9.1 From a report of the *Befehlshaber des rückwärtigen Heersgebietes Nord* providing summary data on Soviet citizens taken prisoner and killed by the security divisions concerned up to 30 September 1941, 29 October 1941

	Prisoners	Shot, killed or hanged	Grand total
281st Security Division			
Red Army men	418	26	444
Partisans	129	174	303
Suspect civilians	686	66	752
Women	32	4	36
Total	1,265	270	1,535
285th Security Division			
Red Army men	9,397 (including action near Luga and Wyritza)	–	9,397
Partisans	140	410	550
Suspect civilians	87	–	87
Women	–	–	–
Total	9,624	410	10,034
207th Security Division			
Red Army men	17,542	1,085 (shot as irregulars)	17,542
Partisans	3,094	187	3,281
Total	20,636	1,272	20,823
Grand total	31,525	1,952	32,392

Source: Norbert Müller, *Okkupation, Raub, Vernichtung – Dokumente zur Besatzungspolitik der faschistischen Wehrmacht auf Sowjetischem Territorium 1941 bis 1944* (Berlin: Militärverlag der DDR, 1980), p. 114.

Certainly, as illustrated below for the region below Leningrad, at no point is it reasonable to state that German forces were fighting a 'partisan war without partisans', as the German historian Heer has put forward, suggesting that German anti-partisan operations were more about a German war of annihilation against the population of the Soviet Union than a security-motivated response to a genuine military threat.[25] Table 9.2 provides the strength of the partisan movement for the Leningrad region throughout the occupation.

The complexities of the partisan war, and in particular differentiating between combatant and non-combatant, a crucial issue in determining 'partisan' losses, are perhaps best illustrated through the following example. In the spring of 1943, the German anti-partisan operation 'Spring Clean' was carried out by troops of the German 281st Security Division in the southern sector of the area occupied by Army Group North, as illustrated in Figure 9.1. Forces

Table 9.2 Partisans and the number of partisan detachments active in the Leningrad region from 10 December 1941 to 15 January 1944

Date	Number of active partisans	Number of detachments	Average detachment size
10.12.41	2,430	59	41
01.01.42	2,391	76	31
01.02.42	3,017	83	36
01.03.42	3,459	89	39
25.03.42	4,095	105	39
[04.42]			
[05.42]			
01.06.42	4,982	60	83
01.07.42	5,024	54	93
20.07.42	5,185	92	56
15.08.42	5,700	102	56
15.09.42	5,001	203	25
15.10.42	5,129	206	25
15.11.42	2,723	46	59
01.12.42	2,472	61	41
01.01.43	2,756	60	46
01.02.43	4,667	67	70
[03.43]			
30.04.43	2,876	64	45
[05.43]			
01.06.43	4,300	65	66
01.07.43	4,415	66	67
01.08.43	4,338	66	66
01.09.43	5,297	75	71
01.10.43	4,836	72	67
01.11.43	11,343	72	158
01.12.43	13,169	77	171
01.01.44	20,662	116	178
15.01.44	25,062	182	138

Source: Hill, *The War Behind the Eastern Front*, p. 165.

committed included Cossack cavalry, available artillery and anti-aircraft guns used in a ground role, and limited armour,[26] apparently supported by aircraft.[27] German operations led to the following report from the 12th Kalinin Partisan Brigade led by Moiseenko:

> 27.4.1943. Partisan brigade commander Moiseenko informs us that the partisan brigades of Maksimenko, Babakov and Karlikov have been broken. They have both dead and wounded, and some taken prisoner. Some of the partisans have made their way to the Soviet rear.[28]

204 *The Soviet Partisan Movement*

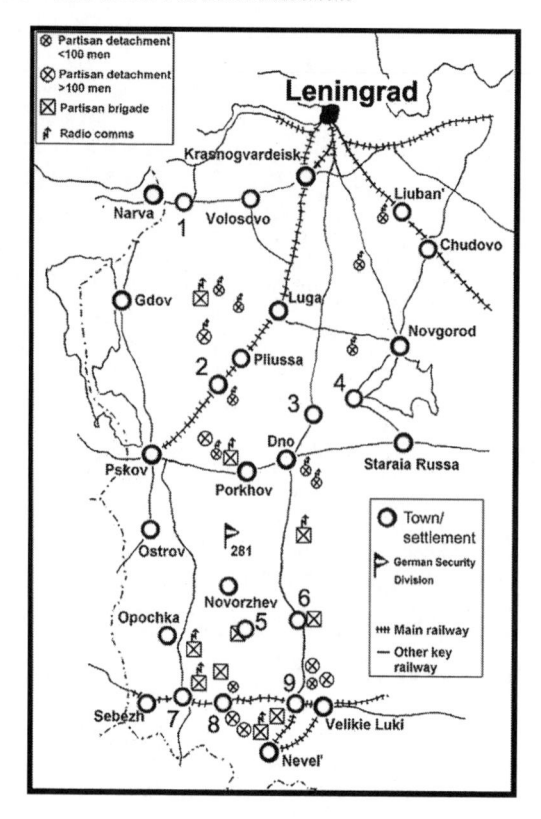

Figure 9.1 Disposition of Soviet partisan detachments on German-occupied territory of the Leningrad region, February 1943.

Key:
1. Kingisepp
2. Strugi Krasnie
3. Sol'tsi
4. Shimsk
5. Kudever'
6. Lokhia
7. Idritsa
8. Pustoshka
9. Novosokol'niki

More detailed Soviet description of the development of the operation adds weight to a conclusion that this operation at least was both targeted at and caused considerable damage to known and significant partisan forces:

> DOCUMENT 129: *To the Head of the Central Headquarters of the Partisan Movement, General-Lieutenant Comrade Ponomarenko P.K. Report on the partisan brigades of Bobakov, Karlikov, and Maksimenko, 12 May 1943*
>
> According to personal reports of those making their way to Soviet lines ... the following has been established:
>
> On 18 April 1943 the enemy conducted offensive operations with from 4–5,000 men against the partisan brigades of Maksimenko, Karlikov, Shipovalov and Moi-

seenko with the aim of completely destroying them and establishing normal movement and other activity in the Novorzhev-Opochka region.

On 19–20 April, after fighting in the region of the villages of Chernoiarovo, Agafonovo, Melikhovo and Gusevo that are situated 12 km south of Novorzhev, the brigades decided to redeploy in an organised manner and move to forest situated in a region ... 2–5 km north of Kudever' ... where the above brigades, with transport for the sick and wounded consisting of up to 50 carts, concentrated.

Having given the partisans the opportunity to evacuate to this area, on 21.4.1943 the enemy resumed offensive operations against the brigades from the Loknia, Bezhantsi, Kudever' and Novorzhev directions with a force of up to 5,000 Germans and a squadron of Russians – Cossack traitors to the Motherland, and artillery. Offensive operations were supported by three aircraft and tanks. Having encircled the partisans in the forest the enemy blocked them in and subjected them to mortar-artillery fire and tightened the encirclement....

Given the difficult situation created, a meeting of the command-political cadres took place, at which it was decided to take up defensive positions and during 21–22 April the brigades took part in intensive defensive fighting with the enemy. Having used up all of their munitions in the fighting it was decided that all the remaining surviving personnel of the brigades would make their way out of encirclement in small groups during the night of 22.4.1943.

...

During the night of 25.4.1943 the brigades were heading for Soviet lines, leaving behind up to 1,500 horses and more than 100 seriously wounded and ill.

During the night of 25.4.1943 having forced the river Puzno and crossing the Loknia-Novosokol'niki railway line ... the partisans came across a strong blocking force of regular German troops, as a result of which partisans of the retreating brigades,... a total of up to 500 men, were scattered in the forest and only with daybreak were small groups and individuals able to cross the front line....

According to command elements crossing the front line a significant proportion of local partisans, after having crossed the Loknia-Novosokol'niki railway line and having come under enemy fire split up in the forest, threw away their weapons and sought refuge in local houses.

(Source: RGASPI f.69.o.1.d.353.ll.14–15)

From Soviet statistics it can be calculated that German forces were operating against, at one time or another during the operation, in the region of 2,455 partisans according to data for 1 March 1943.[29] With the conclusion of the primary operation on 25 April, 281st Security Division claimed to have killed (confirmed) 424 of the enemy, having taken 61 prisoners and seized 'considerable weapons and munitions of all types'.[30] An alternative German source on which the former is based claimed:

> DOCUMENT 130: 281st Security Division. 1a. War diary. 657/43. Secret. Ostrov, 25.4.1943. Re: Operation 'Spring Clean' of the 281st Security Division from 18–22.4.1943
>
> Provisional combat report for Operation 'Spring Clean' of the 281st Security Division in the Kudever' region
>
> ...
>
> 22.4 ...
>   Overall outcome for the period from 18–22.4
>   Enemy losses: 424 bandits shot during the fighting (confirmed), with a further 141 estimated killed, 61 taken prisoner.
>   Spoils: 5 HMGs, 6 LMGs, 7 light mortars, 3 anti-tank rifles, 122 rifles, 11 SMGs, 142 hand grenades, a variety of munitions and explosives, 389 horses and 25 carts.
> ...
>   Our own losses: 11 killed, 45 wounded (apart from 5 killed and 21 wounded from local units)....
>
> (Source: US NA T-315 1872 91–3)

During Operation 'Spring Clean' it is certainly reasonable to assume that more than 100 partisan were killed by troops of 281st Security Division on the basis of weapons recovered and where partisan units admitted 'heavy ... fighting' for the loss of 11 Germans killed and 45 wounded.[31]

Given that the area in which the anti-partisan operation had taken place had already been defined as hostile by the Germans, it is unsurprising that operation 'Spring Clean' was to be followed up by an operation in the Kudever' area in order to properly 'cleanse' the area [*Säuberung*] and in order to gather 'men fit for work and combat between 14 and 65 years old'.[32] The fact that at least some local partisans had abandoned their weapons and taken to the villages, a situation unlikely to escape German attention, could only serve to justify such German operations.

Whilst such German military pressure was often insufficient either to destroy partisan detachments or to force partisans to leave the occupied territory altogether, it still exacted a considerable price on partisan strengths, for little cost to German forces.

Beyond such individual operations in which German losses against lightly armed and poorly supplied partisans tended to be minimal, calculating casualties caused by partisans is not straightforward. That a significant proportion of those casualties inflicted by partisans on the German war machine were not inflicted on security forces such as those employed during 'Spring Clean' is certainly the case. In late 1941 approximately 4,000 partisans of the Leningrad and Kalinin regions fighting against forces of Army Group North faced no more than a total of 30,000 security troops, whose numbers declined dramatically during the winter, as shown below.[33] For the whole of 1942 Leningrad partisans alone claimed to have killed 28,450 Germans and destroyed 70 tanks and 19 aircraft, where partisan strength reached a high of 5,700 on 15 August 1942 from a low of 2,391 on January 1942 (Leningrad region partisan losses for 1942 were no lower than 1,267 killed and 286 missing according to Soviet figures).[34] Yet in 575 anti-partisan 'operations' between 29 December 1941 and 28 September 1942, 281st Security Division, one of three allocated to Army Group North, lost only 161 men, with 128 wounded and 12 missing.[35]

Undoubtedly, many of those killed in partisan attacks other than on trains or on troops in transit by road were not actually German troops that could otherwise have been fighting at the front. Local garrisons of security troops were made up of troops that were certainly not the best the *Wehrmacht* had to offer. The most combat-effective elements of the Security Divisions were soon fighting on the front line, as for example the 368th Infantry (*Jaeger*) Regiment of 281st Security Division, fighting 'almost without interruption' at the front as part of 30th *Jaeger* Division from July 1941. Replacements received by the end of November 1941 were deemed unsuitable for aggressive anti-partisan operations.[36] Increasingly, guard duties were carried out by local collaborators, who would not otherwise have been deployed to the front.

The military effectiveness of the partisan movement cannot reasonably be measured simply in terms of the direct destruction of enemy forces, to a large extent because of problems in calculating the actual casualties brought about specifically by partisan activity. As the above figures provided for Ukrainian partisans suggest, a significant proportion of German losses were undoubtedly brought about during attacks on trains, and losses to front-line units in transit are difficult to distinguish from losses in combat at the front, an area where further detailed research might be revealing.

There are, however, other key measures of partisan military effectiveness – the extent to which partisans tied down German resources in rear-area security that might have been used for some other purpose even if not in front-line combat, and the extent to which their activities disrupted front-line operations, be this through hampering the ability to move reinforcements to where they were needed in a timely manner, and indeed the withdrawal of German forces, and German ability to resupply front-line troops.

As has already been suggested when looking at German losses due to partisan activity, many of those troops committed to anti-partisan work would not otherwise have been deployed at the front at the time they were engaged in anti-partisan work in the absence of the partisan threat (even if, as the German manpower situation deteriorated, fewer combat-effective troops were in front-line combat). Additionally, the numbers of troops committed to anti-partisan work for a sustained period remained relatively small compared to the size of the *Wehrmacht* and the size of the territory concerned throughout the occupation. At the beginning of Operation 'Barbarossa', the *Wehrmacht* allocated nine security divisions to rear-area security, that is 207th, 281st and 285th for Army Group North; 213th, 286th and 403rd for Army Group Centre; and 221st, 444th and 454th for Army Group South, with a total of 15 security divisions being created for service on former Soviet territory.[37] Based on an initial total of in the region of 11,449 men for 281st Security Division on 1 June 1941, this gives a total of approximately 100,000 troops initially committed. The attentions of all three security divisions allocated to Army Group North were, for instance, focused on Russian territory of the Leningrad and Kalinin regions by the end of the year. Even before fighting had begun, 281st Security Division was down to 7,827 men; at the end of 1941, on 21 December, 7,053 men according to its war diary.[38] As noted above, around 4,000 Soviet partisans operating against Army Group North faced no more than 30,000 security troops at the end of 1941, with the security divisions being assisted by forces of the *Reichsführer SS*, in this case elements of *Einsatzgruppe* A and 2nd SS Brigade, for instance.[39] Before the widespread use of collaborators, the situation for the Army Group Centre Rear Area on 5 October 1941, where 'after static rail line guards were posted there were too few troops remaining to mount any offensive action against the partisans or exercise effective control', was certainly not an exaggeration.[40] It is also worth noting that not only were limited numbers of increasingly second-rate troops allocated to rear-area security, but they were also poorly equipped, particularly with regard to transport resources.[41]

Whilst partisan strength dropped dramatically during the winter of 1941–42, the fall in available security forces was even more dramatic. Howell suggests that of 34 battalions initially allocated to rear-area security for Army Group North, all but four were in front-line service by the spring of 1942 – on 22 April 1942 only elements of 207th and 281st Security Divisions were actually engaged in rear-area security duties.[42]

By 1 October 1943, according to Ponomarenko, there were 14 German divisions allocated to rear-area security, of which six were security divisions (201st, 203rd, 207th, 281st, 285th, 286th), four he describes as Luftwaffe field divisions (153rd, 388th, 390th, 391st) that were in fact field training divisions, and four reserve divisions (141st, 143rd, 147th, 151st). In addition, German allies provided security troops – another 14 divisions, nine of which were Hungarian, three Rumanian and two Slovakian, along with 3rd Rumanian Mountain Corps.[43] This list ignores non-divisional units of up to regimental strength, where, for instance, partisans identified 356th Infantry Regiment, apparently of 228th Infantry Division, as operating in the Ostrov region deep in the rear of Army Group North in the summer of 1943, where the division had apparently been disbanded.[44] Whilst all these divisional types had seen or would shortly see front-line service, most were operating in rear-area security roles due to their apparent inadequacies in front-line roles. Despite increasing partisan strength, Army Group North could not field more regular troops against the partisans in late 1943 than late 1941, with somewhere between 25,000 and 30,000 troops in regularly organized units down to below company strength being available for security functions in late 1943.[45]

Anti-partisan operations did on numerous occasions, however, temporarily draw off troops from front-line service, as in the case of the front-line-capable 2nd SS Brigade mentioned above. Partisans, for instance, identified ('confirmed') 27th Infantry Regiment of 12th Infantry Division in the rural Kudever' district of the Army Group Rear Area of Army Group North in December 1943.[46] Even in the autumn of 1941, at least 691st Infantry Regiment of 339th Infantry Division seems to have been deployed in a rear-area security role in the Rear Areas of Army Group Centre, before the crisis period of the Soviet winter counter-offensive of 1941–42.[47]

Many local security functions were carried out by former Soviet collaborators, who undoubtedly suffered heavily in partisan raids and who certainly made up a significant proportion of 'enemy' losses reported by partisans, only sometimes distinguished from German losses. The 281st Security Division alone could claim 778 EKA [*Einwohner-Kampf-Abteilung*] personnel and 480 OD [*Ordnungsdienst*] personnel carrying out security and police functions within its jurisdiction in March 1943.[48] On the territory of Army Group North more reliable security and police units from the Baltic Republics were frequently deployed in significant numbers. Kalinin partisans, for instance, identified the 273rd, 515th and 615th Latvian Police Battalions as operating on the territory of Army Group North in the summer of 1943.[49] Partisan activity also undoubtedly tied down non-combat units such as those identified by partisans in intelligence reports, for example construction and railway units that could have been deployed on other tasks had it not been for acts of sabotage.

A significant proportion of the casualties inflicted by partisans on German and allied forces did not actually damage German front-line operations through depriving them of troops committed permanently to security duties, or indeed draw substantial forces away from front-line duty for sustained periods of time, as was the Soviet intention. Arguably far more significant than killing or tying down second- or even lower-grade units was partisan disruption of German lines of communication through rear areas. Summary data for the Leningrad Headquarters of the Partisan Movement of April 1944 presented in Table 9.3 suggests that Leningrad partisans alone 'destroyed' 1,050 steam locomotives and a staggering 18,643 railway trucks. Ukrainian partisans claimed to have brought about a total of 4,958 train derailments up to 1 September 1944, including 61 armoured trains.[50] Once again, these figures are exaggerated, although damage done to German communications was at times significant.

Much of the damage to German railway communications, broader troop movements and resupply efforts took place either during focused operations such as during the 'War of the Rails' of the summer and autumn of 1943, or later in the war when the numerical balance between partisan and security-force strength was most favourable to the partisans. Of the 1,050 locomotives claimed as 'destroyed' by Leningrad partisans, only 66 were supposedly 'destroyed' during 1941, rising to 266 for 1942 and 440 for 1943, with 278

Table 9.3 From a report of the Leningrad Headquarters of the Partisan Movement on enemy losses, suffered as a result of the activities of partisans of the Leningrad region during the war, 4 April 1944

Destroyed	1941	1942	1943	1944	Total
Rails	–	–	65,363	85,541	58,563
Trains	69	297	466	274	1,106
Locomotives	66	266	440	278	1,050
Railway trucks	870	3,970	5,374	8,429	18,643
Railway trolleys	4	11	3	4	22
Railway bridges	1	20	97	83	201
Road bridges	320	137	447	276	1,180
Telephone lines (km)	20	15	612	1,506	2,153
Telephone exchanges	452	133	4	4	593
Aircraft	71	19	6	5	101
Tanks	70	70	34	53	227
Armoured cars	28	8	6	11	53
Artillery pieces	5	42	31	130	208
Heavy machine guns	30	67	48	32	177
Tractors	48	17	34	18	117
Automobiles	1,632	534	543	1,821	4,530
Horses	253	656	651	1,539	3,099
HQs and garrisons	8	8	94	31	141
Railway stations/halts	5	–	28	15	48
Radio stations	15	22	2	6	45
Germans killed	11,493	28,450	35,985	28,314	104,242
Supply dumps	120	50	111	45	326
Armoured trains	–	1	4	5	10

Source: *V tilu vraga: Bor'ba partisan i podpol'shchikov na okkupirovannoi territorii Leningradskoi oblasti. 1944 g.: Sbornik dokumentov* (Leningrad: Lenizdat, 1985), p. 249.

for 1944 where much of the Leningrad region had been liberated by the spring.[51]

In late 1941, when partisan units remained small in size, German security forces focused on railway security at the expense of other dimensions to rear-area security, given the supply crisis. As Howell notes, on 20 December 1941, 281st Security Division ordered, in order to secure the Pskov–Ostrov–Rezenke and Pskov–Dno railway lines, that 'all bridges and culverts less than 40 feet long were to have double sentries, longer structures to be guarded by a squad of one non-commissioned officer and six men'. In addition,

> all stretches of rail in closed terrain were to have one sentry every 100 yards; in open terrain every 200 yards; sentries were to remain in sight of one another.... This security schedule was not to be deviated from, even if the last man in the division was used.[52]

Only during 1942 would increasingly large, well-trained and equipped partisan units start to do significant damage to the German transportation network in rear areas. In the Army Group North rear areas, partisan attacks on railway lines and bridges increased during the summer of 1942, with a particular increase in the number of partisan attacks being noticed between May and June. From 1 May to 31 July, in the rear of 16th Army partisans destroyed '30 bridges, broke rails in 84 places, and damaged or destroyed 20 locomotives and 113 railroad cars'. Attacks on railway lines were not, however, necessarily on the key transport arteries, and less well-defended road bridges were, at least in the Opochka region, apparently more likely to be hit than rail bridges.[53]

Order Number 00189 of the People's Commissar for Defence entitled 'On the tasks of the Partisan Movement' (Document 128) increased the emphasis of partisans on attacks on railway lines, with, for instance, a series of derailments taking place on key railway lines in the rear areas of Army Group North in September–October 1942, with 16 derailments on the key Pskov–Dno–Staraia Russa line in September and six in October. Nonetheless, this intensity of attack could not be maintained, no doubt to a large extent because partisan strength dropped dramatically during the winter of 1942–43 as it had done during 1941–42, with 5,700 partisans officially accounted for on 15 October 1942 for the Leningrad region, dropping to 2,472 on 1 December 1942. This was in part due to greater German ability to track down partisans in the snow, who were increasingly vulnerable to attack when tied to the shelter of base camps, and vulnerable to the elements when not. Many partisans sought to return to Soviet lines during the winter months, much to the consternation of the Central Headquarters of the Partisan Movement:

> DOCUMENT 131: *From the Central Headquarters of the Partisan Movement ... to the Representative of the Central Headquarters ... on the Kalinin* Front *... and the Representative ... on the Western* Front, *February 1943 (exact date unknown)*
>
> Recently, and despite TsShPD order number 0061 of 6.11.1942 categorically forbidding the voluntary evacuation of partisan units and brigades across the front line, there have been instances of voluntary withdrawal to our rear areas....
> Ponomarenko
>
> (Source: RGASPI f.69.o.1.d.67.l.75)

Even Ponomarenko, head of the Central Headquarters of the Partisan Movement, was forced to admit to Stalin that, before the start of the 'War of the Rails', 'despite the considerable importance of the partisan struggle against [enemy] lines of communication disorganization of enemy movement on the railways has still not reached such an extent as to have operational impact on the German front line'.[54] This would change as an increasingly strong partisan movement was thrown into intensive operations aimed at destroying railway track faster than the Germans could replace it in the summer of 1943.

Ordered on 14 July 1943, what would subsequently be described as the 'War of the Rails' began on 21 July for Orlov partisans and 3 August for Leningrad, Kalinin, Smolensk and Belorussian partisans:

DOCUMENT 132: *Order of the head of the TsShPD on the partisan war of the rails on enemy lines of communication, 14 July 1943*

Through their activities to destroy enemy communications Soviet partisans are rendering considerable assistance to the Red Army in the task of defeating the German occupiers.

...

The huge size of the partisan movement at the current time allows for massive and simultaneous blows against railway lines with the aim of totally disorganizing them and the disruption of enemy front-line operations.

Such a blow should be struck against the enemy through a war of the rails, that is with a massive and simultaneous destruction of rails. The enemy is currently experiencing a shortage of railway track.

Spare rails and many rails from stations and branch lines have been expended on the resurrection of sections blown up by partisans.

...

I order:

1. Partisan formations and detachments in the vicinity of railway lines to conduct systematic and simultaneous destruction of rails on enemy railway lines by breaking rails in half.

...

3. In order to ensure a surprise blow the first operation is to be conducted simultaneously and on the signal of the Central Headquarters, after which activities to destroy rails are to be conducted without respite and with all means.
4. Commanders of partisan detachments are to keep track of and inform partisan headquarters of the buildup of enemy trains for bombing by Soviet aviation.
5. The recording of the number of rails broken by every partisan detachment and brigade.

...

7. Heads of regional and republican headquarters of the partisan movement ... are with all haste to start the supply of materials for and preparations for the operation. Readiness for delivery of the blow is to be communicated by the TsShPD. Orientate yourselves for the conduct of the operation between 27–30 July of this year.

...

P. Ponomarenko

(Source: *RA T.20 (9)*, 1999, pp. 300–302)

By 15 August the TsShPD was communicating the following results from the initial phase of the 'War of the Rails':

DOCUMENT 133: *Communication of the Central Headquarters of the Partisan Movement on a number of results of the operation 'War of the Rails'. 15 August 1943*

The Central Headquarters of the Partisan Movement developed a plan for the disruption of the functioning of enemy railway lines through a massive, systematic destruction of rails.

...

On 3 August 1943 the operation began with a simultaneous blow by Leningrad, Kalinin, Smolensk and Belorussian partisans. Orlov partisans began the operation on 21 July 1943 as directed by the Central Headquarters of the Partisan Movement.

According to figures received up to 13 August 1943, the following rails were destroyed by partisan detachments:

Leningrad region	3,271
Kalinin region	7,224
Smolensk region	8,279
Orlov region	7,935
Belorussian SSR	75,227
Ukrainian SSR	7,000

On the sections of railway below:

Leningrad-Narva	22
Leningrad-Pskov	1,869
Leningrad-Novosokol'niki	476
Pskov-Veimarn	82
Pskov-Rezekne	822
Polotsk-Molodechno	5,834
Polotsk-Novosokol'niki	1,226
Novosokol'niki-Rezekne	6,869
Dugavpils-Vitebsk	2,073
Novosokol'niki-Orsha	793
Krulevshchizna-Lintupi	1,617
Minsk-Vilnius	1,686
Minsk-Smolensk	1,548
Orsha-Lepel'	2,128
Minsk-Gomel'	5,666
Mogilev-Timkovichi	7,179
Luninets-Gomel'	22,013
Luninets-Lida	3,581
Mogilev-Kirov	3,612
Orsha-Unecha	3,033
Orsha-Zhlobin	7,751
Gomel'-Briansk	5,106
Starushki-Bobruisk	8,210
Brest-Luninets	336
Briansk-Kirov	539
Kletnia-Zhukovka	525

Briansk-Roslavl'	121
Unecha-Mikhailovskii Farm	1,150
Briansk-Mikhailovskii Farm	5,648
Navlia-L'gov	421
On the railway lines of the Ukrainian SSR	7,000
Total destroyed	108,936

...

At the same time, in the process of conducting the operation, the following were destroyed:

Railway bridges	57
Bridges on unpaved roads	33
Water towers	8
Water-pressure towers	1
Steam locomotives	17
Wagons and trucks	288
Tank	17
Automobiles	149

In fighting during the conduct of the operation on the railway lines 540 German soldiers and police were killed.

Partisan losses: Killed – 22 persons, wounded – 87 persons.

(Source: *RA T.20 (9)*, 1999, pp. 304–306)

Whilst the above figures are certainly exaggerated, they do give some indication of the areas in which partisan attacks were most heavy. Certainly the rear areas behind Army Group Centre were worst hit as German troops withdrew in the face of the Soviet counter-attack after the German attack on the Kursk salient had been blunted. According to German sources, during the night of 2–3 August partisans behind Army Group Centre, that is in the Army Group Centre Rear Area and *Reichskomissariat* Weissruthenien, set 10,900 demolition charges and mines, 8,422 of which detonated, the remainder disarmed (of which 6,519 detonations were for the Army Group Centre Rear Area). For August the total was 15,977 detonations (12,717 for the Army Group Centre Rear Area) with an additional 4,528 removed by the Germans. According to Howell, the effect of these demolitions 'while never disastrous, was considerable', although a total of 2,951 supply and troop trains were successfully moved during the month in the area concerned.[55]

Across the front, as German fortunes waned at the front and partisan strength increased – the relationship between the two being strong – German and allied forces were only able to provide viable security for an increasingly limited number of railway lines. The onset of winter, in burdening a growing partisan movement with increasingly complex supply issues, had some impact on the frequency and intensity of partisan attacks. However, the tide of the war had clearly turned against Germany and this had an impact on Soviet incitement to join or assist the partisans, or face punishment later. The prospect of Soviet victory gave the partisans new recruits and helped, on the surface at least, ease the tension between hungry partisans and the civilian population on which they depended for most of their food, increasing partisan effectiveness.[56] The State Defence Committee certainly made it plain through partisan units, building on pre-war legislation, that the treasonous behaviour of one family member was enough to implicate the rest of a family, and conversely that the patriotic conduct of a family member, including participation in or at least support for the partisan movement, could exonerate them from the crimes of a close relative:

DOCUMENT 134: *Decree of the State Defence Committee 'On members of the families of traitors', No. GOKO-1926ss. 14 June 1942*

Top Secret

Adult members of the families of persons (military and civilian) sentenced by judicial organs or special tribunal of the NKVD USSR to capital punishment according to Article 58-1 'a' of the criminal code of the RSFSR and equivalent articles of the criminal codes of other union republics – i.e. for espionage in German interests or those of other countries fighting us; for going over to the enemy, betrayal or collaboration with the German occupiers; service in administrative or punitive organs of the German occupiers on territory seized by them; and for attempted treason against the Motherland and treasonous intentions [*izmennicheskie namereniia*] are subject to arrest and exile to isolated regions of the USSR for a term of five years.

The families of those sentenced in absentia to capital punishment ... for voluntary retreat with forces of occupation during the liberation of territory seized by the enemy are also subject to arrest and exile to isolated regions of the USSR for a period of five years.

...

Members of families of traitors to the Motherland are considered to be: Mother, father, husband, wife, sons, daughters and brothers and sisters if they lived together with the traitor against the Motherland or were being supported by him at the time the crime was committed or were being supported by him at the moment of his mobilization in to the army....

Families of traitors to the Motherland are not subject to arrest and exile if, after necessary investigation, it is established that a family member is amongst the ranks of Red Army personnel, partisans, individuals co-operating with the Red Army and partisans during the enemy occupation, and also those awarded orders and medals of the USSR.

(Source: I.N. Kuznetsov, 1997, pp. 69–70)

The order 'On the tasks of the Partisan Movement' also increased emphasis on serving the needs of the Red Army in other ways, in particular in providing intelligence. After a period during which the Red Army, NKVD and Party were all sponsoring partisan units in the German rear during 1941 and into 1942, during the second half of 1942 the organizational structure of the partisan movement under the Central Headquarters of the Partisan

Movement sought to foster links between the partisan movement and Red Army through the military soviets and operational groups at *front* and army level respectively – a process of integration very much along the lines of a model established in the Leningrad region during late 1941.[57] The potential value of partisan intelligence reaching the Red Army through the above organization is obvious but difficult to measure – partisans frequently identified regular and front-line-capable units resting, being redeployed or engaged in anti-partisan operations in the German rear. For instance, the loss of 27th Infantry Regiment to 12th Infantry Division, identified as being in the Kudever' region in December 1943, would have been a major blow to the strength of the division.[58] The effectiveness of this intelligence provision increased as more partisan units were equipped with radios, for instance, the timeliness of intelligence allowing better use of Soviet airpower, although German intelligence also gained a better appreciation of partisan activities at the same time.[59]

Better partisan communications also facilitated attempts to co-ordinate partisan sabotage activities with Red Army operations, a co-operation noticeably more effective by the time of the Soviet winter offensive of 1944 below Leningrad, compared to attempts at co-ordination during the Moscow counter-offensive of 1941–42.[60] Andrianov suggests that the first attempt to co-ordinate partisan attacks with Red Army operations was planned during November for 21–31 December 1941 for operations against German forces in and near Demiansk, although he suggests that the frequency and scale of such co-operation was limited until 1943 to activity barely of operational significance. In 1943, for instance during the summer 'War of the Rails', large-scale partisan activity behind more than one *front* and to a considerable distance behind German lines was of operational and even operational-strategic significance, being geared to the hampering of German movement in the face of the Soviet counter-offensive in the aftermath of the German Operation 'Citadel'.[61]

Whilst the broader impact of the partisan movement on the German economy is not the principal concern of this chapter, it is worth noting that given the extent to which the *Wehrmacht* was forced to 'live off the land' in the east, partisan disruption of the German collection of agricultural products and other resources (e.g. lumber) from the occupied territories of the east is of some significance. As indicated in Table 9.4 as early as 19 June 1942 WiIn Nord considered agricultural activity in all areas of the Army Group North Rear Area to have been at least partially disrupted, with agricultural activity having been considered impossible in a number of districts of the Kalinin region in the south of the area occupied by Army Group North in the border region with Belorussia. It is in this broader economic sense that the partisan movement probably had the most sustained influence on the German military effort, contributing, along with broader German administrative weakness on occupied territory, to the fact that German grain collection from the occupied territories was never as great as had been predicted.[62]

Limited German authority over the hinterland also limited the extent to

Table 9.4 WiIn Nord. Chefgruppe La. Pleskau, 19 June 1942. Situation Report Degree to which the cultivation [*Bewirtschaftung*] of particular districts in the Army Group Rear Area is hampered

Unhindered	Partially hampered	Severely hampered	Impossible {all indicated to be moving towards 'severely hampered'}
	Gdow – eastern sector	Jam	Osmino
	Seredka – eastern sector [arrow to 'severely hampered']	Strugy – western sector	Sebesh – currently
	Karamischewo	Novosselje	Idriza – currently
	Soschichino	Ljady	Pustoschka – currently
	Slawkowitschi	Pljussa	
	Noworschew	Kudewer	
	Opotschka [arrow to 'severely hampered']		
	Krasnoj [arrow to 'severely hampered']		
	Luga		
	Puskinskiy-Gori		

Source: TsGA SPb f.9789.o.1.d.3.l.107.

which German forces could mobilize the local population for labour service for the *Wehrmacht*, and indeed for labour service in the Reich, for which over one million people were mobilized by the *Wehrmacht* during 1942–43, as indicated in Table 9.5. Such unpopular mobilization certainly seems to have increased the number of potential recruits to partisan units; intensive mobilization often coincided with German withdrawal, hence with the increased prospect of SMERSH investigation into the conduct of Soviet citizens during the occupation, which led to a surge in partisan recruitment, as Table 9.2 suggests for the Leningrad region.

These new recruits could increasingly be incorporated into partisan units in relatively safe base areas. German security resources were focused on keeping key railway arteries open, very rapidly to the exclusion of other tasks. In doing so, German forces enjoyed short–medium-term success with limited resources in achieving their aim of keeping key supply arteries to the front open. In focusing on this key task, German forces were, however, despite sporadic large-scale anti-partisan operations such as 'Spring Clean', providing base areas for partisans in the hinterland where Soviet power could be rebuilt and from which increasingly large, well-equipped and organized partisan units could attack and often overwhelm the defences of the precious transport arteries.

Table 9.5 *Ostarbeiter* recruitment/conscription for Army Groups North, Centre and South for 1942 and 1943

	Time period	Ostarbeiter recruited/ conscripted	Approx. population as of March 1943 (millions)	Ostarbeiter as % of total population as of March 1943
Army Group North	1942	50,490		4
	1943	4,557	1.26	Insignificant
Army Group Centre	1942	114,706		2.3
	1943	91,225	c.5.0	1.8
Army Group South	1942	636,603		10.6
	1943	113,780	c.6.0	1.9
Total		1,011,361	12.26	8.3

Source: R.-D. Müller, *Die deutsche Wirtschaftspolitik in den besetzten sowjetischen Gebieten 1941–1943 – Der Abschlussbericht der Wirtschaftstabes Ost* ... (Boppard: Harald Boldt Verlag, 1991), pp. 519 and 549–550.

That the Soviet historiography of the partisan movement inflated the achievements of the partisans whilst at the same time downplaying the human cost of their activities is beyond doubt. However, in 'clinical' terms the Soviet partisan movement was, by Soviet standards, a cost-effective means of causing military and economic damage to the German war effort on the Eastern Front. Even if going as far as to assume that for every officially recognized partisan three or even five unofficial 'partisans' or civilians were killed, then by the standards of the slaughter at the front, a total of around 120,000–180,000 killed for Soviet territory (excluding the Ukraine) compares favourably, given damage done by the partisans to a range of Soviet front-line operations during the war. Soviet forces facing Army Group North alone (taken as the North-Western, Leningrad and Volkhov *Fronts*) suffered 476,450 irrecoverable losses (including 213,557 killed) during 1942 for little territorial gain and where total losses inflicted on Army Group North for 1942 were 259,950, including, however, losses caused by partisan activity.[63]

Guide to further reading

J. Armstrong (ed.), *Soviet Partisans in World War II* (Madison, WI: University of Wisconsin Press, 1964).

Karel C. Berkhoff, *Harvest of Despair – Life and Death in Ukraine under Nazi Rule* (Cambridge, MA: The Belknap Press of Harvard University Press, 2004).

H. Boog, J. Forster, J. Hoffmann, E. Klink, R.-D. Muller, G.R. Ueberschar and E. Osers (eds), *Germany and the Second World War. Volume IV. The Attack on the Soviet Union* (Oxford: Clarendon Press, 1998).

The Soviet Partisan Movement 219

A. Dallin, *German Rule in Russia 1941–1945 – A Study of Occupation Policies* (London: Macmillan, 1981).

A. Dallin, *Odessa, 1941–1944: A Case Study of Soviet Territory under Foreign Rule* (Iasi: Center for Romanian Studies, 1998).

L. Grenkevich, *The Soviet Partisan Movement 1941–1944* (London: Frank Cass, 1999).

Alexander Hill, *The War Behind the Eastern Front – The Soviet Partisan Movement in North-West Russia 1941–1944* (London: Frank Cass, 2005).

E.M. Howell, *The Soviet Partisan Movement 1941–1944*. Department of the Army Pamphlet 20-244 (August 1956), printed in D.S. Detwiler, *World War II German Military Studies*, Volume 18 (New York: Garland, 1979; Eastbourne: Naval and Military Press, 2006).

T. Mulligan, *The Politics of Illusion and Empire – German Occupation Policy in the Soviet Union 1942–1943* (New York: Praeger, 1988).

J. Noakes and G. Pridham, *Nazism 1919–1945 – A Documentary Reader. Volume 3: Foreign Policy, War and Racial Extermination* (Exeter: University of Exeter Press, 1988).

T. Schulte, *The German Army and Nazi Policy in Occupied Russia* (Oxford: Berg, 1989).

Ben Shepherd, *War in the Wild East – The German Army and Soviet Partisans* (Cambridge, MA: Harvard University Press, 2004).

Kenneth Slepyan, *Stalin's Guerrillas – Soviet Partisans in World War II* (Lawrence, KS: University of Kansas Press, 2006).

J. Steinberg, 'The Third Reich Reflected: German Civil Administration in the Occupied Soviet Union, 1941–4', *English Historical Review* (June 1995), pp. 620–651.

K. Ungváry, 'Hungarian Occupation forces in the Ukraine 1941–1942: The Historiographical Context', *JSMS*, Volume 20, Number 1 (January–March 2007), pp. 81–120.

10 The 'Ten "Stalinist" Crushing Blows' of 1944

In early November 1944 in a speech to Moscow Party and Soviet officials Stalin catalogued the victories that the Red Army had scored over the *Wehrmacht* and her allies since the beginning of the year:

> DOCUMENT 135: *Speech delivered by Stalin on the eve of the 27th anniversary of the October Revolution, 6 November 1944*
>
> The decisive successes achieved by the Red Army during the past year and the expulsion of the Germans from the boundaries of our Soviet territory were brought about by a series of crushing blows inflicted by our troops upon the German troops, begun as far back as last January and subsequently developed throughout the course of the year under review.
>
> The first blow was delivered by our troops near Leningrad and Novgorod last January, when the Red Army demolished the Germans' permanent defences and pushed the Germans into the Baltic regions. The result of this blow was the liberation of the Leningrad Region.
>
> The second blow was delivered on the River Bug last February and March, when the Red Army routed the German troops and pushed them beyond the Dnestr. As a result of this blow, the Ukraine on the right bank of the Dnepr was liberated from the German fascist invaders.
>
> The third blow was delivered in the region of the Crimea last April and May, when the German troops were thrown into the Black Sea. As a result of this blow the Crimea and Odessa were liberated from German oppression.
>
> The fourth blow was delivered in the region of Karelia last June, when the Red Army defeated the Finnish troops, liberated Viborg and Petrozavodsk and pushed the Finns into the interior of Finland. The result of this blow was the liberation of the greater part of the Karelo-Finnish Soviet Republic.
>
> The fifth blow was inflicted on the Germans last June and July, when the Red Army utterly routed the German troops at Vitebsk, Bobruisk and Moghilev, and culminated in the surrounding of thirty German divisions near Minsk. As a result of this blow our troops: a) completely liberated the Belorussian Soviet Republic; b) reached the Vistula and liberated a considerable part of the territory of our ally, Poland; c) reached the Niemen and liberated the greater part of the Lithuanian Soviet Republic, and d) forced the Niemen and reached the frontiers of Germany.
>
> The sixth blow was delivered in the region of Western Ukraine last July and August, when the Red Army defeated the German troops at L'vov and hurled them beyond the San

and the Vistula. As a result of this blow: a) Western Ukraine was liberated, and b) our troops forced the Vistula and formed a powerful bridgehead on the other side, west of Sandomierz.

The seventh blow was delivered last August in the region of Kishinev-Iassi, when our troops utterly routed the German and Rumanian troops, and culminated in the surrounding of twenty-two German divisions near Kishinev, not counting the Rumanian divisions. As a result of this blow: a) the Moldavian Soviet Republic was liberated; b) Rumania, Germany's ally, was put out of action and she declared war on Germany and Hungary; c) Germany's ally, Bulgaria, was put out of action and she too declared war on Germany; d) the road was opened for our troops into Hungary, Germany's last ally in Europe, and e) it became possible to extend a helping hand to our ally, Yugoslavia, against the German invaders.

The eighth blow was delivered in the Baltic regions last September and October, when the Red Army defeated the German troops at Tallinn and Riga and expelled them from the Baltic regions. As a result of this blow: a) the Estonian Soviet Republic was liberated; b) the greater part of the Latvian Soviet Republic was liberated; c) Germany's ally, Finland, was put out of action and she declared war on Germany, and d) over thirty German divisions were cut off from Prussia and held between pincers in the area between Tukums and Libau, where our troops are driving the last nail into their coffin.

Last October our troops launched the ninth blow between the Tisa and the Danube, in the region of Hungary, with the object of putting Hungary out of the war and of turning her against Germany. As a result of this blow, which has not yet been completed: a) our troops rendered direct assistance to our ally, Yugoslavia, in expelling the Germans and liberating Belgrade, and b) our troops obtained the opportunity of crossing the Carpathians and of extending a helping hand to our ally, the Czechoslovakian Republic, part of whose territory has already been liberated from the German invaders.

Finally, at the end of last October, a blow was dealt the German troops in North Finland, when the German troops were kicked out of the region of Pechenga and our troops, pursuing the Germans, entered the territory of our ally, Norway.

(Source: Adapted from J.V. Stalin, 1947, pp. 156–160 and Mawdsley, 2005, p. 292).

The first blow mentioned by Stalin, later to become a 'Stalinist' blow in Soviet propaganda, was the 'Leningrad–Novgorod Strategic Offensive' Operation, which began on 14 January and lasted until 1 March 1944. After the siege of Leningrad had been partially lifted in January 1943 (see Chapter 7), during the remainder of 1943 the front before Army Group North had been relatively quiet, although high-intensity, if local, operations near the railway junction of Mga to the south of Lake Ladoga during the summer had kept German troops pinned down at high cost for the attacking Red Army forces, which lost 21,000 men for little gain. In early October, however, forces of the Kalinin *Front* had managed to seize the key railway junction of Nevel', following the seizure of Velikie Luki in January 1943, both on the boundary between Army Groups North and Centre. This penetration threatened the rear of Army Group North, raising the possibility that the Army Group might be cut off by further penetrations on this axis and prompting talk of a withdrawal to the Panther Line (*Ostwall*) positions to the east, running in part along Lake Peipus. These withdrawals had not, however, been undertaken by January 1944, when the Soviet offensive below Leningrad started.[1]

Prior to the start of the offensive, the Soviet 2nd Shock Army had been covertly moved into the Oranienbaum pocket to the east of Leningrad, and it was 2nd Shock that started the offensive as it broke out of the pocket and struck in a south-easterly direction. The next day the Leningrad *Front* joined the offensive, as did forces of the Volkhov *Front* near Novgorod.

Whilst German defences below Leningrad were substantial – German forces had literally had years to consolidate them on many sectors of the front – and the offensive was launched in winter, the Soviet offensive in the region also lacked the drive that was typically exhibited elsewhere. This situation is often attributed in the literature, and quite reasonably so, to the fact that the forces and officers near Leningrad had not accrued the experience of deep penetration operations with increasingly effective combined arms tactics, as had been learnt to the south at considerable cost in human life. Consequently, whilst German forces lost a considerable amount of heavy equipment immediately below Leningrad, the bulk of 18th Army was able to withdraw in good time, including from exposed positions to the south-east of Leningrad in and around Mga – one of the increasingly rare occasions that Hitler sanctioned withdrawal to the west. The after-action report by the commander of the Volkhov *Front* (Document 136) was, therefore, wildly optimistic in claiming the routing [*razgrom*] of the German 18th Army, even if the tally for trophy equipment captured was more realistic and more difficult for commanders to fudge.

DOCUMENT 136: Report of the commander of the Volkhov Front *to the Supreme High Commander on the results of the Novgorod-Luga, Tosno and Liuban'-Chudovo operations of the Volkhov* Front *from 14 January to 12 February 1944, 13 February 1944*

1. Forces of the Volkhov *Front*, together with the Leningrad *Front*, routed [*razgromili*] the enemy's 18th Army and at the current time are mopping up its remnants, at the same time engaged in fighting with 16th Army.

    Completely destroyed were: 28th Light; 1st and 2nd Luftwaffe Field Divisions, the 'SS' Police Division, infantry divisions: 401st, 101st, 95th, 625th, 661st along with 121st Construction and 657th, 236th and 232nd Security Divisions; 657th, 656th and 676th Sapper Battalions and 651st Special Punishment Battalion. The enemy is attempting to reconstitute 28th Light Division from the remnants of other divisions. Routed: 121st, 21st and 8th Light and 15th Latvian Infantry Divisions. The Spanish Legion, Cavalry Regiment 'Nord' and 639th Field-Training Regiment. 212th, 24th, 290th and 13th Luftwaffe Field Divisions suffered heavy losses.

2. During the period from 14 January to 12 February 1944 (28 days of operation) our forces overcame the defensive belt of the enemy in difficult-to-traverse forested and marshy areas to a depth of 140 km, and occupied 779 population centres and the major towns of the Leningrad region: Novgorod, Luga, Mga,

Tosno, Chudovo, Liuban' and the district centres of Oredezh and Batetskaia. 750 km of railway lines were liberated.
3. Trophies seized: Various artillery pieces – 521, ... various machine guns – 1,760, mortars – 243, tanks and armoured cars – 31, rifles and SMGs – 7,465, ... 5 million rifle cartridges, 121,000 anti-tank and anti-personnel mines, ... 538 motor vehicles and tractors, 5 steam locomotives.... In the fighting 82,000 enemy soldiers and officers were killed, 3,200 were taken prisoner, 336 horses seized.
4. Destroyed in the fighting: Various artillery pieces – 562, various machine guns – 2,042, mortars – 335, tanks and armoured cars – 128, rifles and SMGs – 6,440, motor vehicles and tractors – 1,178, ... aircraft – 35.

...

Commander of the forces of the Volkhov *Front*
General of the Army K. Meretskov

(Source: N.L. Volkovskii (ed.), 2004, pp. 620–621)

Whilst many of the units mentioned in Document 136 did not exist as units of the number and type specified, and Soviet assessment of German casualties is perhaps based on extrapolation from the misleading picture of German units 'routed', destroyed or suffering heavy losses, nonetheless 18th Army did suffer heavily in the fighting. According to German sources, from 10 January to March 1944, in opposing the offensive Army Group North incurred losses of 17,772 killed and 69,995 wounded, with 11,154 missing.[2] In February, the Volkhov *Front* was dissolved after Leningrad had finally been declared free on 26 February (see Chapter 7), with the pursuit of German forces towards the Panther Line after the fall of Luga on 12 February being undertaken by forces of the Leningrad *Front* in the north and then with forces of 2nd Baltic *Front* in the south of the region. By the 1 March Soviet forces had reached the outskirts of Pskov and Ostrov to the south of Lake Peipus, but in heavy fighting during March and the first half of April were unable to break through German positions near Pskov, with a similar stalemate setting in to the north of the lake near Narva.[3]

The second blow, and in some ways first in terms of the start date for operations, had been the 'Dnepr–Carpathian Strategic Offensive' Operation actually started before the end of 1943, on 24 December, when forces of the 1st Ukrainian *Front* started the 'Zhitomir-Berdichevskaia' Operation with the aim of destroying the German 4th Panzer Army and providing for the security of the recently recaptured Kiev region and the development of future operations through an advance to the Bug River. The 'Dnepr–Carpathian Strategic Offensive' Operation did not, of course, consist merely of this operation, but in fact a series of *front*-level operations including the subsequent 'Kirovograd', 'Korsun'-Shevchenkovskii', 'Rovno-Lutsk' and 'Nikopol'sk-Krivoi Rog' Operations, the series of operations that lasted until 17 April 1944 and saw the Red Army enter 'foreign', i.e. non-Soviet territory as of 1940.

The 'Korsun'-Shevchenkovskii' Operation is probably the most noted of the operations making up the 'Dnepr–Carpathian Strategic Offensive' Operation in both Western and Soviet literature, given the encirclement of a sizeable German force. As with other operations to a greater or lesser degree, it started with attempts to deceive the enemy as to Soviet intentions – all such activities being covered by the Russian term *maskirovka*. A report on operational 'deception' activities by the 2nd Ukrainian *Front*, produced after the encirclement, gives some idea of the sort of measures being taken by Soviet forces:

DOCUMENT 137: *Report on measures for the operational* maskirovka *of forces of the 2nd Ukrainian* Front *in the 'Korsun'-Shevchenkovskii Offensive' Operation*

1. General situation and plan

After the capture of Kirovograd and the rout of encircled German forces in the Lelekovka region (north-west of Kirovograd) the 5th Guards Tank Army ... moved its formations to the Gruzkoe district (west of Kirovograd).

In the period of preparation for offensive operations against Lebedin and Shpola in order to encircle German forces in the area west of Smela along with forces of the 1st Ukrainian *Front* the 5th Guards Tank Army concentrated in the district of Kamenka, Verbovka, Tomashevka. Artillery support was also concentrated in the same area.

In order to hide preparations for the operation, the relocation of the tank army and in order to mislead the enemy the following deception plan was adopted:

... Tanks and artillery were redeployed to new areas in the main at night and in fog, and were concentrated in forested areas or population centres.

On the front line of 5th Guards Tank Army measures were taken to deceive the enemy into believing that tanks and artillery were concentrated elsewhere.

All of these measures confused the enemy on the principal axis of our attack and hid the redeployment of 5th Guards Tank Army and artillery support from the Gruzkoe district.

2. The development of deception activities

...

The headquarters of engineers decided upon decoy concentration areas and provided for the creation of dummy tanks and artillery pieces, dummy soldiers, false supply dumps and signs of tank and artillery.

The headquarters of armoured forces provided each deception area with two tanks for the imitation of day-to-day activity and the creation of noise and tracks.

The head of communications troops provided for imitation of the work of headquarters' radio units of tank units and formations from tank army down to battalion level.

The head of artillery provided for decoy artillery positions with roaming artillery pieces.

(Source: *SBD 27*, pp. 95–96)

As a result of the operation, at the end of January two German corps had been encircled, a total of six divisions, including one SS, near the town of Korsun'. Hitler, predictably, ordered forces there not to attempt to break out and fantasized that the Korsun' pocket might become a 'Fortress on the Dnepr'. German attempts to punch through to the pocket with 3rd Panzer Corps failed – such a plan had similarly failed in more favourable material circumstances at Stalingrad. Nonetheless, a significant proportion of the personnel from the pocket, even if without the bulk of their equipment, were able to break out across steppe to German lines. German sources claim 36,262 troops escaped from the pocket during the principal breakout on 16–17 February, with more than 4,000 wounded having been flown out before 11 February. The Soviets would eventually claim 18,000 prisoners.[4] Zhukov, the representative of the *Stavka* responsible for the co-ordination of the activities of the two *fronts* involved, was chided by Stalin for the initial failure to seal the pocket.

DOCUMENT 138: *Directive of the Headquarters of the Supreme High Commander Number 220021 to the* Stavka *representative on the destruction of the Korsun' grouping of enemy forces, 12 February 1944, 16:45*

The breakout of enemy forces of the Korsun' grouping from the Steblev salient in the Shenderovka direction took place because:

Firstly, despite my personal instructions, you did not have a thought out general plan for the joint destruction of the Korsun' grouping of the Germans by the 1st and 2nd Ukrainian *Fronts*;

Secondly, the weak 27th Army was not reinforced in good time;

Thirdly, decisive measures were not taken for the destruction of the Steblev enemy salient, from which one could most likely have expected an enemy breakout attempt.

I ought to point out to you, that I placed responsibility on you for the task of co-ordinating the activities of the 1st and 2nd Ukrainian *Fronts*, and it is obvious from your report today that despite the critical circumstances, you are insufficiently well informed on the situation: you are unaware of the enemy occupation of Zhilek and Novo-Buda; you are unaware of Konev's decision on the use of Rotmistrov's 5th Guards Tank Corps for the destruction of the enemy breaking through to Shenderovka.

Forces and resources of the left flank of the 1st Ukrainian *Front* and the left wing of the 2nd Ukrainian *Front* are sufficient to liquidate the enemy penetration and the destruction of the Korsun' grouping.

I demand of you that you focus on the carrying out of this task.
I. Stalin
A. Antonov

(Source: *RA T.16 (5–4)*, 1999, pp. 41–42)

Command of all forces was given to Konev of the 2nd Ukrainian *Front*,[5] and by 17th February, after the principal German breakout from the pocket, he would report:

> DOCUMENT 139: *After battle report of the Commander of forces of the 2nd Ukrainian Front of 17 February 1944 to the Supreme High Commander on the conclusion and results of the destruction* {razgrom} *of the Korsun'-Shevchenkovskii grouping of enemy forces*
>
> I report:
>
> 1. In carrying out your order [of 12 February], on 17 February 1944 forces of the *front* fully defeated [*razgromili*], destroyed and in part imprisoned the encircled enemy grouping, consisting of nine infantry and one Panzer division and a Panzergrenadier brigade.
> 2. All enemy attacks from outside the encirclement to break through to it were successfully repulsed by our forces with the enemy suffering heavy losses in equipment and personnel.
> 3. With the remnants of his strength the enemy, with a force of 8–10 thousand men, from 5–7 artillery batteries and 12–15 tanks from the encircled force started to break out of the encirclement between three and six o'clock on 17 February on the defensive sector of 180th Rifle Division of 27th Army ..., situated to the west and south-west....
> 4. Forces of the *front*: 52nd, 4th Guards and 27th Army, elements of 5th Guards Tank Army and 5th Guards Cavalry Corps smashed the advance. Consequently the enemy, penetrating into the depths of our positions, was broken up in to separate groups, destroyed and captured....
>
> The enemy left all of his heavy equipment....
> Konev...
>
> (Source: Document 5, in 'Korsun'-Shevchenkvskaia operatsiia v dokumentakh (24 ianvaria-17 fevralia 1944 g.)', *Vizh*, Number 2 (1984), p. 44)

Although the fighting around the Korsun' pocket receives much attention in the popular Western literature on the exploits of the *Wehrmacht* on the Eastern Front, the next of the 'Stalinist blows' of 1944 would see far more serious German and Axis losses.

The third blow would see the final liberation of the Crimea by forces of the Independent Maritime Army that had been landed at Kerch' the previous year (see Chapter 6), 4th Ukrainian *Front*, the Black Sea Fleet and Azov Flotilla. German and Rumanian forces holding the peninsula had been cut off from the main body of Axis forces by the Soviet advance in the south of the Ukraine in November 1943, and the defences of the Perekop Isthmus held initial Soviet attempts to retake the territory off the march. By the spring of 1944, up to 165,000 German and 65,000 Rumanian troops holding the Crimea served little strategic purpose – the principal justification for leaving them there in late 1943 – something of a smokescreen for Hitler's obsession for holding territory per se was the claim that the Crimea would have provided a base for Soviet bombing of the crucial Rumanian oilfields. By the spring of 1944, these could conveniently be bombed from

Soviet airfields with 4th Ukrainian *Front* further west, and – indeed, more effectively given the weakness of Soviet strategic bombing – by US bombers based in Italy.

A planned offensive to liberate the Crimea finally began on 8 April and lasted until 12 May 1944. After two days, defences on the Perekop Isthmus had been breached, with Sevastopol' finally falling after a battle lasting less than a week. Belatedly Hitler authorized an evacuation of troops, after some had been pulled out anyway, with up to 130,000 being evacuated by sea and a further 21,000 by air – an embarrassment for the Soviet side given the superiority of the Black Sea Fleet, now with superior air cover compared to 1941, over the paltry German and Rumanian naval forces in the region. Nonetheless, 17th Army defending the Crimea had incurred losses of around 53,500 men killed, missing or captured from 8 April to 13 May 1944, with a further 22,000 Rumanian losses.[6] Soviet forces had lost considerably fewer men as irrecoverable losses (see Table 10.4 below) in what had ended up being an unusually economical operation by Soviet standards.

As was the case in the North Caucasus, in the Crimea in May 1944 the returning Soviet security services (now the NKVD and NKGB) set about punishing the indigenous population en masse for collaboration with the Germans. A GKO decree of 11 May 1944 required that all Tatars be deported from the Crimea to the Uzbek SSR.[7] By 20 May, after a two-day operation, the head of the NKVD, Beria, received the following:

DOCUMENT 140: *Telegram from the Deputy People's Commissar NKGB B.Z. Kobulov and Deputy People's Commissar NKVD I.A. Serov to the People's Commissar NKVD L.P. Beria on the conclusion of the operation for the deportation of the Crimean Tatars, 20 May 1944*

With this telegram I am reporting, that ... the operation for the deportation of the Crimean Tatars finished today, 18 May, at 16:00. A total of 180,014 persons were deported, loaded into 67 trains, of which 63 trains have already been dispatched to their final destinations, with the remaining four to be similarly dispatched today.

In addition, the District Military Commissariats of the Crimea have mobilized six thousands Tatars of conscription age....

Of the 8,000 special contingent sent on your instructions for use by the Moscow-Coal Trust 5,000 are Tatars. Hence, 191,044 persons of Tatar nationality have been deported from the Crimean ASSR.

During the deportation 1,137 persons from amongst anti-Soviet elements were arrested, and during the period of the operation 5,989.

During the deportation of the Tatars the following weapons were seized: mortars – 10, machine-guns – 173, SMGs – 192, rifles – 2,650, munitions [*boepripasi*] – 45,603.

In total during the period of the operation the following were seized: mortars – 49, machine-guns – 622, SMGs – 724, rifles – 9,888, and munitions – 327,887 items....
Simferopol. Kobulov, Serov

(Source: N.L. Pobol' and P.M. Polian, 2005, pp. 501–502)

The fourth blow would lead to Finland withdrawing from the war, the Finns having put out tentative peace feelers in February 1944, but were under heavy German pressure to remain in the war. In the summer of 1941 Finnish troops had advanced to the 1940 Finnish border, stopped and dug in. The Soviet 'Viborg–Petrozavodsk Offensive' Operation, which took place from 10 June to 9 August 1944, caught the Finns off guard. This was certainly not going to be a repeat of the Soviet military debacle of the winter of 1939–40, partly because it was not winter, but also because the Red Army was now a very different creature. Within only a fortnight Soviet troops north of Leningrad had advanced as far as Viborg and what was the border in June 1941, and a second phase of Soviet operations saw Soviet troops to the east advance from the River Svir' to the Karelian capital, Petrozavodsk. Whilst the success of Soviet operations in Karelia was certainly a factor in the Finns seeking, with far more resolve than in February, to extricate themselves from the war, the success of Soviet troops against forces of Army Group North to the south during July was also important in physically isolating the Finns from their German allies. In late August the decision was taken to leave the war; in early September the breaking off of diplomatic relations with Germany was followed by an armistice in which the Soviet Union added the Petsamo region (still in German hands), reparations and a base outside Helsinki to the spoils of 1940, but without Finland being subject to full Soviet occupation.[8]

The fifth blow is arguably individually the most significant of the 'Stalinist blows' of 1944, seeing the effective destruction of Army Group Centre as a fighting force worthy of the Army Group designation.

Between 7 August and 2 October 1943 Soviet forces had engaged in heavy fighting with Army Group Centre (Operation 'Suvorov') that saw the final recapture of Smolensk on 25 September and the rail junction of Nevel' further north on the boundary between the German Army Groups North and South, but at the heavy cost of 107,645 irrecoverable losses, which at this stage of the war with Soviet forces advancing meant mostly killed rather than POWs.[9] Subsequently, the focus of Soviet attentions had been to the north and south, a trend that German intelligence saw as likely to continue during May and June 1944. Army Group Centre remained relatively weak, particularly in armour despite the inevitable pleas from commanders lower in the chain of command, who were at least aware that something was afoot from the forward deployment of infantry and artillery before their positions, even if they were unaware of the preparations taking place in the Soviet rear. Such junior concerns could be dismissed as predictable bleating from those who were not concerned with the broader picture, particularly given that the German command not only had Soviet operations to the north and south on the Eastern Front to worry about, but also Allied operations in Italy and, after 6th June 1944, what in Soviet terms constituted a genuine 'Second Front' in France. Glantz and House note that when a battalion commander of the German 12th Infantry Division of Army Group Centre described the threat before his division to General Martinek of 39th Panzer Corps whilst he was inspecting the unit, the latter cited the proverb 'Whom God would destroy, he first strikes blind'; in fact, it would take days for the German command to fully appreciate the significance of Soviet operations against the Army Group. Operation 'Bagration' began in earnest on 23 June 1944, at which point in the war the front-line situation in the East was as illustrated in Figure 10.1.[10]

In the summer of 1944, Soviet forces were able to concentrate tremendous material resources against German forces, assisted by increasingly sophisticated *maskirovka*, counter-intelligence against German stay-behind agents and the fact that German aerial reconnaissance was increasingly hampered by Soviet air superiority where it mattered.

The Red Army was able, in considerable secrecy, to concentrate overwhelming force on the key axes. As an illustration of Soviet ability to concentrate force on the key axes of attack, Table 10.1 provides the correlation of forces on the axis of attack of 11th Guards Army of 3rd Belorussian *Front* to the north of Minsk. It is important to note that the correlation for tanks

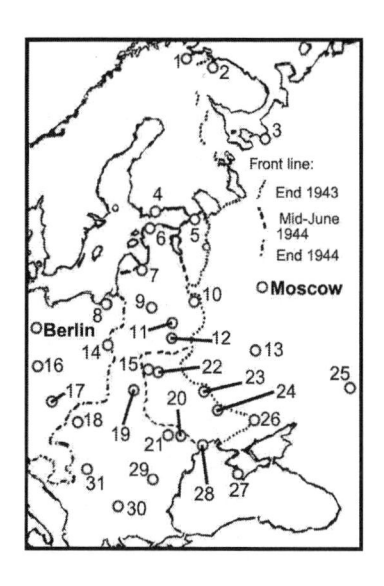

Figure 10.1 Changes in the front line from late 1943 to the end of 1944.
Key:

1. Kirkenes
2. Murmansk
3. Arkhangel'sk
4. Helsinki
5. Leningrad
6. Tallin
7. Riga
8. Königsberg
9. Vilnius
10. Vitebsk
11. Minsk
12. Bobruisk
13. Kursk
14. Warsaw
15. Lutsk
16. Prague
17. Vienna
18. Budapest
19. L'vov
20. Kishinev
21. Iassi
22. Rovno
23. Korsun'-Shevchenkovskii
24. Kirovgrad
25. Stalingrad
26. Zaporozh'e
27. Sevastopol'
28. Odessa
29. Bucharest
30. Sofia
31. Belgrade

Table 10.1 Correlation of forces on the principal axis of attack (Orsha axis) of 11th Guards Army (15 km width) of 3rd Belorussian *Front* on 23 June 1944

Forces and weapons	Enemy		Soviet forces		Superiority over enemy
	Density per 1 km frontage	Overall	Density per 1 km of frontage	Overall	
Divisions	10 km per division	2 divisions + 1 regiment + 2 battalions	1.4 km per division	11	–
Combat troops	1,888	28,320	7,915	118,729	4.2:1
MMGs/HMGs	120	1,800	274	4,107	2.3:1
Mortars	14.5	218	77.4	1,161	5.3:1
AT guns	12	181	32	482	2.7:1
Artillery (76 mm and above)	14.6	220	80	1,193	5.4:1
RS	3.6	54	24	360	6.6:1
Tanks and SPs	4.7	70	24.7	371	5.3:1

Source: David M. Glantz and Harold S. Orenstein (trans. and eds.), *Belorussia 1944: The Soviet General Staff Study* (London/Portland, OR: Frank Cass, 2001), p. 48.

and self-propelled guns does not include those forces allocated for the development of the penetration of German defences. The total strengths for Army Group Centre and the forces of the 1st–3rd Belorussian and 1st Baltic *Fronts* facing them during June before the commencement of the Soviet offensive are provided in Table 10.2.

With the meagre resources, particularly armour, available to Army Group Centre (where the so-called 3rd Panzer Army was reliant for mobility on 60,000 horses!), German forces could not hope to mount any sort of mobile defence between the fortified towns [*feste Plätze*] that Hitler had ordered be held rather than allow a withdrawal westwards. As the offensive got underway, Soviet mobile forces penetrated deep into the German defences, bypassing centres of resistance for later reduction and then pressing on in pursuit of those German troops that had escaped encirclement to the west, well beyond the sort of distances it was expected Soviet troops would be able to pursue them without some sort of halt for consolidation. Minsk, capital of the Belorussian SSR, fell on 3 July, leaving a huge German pocket, the bulk of 4th Army, to the east. Soviet reinforcement during the operation took forces committed to over two million, as shown in Table 10.4 below.[11]

Between 22 June and 10 July, German forces of Army Group Centre lost in the region of 264,444 men according to statistics compiled during 1944, of whom 6,622 were counted as killed, 22,165 wounded and 235,657 missing – mainly killed and POWs. The German 4th Army suffered most heavily, with 5,315 recorded as killed, 16,870 wounded and 108,485 missing. A total of at least 28 German divisions had ceased to exist as effective fighting units; Soviet sources claimed 25 German divisions 'routed' [*razgromleno*] or completely destroyed during June and 28 during July. Not that Soviet losses were light – as Table 10.4 below shows, during an operation

Table 10.2 Strengths of Army Group Centre and the forces of the 1st–3rd Belorussian and 1st Baltic *Fronts* facing them during June 1944

	Soviet 1st Baltic, 2nd and 3rd Belorussian and 1st Belorussian (left wing)	German 'White Russian Balcony' (4th and 9th Armies and 3rd Panzer Army)
Personnel	1,254,300 (22.06.1944)	336,573 (01.06.1944)
Artillery pieces	4,230 45–57 mm AT, 10,563 76 mm+ field artillery, 11,514 82–120 mm mortars, 2,306 RS launchers, 2,303 AA	2,589
Tanks	2,715	118
Self-propelled guns	1,355 (SAU)	377 (*Sturmgeshütze*)
Aircraft	5,327	602

Sources: *DDRudZW*8, p. 532 and 'Belorusskaia operatsiia v tsifrakh', *Vizh*, Number 6 (1964), p. 77.

Table 10.3 Number and origin of vehicles in the Red Army vehicle park 1941–45 (thousands)

Vehicle	22 June 1941	1 January 1942	1 January 1943	1 January 1944	1 January 1945	1 May 1945
Domestic	272.6	317.1	378.8	387.0	395.2	385.7
Percentage of total park	100.0	99.6	99.7	77.9	63.6	58.1
Imported	–	Negligible	22.0	94.1	191.3	218.1
Percentage of total park	–	Negligible	5.4	19.0	30.4	32.8
Captured	–	1.4	3.7	14.9	34.7	60.6
Percentage of total park	–	0.4	0.9	3.9	6.0	9.1
Total	272.6	318.5	404.5	496.0	621.2	664.4
Of which replacement of losses during previous period	–	159.0	66.2	67.0	32.6	27.0
Soviet production during previous period:						
Lorries	–	59.3*	32.4	46.7	55.2	–
Cars	–	5.5	2.6	2.6	5.4	–
Allied deliveries during previous period	–	0.4	32.5	95.1	139.6	–

Sources: Vorsin, 'Motor Vehicle Transport Deliveries through "Lend-Lease"', pp. 164 and 169; Krivosheev, *Soviet Casualties and Combat Losses*, p. 257; and Harrison, *Accounting for War*, p. 197.

Note
*Annual production for 1941 (see Table 8.7) divided by two.

Table 10.4 Soviet strategic offensive operations and losses during 1944

Strategic offensive operation	Principal forces involved	Numerical strength	Max. distance advanced/time frame	Irrecoverable losses	Total losses (inc. sick and wounded)
'Dnepr–Carpathian'	1st, 2nd, 3 rd, 4th Ukrainian *Fronts* (+15.03–05.04 2nd Belorussian *Front*)	2,406,100	450 km/116 days	270,198	1,109,528
'Leningrad–Novgorod'	Leningrad and Volkhov *Fronts*, Baltic Fleet (+ 1st Shock Army, 2nd Baltic *Front* 14.01–10.02, and 2nd Baltic *Front* 10.02–01.03)	822,100	280 km/48 days	76,686	313,953
'Crimean'	4th Ukrainian *Front*, Independent Maritime Army, 4th Air Army, Black Sea Fleet, Azov Flotilla	462,400	260 km/35 days	17,754	84,819
'Viborg–Petrozavodsk'	Karelian and Leningrad *Fronts*, Baltic Fleet and Ladoga and Onega Flotillas	451,000	250 km/61 days	23,674	96,375
'Belorussian'	1st, 2nd, 3rd Belorussian and 1st Baltic *Fronts*, Dnepr Flotilla	2,331,700	600 km/68 days	178,507	765,815
'L'vov–Sandomierz'	1st Ukrainian *Front*	1,002,200	350 km/48 days	65,100	289,296

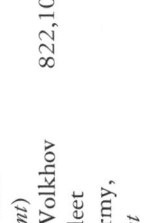

Table 10.4 continued

Strategic offensive operation	Principal forces involved	Numerical strength	Max. distance advanced/time frame	Irrecoverable losses	Total losses (inc. sick and wounded)
'Iassi–Kishinev'	2nd, 3rd Ukrainian *Fronts*, Black Sea Fleet, Danube Flotilla	1,314,200	320 km/10 days	13,197	67,130
'Baltic'	Leningrad *Front*, 1st, 2nd, 3rd Baltic *Fronts* (14.09–20.10.44), 39th Army, 3rd Belorussian *Front* (01.10–31.10.44) and Baltic Fleet	1,546,400	300 km/72 days	61,468	280,090
'East Carpathian', 'Belgrade' and 'Budapest (to 13.02.45) Strategic Offensive' Operations	1st and 4th Ukrainian *Fronts* and 1st Czechoslovak Army Corps	378,000	110 km/51 days	28,473	131,910
	2nd and 3rd Ukrainian *Fronts*, Danube Flotilla	300,000	200 km/23 days	4,350	18,838
	2nd and 3rd Ukrainian *Fronts*, Danube Flotilla	719,500	400 km/108 days	80,026	320,082
'Petsamo–Kirkenes'	Karelian *Front* and Northern Fleet	133,500	150 km/23 days	6,084	21,233
Totals				825,517	3,499,069

Source: Krivosheev, *Soviet Casualties and Combat Losses*, pp. 140–152.

extending officially until the end of August Soviet forces lost 178,507 personnel as irrecoverable losses, losing a staggering 2,957 tanks and self-propelled guns during the operation.[12]

In the end it was logistical problems as much as German resistance that halted the Soviet advance – hardly surprising with supply lines extending as much as 400 km from principal supply bases to forward units. As the Soviet General Staff Study on the operation comments with regard to the Soviet 43rd Army:

DOCUMENT 141: *Extract from the Soviet General Staff study on the 'Belorussian Strategic Offensive' Operation ('Bagration') on supply issues*

With the lines of communication so stretched out, shortcomings in motor vehicle transport were sharply felt.

To provide the rapidly advancing forces with all necessities, decisive measures were undertaken to mobilize motor vehicle and cart transport.... For example, the 43rd Army was forced to resort to transporting divisional artillery by horse, and having freed-up motor vehicles to transport cargoes, to create motor vehicle supply groups from divisional motor transport, mobilize local cart transport, organize a cart battalion with 1,000 carts, and exploit captured motor vehicles more extensively.

Considerable difficulties also arose during the operation in connection with providing forces and rear area services with POL (petroleum, oil and lubricants) products. Fuel reserves continuously declined, and by 14 July the 43rd Army has only a total of 0.5 petrol refuellings and 0.2 motor oil replenishments. This led to interruptions in motor-vehicle transport and in the resupply of armies with ammunition.

(Source: D.M. Glantz and H.S. Orenstein (eds. and trans.), *Belorussia 1944*, 2001, p. 208).

Nonetheless, in one fell swoop Belorrussia had been all but liberated and the 'Lublin–Brest' Operation in July and early August saw the Red Army advance deep into Polish territory, with the town of Lublin falling to Soviet forces on 24 July 1944 and a further advance taking the Red Army to the gates of Warsaw, seizing bridgeheads to the north and south of the city over the Vistula. Soviet lead units approached the fortified suburb of Praga, part of the city of Warsaw but on the eastern bank of the Vistula where the remainder was on the western side, on 31 July 1944; the following day saw the start of the Warsaw Uprising by the Polish Home Army tied to the government in exile in London rather than the Soviet-sponsored Polish Committee that had taken up seat in Lublin after its capture by the Red Army. Soviet assistance to the uprising was limited – Soviet forces did not punch through to the insurgents in any strength, and only started regular airdrops of supplies and munitions in mid-September. A single battalion of Soviet-sponsored Polish troops did make it across the Vistula to aid the uprising, according to Document 142:

> DOCUMENT 142: *From a report of member of the Military Soviet of the 1st Belorussian Front, General-Lieutenant K.F. Telegin to the Main Political Directorate of the Red Army on the situation in Warsaw and assistance to the insurgents (by direct transmission), 16 September 1944, 14:00–15:00*
>
> This is General-Lieutenant Shikin.
> Greetings Comrade Telegin!
> I would like to report what you know about the situation in Warsaw as it stands today.
> Greetings! This is Telegin.
> Reporting on the situation in Warsaw.
> 1. Reconnaissance troops of the 1st Polish Army managed this evening to break through to the western bank of the Vistula in the region of the southern bridge. A Colonel Radoslav was brought to our side of the river by the scouts along with two rank-and-file insurgents.
> Radoslav is the leader of a group of insurgents about 150-strong, continuing to hold out in that area, he himself and his people belonging to the Security Corps, loyal to the Lublin government....
> From the start of our offensive operations the Germans increased their stranglehold on the district, bombing and shelling daily and using tanks against the insurgents, inflicting significant losses on the insurgents and pressing them in to a single quarter against the river (Quarter Number 71 of the plan of Warsaw). The situation for the group became critical.
> Today a single battalion of the Polish Army was sent across the other side of the river, and cleared Quarter Number 71 of Germans and firmly holds it along with the insurgents....
>
> (Source: *Velikaia Otechestvennaia voina*, 1999, kn.3, p. 461)

Whilst Soviet supply lines were seriously extended and Soviet forces faced stiff German opposition in the region, nonetheless Soviet forces probably could have broken into the city in late August or September had there been compelling reason to do so. There was however, no compelling reason to squander resources on a frontal assault on a major city in order to save insurgents whose uprising was timed to seize the city just before the arrival of Red Army troops, to the political detriment of the position of the pro-Soviet Polish Committee in Lublin. Soviet troops would not advance on this sector of the front again until early 1945.[13]

The 'L'vov–Sandomierz Strategic Offensive' Operation became the sixth blow of 1944, and saw Soviet mechanized and armoured forces similarly advancing large distances in short periods of time, in this instance as much as 50–65 km per day on the approaches to the Vistula River much further south, over which they were able to seize a bridgehead at Sandomierz. The operation saw the encirclement of a significant German force consisting of *Korpsabteilung* C of 13th Corps, made up of three units of regimental strength, along with an infantry division, security division, and most noted in the wider Western literature, the 14th Waffen SS Division, 'Galicia', a

The 'Ten "Stalinist" Crushing Blows' of 1944   237

Figure 10.2 Rail transport and the Soviet 'L'vov–Peremishl'' Operation, July 1944 (see Document 142).

unit drawing on what in Soviet terms were western Ukrainians, but more importantly marking a volte-face in German and particularly SS policy on the deployment of substantial units of eastern origin in front-line roles. The pocket saw a German loss of 40,000 men and much equipment.[14]

Given the distances being advanced by Soviet forces, as in the case of the 'Belorussian' Operation, careful logistical preparations were important for the Red Army to be able to advance as far as it could in a single operational bound, as is apparent from Documents 85 (Chapter 6) and 142 (below). Whilst Document 86 above is concerned with transport from railheads to front-line troops, Document 143 is concerned with the maximization of railway capacity to railheads as deep in newly liberated territory as possible during the 'L'vov–Sandomierz' (or 'L'vov–Peremishl'') Operation, and then the transfer of this material to front-line troops by road. Of particular note in this document, to which Figure 10.2 relates, and something that frequently appears in similar documents, is the extent to which German forces had developed the capacity of the Soviet rail system on occupied territory over that which had existed in the summer of 1941:

DOCUMENT 143: *Rail and road transport in order to provide material support for Soviet forces during the 'L'vov–Peremishl'' Operation, July 1944*

Material Support
  ... The plan envisioned ... :
...
  All rear service area organs were redeployed closer to the forces prior to the offensive. The rear service areas of larger formations were partially relocated in the rear service regions of smaller formations (the *front*'s rear service units to the army rear service areas and the army rear service units to the forces' rear service area):

The *front* was based on four railway lines ...:

1. Kiev-Zhitomir-Novograd-Volinskii-Shepetovka-Ternopol';
2. Kiev-Fastov-Berdichev-Shepetovka-Staro-Konstantinov-Grechani;
3. Kazatin-Zhmerinka-Grechani-Ternopol'; and
4. Shepetovka-Zdolbunov-Kivertse.

In addition, two sets of trains per day were provided for the 1st Ukrainian *Front* along the line running from Zhmerinka to Mogilev-Podol'skii, Sadagura and Kolomiia.... The *front* had five motor-vehicle roads at its disposal.... In addition, each army had its own motor-vehicle road.

In preparing railway lines for the 1st Ukrainian *Front's* offensive operation, primary attention was focused on increasing the carrying capacity of the railway sectors. The following measures were undertaken to this end:

Restoration of the secondary route in the Kazatin-Zhmerinka sector, which increased the carrying capacity of the entire line (Kazatin-Zhmerinka-Ternopol');

Restoration of the railway bridge across the Dnestr River at Zaleshchiki; ...

As a result of these measures we succeeded in increasing the carrying capacity of the railway sector by a factor of 1.5–2. The average capacity of two-way sectors was 24 pairs of trains a day (12 for one-way sectors). The capacity in individual sectors (Shepetovka-Zdolbunov) was 36 pairs of trains.

The training of railway units for swift restoration of railway lines during the operation was an important mission. Air reconnaissance, during which the principal railway junctions were photographed, was conducted to obtain data on the condition of railway sectors on enemy territory and the travel capacity of junctions and large stations. Aerial photography established, that in comparison with 1941, in many sectors the enemy had done considerable work to develop travel capacity.... Table 7 shows which sectors were to be restored, their length, and their rate of restoration.

In all, the *front* had at its disposal 56,331 lorries (74 percent of those authorized), of

Sector	Sector length (km)	Restoration period (days)	Rate of restoration (km/day)
Zviniache–Saperzhanka–L'vov	116	12	9.7
Saperzhanka–Kristinopol'–Rava Russkaia	90	9	10.0
Radzivilov–Krasne	55	6	9.2
Ternopol'–Krasne–L'vov	133	14	9.5

which 50 percent were placed in reserve. A great deal of repair work was done on motor-vehicle transport to bring it in to order. The manufacture and restoration of deficient parts on the spot played a significant role in the repair of motor-vehicle transport.... As a result of all this repair work, the motor-vehicle park achieved 91 percent technical readiness.

Road work also consumed a large quantity of forces and equipment....

(Source: D.M. Glantz and H.S. Orenstein (trans. and eds.), *The Battle for L'vov, July 1944*, 2002, pp. 36–39)

The growth in the Red Army vehicle park during the war, facilitating the bounding Soviet advance by 1944, is apparent in Table 10.3.

It is worth noting that, given the dramatic increase in size of the Red Army from a list strength of 3,334,400 for the third quarter of 1941 to a high list strength of 6,714,300 for the third quarter of 1944,[15] the increase in available vehicles was proportionally not dramatically greater than the increase in manpower, even if imported motor vehicles were typically larger and had a greater capacity than Soviet vehicles available in 1941. Consequently, therefore, the considerable reliance that the Red Army, as did the *Wehrmacht*, placed on horses and on the infantry marching from railheads continued throughout the war. Table 10.3 also highlights that a considerable number of motor vehicles that were used by the Red Army were drawn from the wider Soviet economy rather than new Soviet production, Allied imports or captured stocks (see Chapter 8).

As the fourth blow, the seventh 'Stalinist blow' would result in the loss of another German ally in the east, in this case Rumania. The brief 'Iassi–Kishinev Strategic Offensive' Operation lasted from 20 to 29 August 1944. Whilst the operation has received relatively little attention from historians, and Soviet success was achieved where the Soviet numerical advantage was, where it mattered, overwhelming – by now the norm – it was nonetheless a significant operational-strategic achievement in a very short space of time – perhaps even strategic if knocking Rumania out of the war is considered, although it was not expected by either the Germans or the Soviets that Rumania would crumple so quickly.

Whilst the *Wehrmacht* was still millions strong on paper, in the absence of the armoured forces for a mobile or elastic defence and particularly given Hitler's obsession with holding ground per se, it was forced to commit the bulk of front-line troops to creating some sort of defensive line, based on strongpoints, with limited and typically somewhat less than mobile reserves. The first line of German defences was inevitably poorly manned, with Soviet reconnaissance forces often penetrating deeply into them before the start of primary operations. This German practice did serve some purpose, providing something of a tripwire in the event of a major assault. Nonetheless, with the low strength and poor mobility of German forces, combined with often poor operational-strategic dispositions – occupied with a view to holding onto territory rather than sound defence, in this case with the political concern for Rumanian reaction to the loss of those territories acquired from the Soviet Union after June 1941 – the inevitable encirclements of the last few months continued.

In the case of the Soviet 'Iassi–Kishinev Strategic Offensive' Operation, most of the reformed German 6th Army was to be encircled; the previous formation having been lost at Stalingrad. The fact that the Soviet 2nd and 3rd Ukrainian *Fronts* were considerably weaker than they had been only a few months before, having lost amongst other formations 5th Guards Tank Army, might have lulled the German High Command into a false sense of security on this sector of the front, but the German Army Group South Ukraine had lost numerous divisions, including the bulk of its armour, in the light of the collapse of Army Group Centre to the north.

As the Soviet operation broke through German and Rumanian defences on the far left and right of the principal fortified positions of the 'Trajan' and associated positions, there was little German and Rumanian forces could do as forces of the 2nd Ukrainian *Front* raced southwards to the west of Iassi as forces of 3rd Ukrainian *Front* pushed south-west and east from bridgeheads over the Dnestr. Army Group South Ukraine had only two German panzer (13th and 20th) and one Rumanian armoured (1st Rumanian) division and the 10th Panzer Grenadier Division by 15 August, where the Soviet 2nd Ukrainian *Front*'s mobile force alone could deploy 6th Tank Army along with 18th and 23rd Tank Corps. The two *fronts* together deployed a modest but nonetheless overwhelming total of 1,428 tanks and 446 SPs, against the 155 tanks and 324 SPs of Army Group South Ukraine as of 1 August, down from 424 tanks and 430 SPs on 11 July. Only three days into the operation, the Rumanian dictator Marshal Antonescu was overthrown in the name of the young king, and very soon Rumania was fighting on the side of the Allies and the Soviet Union, albeit paying particular attention to territorial squabbles with its old rival Hungary that remained allied with Germany.[16]

The eighth blow saw the 'liberation' of the bulk of the Baltic Republics by Soviet troops in the period from 14 September to 24 November 1944; not that the bulk of the local population probably saw it in such terms, in a region where collaboration with the Germans was relatively enthusiastic, including participation in the foreign-manned Waffen SS units that had appeared as German fortunes waned. On 14 September Soviet forces of the Leningrad *Front*, now freed from the responsibility of dealing with Finland, started the process of 'liberating' Estonia, striking from jumping-off points west of Narva (captured in July) and near Tartu (taken in August), with Tallinn falling by 23 September. Subsequent operations saw Soviet troops push on to the coast to the west and amphibious operations saw the recapture of most of the Baltic islands, with a German garrison on the largest of these holding out until late November before being evacuated by sea (timidity in the use of Soviet naval forces not being confined to the Arctic or Black Seas). Whilst being pushed back by forces of the Leningrad *Front*, a more serious threat for the survival of Army Group North had developed in the south, where during the later stages of the 'Belorussian Strategic Offensive' Operation, in penetrating as far as the gates of Riga, Soviet forces now threatened to cut Army Group North off by land from Army Group Centre and the Reich. Heavy defences for the city of Riga and a fresh infusion of armour from Army Group Centre prevented this taking place in late September, but German forces were not in a position to stop Soviet forces redeploying to strike westwards towards the coast, with Soviet lead units having penetrated to the coast north of Memel by 10 October after only five days of operations; Memel itself held out until the end of the year when much of the garrison was evacuated by sea. Army Group North was now finally isolated, at least by land, and certainly no longer able to make a major contribution to the German war effort as an entity. However, the German navy (or *Kriegsmarine*) was able to sustain the remaining forces of what became Army Group Kurland that had retreated into the Kurland Peninsula. Despite the pulling out of much of the Army Group's manpower as the situation deteriorated to the south, at the end of the war more than 200,000 German troops in the pocket were taken prisoner.[17]

In the far south, the ninth blow actually consisted of more than one strategic offensive operation, the 'East Carpathian' and 'Belgrade Strategic Offensive' Operations, taking place from 8 September to 28 October and 28 September to 20 October respectively, followed by the 'Budapest Strategic Offensive' Operation that started on 29 October 1944 and saw Soviet troops bogged down in fierce fighting until 13 February 1945.

The 'East Carpathian Strategic Offensive' Operation aimed to destroy German forces in the East Carpathian region and link up with the abortive Slovak uprising against the Germans. Had the uprising and the Soviet operations somewhat dependent on it been more successful, it would have allowed Soviet forces to avoid and isolate Hungary in their drive to secure Eastern Europe. According to Soviet accounts the failure of the Slovak uprising to draw in key Slovak army units (Slovakia had been given a measure of independence under German overlordship), in particular the 'Slovak Corps' based around the towns of Prešov and Košice and ideally situated and intended to secure key mountain passes for advancing Soviet troops, was a key factor. That the Germans were able to disarm the corps was a major factor in the failure of Soviet operations to break through the stiffly defended mountain passes to pockets of territory held by the rebels deep in the German rear, although the fact that Soviet operations were launched with relatively little preparation on the back of the 'L'vov–Sandomierz' Operation and without the overwhelming superiority in manpower in difficult mountainous terrain was also important.[18]

In the aftermath of the Rumanian collapse and the failure of the 'East Carpathian Strategic Offensive' Operation and Slovak uprising, Soviet forces continued their advance towards Austria and the Reich through Hungary. Initially, Soviet forces were able to advance quickly through open country along the Rumanian border in early October, and it was hoped that the Rumanian collapse would be mirrored in Hungary. However, whilst representatives of the conservative Horthy government negotiated a separate peace with the Soviet Union in Moscow – the intention to seek peace being announced by radio on 15 October – SS 'commandos' toppled the government by seizing Horthy's headquarters in Budapest and facilitated the establishment of a fascist Hungarian government. Despite some defections to the Soviets, the bulk of the Hungarian Army continued to fight for the Axis alongside German units – and against Hungary's local rival Rumania.

With Soviet patience for a Hungarian collapse exhausted, the first attempt to seize Budapest, on a narrow front with a force based on two mechanized corps of 46th Army of Malinovskii's 2nd Ukrainian *Front*, started on 28 October; on 4 November the *Stavka* noted the poor chances of success for the operation without support, against what were strong Axis (German and Hungarian) forces in the region:

DOCUMENT 144: *Directive of the* Stavka *VGK Number 220256 to the Command of forces of the 2nd Ukrainian* Front *on the organization of the advance on Budapest, 4 November 1944, 20:00*

The Headquarters of the Supreme High Commander considers an attack on a narrow front with a force of only two mechanized corps with only limited infantry could lead to unjustified losses and place forces active on that axis under threat of flank attack by enemy forces from the north-east.

Given this, the *Stavka* orders:

1. That the right wing of the *front* (7th Guards, 53rd, 27th and 40th Armies) be moved to the western bank of the River Tisa with the aim of conducting an advance on a wide front and destroying the Budapest grouping of enemy forces with a blow by the right wing of the *front* from the north and north-east in co-operation with a blow by the left wing of the *front* (46th Army and 2nd and 4th Guards Mechanized Corps) from the south.

(Source: *RA T.16 (5–4)*, 1999, p. 165)

After further abortive attempts to seize Budapest by the 2nd Ukrainian *Front*, forces of the 3rd Ukrainian *Front* were to participate in the capture of Budapest and destruction of Axis forces in the region, having first crossed the Danube, to the south-west of Budapest.

DOCUMENT 145: *Directive of the* Stavka *VGK Number 220280 to the Command of forces of the 2nd and 3rd Ukrainian* Fronts *and* Stavka *representative on the transfer of 46th Army and on the tasks of the* fronts *in the capture of Budapest, 12 December 1944, 04:00*

The Headquarters of the Supreme High Commander orders:

1. Shlemin's 46th Army consisting of ten rifle divisions, 2nd Guards Mechanized Brigade, 7th Breakthrough Artillery Division and with all army support units,... is to be transferred from 2nd Ukrainian *Front* to 3rd Ukrainian *Front*....

3. With the forces of the 2nd and 3rd Ukrainian *Fronts* the Budapest group of enemy forces is to be destroyed and the city of Budapest captured, for which:
   a) The command of forces of the 2nd Ukrainian *Front*, continuing the advance by its left wing on Budapest, with a force of two-three rifle corps, 6th Guards Tank Army and Group Pliev,... is to strike [to the east of Budapest] ... with the aim of occupying the northern bank of the Danube on the Nesmei-Esztergom sector and to prevent the retreat of the Budapest enemy grouping to the north-west;...

b) The command of forces of the 3rd Ukrainian *Front* is to strike from the Lake Velence region [between Lake Balaton and Budapest] in the direction of Bicske with 46th and 4th Guards Armies, with 18th Tank Corps, 2nd Guards Mechanized Corps, 7th Mechanized Corps and 5th Guards Cavalry Corps, with the aim of moving round the enemy Budapest grouping from the west. Part of the force committed is to advance on Budapest from the west and in co-ordination with the left wing of the 2nd Ukrainian *Front* capture it.
4. The advance is to start ... 19–20.12.1944.
5. Plans for the operation are to be submitted to the General Headquarters 15.12.1944.

(Source: *RA T.16 (5–4)*, 1999, p. 181)

Budapest was finally encircled on 26 December, but with the city prepared for a stubborn defence that would see much of it destroyed and the loss of many civilian in addition to military lives, this would be the first time that the Red Army would have to besiege a major enemy city.

DOCUMENT 146: *Directive of the* Stavka *VGK Number 220286 to the Commanders of forces of the 2nd and 3rd Ukrainian* Fronts *on the use of artillery in the fighting for Budapest, 26 December 1944, 22:10*

According to available information the Germans have decided to hold the city of Budapest for as long as possible, having fortified major buildings in advance and having occupied all positions in the city suited for defence.

In order that the Germans do not have the possibility of carrying out this plan, to avoid heavy casualties to our forces and speed up the capitulation of the group of German forces encircled in Budapest, the Headquarters of the Supreme High Commander orders that for the destruction of the enemy spread around major buildings across Budapest, and also in the fortress on the western bank of the Danube, artillery of all calibers is to be used, including the largest, as well as airpower and groups of sappers. Artillery of all calibers, up to and including the largest, is also to be used to accompanying the infantry in street fighting with the aim of destroying centres [*ochagi*] of resistance with direct artillery fire.

(Source: *RA T.16 (5–4)*, 1999, p. 184)

The western part of the city, Buda, finally fell on 13 February 1945 – leaving only ruins.[19] The region had not seen the end of bloodshed, however, since the last significant counter-offensive by German forces would take place in the Lake Balaton region in March 1945 (see Chapter 12), causing little trouble to Soviet forces whilst finally wiping out the last remnants of German armoured forces, by this time hopelessly short of fuel.

The last of the 'Stalinist' blows of 1944 took place in the far north with the 'Petsamo–Kirkenes Strategic Offensive' Operation, lasting from 7 to 29 October 1944 and seeing the liberation of Soviet Arctic territory and Soviet troops occupying the Finnmark region of northern Norway. German troops of 20th Mountain Army were in the process of beginning evacuation from the region when the Soviet offensive started – German stockpiles of nickel, the mining of which was now the principal reason for holding on to the Petsamo region, having been deemed sufficient to allow the more expedient use of forces for the defence of naval bases on the Norwegian coast (for offensives by new German submarine types now no longer able to operate from French bases).[20]

Despite the availability of more than 300 large and medium vessels to the Northern Fleet, including the battleship *Arkhangel'sk* and cruiser *Murmansk*, supported by more than 563 aircraft for the Fleet alone, the Northern Fleet was unable to prevent the withdrawal of considerable German assets by sea, just as the Soviet 14th Army and marines of the Northern Fleet were unable to prevent the withdrawal of German forces westwards from the Petsamo region. The battleship *Arkhangel'sk*, actually the British battleship *Royal Sovereign* provided to the Soviet Union in lieu of Italian warships as reparations after the Italian surrender, 'lay idle' at the Northern Fleet's base during October, with the cruiser *Murmansk* (the US *Milwaukee*) apparently not once having put out to sea. Aircraft of the Northern Fleet were able to inflict significant losses on German shipping, but opportunity was undoubtedly lost to use surface and submarine forces to good effect. Most probably, as the Russian historian Suprun notes, limited use of naval assets was due to fear of losing vessels, particularly late in the war, and what he describes as the 'Beria syndrome' – particularly in the aftermath of losses in the Black Sea in October 1943 (see Chapter 6).[21] Document 147 provides details of Red Army losses and some indication of German losses during ground operations.

DOCUMENT 147: *War Diary of 14th Army for October 1944*

...

Losses of Army forces during the period of offensive operations:
During the month of October 1944 army losses were:

Killed	a) Officers	367
	b) Sergeants	1,335
	c) Ranks	3,105
Missing	a) Officers	6
	b) Sergeants	86
	c) Ranks	238
Wounded	a) Officers	809
	b) Sergeants	2,820
	c) Ranks	7,007
Sickness with hospital evacuation	a) Officers	139
	b) Sergeants	512
	c) Ranks	1,777

Date	Establishment number of beds	Beds made available	Beds occupied	Subject to evacuation to the deep rear
As of 6.10.44	5,795	5,795	1,375	203
11.10.44	6,225	7,013	2,908	839
15.10.44	6,785	8,519	4,828	1,962
20.10.44	6,815	8,523	5,312	2,099
25.10.44	7,345	10,912	5,860	2,088
31.10.44	8,875	10,097	5,757	1,198

...

A significant role in the transfer of troops across water obstacles and the seizing of bridgeheads was played by special purpose motorized battalions (Ford amphibian vehicles).

Results of the activities of engineer and sapper units:

In facilitating the advance of forces of the army, and their forward movement and passage across water obstacles engineer and sapper units:

Cleared mines from a) 107 square km of territory, b) 598 km of road, c) 357 buildings and fortifications. Enemy mines cleared 15,671, including 11,482 anti-tank mines.

...

Permanent bridges erected – 34

Pontoon bridges erected – 29

Bridges repaired – 6

Quays repaired – 3

Footbridges constructed – 32

...

Use of medical facilities of the army:

From 28.10.44 the evacuation of wounded by sea via the port of Linakhamari began.

...

Overall results of army offensive operations:

...

During the period from 7 to 29.10.44, during offensive operations, the following losses were inflicted on the enemy:

Destroyed:

Artillery pieces of various calibers – 257

...

Rifles and SMGs – 7,000

...

Horses – 2,150

...

Aircraft – 127

Tanks – 12

Radio stations – 36

During offensive operations the enemy lost (killed) 28,910 soldiers and officers.

Captured:

Artillery pieces of various calibers – 210

...

> Rifles and SMGs – 7,395
> ...
> Horses – 450
> ...
> Aircraft – 17
> Tanks – 5
> Radio stations – 19
> ...
> 1,579 soldiers were taken prisoner, including:
>
> a) Died of wounds during evacuation – 341
> b) Destroyed [*unichtozheno*] given the impossibility of evacuation – 212
> ...
>
> (Source: A.A. Gorter *et al.*, 2005, pp. 218–245)

The year 1944 had seen Soviet troops recapture almost all the territory incorporated into the Soviet Union in 1940 and saw the heart ripped out of the *Wehrmacht* and the loss of two German allies in the far north and far south of the theatre of operations. Soviet losses had continued to be horrific throughout 1944, as Table 10.4 indicates, but from a purely military viewpoint at least the Red Army had much to show for them. Soviet forces were now within striking distance of the Reich, and the end of the war was at least in sight.

Guide to further reading

'1st Ukrainian Front's L'vov-Perymyshl' Operation (July–August 1944)' [Documents], *JSMS*, Volume 9, Number 1 (March 1996), pp. 198–252.

James F. Gebhardt, *The Petsamo-Kirkenes Operation: Soviet Breakthrough and Pursuit in the Arctic, October 1944*, Leavenworth papers, Number 17 (Combat Studies Institute, U.S. Army Command and General Staff College, 1990).

David M. Glantz, 'The Red Army's Lublin-Brest Offensive and Advance on Warsaw (18 July–30 September 1944): An Overview and Documentary Survey', *JSMS*, Volume 19, Number 2 (June 2006), pp. 401–441.

David M. Glantz, *Red Storm over the Balkans: The Failed Soviet Invasion of Rumania, Spring 1944* (Lawrence, KS: University Press of Kansas, 2007).

David M. Glantz and Harold S. Orenstein (trans. and eds.), *Belorussia 1944: The Soviet General Staff Study* (London/Portland, OR: Frank Cass, 2001).

David M. Glantz and Harold S. Orenstein (trans. and eds.), *The Battle for L'vov, July 1944: The Soviet General Staff Study* (London/Portland, OR: Frank Cass, 2002).

David M. Glantz and Harold S. Orenstein (trans. and eds.), *The Battle for the Ukraine: The Red Army's Korsun'-Shevchenkovskii Offensive, 1944* (The Soviet General Staff Study) (London/Portland, OR: Frank Cass, 2003).

Steven H. Newton, *Retreat from Leningrad: Army Group North, 1944–1945* (Atglen, PA: Schiffer Publishing, 1995).

Krisztián Ungváry, trans. Ladislaus Löb, *The Siege of Budapest: One Hundred Days in World War II* (New Haven, CT: Yale University Press, 2005).

11 From the Vistula to Berlin
The end of the Reich

At the end of 1944, despite still being relatively bogged down in Hungary in the south, the Red Army was readying itself for the final blows of the war on the principal Berlin axis, operations that had been in the planning phase from October 1944. In November, Zhukov took over command of the 1st Belorussian *Front* standing before Warsaw from Rokossovskii, who took over 2nd Belorussian *Front* on Zhukov's right flank facing the southern portion of East Prussia (Pomerania).[1] To the south of 1st Belorussian *Front* was Konev's 1st Ukrainian *Front* that had seized the Sandomierz bridgehead over the Vistula, threatening southern Poland.

The Red Army that was poised at the gates of Warsaw was larger, more confident, better equipped and more far more capable a machine compared to its *Wehrmacht* nemesis than it had been in 1941. The Red Army and its leadership, tempered by more than three years of war, were also far more trusted by Stalin. Whilst discipline remained harsh, gone were the commissars of the period of defeat to the eve of the Stalingrad counter-offensive (see Documents 30 and 84, Chapters 3 and 5 respectively), all Soviet military leaders were now officers rather than simply command elements (see Chapter 5) and at the end of 1944 officers and ranks alike could be trusted to press home their attack with, in the main, only the mechanisms for maintaining discipline that could be expected in most armies. On 29 October 1944 the blocking detachments that had encouraged hundreds of thousands of Red Army men forward to their deaths were dissolved.

DOCUMENT 148: *Order of the People's Commissar of Defence Number 0349, 29 October 1944 (on the dissolution of independent blocking detachments)*

In line with changes in the general situation at the front the necessity for the future sustaining of blocking detachments has subsided.
 I order:

1. Independent blocking detachments are to be dissolved by 13 November 1944. Personnel from the dissolved detachments are to be used as replacements for rifle divisions.

2. You are to report on the dissolution of the blocking detachments by 20 November 1944.

People's Commissar of Defence
Marshal of the Soviet Union I. Stalin.

(Source: O.A. Rzheshevskii, 1990, pp. 452–453)

However, whilst those that had survived the slaughter of the war to date enjoyed a certain trust, those that had been taken prisoner during the first cataclysmic weeks and months of the war, many of whom had survived the horror of German POW camps during the winter of 1941–42, and a substantial number captured during the summer retreat in the south during 1942, were not so fortunate. Branded as traitors thanks to Order Number 270 of 16 August 1941 (see Document 33, Chapter 3), many POWs and indeed *Ostarbeiter* (see Table 9.5), would find themselves under the suspicious eyes of the NKVD:

DOCUMENT 149: *Special communiqué by L.P. Beria to I.V. Stalin, V.M. Molotov and G.M. Malenkov on the work of verification-filtration points for the processing of Soviet citizens, 2 January 1945*

The NKVD of the USSR reports, that for the time during which checking-filtration points for the processing of Soviet citizens returning to the Motherland have been functioning, as of 30 December 1944 96,956 persons have been received and processed.
...
Of this number 38,428 persons have been provided with authorization and sent on to places of permanent residency; 5,827 persons of conscription age have been handed over to *voenkomati*; and 43,693 persons have been sent for the conduct of further verification to special camps of the NKVD.
Of those checked 153 persons have been uncovered and arrested as German stooges, traitors and betrayers of the Motherland.

(Source: *Lubianka*, 2006, p. 485)

Able-bodied men were certainly in high demand with the Red Army. It was certainly the case that many formations were in the position of the divisions of the Soviet 8th Army of 1st Belorussian *Front* described by Shtemenko, where, having reached the Oder during the 'Vistula–Oder' Operation, they could only apparently muster 'two battalions apiece, with only 22–45 men per company'.[2]

Whilst Red Army manpower shortages meant that suitable returnees from German captivity or labour service would be sent to the Red Army, the Red Army faced an opponent that was now resorting to throwing even less military-capable personnel into front-line combat, in form of the *Volkssturm*, than the Soviet Union had with the *opolcheniia* or militia of 1941. The increasingly poorly trained and equipped bulk of the *Wehrmacht* could do little but delay the Soviet tide and inflict more agony on a Red Army that had already suffered losses that had not been, and thankfully have yet to be, suffered by any army in a single war. A dwindling pool of German mobile units formed around a battle-hardened core of veterans was now only able to launch counter-attacks penetrating at best tens of kilometres behind the Soviet front line. However, it would still take the Red Army, aided by her allies in the West, another four months to finally bring the war to an end. German forces were now fighting on home territory, far more urbanized and suited to the defence than the vast expenses of most of the Soviet Union, and were fearful of Soviet occupation. Whilst the Panzer divisions were but shadows of their 1943 equivalents, and the Luftwaffe increasingly absent from the skies, the still-numerous German infantry, equipped with a plethora of anti-tank weapons, would take an exacting toll on Red Army personnel desperate to survive what would clearly be the last months of the war.

On 12 January 1945, forces of the 1st Ukrainian *Front* began the dramatic 'Visula–Oder Strategic Offensive' Operation with the 'Sandomierz–Silesian' Operation, advancing rapidly towards the Oder River in Silesia and destroying 4th Panzer Army in the process. At the same time, 3rd Belorussian *Front* (Cherniakhovsksii) attacked German forces in East Prussia as Rokossovskii's 2nd Belorussian *Front* attacked in Pomerania. All of these attacks were geared to paralysing German ability to shift forces to meet the Soviet threat on any particular axis, in particular the key Berlin axis, on which the Soviet advance by 1st Belorussian *Front* began on 14 January.

By this stage of the war, the Soviet numerical advantage was so overwhelming that, even with those forces tied down besieging fortified towns and cities or dealing with local German counter-offensive operations, the Red Army could launch multi-*front* operations that could bound forward until a combination of extended supply lines and the need for replacement troops in the face of stiffening enemy resistance brought a halt. Table 11.1 gives Soviet forces for the 1st Belorussian and Ukrainian *Fronts* at the start of the 'Vistula–Oder' Operation. Overwhelming Soviet superiority is further highlighted by the resources that could be thrown into operations away from the principal axis, for example in the 'East Prussian' Operation in Table 11.2.

On paper, in terms of numbers of divisions, the German Army Group A, facing 1st Belorussian *Front*, did not look anything like as weak as it was in reality. Table 11.3 gives the strength in terms of divisions and brigades of Army Group A, according to Soviet sources, at the start of the Soviet 'Vistula–Oder' Operation. However, not only were German divisions hopelessly understrength, but short of fuel and operating in an environment where Soviet air superiority meant that limited reserves were vulnerable whilst moving up to face an enemy penetration if they were deployed too far back where they would have some room to manoeuvre. Forward deployment,

Table 11.1 Operational density of infantry, tanks and artillery of Soviet forces at the beginning of the 'Vistula–Oder' Operation, January 1945

Front		1st Belorussian	1st Ukrainian
Width (km)	Overall	230	250
	Breakthrough sector	30 (excluding 4 km breakthrough sector for 47th Army)	36 (excluding 3 km breakthrough sector for 60th Army)
Number of rifle divisions	Overall	68	66
	Breakthrough sector	37	34
Concentration of infantry (km per rifle division)	Overall	3.4	3.8
	Breakthrough sector	0.8	1.06
Number of guns and mortars (excluding AT, RS and AA)	Overall	13,706	13,717
	Breakthrough sector	7,318	8,626
Concentration of artillery for 1 km of front	Overall	60	55
	Breakthrough sector	244	239
Number of tanks and SPs	Overall	3,220	3,244
	Breakthrough sector	2,942	3,181
Concentration of tanks and SPs for 1 km of front	Overall	14	13
	Breakthrough sector	98	88

Source: 'Vislo-Oderskaia operatsiia v tsifrakh', *Vizh*, Number 1 (1965), p. 75.

Table 11.2 Soviet forces at the start of the 'East Prussian' Operation (as of 10 January 1945)

Resources	3rd Belorussian	2nd Belorussian	43rd Army (1st Baltic Front)	Total frontline/total including rear area services
Personnel (frontline)	483,978	671,016	67,662	1,222,656/1,669,105
Tanks	836	1,178	21	2,035
SPs	762	1,017	45	1,824
AT (45–57 mm)	1,611	2,088	286	3,985
Artillery (76 mm+)	4,213	5,793	778	10,784
Mortars (82–120 mm)	4,490	5,411	756	10,657
RS batteries	567	970	26	1,563
AA	704	1,026	114	1,844
Motor vehicles	23,069	32,864	3,948	59,881

Source: 'Vostochno-Prusskaia operatsiia v tsifrakh', *Vizh*, Number 2 (1965), pp. 81–82.

however, would mean that they might very well not engage the principal Soviet thrust and faced encirclement if engaged with Soviet supporting thrusts, as would be the case with 16th and 17th Panzer Divisions of 24th Panzer Corps deployed near the Sandomierz bridgehead at the start of the 'Vistula–Oder' Operation.[3]

Not that the *Wehrmacht* had sufficient mobile reserves to effectively halt major Soviet thrusts even if they could be positioned appropriately: not only had precious armoured forces just been squandered in the west during the December 1944 Ardennes offensive, but also in Hungary in January when at the beginning of January 1945 4th SS Panzer Corps, transferred from Army Group Centre (which together with Army Group A defended the key Berlin axis), attempted to relieve Budapest, the fall of which would not take place until 13 February, when 2nd Ukrainian *Front* could report as follows:

> DOCUMENT 150: *From a combat report of the command of the 2nd Ukrainian* Front *to the Supreme High Command on the liberation of Budapest, 13 February 1945*
>
> I report: forces of the left wing of the *front*, having broken through a range of strong fortified defensive lines both on the approaches to and within the city of Budapest, as a result of fierce street fighting over many days, having to storm every building and block, by 10:00 on 13 February of the current year defeated the encircled enemy grouping ..., fully occupying the capital of Hungary, the city of Budapest – one of the most important rail and road centres of Europe....

Table 11.3 Grouping and operational density of German forces at the start of the Soviet 'Vistula-Oder' Operation, January 1945

Army		9th	4th	17th (and one division facing 4th Ukrainian Front)	Army Group A reserves	Total for Army Group A (excluding 1st Panzer Army and 1st Hungarian Army facing 4th Ukrainian Front)
Number of units	Infantry divisions (all types)	8	7	5	2	22
	Panzer divisions	–	–	–	4	4
	Motorized divisions	–	–	–	2	2
	Infantry brigades	1	1	–	–	2
	Total divisions	8	7	5	8	28
	Total brigades	1	1	–	–	2
Width of *front* (in km)		230	160	90	–	480
Number of km per division		27	23	18	–	17

Source: 'Vislo-Oderskaia operatsiia v tsifrakh', p. 72.

> An enemy group of up to 7,000 persons breaking out is being successfully destroyed in the forests to the north-west of Budapest.
>
> During the period of struggle for the capture of Budapest by forces of the *front*, of the encircled enemy group the following were destroyed: soldiers and officers – 49,982, tanks and self-propelled guns – 203, artillery pieces of various calibers – 367, armoured cars and armoured personnel carriers – 253,... aircraft – 189.
>
> According to incomplete figures, 127,202 soldiers and officers have been captured, tanks and SPs – 269, artillery pieces of various calibers – 1,257, armoured cars and armoured personnel carriers – 83,... aircraft – 15,... motor vehicles – 5,153, horses – 1,585....
>
> (Source: O.A. Rzheshevskii, 1990, p. 453)

It is difficult to argue that the holding of Budapest had a significant influence on the length that the Third Reich survived, and German operations in the region continued to have little apparent purpose even after its fall. At the beginning of March 1945, remaining assets of the 6th SS Panzer Army, having been pulled out of the west after the Ardennes offensive, would strike Soviet forces in the Lake Balaton region to the south-west of Budapest, along with yet another reformation of 6th Army, and to little gain.

To the north, the collapse of the German Army Group A in the face of 1st Belorussian and 1st Ukrainian *Fronts* had meant that from about 18 January Soviet forward elements could aim to race forward to breach the Oder River running in a north-westerly direction from south-western Poland towards Berlin, along which German forces were attempting to form some sort of defensive line. The redeployment of the German Grossdeutschland Panzer Corps from East Prussia to Lodz to the south-west of Warsaw, at which lead elements detrained on 16 January, did little to relieve the situation; follow-on elements did not even make it to Lodz as their trains were intercepted by advancing Soviet forces. Elements of the German 4th and 9th Armies making it to the Oder were not given any reprieve, being thrown back into the fighting to hold some sort of Oder line, along with forces pulled out of the Kurland pocket by sea.

Soviet General Staff plans for operations in Germany of October–November 1944 had contemplated that Soviet forces would take Berlin in a two-stage but near continuous operation lasting 45 days. Despite Zhukov's suggestion that his forces press on beyond the Oder in February, supported with Konev's agreement by the continued advance of Konev's forces to the south towards the Elbe River, the advance of 1st Belorussian *Front* was halted in early February. Konev's forces continued to advance to the Western Neisse River, running southwards from the section of the Oder before Berlin, and then also halted. Whilst the manifold possible reasons for the halt are discussed by Mawdsley in some detail,[4] Shtemenko had the following to say on the matter in his memoirs:

> **DOCUMENT 151:** *Comment by the then head of the operations department of the Soviet General Staff Shtemenko on the reasons for the halt of the 1st Belorussian* Front *along the Oder at the beginning of February 1945*
>
> On February 1st, 1945, the 5th Assault [Shock] Army, and then the 8th Guards Army, of the 1st Belorussian *Front*, struck across the Oder and secured some not very large bridgeheads near the fortress of Küstrin. The fortress itself however remained in enemy hands....
> On this [Oder] line the Soviet armies were stopped.
> The operational situation was developing unfavourably to us. The 1st Belorussian *Front*, which was straining towards Berlin, but at present lacked the strength to capture it, had pushed ahead. On the Berlin sector it had, in effect, only four field armies and two tank armies, all of them under strength.... Two of them ... had been compelled to leave some of their forces to deal with the encircled garrison at Poznan, and another ... had to maintain the siege of Küstrin while simultaneously attacking Berlin.
>
> (Source: S.M. Shtemenko, 1970, pp. 308–309)

Shtemenko goes on to highlight a number of reasons for the halt other than the supposedly weak Soviet spearhead on the Oder, such as:

1 A growing threat to the extended flanks of 1st Belorussian *Front* from German forces to the north, in Pomerania, against which Zhukov was forced to turn his attention. On 17 February German forces in fact launched a counter-attack from the Stargard area.
2 A poor supply situation that meant that supplies were being shipped by road from railheads east of the Vistula, particularly hampering the effectiveness of Soviet artillery support.
3 Growing Luftwaffe activity from permanent airfields in the Berlin area where VVS aircraft were operating from hastily prepared forward bases in poor weather conditions.[5]

In his memoirs Zhukov also notes that, despite weak German defences for Berlin at the end of January, Soviet intelligence, now considerably weaker than it had been on former pre-1940 Soviet territory where human intelligence from partisans was of considerable value (see Chapter 9), indicated that four Panzer and up to 5–6 infantry divisions were being transferred from the West, with other units being transferred from the Baltic Republics and East Prussia.[6] Certainly, in the absence of concrete intelligence as to where some of these units that were actually being transferred were being sent, it would have made sense to assume that they were all destined for the defence of Berlin – now only 60–80 km from the front-line along the Oder.

Soviet forces of 1st, 2nd and 3rd Belorussian *Fronts* would spend February and March in operations in Pomerania and East Prussia, fighting what had been Army Group Centre, now cut off from the main German force along with what was now Army Group Kurland. At the same time 1st Ukrainian *Front* continued operations in Silesia. The semi-official post-Soviet Russian-language history of the Great Patriotic War has the following to say about operations during this period:

> DOCUMENT 152: *Concluding remarks on Soviet operations in Eastern Pomerania and Silesia during February and March 1945 from the semi-official post-Soviet Russian-language history of the Great Patriotic War*
>
> Having defeated major enemy forces in Eastern Pomerania and Silesia, the Red Army had thwarted the intention of the German High Command to strike a blow on the flanks of our forces on the approaches to Berlin. Having seized a line along the Oder and Niesse Rivers they had created favourable circumstances for the final blows against Germany and in Czechoslovakia. Now, having liberated Pomerania and Silesia Soviet forces at last had the possibility of continuing the advance on the Berlin axis.
> (Source: *Velikaia Otechestvennaia voina ... Kniga tret'ia.* 1999, p. 252)

Whether such a cautious approach was necessary is certainly debatable – Soviet forces would lose thousands of men in the destruction of German forces in eastern Pomerania and in the reduction of fortified German positions in East Prussia. Such Soviet operations did, however, create the situation whereby German formations with at least limited mobility that had been substantial in February–March, and continued to appear on Hitler's maps as such, were now of little or no operational significance. Also important, however, was the fact that in the west, by the time the Red Army resumed its advance on Berlin, the Allies had crossed the Rhine and contributed to the stranglehold on the heart of the Reich.

Whilst the need to protect the flanks of the principal thrust by Soviet forces on the Berlin axis provided understandable grounds for delay in the capture of Berlin, this need only have concerned German forces with some sort of mobility, not those units bottled up in fortress cities that were not on major road and rail junctions along principal axes of advance, the capture of which would contribute to easing Soviet supply problems. The eventual capture of the fortress city of Königsberg, on the back of successful operations by Cherniakovskii's 3rd Belorussian *Front* against German forces of Army Group North (previously Army Group Centre until it was cut off from the principal Berlin axis in mid-January), constituted a major and arguably unnecessary operation that would not see the city fall until 10 April 1945, and with the loss of thousands of Soviet lives.

Before Cherniakhovskii, like Vatunin another young rising star, was killed by German artillery on 18 February, forces of the 3rd Belorussian *Front* had reached the city and succeeded in cutting it off from the sea via Pillau. Details of the defences of the city are provided in Document 153: fighting in such urban conditions even without particularly thoroughly prepared defences had proved so effective in whittling down the strength of the

German 6th Army and elements of 4th Panzer Army in the autumn and winter of 1942 at Stalingrad that fortresses such as Königsberg would similarly soak up Soviet resources.

> DOCUMENT 153: *Details of the German defences of Königsberg from guidelines from the operational department of the headquarters of 11th Guards Army on the storming of the city and fortress, 10 February 1945*
>
> NKO SSSR. Operational department of the headquarters of the 11th Guards Army, Number 076, 10 February 1945....
>
> I. Introduction
>
> ...
>
> The carrying out of this task is associated with a new form of operations for us – ... street fighting, with the following specific characteristics:
>
> a) Limited vision and fields of fire;
> b) The possible use by the enemy of all types of engineered defensive works and positions based on existing structures;
> c) The impossibility of the widespread use of large units of infantry and tanks; additionally, fighting within the city will inevitably break in to a series of individual encounters; the result of such fighting will frequently be decided by independent activity by small units acting on their own initiative, especially assault groups;
> d) Complexity in the use of artillery and tanks;
> e) Complexity in the observation and direction of the activities of units.
>
> ...
>
> II. Characteristics of the defences of Königsberg
>
> The fortress of Königsberg consists of two citadels and two defensive belts.
>
> The outer defensive belt is 6–7 kilometres from the centre of the city.... It consists of 12 basic and three additional forts and a system of established and field fortifications.
>
> ...
>
> Each fort has ramparts with open firepoints and strongpoints for direct fire by 9–10 anti-tank and field artillery pieces for each.
>
> In front of each fort there is an anti-tank ditch ten metres wide and three metres deep. In the gaps between forts one-two lines of trenches have been dug, protected on some sectors by barbed-wire obstacles and minefields. On particularly important sectors there are, in addition, machine-gun bunkers [DOT and DZOT].
>
> The internal defensive belt extends from the external side of the ring road and consists of 24 earthen forts with prepared firepoints and bunkers for personnel.
>
> Directly inside the city for its complete depth the enemy has created strongpoints, consisting of separate brick buildings suited to the defence and whole city blocks.
>
> In every strongpoint there is two-level defence – on the lower floors there are positions to fire along the streets and on the upper floor and in lofts there are positions for firing on the streets, courtyards and neighbouring buildings from above.
>
> The approaches to the strongpoints and the gaps between them are covered by a system of ditches, obstacles and barricades, mined streets and objects.
>
> The southern sector of the outer ring is defended by units of the 69th, 549th and 56th Infantry Divisions, 73rd and 74th Fortress Machine-Gun Battalions and by elements of 6th and Grossdeutschland Panzer Divisions.
>
> (Source: *SBD 1*, pp. 93–95)

From the Vistula to Berlin 257

Before the final storming of the fortress city in April, two divisions of German reinforcements pulled out of Memel allowed German forces to re-establish the link between port and city in mid-February, with another German pocket having by this time formed to the south-west of the city centred on the town of Heiligenbeil – it was during the reduction of this pocket that Cherniakhovskii was killed. Under Vasilevskii's command 3rd Belorussian *Front* regrouped and on 12 March set about destroying the German East Prussian pockets along the coast. Whilst by 29 March the Heiligenbeil pocket had been destroyed, some troops made it across the water to Königsberg, the final assault on which had started on 6 April. By this point Soviet forces had accrued considerable experience in the reduction of such fortified urban areas – experience bought at the cost of tens of thousands of lives and literally thousands of armoured vehicles, the use of which in urban fighting requiring particularly close co-operation between arms if losses were to be kept in check. The following four documents highlight some of the problems of and 'solutions' developed for fighting in urban areas:

DOCUMENT 154: *Directive to armoured and mechanized forces of the 1st Belorussian* Front *on the organization and conduct of fighting for German cities and major towns, 20 February 1945*

...

2. Tanks and self-propelled guns are used in the main as part of assault groups (a reinforced rifle platoon or company) and assault detachments (up to a reinforced rifle battalion). 2–3 tanks or self-propelled guns are allocated to an assault group. A company of tanks or battery of self-propelled guns is to be allocated to an assault detachment.

3. Tanks and self-propelled guns operating with assault groups or detachments are to advance with the group (detachment), supporting them with fire from a position along the street.... Particular attention is to be paid to the use of concentrated machine-gun fire. The distance between tanks and self-propelled guns moving along a street should provide for support for the lead tank in order to protect it from the throwing of grenades, Molotov cocktails and from destruction by *Panzerfaust*. The normal distance should be considered 75–100 m. Under no circumstances should tanks and self-propelled guns advance 'bumper-to-bumper'. If one tank advances along the left side of the street, firing upon houses on the right side of the street, then the other advances along the left side. All tank hatches should be closed.

...

5. ... Buildings of average strength and enemy-occupied barricades are to be destroyed by fire from tanks and self-propelled guns (76 and 85 mm). For the destruction of particularly strong buildings heavy tanks are to be used (IS-122) and heavy assault guns (ISU-122, ISU-152).

Flame tanks are to be used, supported by artillery and battle tanks, for the flushing out of the garrisons of strongpoints, DZOT, DOT.

...

9. In street fighting the carefully organized observation and reconnaissance of objectives is of decisive significance; from this starting point efforts by commanders of all ranks should be directed towards the realization of close co-operation with the infantry.

...

10. In organizing this co-operation the question of target identification, the identification of positions reached by the infantry and reliable communications with the infantry are to be carefully worked out. In street fighting such means as coloured rockets and tracer fire are to be put down by the infantry in the direction of targets identified. Communication via runners acquires particular significance in street fighting....

11. Each tank or self-propelled gun is to be reinforced by a covering group of 4–5 men with SMGs for the constant protection of the vehicle and destruction of groups of enemy tank hunters armed with *Panzerfaust* grenade launchers.

(Source: *SBD 10*, pp. 98–101)

DOCUMENT 155: *Temporary instructions of the Command of 6th Army of 11 March 1945 on the use of tanks and self-propelled guns in street fighting (based on experience of street fighting for the city of Breslau)*

I. The Enemy

In the fighting for the city of Breslau the enemy has shown stubborn resistance to the advance by our forces. All brick or stone buildings were prepared for defence, streets and squares criss-crossed with obstacles and barricades. Tightly packed buildings within blocks or thick brick or stone walls along streets and within blocks exclude the possibility of maneuver by tanks and self-propelled guns within city blocks.

On barricades, against obstacles, in the cellars of buildings and on the ground and higher floors of buildings the enemy positions small-caliber cannon, machine-guns and sub-machine gunners with *Panzerfausts* and grenades, the last two being used in large quantities and are one of the principal enemy means in the struggle with our tanks and SPs.

On the appearance of our tanks and SPs on enemy-occupied streets, the enemy fires *Panzerfausts* at our vehicles from the upper floors of buildings.

...

III. The role of tanks and SPs as part of an assault battalion

1. Experience of recent days in the city of Breslau has shown, that it is most appropriate to use tanks and SPs in a decentralized manner in street fighting, that is groups of 2–3 vehicles as part of the assault battalions of regiments, in close co-operation with artillery, sappers and flamethrowers.
2. Tanks and SPs, advancing in appropriate order 100–200 m behind the infantry, with 20–30 m between each tank, are to destroy enemy firepoints, machine gunners and troops equipped with *Panzerfausts* spread throughout buildings through the destruction of the walls of buildings and other structures with direct fire.
3. Typically one tank or SP is firing, and behind it an advancing SP (tank) observes

the enemy and is prepared to open fire on buildings from which the first SP is fired upon by *Panzerfausts*.
4. ... tanks and SPs ... should be no closer than 150 m from enemy forward positions....
5. The movement of tanks and SPs from one firing position to another is carried out when the infantry have cleared all floors of a [nearby] building of the enemy and where the subsequent firing position and approaches to it have been reconnoitered and checked by sappers.

...

9. Street junctions should be crossed by tanks and SPs at maximum speed in order to avoid destruction by enemy flanking fire and only after careful observation and reconnaissance.

(Source: *SBD 21*, pp. 145–147)

DOCUMENT 156: *Directive to forces of the 8th Guards Army on the capture and blockading of buildings turned into strongpoints by the Germans (on the basis of experience in fighting for Poznan), 16 February 1945*

1. The choice of objective for attack
...
   b) In the first instance it follows that the following should be chosen:
      - objectives where their fall would force the enemy to vacate a number of other buildings;
      - objectives that might be suitable starting points for further offensive operations.
   c) As a rule, buildings that are connected to other buildings should be attacked simultaneously. In order to hinder enemy fire support and counter-attack from nearby buildings, on the flanks of attacking units covering fire should be provided or flanks should be screened by smoke.
2. Reconnaissance of the object under attack and approaches to it
   a) Any sort of attack should be preceded by well-organised reconnaissance.
...
5. The timing of the start of an attack
   a) The best time to seize a building is the period before dawn, in order that the approach to the objective be covered by darkness, as the attack itself, and the battle within the objective and its consolidation be carried out in daylight....
6. Forces and resources to be allocated to the attack, and the subdivision of them into groups
   a) In the struggle for the capture of a building where reliance is on surprise a small group of carefully-picked soldiers and NCOs is required, along with an officer. In circumstances where the element of surprise is missing the assault group should be sizeable, as available fire-support and reserves.
   b) ... in all instances an assault group should include artillery up to 152 mm calibre for direct fire, sappers for the creation of access points, flamethrowers ..., tanks or self-propelled guns....

c) The assault group should be split into subgroups:
- a number of assault subgroups (of three-five men) ...
- a number of covering subgroups (of five-seven men) ...
- a support group consisting of artillery, tanks and self-propelled guns ...
- a reserve group....

(Source: *SBD 11*, pp. 23–26)

DOCUMENT 157: *Directive of the 2nd Ukrainian* Front *on the use of artillery in street fighting for major population centres, April 1945*

In the fighting for Budapest there were a number of specific uses of artillery that should be considered in the conduct of street fighting for major population centres.
...
III. Methods for using artillery in street fighting

1. ...
    A variety of artillery resources should accompany assault groups for use against a variety of targets. Small calibre and regimental artillery should fire upon windows, embrasures, through holes in walls and such, and 76 mm guns and 122 mm howitzers should destroy the walls of buildings and cellars....
    For the destruction of major buildings 152 and 203 mm artillery pieces should be used.... At the same time mortars should be used to provide covering fire in order to destroy the enemy in attics and courtyards, for the isolation of buildings under attack, and also for firing upon streets running transversely.
2. Varied munitions should be used against buildings: through windows and holes high explosive rounds should be used, against walls armour-piercing and bunker-busting munitions. For the creation of fires within buildings hollow-charge projectiles for 76 mm guns and 122 mm howitzers should be used.
    For firing upon windows in multi-level buildings 37 mm anti-aircraft guns should be deployed....

(Source: *SBD 4*, pp. 95–98)

The fortress city of Königsberg finally fell on 10 April after intense street fighting, yielding over 90,000 prisoners, but still leaving a pocket to the west of the city on the Samland Peninsula, containing nine German divisions, the destruction of which, culminating in the capture of the port and naval base of Pillau, took place between 13 and 25 April. Perhaps the only argument that might be put forward for these costly operations was to prevent forces being transferred to the principal axis – as indeed troops had been from Kurland. Had the Soviet Baltic Fleet, run down after its retreat to Kronstadt and Leningrad during the first weeks of the war, been more effectively used (with the acceptance of at least some losses of shipping, which could have been limited by the Soviet air superiority in the region), then the withdrawal could have been more effectively hampered and the Baltic pockets contained. In reality Soviet surface vessels of any size did not

Table 11.4 Soviet losses of personnel and equipment during the 'Vistula–Oder', 'East Prussian' and 'East Pomeranian Strategic Offensive' Operations, January–April 1945

Operation		'Vistula–Oder' (12 January–3 February 1945)	'East Prussian' (13 January–25 April 1945)	'East Pomeranian' (10 February–4 April 1945)	Totals
Personnel	Strength	2,203,600	1,669,100	996,100	–
	Irrecoverable losses	43,476	126,464	55,315	225,255
	Total losses (inc. sick and wounded)	194,191	584,778	234,360	1,013,329
Selected equipment losses	Tanks and SPs	1,267	3,525	1,027	5,819
	Combat aircraft	343	1,450	1,073	2,866

Source: Krivosheev, *Soviet Casualties and Combat Losses*, pp. 154–156 and 263.

interfere with German shipping in the southern Baltic, even if Soviet submarines took their toll on German transports involved in evacuations from East Prussia, with the loss of many civilian lives.

Soviet losses of personnel and equipment during the 'Vistula–Oder', 'East Prussian' and 'East Pomeranian Strategic Offensive' Operations running from January into April 1945 are provided in Table 11.4. Whilst the Red Army had made great strides in the use of tanks and their co-ordination with infantry and artillery, including in urban environments, it is tempting to argue that many of the issues identified in Document 158 below, which contributed to the continued high losses for the Red Army, were as a result of cultural factors that could not easily be dealt with, even with appropriate changes in force structure and organization:

DOCUMENT 158: *Order Number 052 of 27 February 1945 to forces of 1st Shock Army on the organization and conduct of preparations for operations in March 1945*

Recent attacks by forces of the army during the February operation of 1945 have shown that many units participating in the breakthrough of enemy defences suffer from a number of inadequacies in their preparations and training in order to be able to conduct offensive operations in complex military conditions and with stubborn enemy resistance.

The basic and substantial inadequacies have been as follows:

...

2. Regimental and battalion artillery as a rule lags behind the advancing infantry, limiting the rate of advance by the infantry, which sometimes gives the enemy the opportunity to solidify his tactical defence in the rear and prevent our units reaching objectives for a given day.
3. The infantry is unable to independently deal with enemy counterattacks with tanks and self-propelled guns with the weapons provided. Amongst infantry and artillery units there have been instances of tank fright.

...

6. The artillery has not learned to independently engage enemy firepoints in order to support the infantry's advance. Artillery officers are not good at following the course of the fighting and poorly and belatedly react to enemy fire and counterattacks.... As a rule, commanders of artillery units wait for fire requests or tasks from officers of the rifle formations, and the latter do not call up artillery fire directly from attached or supporting artillery units, but through senior infantry officers.

...

8. Units do not know to how use radio communications appropriately, with radio being particularly poorly used at regiment-battalion level. As a rule the bulk of radio exchanges are conducted in open text.

(Source: *SBD 13*, pp. 121–122)

Perhaps the only issue identified in Document 175 that could have been dealt with without major changes in military and to some extent broader Soviet culture was the capability of Soviet infantry against tanks. The legendary Russian initiative and 'make-do' might have been acceptable in pursuit of clearly defined goals established by higher authority, but initiative amending or deviating from goals set from above was a risk that was typically not worth taking. Certainly routeing fire-support requests through senior officers would allow someone else to take the blame for friendly-fire incidents, and at the same time make it more likely that fire support would be provided by artillery officers seeking the appropriate level of authorization before risking being blamed for firing upon their own forces. As for the capability of Soviet infantry against the relatively few effective German tanks and self-propelled guns, those who have miniature wargamed will appreciate the extent to which, after tank armour increased significantly as the war progressed and Soviet anti-tank rifles became all but obsolete, Soviet infantry lacked the capability to engage enemy tanks with the equivalent of the German *Panzerschreck* or *Panzerfaust*, US Bazooka or even British PIAT.[7] Their ability to draw on anti-tank and artillery resources for the destruction of the limited number of enemy tanks, tank hunters and assault guns would have been improved by better use of by now relatively abundant communications resources. Soviet fear of enemy interception of radio communications, whether or not the enemy would have time to use uncoded communications to their advantage before the information was redundant, along with broader issues surrounding lower-level initiative, seems to have limited the effective use of radio communications.

Nonetheless, despite the continued failings of the Red Army and high casualties, what was undoubtedly a Soviet juggernaut ploughed on. Whilst it was by no means certain that the capture of Berlin would mean the end of German resistance given rumours of a German 'Alpine redoubt' to which Hitler would presumably retreat, the capture of Berlin would nonetheless have been an immense psychological blow to German society with or without Hitler's death there. It would also bring prestige to a Red Army that had borne the brunt of the fighting against German land forces since the summer of 1941, and ensure the Soviet Union a powerful position in post-war Germany and indeed Central Europe.

In late March 1945 the *Stavka* began planning operations against Berlin in a climate of increasing mistrust between Stalin and the Allies, with fears that separate peace agreements between the Germans and the Allies in the west, or at least a German collapse in the west, whether in collusion with the Allies or not, would allow Allied forces to launch themselves from their Rhine bridgeheads towards Berlin.[8]

Initial orders for the capture of Berlin, on the approaches to which Soviet forces remained along the Oder and Neisse Rivers as in Figure 11.1, were issued to 1st Belorussian *Front* under Zhukov's command as shown in Document 159.

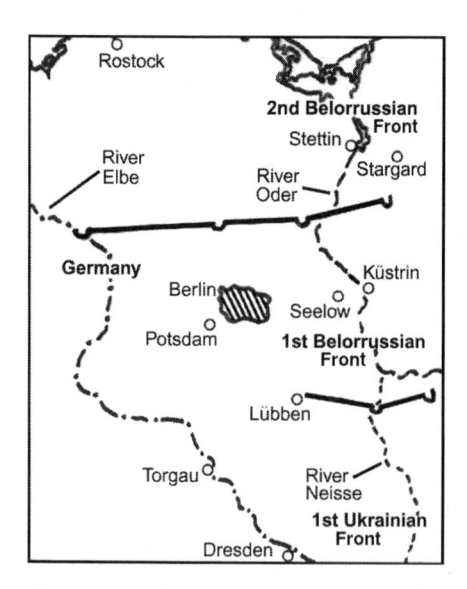

Figure 11.1 The 'Berlin' ('Strategic Offensive') Operation 16 April to 8 May 1945.

DOCUMENT 159: *Directive of the* Stavka VGK *Number 11059 to the command of forces of the 1st Belorussian* Front *on preparations and the conduct of operations for the capture of Berlin, 2 April 1945*

The Headquarters of the Supreme High Command orders:

1. To prepare and conduct an offensive operation with the aim of capturing the capital of Germany, the city of Berlin, and no later than on the twelfth-fifteenth day of the operation take up positions along the Elbe River.
2. The principal thrust is to be struck from the bridgehead on the River Oder west of Küstrin with the forces of four regular and two tank armies.

    On the breakthrough sector five-six artillery breakthrough divisions are to be used, creating an artillery concentration of no less than 250 guns of 76 mm and above for one kilometer of front to be broken through.
3. For support of the principal grouping of the *front* from the north and south two supporting blows are to be struck with a force of two armies for each. The first – from the region north-west of Berwalde in the general direction of Eberswalde ... ; the second from the bridgeheads on the River Oder north and south of Frankfurt on the Oder in the general direction of Fürstenwalde, Potsdam, Brandenburg, enveloping Berlin from the south.
4. Tank armies are to be introduced on the axis of the principal thrust after breaking through defences in order to provide for the success of the envelopment of Berlin from the north and north-east.
5. Second-echelon armies are to be used for the development of success on the principal axis.

(Source: *RA T.16 (5–4)*, 1999, p. 223)

Zhukov's 1st Belorussian *Front* was to be supported by both Konev's 1st Ukrainian *Front* to the south and Rokossovskii's 2nd Belorussian *Front* to the north along the Baltic coast, both of which were to press on to the Elbe River to the west of Berlin. Zhukov had the following to say on the planning for the Berlin operation in his memoirs:

DOCUMENT 160: *Extracts from the memoirs of Marshal Zhukov on the planning of the Soviet Berlin offensive of April 1945*

On 1 April the Supreme High Commander heard A.I. Antonov's report on the overall plan for the Berlin operation, and then my report on the offensive plans of 1st Belorussian *Front* and I.S. Konev's plan for offensive operations by 1st Ukrainian *Front*.

The Supreme Commander did not agree with the dividing line between 1st Belorussian and 1st Ukrainian *Fronts* indicated on the *Genshtab* map by a line from Gross Gastrose to Potsdam and he crossed out the boundary line from the Niesse to Potsdam and accentuated the line only as far as Lübben.

He then directed Marshal I.S. Konev:

In the event of stubborn resistance by the enemy of the eastern approaches to Berlin, as will probably be the case, and the possibly holding up of the offensive by 1st Belorussian *Front*, 1st Ukrainian *Front* is to be prepared to strike a blow with its tank armies from the south towards Berlin.

...

It was decided that the advance on Berlin was to start on 16 April, without waiting for 2nd Belorussian *Front*'s participation, which, by all confirmed accounts, would not be in a position to advance from the Oder any earlier than 20 April.

On the night of 2 April at the *Stavka* and in my presence the Supreme Commander signed the directive of the 1st Belorussian *Front* for the preparation and conduct of the operation....

(Source: G.K. Zhukov, 1995, pp. 226–227)

Red Army victory was guaranteed by the overwhelming force that was deployed by the three *fronts* committed to the operation, as indicated in Table 11.5.

The principal German forces facing the Soviet offensive against Berlin were 3rd Panzer Army to the north-east, 9th Army in the centre immediately to the east of Berlin and 4th Panzer Army to the south-east. According to Soviet figures, 3rd Panzer Army could field a total of 12 divisions, of which six were standard infantry and two motorized, but, despite its designation, none were Panzer; 9th Army could field a total of 16 divisions, of which nine were standard infantry, along with one Panzer and four motorized; and 4th Panzer Army could field a total of 13 divisions, of which nine were standard infantry, one Panzer and one motorized. According to Mawdsley, 3rd Panzer could field 242 tanks and 9th Army 512 tanks, for which fuel was scarce with no sizeable reserves in rear areas. Table 11.4 above gives Soviet forces to be committed at the beginning of the Soviet operation and not total forces available to the three *fronts* – a total in fact, as noted in a footnote to the Soviet table on which Table 11.5 is based, of 6,250 tanks and self-propelled guns, if those initially in rear areas are considered.[9]

After forces of 1st Belorussian *Front* had redeployed from operations in Pomerania after 29 March, the last major offensive of the war in the west actually began on 14 April 1945 with reconnaissance-in-force[10] by elements of 1st Belorussian and 1st Ukrainian *Fronts*. The principal attack began for these two *fronts*, as planned, on 16 April, followed by 2nd Belorussian *Front* to the north on 18 April. As in Document 159 above, the principal thrust was to be by 1st Belorussian *Front* on the most direct route to Berlin, that is, from the Küstrin bridgehead westwards through German positions on the Seelow Heights, by now thoroughly prepared for defence. The Soviet attack began in darkness, as described in Zhukov's memoirs:

> DOCUMENT 161: *Description by Marshal Zhukov of the start of principal offensive operations by 1st Belorussian* Front *on 16 April against German positions on the Berlin axis*
>
> At precisely three minutes prior to the start of the artillery preparation we all left the dugout and took up our positions in the observation post....
>
> From there, during the day one could see all of the territory along the Oder. At this time early morning mist hung in the air. I glanced at my watch: it was precisely 5 o'clock.
>
> At that very moment the area was brightly lit up by the firing of the many thousands of artillery pieces, mortars and our legendary *Katiushas*, on the heels of which the sound of the shots rang out and the immense force of the explosions of the shells and bombs reverberated around us. In the air the perpetual drone of bombers grew in strength.
>
> From enemy positions there were a few bursts of machine gun fire during the first seconds, and then they fell silent.... During the powerful 30-minute artillery preparation the enemy did not fire once. This was testimony to his full suppression and disarray of the defensive system. As a result it was decided to cut short the time for the artillery preparation and with haste start the general offensive.
>
> Thousands of multicoloured rockets howled. On this signal 140 searchlights came to life, situated every 200 metres. More than 100 billion candles lit up the battlefield, blinding the enemy and picking out objectives for our tanks and infantry out of the darkness. It was a picture of colossal and impressive force, and perhaps, during the whole of my life, I do not recall an equivalent sensation.
>
> The artillery still further increased its fire, and the infantry and tanks threw themselves forward in unison.... By daybreak our forces had occupied the forward positions and started to attack the second line.
>
> (Source: G.K. Zhukov, 1995, pp. 243–244)

Whilst Mawdsley suggests that Zhukov's 'tactical innovation' in the use of searchlights had little impact, Glantz and House suggest that the searchlights actually 'added to the confusion' of darkness, fog and smoke, going on to suggest that the Soviet artillery preparation – all 2,450 railway wagons or

Table 11.5 Forces of 1st and 2nd Belorussian and 1st Ukrainian *Fronts* at the start of the 'Berlin' Operation

Forces	Fronts			Totals (including army and front *rear-areas*)
	2nd Belorussian	1st Belorussian	1st Ukrainian	
Personnel	314,000	768,100	511,700	1,593,800 (*c.* 2,500,000)
Tanks	644	1,795	1,388	3,827
SPs	307	1,360	667	2,334
AT guns	770	2,306	1,444	4,520
Field artillery (76 mm +)	3,172	7,442	5,040	15,654
Mortars (82 mm +)	2,770	7,186	5,225	15,181
RS launchers	807	1,531	917	3,255
AA guns	801	1,665	945	3,411
Motor vehicles	21,846	44,332	29,205	95,383
Aircraft (serviceable) – of which:	1,360	3,188	2,148	6,696
Fighters	602	1,567	1,106	3,275
Ground-attack	449	731	529	1,709
Bombers	283	762 (+800 with 18th Long-Range Air Army)	422	1,467
Reconnaissance	26	128	91	245

Source: 'Berlinskaia operatsiia v tsifrakh', *Vizh*, Number 4 (1965), p. 81.

almost 98,000 tons-worth of it according to Zhukov – caused more problems than it solved in churning up the terrain for the Soviet tanks, with Soviet forces not having progressed up the actual heights – poor going for the tanks – by late morning.[11]

With Zhukov's 1st Belorussian *Front* apparently still bogged down in the German defences on 17 April, in not establishing a clear demarcation of responsibilities between 1st Belorussian *Front* and 1st Ukrainian *Front* to the south, as Zhukov noted above, Stalin gave Konev the opportunity to race Zhukov's forces for Berlin, and indeed even Rokossovskii's 2nd Belorussian *Front* was directed towards Berlin on 18 April. Konev apparently issued the following order in the early hours of 18 April:

> DOCUMENT 162: *Directive Number 00215 of the 1st Ukrainian* Front *on the redirection of forces towards Berlin, 18 April 1945, 02:47*
>
> In carrying out the orders of the Supreme High Command I order:
>
> 1. The command of the 3rd Guards Tank Army: During the night of 17–18 April 1945 force the River Spree and develop a powerful thrust in the general direction of ... the southern suburbs of Berlin. The task of the Army is to break through to the city of Berlin from the south on the night of 20–21 April 1945.
> 2. The command of the 4th Tank Army: During the night of 17–18 April force the River Spree north of Spremberg and develop a powerful thrust in the general direction of ... Luckenwalde. The task of the Army is to have seized the Beelitz, Treuenbritzen, Luckenwalde region by the end of 20 April 1945. During the night of 21 April Potsdam and the south-western portion of Berlin are to be occupied. The redirection of the Army in the direction of Potsdam in the Treuenbritzen region is to be supported by 5th Mechanized Corps. Reconnaissance is to be conducted in the Senftenberg, Finsterwalde, Hertsberg directions.
> 3. On the principal axis the armoured fist is to push forward boldly and decisively. Towns and major centres of population are to be avoided as is getting caught up in sustained frontal attacks. I require that you are fully aware, that the success of tank armies depends on bold maneuver and decisive action.
>
> Point 3 is to be passed down to commanders of corps and brigades.
> ...
> Commander of the 1st Ukrainian *Front*, Konev.
>
> (Source: I.S. Konev, 1966, p. 119)

However, by 18 April 1st Belorussian *Front* had overcome the Seelow defences and by 25 April 2nd Belorussian *Front* was once again directed to head due west rather than towards Berlin. By 24 April, forces of 1st Belorussian *Front* had wheeled round the city from the north and met up with elements of 1st Ukrainian *Front* to the south, encircling Berlin, where unbeknown to Soviet forces Hitler had chosen to remain.

Towards the end of the war in the west, it is worth taking stock not only of how Stalin's leadership style had changed, but how those surrounding him and participating in day-to-day decision making had changed. To start with, the *Stavka* was no longer dominated by the old guard of the 1930s, as it had been in the summer of 1941 (see Document 25, Chapter 3). On 17 February 1945, *Stavka* membership was as follows:

> DOCUMENT 163: *Decree of the State Defence Committee Number 7550s on the composition of the* Stavka *VGK, 17 February 1945*
>
> Contrary to the Decree of the State Defence Committee of 10 July 1941 the *Stavka* of the Supreme High Command is made up of the following:

The Supreme High Commander and People's Commissar for Defence, Marshal of the Soviet Union I.V. Stalin;
Deputy People's Commissar for Defence and Marshal of the Soviet Union G.K. Zhukov;
Deputy People's Commissar for Defence and Marshal of the Soviet Union A.M. Vasilevskii;
Deputy People's Commissar for Defence and General of the Army N.A. Bulganin;
Head of the *Genshtab* of the Red Army and General of the Army A.I. Antonov;
Head of the Navy and People's Commissar for the Navy Admiral of the Fleet N.G. Kuznetsov.

Chairman of the State Defence Committee, I. Stalin

(Source: I.A. Gor'kov, 2002, p. 536)

Document 181 provides a list of visitors to Stalin in his Kremlin office for the period from 25 April – the date on which Soviet and American forces met on the Elbe River – and 2 May, the day on which the Berlin garrison would finally surrender.

DOCUMENT 164: Visitors to Stalin in his Kremlin office, 25 April {US-Soviet meeting on the Elbe River} to 2 May {surrender of the Berlin garrison} 1945

25 April 1945
Beria	22:40–00:30
Vishinskii	23:35–00:15
Malenkov	00:20–00:50
Mikoian	00:20–00:50
Khrushchev	00:30–00:50

26 April 1945
Vishinskii	22:15–23:30
Bulganin	22:40–23:30 (GKO)
Antonov	22:40–23:30
Shtemenko	22:40–23:30
Malenkov	00:05–00:10
Beria	00:05–00:10

28 April 1945
Beria	23:20–23:35
Malenkov	23:20–23:35
Antonov	23:30–01:05
Bulganin	23:30–01:15
Voronov	23:30–23:35 (NKO)
Shtemenko	23:30–01:05
Osokin	23:30–23:35 (?)
Vishinskii	24:00–01:00
Beria	00:30–01:15

Malenkov	00:30–01:15
Voronov	00:30–00:40
Osokin	00:30–00:40
30 April 1945	
Malenkov	19:30–20:15
Beria	19:30–20:15
Vishinskii	19:30–20:15
2 May 1945	
Vishinskii	17:10–19:15
Beria	17:55–19:25
Malenkov	17:55–19:25
Serov	18:45–19:15 (NKVD)
Meshchik	19:00–19:15 (?)
Antonov	19:00–19:15
Shtemenko	19:00–19:25

(Source: I.A. Gor'kov, 2002, pp. 466–467)

Whilst Document 181 does not cover Stalin's meetings elsewhere, in particular at the People's Commissariat for Defence, nonetheless it does highlight the importance of the General Staff in military decision making with frequent visits by General Staff officers such as Shtemenko, head of the operations department of the *Genshtab* from May 1943, and Antonov, a predecessor of Shtemenko as head of the operations department, and from February 1945 head of the *Genshtab* as a whole. Heads of the different 'arms' and services such as Voronov, head of the Main Artillery Board of the Red Army (and previously of the PVO), unsurprisingly continued to make frequent visits, with some notable changes in personnel: Zhigarev, head of the VVS in June 1941 having been moved to command the VVS of the Far-Eastern Front in April 1942, not having escaped responsibility for the virtual destruction of the VVS during the first days of 'Barbarossa', but did escape with his life and relatively minor demotion, to be replaced by Novikov. Novikov's less frequent appearances in the list of visitors to Stalin's Kremlin office can be explained by the almost total Soviet air supremacy by April 1945. Kuznetsov remained in command of the navy, but headed a force that had very much a peripheral role in Soviet victory and had a tarnished reputation with Stalin through heavy losses of major units in the retreats of 1941 and 1942 and the subsequent apparent squandering of major units (for example, see Document 95, Chapter 6).

Notably absent are many of Stalin's closest colleagues or even cronies of the Civil War era or, in the case of Mekhlis, the 1920s. Where applicable all had tarnished their reputations as military leaders during 1941–42, even if not losing Stalin's 'trust'. Voroshilov lost his place on the State Defence Committee in November 1944, having been excluded from decision making for some time. Of Stalin's peers, only Malenkov, Molotov, Beria, Vishinskii and, to a slightly lesser extent, Mikoian remained prominent; Malenkov, Molotov and Beria being part of a Politburo-dominated inner core of the State Defence Committee that tended to meet in Stalin's Kremlin office. Whilst not making the inner core, capable organizers such as Mikoian and Vosnesenskii retained prominence throughout the war. Although not appearing in Document 164 above, it is worth noting that, of the post-Great Purges 'old guard', Timoshenko had a least preserved a position as a *Stavka* representative at *front* headquarters level in 1945, even if he was no longer at the heart of decision making.

Beria, head of the NKVD, and along with Malenkov and Molotov as close as Stalin got to friendship, remained particularly prominent throughout the war and, by Stalin's standards, trusted, but even he had seen a no doubt suspicious or at least cautious Stalin chip away at his empire or dilute his authority (although the repeated separation of the NKGB from NKVD in 1943 left the latter in the hands of Beria's trusted ally Merkulov until 1946), for instance, in removing counter-intelligence in the armed forces from his empire (the special sections of the NKVD becoming the NKO-run SMERSH).[12]

The entrusting of counter-intelligence in the Red Army to the NKO was certainly symptomatic of the general improvement in trust of the Red Army and the rise of a younger generation of leaders such as Zhukov and Bulganin (the latter gaining a place on the GKO in place of Voroshilov in November 1944, and indeed becoming something of a core member), and on their heels figures such as Rokossovskii and Konev, whose personal ascendancies ran alongside that of the *Genshtab* and the Red Army as a whole. Vatunin, very much a rising star whose name appears more than once in entries for 1941, and who was at the time head of the operations department of the *Genshtab*, was killed whilst commanding the 1st Ukrainian *Front* in 1944.[13]

On 26 April Soviet forces set about the destruction of the Berlin garrison and capture of Berlin, with Soviet reconnaissance troops raising the Soviet red banner over the Reichstag on 30 April, even if fighting for the Reichstag continued until the morning of 1 May. The Soviet command was informed of Hitler's suicide of 30 April the following day during negotiations for surrender with the new German Chief-of-Staff, General Krebs – a surrender forced on the Berlin garrison if not the entire *Wehrmacht* the next day.[14]

DOCUMENT 165: *From a combat report of the command of the 1st Belorussian* Front *on the military activities of forces of the* front *and the capture of Berlin, 3 May 1945*

1. On the left wing of the *front* the enemy continues to retreat in a westerly direction, offering only weak resistance to our advancing forces.

    The encircled garrison of Berlin, led by General of Artillery Weidling, along with his headquarters, ceased resistance and gave themselves up to our forces. Isolated groups of the encircled garrison that are attempting to break out in a westerly direction are being destroyed by our forces in the Spandau region and further west.

2. Having broken the resistance of the encircled enemy forces of the *front* have fully occupied the German capital – the city of Berlin.... According to provisional figures for 2.5.1945 from the enemy forces of the Berlin garrison more than

> 64,000 soldiers and officers have been taken prisoner.... The tallying up of POWs in Berlin continues.
>
> On the left wing of the *front* forces continue to forcibly advance and, encountering only weak enemy resistance within a single day have advanced 50 km in the Wilsnack region (12 km south-east of Wittenberg) and forward units have linked up with American forces.
>
> ...
>
> Commander of the forces of the 1st Belorussian *Front*, Marshal of the Soviet Union G. Zhukov
>
> (Source: O.A. Rzheshevskii, 1990, p. 455)

Despite the fall of Berlin, Hitler's death and the final surrenders of the *Wehrmacht* of 7 and 8 May,[15] sporadic German resistance continued for days, with particularly heavy fighting in and around the Czechoslovak capital Prague taking place on 9 May.

> DOCUMENT 166: *From the combat report of the headquarters of 4th Guards Tank Army to the commander of forces of 1st Ukrainian* Front *Marshal of the Soviet Union I.S. Konev, 9 May 1945, 21:30*
>
> 1. During the morning and first half of the day on 9.5.1945 groups of SS of the Führer [*begleit*] Regiment, Das Reich Panzer Division, 20th Police Regiment and an SS security battalion along with two construction battalions and other units resisted the activities of our forces in the Prague region.
> 2. Forces of the 4th Guards Tank Army continued to forcibly develop their advance on Prague and at 04:00 on 9.5.1945, with the 62nd and 63rd Tank Brigades, 10th Tank Corps and 70th Self-propelled Artillery Brigade, broke in to the city and fought groups of SS in order to clear the city. By 12:30 the city of Prague had been fully cleared....
>
>   During 9.5.1945 forces of the army captured the following on the approaches to and in Prague: 35 serviceable aircraft in the eastern suburbs of Prague, up to 500 motor vehicles and more than 5,000 POWs. The surrender of enemy forces continues.
>
> (Source: O.A. Rzheshevskii, 1990, p. 455)

Some of those engaged in the fighting around Prague during the last days of the war in the west would not, however, get to savour the end of the war against Nazi Germany for long, as they would be redeployed to the Far East.

Guide to further reading

Anthony Beevor, *Berlin: The Downfall, 1945* (New York: Viking, 2002) and other editions.
O.A. Rzheshevskii, 'The Race for Berlin', *JSMS*, Volume 8, Number 3 (September 1995), pp. 566–579.
Tony Le Tissier, *Zhukov at the Oder: The Decisive Battle for Berlin* (New York: Praeger, 1996) and other editions.

12 The Soviet invasion of Manchuria

After the liberation of Prague brought the war in the west against Nazi Germany to an end, as a result of agreement confirmed at the February 1945 inter-Allied Yalta conference, Soviet forces were to be committed to the war in the Far East against Japan within three months of the defeat of Nazi Germany. Whilst the possibility remained for Soviet participation in an assault on the Japanese home islands, in the first instance Soviet troops would be committed to operations in Manchuria, on Sakhalin and the Kurile Islands.

In order to build up substantial forces for the war against Japan, between May and 8 August 1945 the Soviet Union transferred more than 403,000 men, 2,119 tanks and self-propelled guns, 17,374 motor vehicles and 36,000 horses to the Far East from the west via the Trans-Siberian Railway.[1] The Japanese were aware that the Soviet Union was amassing troops in the Far East during the summer of 1945 and certainly expected eventual Soviet operations against them. Whilst some were unconvinced of the sincerity or practicality of the Soviet Yalta commitment to participate in the war in the Far East within three months of the defeat of Nazi Germany, the Soviet failure to promptly renew the April 1941 neutrality pact in April 1945 understandably heightened concerns. Actual Soviet strength in the region by August was, however, underestimated by Japanese intelligence by as much as 30–50 per cent, allowing many Japanese planners and intelligence officers to convince themselves that a Soviet invasion was not imminent, given their assessments of the forces required for such an undertaking. Less favourable assessments of the situation and the recall of Soviet embassy personnel and their dependants from Japan on 24 July 1945 had failed to significantly increase Japanese front-line readiness.[2] Shortly after the pulling out of embassy personnel Soviet forces were to finalize plans for the invasion of Manchuria.

DOCUMENT 167: *From a directive of the* Stavka VGK *to forces of the Far Eastern* Front, *28 July 1945*

... the Headquarters of the Supreme High Command orders:

1. By 1 August to have undertaken and completed all the necessary preparations amongst forces of the *front* for the organization [*gruppirovka*] of troops,... with the aim, on the special order of the Supreme High Command, to undertake offensive operations.
2. During preparations for the operation you are to make sure of the following:
   a) The aim of the operation is to be: active co-operation with forces of the Trans-Baikal *Front* and the *Primorskaia* [coastal] group of forces in the total defeat of the Japanese Kwantung Army and capture the Harbin region.
   b) The conduct of offensive operations on the Sungari axis by forces of 15th Army in co-operation with the Amur Flotilla.

   No less than three rifle divisions are to be allotted to the conduct of the operation, along with the bulk of the artillery of the High Command, tanks, aircraft and bridging equipment, with the first task being the forcing of the Amur River, the capture of the Tungchiang Fortified District and by the 23rd day to have reached the Chiamussu region.

   For future development you should consider operations along the River Sungari towards Harbin.

   ...

6. All preparations are to be conducted in the strictest secrecy.

   Access to full operational plans is to be given to: the commander, members of the military soviet, the head of *front* headquarters and the heads of the operational divisions of *front* headquarters.

   Heads of different elements of forces and their support staff are to be allowed to prepare specific elements of the plan without familiarization with the general tasks of the front.

   Commanders of armies are to be given instructions in person in oral form....

   Rules for access to army-level plans are to be as those for *fronts*.

   All documentation for plans of military operations is to be stored in the personal safes of military commanders of *fronts* and armies.

7. Correspondence and conversations on questions concerned with the plan for the operation are to be conducted solely through the head of the General Headquarters of the Red Army.

Stavka of the Supreme High Command
I. Stalin
Antonov

(Source: O.A. Rzheshevskii, 1990, p. 456)

On 7 August, no doubt in light of the United States dropping the first atomic bomb on Hiroshima on 6 August, orders went out for Soviet forces in the Far East to finally ready themselves for offensive operations only two days later on 9 August.[3] Table 12.1 provides Soviet figures for manpower committed at the start of the operation, along with equipment available to them. According to figures provided by Krivosheev, 638,300 troops of the Trans-Baikal *Front*, 334,700 of the 2nd Far-Eastern *Front* and 586,500 of the 1st Far-Eastern *Front*, in addition to naval forces and a small Mongolian force, participated in the 'Manchurian Strategic Offensive' Operation.[4]

According to figures provided by Glantz, the Japanese forces in Table 12.2 were available to defend against Soviet attack. Despite on paper seeming an impressive force, experienced Japanese troops had long since been transferred to meet the US and British threat elsewhere, along with more capable air assets. Replacement troops were at best poorly trained, and in fact the Japanese did not consider any of the infantry divisions available to face the Soviets as combat-ready.[5]

In terms of armour, Japanese weakness was more pronounced than in terms of manpower. The Soviet 1st Far-Eastern *Front* alone could deploy a total of 1,809 tanks and self-propelled guns, of which 18 were KV, 560 T-34, 390 T-26, 186 BT-7, 189 ISU-152, 63 SU-100 and 403 SU-76. The bulk of this strength would be deployed on the key Mutanchiang axis, where 1st Red Banner and 5th Armies would strike with forces including 1,094 tanks and self-propelled guns. Much of this strength would be used to support rifle divisions, with each rifle division on the principal axis being provided with a 65-tank armoured brigade and a 21-strong ISU-152 self-propelled gun regiment, which, along with their independent SU-76 self-propelled gun sections gave a rifle division a total of 99 tanks and self-propelled guns. Deeper penetration operations were, according to what was now standard practice, to be conducted by a forward mobile group, 10th Mechanized Corps, consisting of one tank and two mechanized brigades, along with three self-propelled artillery and an independent tank and Guards mechanized regiment, an independent communications battalion and other supporting units, with 110 T-34, 31 BT-7, 110 T-26, 63 SU-100 and 57 SU-76.[6]

The 1,155 tanks available to the Japanese were not concentrated in units of significant size apart from two brigades, and models available were vastly inferior to the T-34s that were the mainstay of Soviet forces in the Far East. Such was the weakness of Japanese tanks armed at best with a 57 mm main gun but more typically 37 mm, that the Soviet Union could deploy T-26s and BT-7s that had been in the Far East since before the German invasion of June 1941. Whilst Japanese artillery remained a threat, as regarding specifically anti-tank weapons her infantry divisions could at best field 37 mm anti-tanks guns, which would require a lucky hit to knock out a T-34.[7]

Soviet air support was also not only qualitatively but quantitatively far superior to that available to the Japanese, the latter apparent by comparing

Table 12.1 Troops and military equipment of the Trans-Baikal and 1st and 2nd Far Eastern *Fronts* at the start of the 'Manchurian' Operation

	Trans-Baikal Front	*1st Far Eastern* Front	*2nd Far Eastern* Front	*Total*
Personnel	654,000	586,589	337,096	1,577,725
Personnel in frontline units	416,000	404,056	238,926	1,058,982
Personnel in rear-area units	238,040	182,533	98,170	518,743
Tanks	1,751	1,201	752	3,704
Self-propelled guns	665	659	528	1,852
Anti-tank guns (45 and 57 mm)	1,360	1,539	808	3,707
Field-artillery (76 mm and above)	3,075	3,743	1,604	8,422
Mortars (all types)	3,922	4,879	2,829	11,630
RS launchers	583	516	72	1,171
AA guns	601	504	1,280	2,385

Source: 'Kampaniia Sovetskikh Vooruzhennikh Sil na Dal'nem Vostoke v 1945 g. (Fakti i tsifri)', *Vizh*, Number 8 (1965), p. 68.

Table 12.2 Japanese forces facing the Soviets in the Far East, summer 1945

Total Japanese strength	1,217,000 men, 1,155 tanks, 5,360 guns, 1,800 aircraft			
Made up of	993,000 Japanese		214,000 auxiliaries	
	713,000 in Manchuria (Kwantung Army)	280,000 in southern Korea and on Sakhalin and the Kuriles	170,000 Munchukuoan Army	44,000 Inner-Mongolian Forces

Source: Glantz, *August Storm: The Soviet 1945 Strategic Offensive in Manchuria*, p. 28.

Table 12.3 Aircraft strengths of Soviet *fronts* and naval forces at the start of the 'Manchurian Strategic Offensive' Operation

Aircraft type	Trans-Baikal Front (12th Air Army)	1st Far Eastern Front (9th Air Army)	2nd Far Eastern Front (10th Air Army)	Pacific Fleet	Northern Pacific Flotilla	Totals
Fighters	499	536	823	461	178	2,497
Ground-attack	197	193	178	194	46	808
Bombers	440	352	198	342	62	1,364
Torpedo	–	–	–	138	–	138
Reconnaissance	40	62	40	84	31	257
Artillery-spotter	–	35	39	–	–	74
Transport	189	15	24	–	–	228

Source: 'Kampaniia Sovetskikh Vooruzhennikh Sil na Dal'nem Vostoke', p. 68.

overall Japanese strength above to Soviet strength in Table 12.3. However, Drea suggests that the Kwantung Army actually had only 180 combat aircraft.[8] According to Marshal P.S. Kirsanov, Soviet superiority in the air was further enhanced by the fact that, presumably after the start of hostilities, the Japanese command pulled back the bulk of their limited air assets to bases in South Korean and Japan, meaning that Soviet air forces met even less opposition than expected and could focus more on the support of ground troops.[9]

In order to capture Manchuria, and in the process destroy the Kwantung Army, the broad Soviet plan was, as summarized by Glantz and along the lines outlined in Document 167, that:

> The Trans-Baikal *Front* would attack eastward into western Manchuria, while the 1st Far Eastern *Front* would attack westward into eastern

Manchuria. These two attacks would converge in the Mukden, Changchun, Harbin, and Kirin areas of south central Manchuria. The 2nd Far Eastern *Front* would conduct a supporting attack into northern Manchuria, driving southward to Harbin and Tsitsihar. Timing of on-order operations against southern Sakhalin Island and the Kuriles would depend on the progress of the main attacks.[10]

Hence Soviet forces of the Trans-Baikal *Front* and 1st Far Eastern *Front* were to encircle the bulk of the Kwantung Army through bold deep penetration operations, particularly by the Trans-Baikal *Front* in the west, assisted by operations of 2nd Far Eastern *Front* that would pin Japanese forces and contribute to the prevention of their orderly withdrawal (see Figure 12.1). Having encircled the bulk of the Kwantung Army the Trans-Baikal and 1st Far Eastern *Fronts* were to advance on the Laiotung Peninsula and Port Arthur, lost to Russia, as south Sakhalin, after defeat in the Russo-Japanese War of 1904–05. As it happened, the second phase of the Soviet operation would barely get started before Japanese forces capitulated.[11]

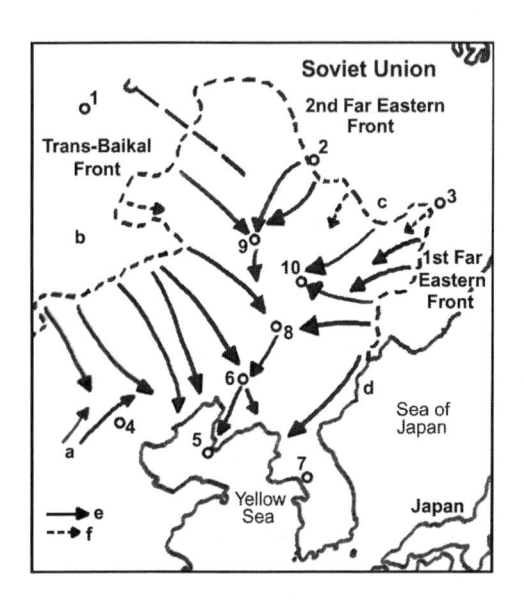

Figure 12.1 The Soviet 'Manchurian Strategic Offensive' Operation, 9 August to 2 September 1945.

Key:

1. Chita
2. Blagoveshchensk
3. Khabarovsk
4. Peking
5. Port Arthur
6. Mukden
7. Seoul
8. Changchun
9. Tsitsihar
10. Harbin

a. Chinese forces
b. Mongolia
c. Amur Flotilla
d. Far Eastern Fleet
e. Soviet advance
f. Japanese retreat

Having gained tactical and operational surprise during the invasion of Manchuria on 9 August 1945, with the successful development of operations on the mainland Soviet forces commenced operations against Japanese forces on South Sakhalin with forces of 16th Army of the 2nd Far Eastern *Front* in co-operation with the Northern Pacific Flotilla of the Soviet Pacific Fleet on 11 August, to be followed by landings on the Kurile Islands by forces of 2nd Far Eastern *Front* and the Pacific Fleet from 18 August.[12]

Whilst Soviet forces had gained tactical and operational surprise in Manchuria, the Japanese did at least have plans on how to deal with a Soviet invasion that was expected eventually, even if not until the spring of 1946 according to some, more optimistic estimates of the summer of 1945.[13] Faced with superior forces the Japanese were well aware that holding the Red Army on the borders was not feasible for any sustained period, and hence the eventual Japanese plan was to hold key fortified positions, for instance the particularly dense fortifications in the Eastern Highlands facing 1st Far Eastern *Front*, and key positions covering the passes through the Greater Khingan Mountains across which forces of the Trans-Baikal *Front* would have to advance, both to delay the Soviet advance and whittle down Soviet strength. The bulk of Japanese forces were to conduct an orderly withdrawal into the southern portion of the interior where Soviet forces, with their strength sapped and at the end of extended supply lines, could be held.[14]

The Soviet advance was, in reality, more successful that Soviet or Japanese expectations.

Despite having to advance across mountainous terrain following by the barren expanses of the Central Plains, with poor lines of communications and in particular problems in keeping troops and vehicles supplied with water, the advance of the Trans-Baikal *Front* was particularly dramatic in its speed and depth. Bypassing key Japanese positions, as Glantz notes, 6th Guards Tank Army had proved able to cover 350 km of rough terrain in only three days after the start of operations on 9 August. After 12 August, with Soviet troops deep in the Japanese rear, 'only logistical difficulties limited the Soviet advance', with Japanese troops unable to form any sort of viable defensive line.[15]

The dramatic rate of the advance of the Trans-Baikal *Front* was assisted by the fact that, in the face of weak Japanese anti-tank capabilities and the concentration of the bulk of Japanese forces in the region along a particularly limited number of avenues of advance, this *front* could deploy tanks in the first echelons of the attack without fear of them being bogged down in the sort of anti-tank defences faced in the West, with the subsequent advance greatly assisted by Soviet airpower:

> DOCUMENT 168: *Extract from the entry in the* Soviet Military Encyclopedia *on the 'Manchurian Operation' of 1945*
>
> One specific dimension to the operational organization of forces of the Trans-Baikal *Front* was the large number of tank armies and cavalry mechanized groups in the first echelon, which played a major role in the achievement of the rapid rate of advance of the troops. Aviation was certainly a powerful military resource that had significant impact on the course of operations, with more than 22,000 sorties being launched. Aviation was widely used for reconnaissance, the dropping of troops and the delivery of supplies, and especially fuel for the tank armies. During the operation 16,500 men, about 2,780 tons of fuel, 563 tons of munitions and about 1,500 tons of other supplies were delivered by air.
>
> (Source: *SVE* 5, p. 130)

Unsurprisingly it was the Trans-Baikal *Front* which received the bulk of the fuel flown in by air to sustain the advance – a total of 2,456 tons.[16]

As forces of the Trans-Baikal *Front* advanced across the mountains and broke in to the Central Plain, forces of the 1st Far Eastern *Front* faced denser Japanese defences. Indeed, relatively few Japanese troops were in the west given the perception that the terrain and associated logistical problems made large-scale Soviet operations there unlikely. Despite the greater concentration of Japanese forces on the eastern sector of the front, in well-prepared positions, as Glantz notes, 'forward detachments of reinforced tank brigades swept through and around Japanese defensive lines, preempting any systematic defense. Follow-on rifle forces crushed or bypassed any established defences.'[17]

With Soviet forces deep in the heart of Manchuria the widespread surrender of Japanese forces began, according to Soviet sources, on 19 August. Between 18 and 27 August Soviet forces were either transported in by air or forward mobile detachments of the ground forces sent in to towns such as Harbin, Mukden and Port Arthur, as yet still not occupied by Soviet forces, in order to 'speed up' the surrender of Japanese forces and 'prevent them from evacuating or from damaging material assets' before the final Japanese surrender on 2 September.[18] In the light of the Japanese capitulation proposed Soviet landings on the northern Japanese island of Hokkaido did not take place.

The success of Soviet operations and the inadequacy of Japanese forces in Manchuria against a Red Army schooled in and equipped for the war in the West are illustrated by figures, at the time they were reported provisional, provided by 1st Far Eastern *Front* for enemy and its own losses for the period from 9 August to 1 September 1945:

DOCUMENT 169: *Report of the command of forces of the 1st Far Eastern* Front *to the High Command of Soviet forces in the Far East on enemy losses, trophy items captured and losses of Soviet forces from 9 August to 1 September 1945, 2 September 1945*

I report:

1. Overall enemy losses are 322,500 soldiers, officers and generals, of whom more than 65,000 soldiers and officers were killed during the fighting of the period from 9.8 to 20.8, and in fact in the Mutanchiang region, according to General-Lieutenant Shimizu Noritsune in command of 5th Army, more than 40,000 soldiers and officers were killed.

    For the whole period from 9.8. to 1.9.45 257,225 men were captured, of whom 43 were generals, 8,058 officers and 249,124 men.

    Amongst those captured officers and men are: 236,216 Japanese; 9,297 Manchurians; 6,788 Koreans; 4,924 Chinese.

    Amongst the captured generals: Commander of the 1st Army Group General Kita Seiichi;...

    During the actual fighting 1st Far Eastern *Front* took more than 7,000 prisoners, the remainder giving themselves up after the capitulation of the Japanese Army....

2. For the period from 9.8 to 1.9.45 forces of the 1st Far Eastern *Front* captured the following trophy items:

    Aircraft of various types – 359 (of which some were serviceable)
        Tanks – 120
        Armoured cars – 18
        Artillery pieces of various calibers – 705
        Self-propelled guns – 15
        Mortars and grenade launchers – 1,117
        LMGs – 1,651
        HMGs – 881
        Motor vehicles – 1,417
        Steam locomotives – 35
        Railway trucks – 5,526
        Tractors – 51
        Horses – 6,948
    Supply dumps of various types – 441 and a lot of other military supplies
    The tallying up of trophy items continues.

3. Forces of the 1st Far Eastern *Front* lost 17,225 men in the period from 9.8 to 1.9.45, of whom: 3,254 were killed and 13,867 wounded.

    Losses of horses were 260.

    Material losses were: artillery pieces – 8, mortars – 17, tanks and armoured cars hit my artillery fire and burnt out on the battlefield – 31. Aircraft (shot down in aerial combat, by AA fire or destroyed on the ground) – 53. Losses due to accidents or catastrophes – 12. Total aircraft lost – 65.

Meretskov

(Source: *RA T.18 7(2)*, 2000, pp. 130–131)

The Soviet Union suffered a total of 12,031 irrecoverable personnel losses during the 'Manchurian Strategic Offensive' Operation as a whole between 9 August and 2 September 1945, during which, according to Krivosheev, total losses of tanks and self-propelled guns for three *fronts* were only 78.[19] According to Soviet sources, a total of 83,737 Japanese troops were killed and 594,000 taken prisoner during the 'Manchurian' Operation as a whole.[20] Japanese sources suggest that in the region of 21,000 Japanese troops were in fact killed.[21]

In Manchuria, Soviet forces gained the upper hand over the Japanese on a number of levels from the operational-strategic down to the tactical. At the operational-strategic level they had achieved surprise, particularly in the west, thanks to their ability to deploy troops over terrain and distances well beyond Japanese expectations and planning. This ability to deploy and sustain large mechanized forces across difficult terrain contributed to Japanese paralysis at an operational level, where Japanese forces proved unable, even in the east, to block or counter-attack against the flanks of Soviet penetrations with any strength. At the tactical level, Soviet forces used 'small, task-oriented assault groups with heavy engineer and firepower support' rather than the human waves that had characterized Soviet tactics at the beginning of the Great Patriotic War, and where possible probed, bypassed and penetrated through the cracks of even more dense defences rather than hurling themselves against them. Relying more on machines than human lives, Soviet commanders exercised initiative much further down the chain of command than they had done earlier in the war.[22]

The rivers of blood spilled over years in the war against Nazi Germany had at least contributed to what, by Soviet standards, was a relatively bloodless success in the east, even if lives lost there might seem to have been lost to little purpose compared to the increasingly obvious need to defeat Nazi Germany as the true nature of the regime was revealed to Soviet citizens after June 1941.

Guide to further reading

Edward J. Drea, 'Missing Intentions: Japanese Intelligence and the Soviet Invasion of Manchuria, 1945', *Military Affairs* (April 1984), pp. 66–73.

David Glantz, *August Storm: The Soviet 1945 Strategic Offensive in Manchuria*, Leavenworth Paper Number 7 (Fort Leavenworth, KS: Combat Studies Institute, US Army Command and General Staff College, February 1983).

David Glantz, *August Storm: Soviet Tactical and Operational Combat in Manchuria, 1945*, Leavenworth Paper Number 8 (Fort Leavenworth, KS: Combat Studies Institute, US Army Command and General Staff College, June 1983).

David Glantz, *Soviet Operational and Tactical Combat in Manchuria, 1945: 'August Storm'* (London: Frank Cass, 2003).

Conclusion

By the end of the Great Patriotic War, the Soviet Union had undoubtedly recovered the Great Power status that its Tsarist predecessor had last most obviously enjoyed from about 1813–14 until the Crimean War of 1853–56. Whilst Soviet victories at the end of the Great Patriotic War continued to be won at horrendous human cost, they were nonetheless arguably being won (particularly given the fact that Soviet forces faced a prepared enemy on the defensive in an increasingly built-up landscape) more economically in terms of the shedding of Soviet blood than they had been earlier in the war. This was to a large extent thanks to the recovery of the Soviet armaments industry after the shock of invasion and associated loss of territory, but also because the resultant equipment was being used more effectively. Soviet losses of men and material continued, however, to be staggering until the end of the war, particularly when compared to those of British, Canadian and American forces in the west – losses on a scale not simply explainable by the greater scale and ferocity with which the war was being fought in the east. Alongside the 557,643 Soviet troops killed in action or dying during casualty evacuation from January–May 1945, more than total British and Commonwealth losses for the whole war, during the same period the Red Army lost 13,700 tanks and self-propelled guns and 27,000 motor vehicles.[1]

Whilst the Red Army certainly remained the massive and slightly unwieldy juggernaut of the German memoir-influenced Western historiography of the 1950s and 1960s,[2] it was no longer quite such the crude instrument that had whittled down German strength during the summer of 1941 and eventually halted the increasingly feeble German spearheads before Moscow. Later in the war, unsupported or at best poorly supported frontal assaults by Soviet infantry were increasingly infrequent and tanks were no longer being thrown into battle in battalion-sized packets, instead being deployed en masse but in genuinely combined-arms tank and mechanized corps and indeed armies, able to make deep penetrations into multi-layered if weakly manned German defences that could no longer depend on powerful mobile reserves. Such Soviet penetrations were increasingly spearheaded by mobile groups led by officers showing an initiative that few would have been willing to show in the political climate engendered by the purges at the start of the war. Nonetheless, the thousands of Soviet troops killed in capturing fortified cities such as Königsberg and Budapest did so for little military purpose.

In the light of the strength of the Soviet war machine during the second half of the war in the east, it is easy to forget that Soviet and indeed Allied victory was not and certainly had not always been all but inevitable. Ignoring Hitler's decision to turn his attentions eastwards in 1941 rather than knocking Britain out of the war[3] – one counter-factual that might very well have influenced the outcome of the war in a single stroke, it is important to note, as Overy does in *Why the Allies Won*, that:

> Battles are not pre-ordained. If they were, no one would bother to fight them. The decisive engagement at Midway Island was won because ten American bombs out of the hundreds dropped fell on the right target.... The bombing offensive, almost brought to a halt in the winter of 1943–4, was saved by the addition of long-range fuel tanks to escort fighters, a tiny expense in the overall cost of the bombing campaign.[4]

However, whilst German victory might have seemed very much a possible outcome in the early summer of 1941, at the beginning of the Great Patriotic War German strength, no matter how it is measured, was certainly nothing like as overwhelming as Allied strength in 1944–45. Short of the invention of a wonder weapon such as the atomic bomb, the like of which Hitler dreamt and only the vast resources of the United States could develop in time to deploy against Japan in August 1945, the chances of a surprise German victory were diminishing rapidly during 1943 and particularly in 1944. The benefit of counter-factuals is that they bring us to consider the relative importance of variables in what did happen, and the list of what Allied powers might have done differently in 1939–42 to prevent German successes is far longer than any list that can be devised as to what Germany could have done differently in late 1943–45 in order to stave off defeat.

By the time of the Allied landings in Normandy, Soviet ascendancy in the east was obvious and German defeat a question of 'when' rather than 'whether'. Once the Soviet Union became embroiled in the Second World War, the bulk of German divisions was undoubtedly fighting and destroyed on the Eastern Front. The concluding volume of the Khrushchev-era official Soviet history of the Great Patriotic War provides the data in Table C.1 to illustrate the extent to which, throughout the war, the bulk of German ground forces at least were concentrated against the Soviet Union. The data presented certainly highlights the basic fact that the bulk of German ground forces fought the Red Army from June 1941 throughout the war, even if the June 1944 invasion of Normandy led to the fact that by 1 January 1945, the Western Allies were facing more than 37 per cent of German ground strength measured in divisional equivalents. However, German resources thrown into the closing stages of the campaign in North Africa and the air war in the Mediterranean and then over Europe from 1942 onwards were substantial, the latter tying down increasing German resources from 1943 onwards.[5] However, as figures provided by Mawsdley suggest, the Soviet Union was certainly killing far more German 'military personnel' than the Western Allies between the third quarter of 1941 and third quarter of 1944, with the final quarter of 1944 being the only possible exception where 223,000 German troops were killed in the 'East', compared to 224,000 on other fronts.[6] With the exception of the Italians, Germany's allies were also tied down on the Eastern Front. However, the Soviet official history certainly exaggerates the importance of the Red Army holding down German allies in the East where the Finns, Rumanians and Hungarians were not interested in fighting, and indeed keen not to fight, the Western allies – in the case of the Finns, and to a lesser extent Rumanians, the key concern was regaining territory lost to the Soviet Union in 1940.[7]

Despite the recent rediscovery of the contribution of the Red Army to the defeat of Nazi Germany in the Western popular historiography of the war, there is no doubt when considering the Western Front and Allied aid to the Soviet Union that Nazi Germany and her allies was defeated by a genuine coalition of powers that held together throughout the war, despite Hitler's hopes of driving a wedge between its disparate elements. Whilst the Western Allies only belatedly committed sufficient land forces to occupy a significant proportion of German divisions, and the Soviet Union almost alone faced significant German land forces before the spring of 1943, the Western-Allied contribution to the defeat of Germany even before D-Day nonetheless went beyond strategic bombing and the air war. Allied aid had certainly been important in helping the Soviet Union survive the winter of 1941–42, had allowed Soviet industry to focus on the production of key weapons systems and increasingly had a major impact on Red Army mobility and communications, even if the chances are that without this aid the Red Army would still have held Moscow and gradually pushed the German invaders back. That Japanese forces did not take advantage of German invasion and attack the USSR from Manchuria in late 1941 or the autumn of 1942 owes much to the success of Soviet arms at Lake Khasan and Khalkin Gol in 1938 and 1939 respectively, but also to the commitment of better elements of Japanese air and ground forces to the war against the Western Allies after December 1941.

Whilst the Red Army held the *Wehrmacht* before Moscow and Stalingrad and then pushed it back at least in part beyond the pre-1939 Soviet border before D-Day, during this period the Western Allies were nonetheless gathering strength and indeed the will before, in June 1944, finally making a major land commitment to the war – the 'Second Front' for which Stalin had been pushing for some time. Whilst operations in Sicily and Italy from July and September 1943 respectively failed to draw off sizeable German assets, it has to be remembered that the United States was engaged in a war on two fronts, and in the lead up to D-Day the Western Allies were

Table C.1 German divisional equivalents on the 'Soviet–German', 'other fronts' or on 'occupied territory or in Germany' according to the Soviet Khrushchev-era official history of the Great Patriotic War

Date	Total German 'divisions'	'On Soviet–German front'	% of total German divisions	'On other fronts'	% of total German divisions	On 'occupied territory or in Germany'	% of total German divisions
22 June 1941	217.5	153	70.3	2	0.9	62.5	28.8
1 May 1942	236.5	181.5	77	3	1.1	52	21.9
1 July 1943	297	196	66	8	2.7	93	31.3
1 January 1944	318	201	63.3	19.5	6.1	97.5	30.6
1 June 1944	326.5	181.5	55.6	81.5	25	63.5	19.4
1 January 1945	314.5	179	57	119	37.8	16.5	5.2

Source: *Istoriia Velikoi Otechestvennoi voini.... Tom shestoi. Itogi...*, p. 26.

building up resources for an amphibious assault on enemy-held shores on a scale without precedent. Subsequent Soviet claims of Allied prevarication may have contained some truth – the Allies were not going to launch themselves at Normandy without due preparation just to please Stalin. However, in some ways the Western Allies were doing what Stalin had been doing from September 1939 until the German-led invasion – building up resources with the knowledge that premature commitment was unnecessary with German forces committed elsewhere. One might also argue, however, that Soviet commitment to dealing with the National Socialist threat had been more serious than that of the Western powers during the 1930s, and in particular by September 1938, prompting the signing of the Nazi–Soviet Pact to buy time – both the Western allies and the Soviet Union could certainly make claims that the other had vacillated and stood by at key moments when their earlier intervention could have been significant.

In terms of what actually happened, the Soviet Union paid a far higher human and material cost during the war than her Allies, albeit one that might have been reduced had it not been for the Great Purges and failure to take relatively rudimentary preparations to meet German invasion. In explaining why this was the case and moving beyond tactical and operational practice, it has to be borne in mind that whilst the Soviet Union did not join the war until June 1941, Soviet forces could not retreat behind the English Channel but were locked in continuous combat for almost the next four years, on a scale that would only be matched in the west in the latter stages of the war, and in combat of a far more sustained ferocity.

The scale of killing on the Eastern Front, particularly if the Final Solution is included, has seen no equal in history to date. Estimates of total Soviet losses have risen since the end of the war, when in 1946 Soviet losses were publicly admitted to having been seven million killed, despite the regime being aware of at least 15 million deaths. The official figure for losses was increased to 20 million or more under Khrushchev and Brezhnev, increasing again to 26–27 million or more during Gorbachev's *perestroika*. It was during this period that a commission of the Ministry of Defence, working in co-operation with other agencies, would report that 8,668,400 Soviet military personnel were either killed, died of wounds or did not return from captivity – a figure taken as undermining the total Soviet figure of 20 million killed and leading to a figure of 27 million Soviet deaths as a result of the war being announced by Gorbachev on the eve of Victory Day (9 May) in 1990. This figure has been widely accepted since then.[8] Of these 8,668,400 Krivosheev suggests that 5,177,410 were killed in action or died during casualty evacuation in the war against Germany, with a further 1,100,327 dying in hospital of wounds and 540,580 as non-combat losses, due, for example, to disease and accidents.[9]

In the region of 4,559,000 Soviet troops were accounted for as missing in action or POWs during the war, according to figures once again provided by Krivosheev; Streit suggests that 3,350,000 POWs were taken in 1941 alone, of whom nearly 60 per cent had died by 1 February 1942.[10] As Krivosheev discusses, not all of these were Red Army personnel – indeed German claims for POWs taken often exceeded Red Army forces in a given area, with many construction workers and other auxiliary personnel under army supervision not appearing in Red Army statistics for losses but counting as POWs in German statistics. Additionally, according to Krivosheev, many liable for military service who found themselves on Axis-occupied territory were also apparently imprisoned, although a significant number of non-Russian POWs and even some Russians, possibly wounded, were subsequently released back into the population.[11] According to Soviet statistics, there were 1,836,000 POW returnees to the Soviet Union from German camps at the end of the war, and a further 939,700 had been redrafted into the Red Army either from camps or having been released into the civilian population of occupied territory during the war, leaving 1,783,300 from the 4,559,000 total, of whom 673,000 died in captivity according to German figures and with about half of the remainder having died in German captivity according to Krivosheev – perhaps these individuals being the 'approximately 600,000' POWs that would fall victim to SS extermination, according to Streit. That leaves 500,000 of those 'missing' who had, according to Krivosheev, in fact largely been killed.[12] Whilst assessment of who died and how during the Great Patriotic War is a complex problem with no conclusive figures,[13] the finer calculations do not change the broad thrust of the statistics – that tens of hundreds of thousands of Soviet service personnel died during battle or as a result of wounds sustained, with hundreds of thousands more dying in German captivity.

War-related civilian losses are an even more complex issue given the sheer scale of population displacement during the war in the east making it difficult to keep track of population, some of whom were killed by military action, in German atrocities, as part of the Final Solution or died of starvation on both sides of the front line in both German and NKVD camps, even if many deaths in the latter were ultimately the result of German action given that wartime mortality rates in the camps far exceeded those immediately before and after the war.[14]

To losses of human life and the demographic implications of a low wartime birth-rate have to be added reduced numbers of livestock and horses; the slaughter of the latter at the front was significant owing to the reliance that both sides placed on horse-drawn transport and given that their importance for agriculture had increased during the war due to the loss of male labour to the Red Army[15] and reallocation of tractor production to tanks.[16] As a result of the fighting and scorched-earth policies on both sides, but particularly wholesale by Germany in retreat, damage to infrastructure and other material assets, whether industrial or housing stock, was tremendous. According to Soviet figures 1,710 towns and other urban settlements were 'fully or partially reduced to ruins or razed, along with 70,000 villages and hamlets'; Stalingrad, Sevastopol', Novorossiisk and Kerch' were all but ruins. Along with damage to industrial concerns that could not be evacuated, thousands of kilometres of railway line, hundreds of bridges and vast quantities of agricultural equipment had been destroyed.[17] Soviet recovery, both demographically and materially, would be a long process.[18]

German military deaths, whilst colossal by the standards of Britain and the United States, were significantly lower than those for the Soviet Union, particularly when considering that Germany was fighting against the Western Allies as well as the Soviet Union, and even if Soviet deaths amongst POWs are not considered. According to figures provided by Mawdsley, 2,742,000 German military personnel were killed in the 'East' from the third quarter of 1941 to the end of 1944, compared to 766,000 on 'other fronts' for the same period, with a further 147,000 killed prior to this period. Total German losses for 1945 are given as 1,230,000. This leaves us with a figure of 4,885,000 for the war as a whole.[19] Amongst other figures, Krivosheev gives a figure of 2,007,000 killed on the Eastern Front to the end of April 1945 according to an OKH memorandum of 10 May 1945, excluding deaths amongst POWs, given as 450,600 for the war in the east as a whole according to Soviet figures. This figure does not include deaths amongst those counted as missing in action – 2,610,000 being counted as missing or POWs in the OKH figures. If subtracting 1,939,000 German returnees from Soviet captivity and 450,600 that died in captivity according to Soviet figures then this leaves another 220,400 unaccounted for in this rather crude analysis, many undoubtedly killed.[20] Either way, the number of German troops that were killed in action and died as Soviet POWs was far lower than the corresponding figures for Soviet forces, although the addition of casualties from amongst Germany's allies does change the picture to some extent.[21]

The horrendous loss of human life on the Eastern as compared to the Western Front, not counting the millions of maimed and other wounded, certainly owed much to German National Socialist ideology, whether most obviously in the Final Solution, in the more complex issue of Soviet POW deaths and in particular during the winter of 1941–42, or simply in the uncompromising manner in which the Nazi leadership prosecuted a war inspired not only by racial ideology but vehement anti-communism. At the same time Nazi Germany was fighting a regime that, whilst lacking the same racial-ideological component, not only saw fascism as the most threatening form of capitalism (as it was indeed proving), but that had been willing to sanction the sacrificing of hundreds of thousands of its own citizens in an attempt to eradicate real, potential and imagined opposition during the Great Purges. It is therefore no surprise that Stalin and his regime squandered human life, particularly during the first half of the war before it became more scarce, with abandon, much as Hitler would be willing to squander German lives as Nazi fortunes waned as the war progressed. That lives were squandered in order to defend the Soviet Union from what, as German occupation policies soon proved, a threat even more brutal than the Stalinist regime, goes some way to legitimize Soviet losses – the end justifying the means – but that does not change the fact that German resources, including significant numbers of divisions late in the war, were being more effectively destroyed in human-cost terms by the Western Allies, the difference arguably not explained alone by systemic and broader cultural factors.

Both Hitler and Stalin are inevitably the focus of more attention in military-historical literature than other wartime leaders such as Churchill and Roosevelt, given the extent to which they personally were able and willing to make decisions, with little consultation and often then with 'yes' men in their entourages, that could send hundreds of thousands of men to their deaths. However, whilst Hitler's tendencies in this direction became more extreme as the German position deteriorated, after the Soviet position had improved with the Soviet counter-offensive below Moscow Stalin's leadership would show the opposite trend. Having held much of the responsibility for lack of Soviet short-term preparations to meet the invasion, the decision not to pull troops back from Kiev in the summer of 1941 and the decision to undertake a sustained counter-offensive across a broad front after more localized successes at the gates of Moscow, near Tikhvin and Rostov-on-Don, Stalin started both to consult more widely and learn from mistakes. The influence of his pre-war and often Civil War cronies such as Voroshilov and the old guard such as Budennii declined rapidly, making way for capable commanders such as Zhukov, Vasilevskii, Konev and Rokossovskii[22] as Hitler was dismissing competent commanders one by one. Hence, whilst taking much of the blame for the debacles of the summer and autumn of 1941 and summer of 1942, Stalin could legitimately claim some credit both personally and in recognizing able subordinates for eventual Soviet military victory, aided by economic foundations laid down during the Five-Year Plans that Stalin had personally driven forward, once again amidst considerable human, particularly peasant, suffering.[23] Perhaps one of Stalin's greater successes was the realization that the Soviet people were often not fighting for Stalin and socialism per se, but for *Rodina* – the motherland, and *narod* – the people, often tied to family, friends and comrades-in-arms, with the Russians more the vanguard of the Soviet people than of the proletariat.[24]

During the 1930s the Soviet Union was perhaps the most 'militarized' (in the broadest possible sense) society in the world when one takes into account such factors as defence and related spending, the size and equipment of its armed forces, the importance of foreign threats in propaganda and the scale of conscription and military training or preparation for non-regular troops. In order to play a crucial role in the defeat of Nazi Germany, as is apparent in the material presented in this reader, the importance of the creation and deployment of military power in Soviet society increased during the Great Patriotic War to a level without comparison in the West with the possible exception of the last months of the Nazi regime. Having defeated Nazi

Germany, with an Eastern European empire to hold on to and with challenging capitalist hegemony with the assistance of military power, even if by proxy, being a real possibility and ideological obligation, the Soviet superpower continued to use a vast proportion of the state budget on defence spending. Maintenance of her newly re-acquired Great Power or superpower status was, initially from the end of the war up until the mid-1950s at least, at the expense of the peasantry as had been the case in the 1930s. Increasingly, defence spending was one of a number of major economic burdens on the shoulders of an increasingly inefficient system in which resources were also being thrown at the agricultural sector and attempts to provide Soviet 'consumers' with the housing and other consumer goods to placate them in a society less reliant on terror as a basic tool of governance and motivational tool than it had been under Stalin. As foreign-currency oil revenues collapsed in the mid-1980s, the scale of the economic burden of maintaining a Soviet military might, sustained increasingly ineffectively for new generations by pride in wartime achievements, became apparent. Residual Soviet pride in the achievements of the Great Patriotic War won at such high cost could not prop up Soviet hegemony in Eastern Europe nor indeed the Soviet Union itself, but pride in wartime achievements remained a significant element in attempts by the Putin regime to rekindle Russian national pride, despite the fact that the Great Patriotic War had ended more than 60 years before.

Chronology of key events

1917–38

October 1917	The Bolsheviks seize power in Petrograd – the October Revolution
1917–21	The Russian Civil War is fought by the Bolsheviks against internal opponents and foreign 'intervention'
1921	The New Economic Policy is introduced into Russia
1924	Death of Lenin
	The Soviet Union is officially established
1928	Official start of the First Five-Year Plan for the development of the Soviet economy
1929–30	Period of mass collectivization of Soviet agriculture
1931	Japanese invasion of Manchuria
1933	Adolf Hitler comes to power in Germany
1934	The Soviet Union joins the League of Nations in an attempt to check the rise of Nazi Germany
1935	The Soviet Union sign mutual-assistance treaties with France and Czechoslovakia
1936	Germany reoccupies the Rhineland
1936–38	Period of the 'Great Purges' in the Soviet Union
1937	'Dual command' is reintroduced in the Red Army
March 1938	German *Anschluss* with Austria
July–August 1938	Border clash between Soviet and Japanese forces at Lake Khasan at the junction between Korea, Manchuria and the Soviet Union
September 1938	Germany acquires the Sudeten region of Czechoslovakia at the Munich Conference

1939

March	Germany seizes the remainder of Czechoslovakia
April	Britain and France make guarantees for Polish security
Summer	Abortive negotiations between Britain, France and the Soviet Union over containing Nazi Germany
August	Major clash between Soviet and Japanese forces at Khalkin-Gol on the border between Mongolia and Manchuria is a Soviet victory
23 August	Nazi–Soviet Non-Aggression Pact
1 September	Germany invades Poland
3 September	Britain and France declare war on Germany
17 September	The Soviet Union invades Poland
28 September	German–Soviet Treaty, with secret protocols, sees Germany and the Soviet Union carve up Eastern Europe
30 November	Soviet invasion of Finland

1940

12 March	Soviet peace treaty with Finland
April	German forces seize Denmark and Norway
May–June	German forces seize the Low Countries and France
June	Soviet forces move into the Baltic Republics and the Soviet Union acquires Bessarabia and northern Bukovina from Rumania
July–October	The Battle of Britain
12 August	'Unitary command' is introduced in the Red Army
September	Italian forces invade Egypt
18 December	Initial German order (Directive Number 21) for Operation 'Barbarossa' – the invasion of the Soviet Union – signed by Hitler

1941

April	Soviet–Japanese Neutrality Pact
5 May	Stalin speech to graduating officers on the need for a new 'offensive' orientation for the Red Army
15 May	Plan for the strategic deployment of the Red Army proposes pre-emptive offensive action against German forces on the Soviet border
14 June	TASS communiqué published in *Pravda* denying aggressive intentions on the part of the Soviet Union or Nazi Germany towards the other

22 June	(a.m.) The German invasion of the Soviet Union, Operation 'Barbarossa', begins. (p.m.) Red Army ordered to counter-attack
23 June	Headquarters of the High Command [*Stavka* GK] created for the co-ordination of the Soviet military, headed by Timoshenko
23–29 June	Major tank engagements in the Dubno, Brodi, Lutsk and Rovno regions between Soviet mechanized forces of the South-Western *Front* and 1st Panzer Group of Army Group South
24 June	Council for Evacuation created to organize the removal of industry from areas threatened by the German advance
28 June	Minsk, capital of Belorussia, falls to German forces of Army Group Centre
29–30 June	Stalin, in crisis, retreats to his *dacha*
30 June	Creation of the State Defence Committee [GKO] under Stalin for the co-ordination of the Soviet war effort
	Creation of the first seven militia divisions [*narodnogo opolcheniia*] in Leningrad
3 July	Stalin makes his first radio speech of the war to the Soviet people, addressing them as 'brothers and sisters'
5 July	*Stavka* GK orders the creation of the Luga defence line for the defence of Leningrad from the south
9 July	Pskov falls to German forces of Army Group North
10 July	Headquarters of the Supreme Command [*Stavka* VK] replaces the *Stavka* GK as Stalin replaces Timoshenko as head of the Red Army and *Stavka*
	The GKO orders the creation of *napravlenie* commands for the co-ordination of multiple *fronts*, namely the North-Western under Voroshilov (to 27 August 1941); Western under Timoshenko (to 10 September 1941 and again from 1 February–5 May 1942 under Zhukov); and South-Western initially under Budennii (to 23 June 1942, with the exception of 1 October to 24 December 1941)
	Start of what became known in the Soviet Union as the 'Battle of Smolensk', primarily fought by forces of the Western *Front*, lasting until 10 September 1941 and culminating in the El'nia counter-attack
12 July	Agreement between the United Kingdom and Soviet Union on joint action in the war against Germany

Chronology of key events

16 July	'Dual command' reintroduced into the Red Army
	GKO decree on the construction of the Mozhaisk defence line for the defence of Moscow
	Smolensk falls to German forces of Army Group Centre
17 July	Military counter-intelligence (special sections) transferred from the NKO to NKVD
18 July	Party decree on 'the organization of the struggle in the rear of German forces' seeks to develop partisan activity under Party auspices
30 July	German order (Führer Directive Number 34) leads to Army Group Centre going over to the defensive on the Moscow axis
8 August	Headquarters of the Supreme High Command [*Stavka* VGK] replaces *Stavka* GK as Stalin becomes Supreme High Commander of Soviet forces
12 August	Soviet counter-attack by forces of the North-Western *Front* south-east of Staraia Russa
16 August	Order Number 270 of the *Stavka* VGK makes the surrender of Red Army personnel tantamount to treason
30 August	German forces of Army Group North sever rail communications between Leningrad and the rest of the Soviet Union
	Soviet 'El'nia' Operation by forces of the Reserve *Front*
31 August	The first significant British convoy delivers aid to the Soviet port of Arkhangel'sk
8 September	German forces of Army Group North reach Lake Ladoga and capture Schlissel'berg, cutting off land communications between Leningrad and the rest of the Soviet Union. The siege or blockade of Leningrad begins
	Soviet forces destroy the El'nia bridgehead near Smolensk of forces of Army Group Centre
19 September	German forces capture Kiev, capital of the Ukraine
30 September	Start of Soviet 'Moscow Strategic Defensive' Operation (to 5 December 1941) in the face of German operations by 2nd Panzer Group as a precursor to the start of the principal phase of Operation 'Typhoon'
2 October	The German advance on Moscow resumes with the start of the principal phase of Operation 'Typhoon' by 3rd and 4th Panzer Groups
5 October	German forces of 2nd Panzer Group take Briansk

7 October	German forces of 2nd Panzer Group take Orel and 3rd Panzer Group take Viaz'ma
14 October	German forces of 3rd Panzer Group take Kalinin
15 October	GKO decree on the evacuation of Moscow
16 October	Rumanian and German forces capture Odessa
25 October	German 6th Army takes Khar'kov
7 November	Soviet Revolution Day parade takes place in Moscow with troops drawn off from and returning immediately to the front line
	US Lend-Lease aid is formally extended to the Soviet Union
15 November	Final German push on Moscow begins
17 November	*Stavka* VGK order on a 'scorched-earth' policy as Soviet forces retreat before Moscow
	Soviet forces begin the 'Rostov Strategic Offensive' Operation in the south (to 2 December 1941)
20 November	German forces of Army Group South capture Rostov-on-Don
26 November	British intercepts indicate that German forces encountered British-supplied tanks in Soviet service for the first time
29 November	Soviet forces of the Southern and Trans-Caucasian *Fronts* recapture Rostov-on-Don
5 December	Start of the 'Moscow Strategic Offensive' Operation by Soviet forces, primarily the Western and Kalinin *Fronts*
7 December	Japanese forces attack the US naval base at Pearl Harbor
8 December	German forces go over to the defensive below Moscow
9 December	Soviet forces recapture Tikhvin, preventing German forces from linking up with the Finns on the River Svir' and cutting Soviet forces off from the Lake Ladoga lifeline to Leningrad
11 December	Germany declares war on the United States
16 December	Kalinin is recaptured by Soviet forces of the Kalinin *Front*
	Hitler orders that German forces stand fast in the face of the Soviet counter-offensive below Moscow
25 December	Start of the Soviet 'Kerch'–Feodosia Amphibious' Operation in the Crimea by the Trans-Caucasian *Front*

1942

8 January	The Soviet 'Moscow Strategic Offensive' Operation develops into the overambitious 'Rzhev–Viaz'ma Strategic Offensive' Operation that lasts until 20 April 1942
17 March	The Soviet 2nd Shock Army and much of 59th Army are encircled in operations below Leningrad
5 April	German Führer Directive Number 41 for offensive operations in the south
12–29 May	Significant encirclement of Soviet forces during offensive operations near Khar'kov
30 May	Creation of a Central Headquarters for the Partisan Movement (TsShPD) to organize and co-ordinate partisan activity
28 June	Operation 'Blau', the German summer offensive of Army Group South begins – the beginning of the Soviet 'Voronezh–Voroshilovgrad Strategic Defensive' Operation to 24 July 1942
4 July	Sevastopol' captured by the German 11th Army
	The British convoy to Arkhangel'sk PQ-17 scatters in the face of German attacks and the threat from *Tirpitz*, resulting in the loss of most of its merchant ships and the temporary cessation of convoys
6 July	Voronezh captured by the German 6th Army
17 July	Beginning of the Soviet 'Stalingrad Strategic Defensive' Operation, to 18 November 1942
23 July	German Directive Number 45 for the continuation of Operation '*Braunschweig*' (the Caucasus offensive) directs Army Group A towards the Caucasus and B towards Stalingrad
	German forces recapture Rostov-on-Don
25 July	Beginning of the Soviet 'North Caucasus Strategic Defensive' Operation that lasts until 31 December 1942
28 July	Order Number 227 of the People's Commissar for Defence calls for 'not a step back' in the face of the renewed German advance
30 July	'Rzhev–Sichevka' Operation of Soviet forces of the Kalinin and Western *Fronts* against Army Group Centre to 23 August 1942
19 August	'Siniavino' Operation of Soviet forces of the Leningrad and Volkhov *Fronts* seeks to de-blockade Leningrad, to 10 October 1942
	British and Canadian forces raid Dieppe

1 September	German forces reach the outskirts of Stalingrad
5 September	Order Number 189 of the People's Commissar for Defence 'on the tasks of the partisan movement' seeks to make the partisan movement more valuable to the Red Army
7 September	German forces capture the Black Sea port of Novorossiisk
9 October	'Unitary command' is re-established in the Red Army
14 October	German offensive operations within Stalingrad see most of the city in German hands by the end of the day
23 October	Start of Allied offensive operations at El Alamein
8 November	Operation 'Torch' – British–US landings in north-west Africa
19 November	Soviet forces begin Operation 'Uranus', the initial encirclement of German forces at Stalingrad and the first phase of the 'Stalingrad Strategic Offensive' Operation by forces of the South-Western, Don and Stalingrad *Fronts*
24 November	Soviet forces encircle the German 6th Army along with elements of 4th Panzer Army when Soviet spearheads link up at Kalach-on-Don
25 November	Soviet forces of the Kalinin and Western *Fronts* begin Operation 'Mars' against the German Army Group Centre, to 20 December 1942
16 December	Soviet forces launch scaled-down operations (Operation 'Little Saturn') for the destruction of German forces of Army Groups A and B in the south
27 December	Hitler authorizes the withdrawal of Army Group A from the North Caucasus

1943

13 January	Beginning of the Soviet 'Voronezh–Khar'kov Strategic Offensive' Operation by forces of the Briansk, Voronezh and South-Western *Fronts* that sees the effective destruction of 2nd Hungarian and 8th Italian Armies (to 3 March 1943)
18 January	Leningrad blockade partially lifted with the recapture of Schlissel'berg during Operation 'Spark' of the Leningrad and Volkhov *Fronts*
25 January	Soviet forces of the Voronezh *Front* recapture Voronezh

Chronology of key events 299

2 February	German forces of 6th Army at Stalingrad surrender Soviet offensive operations directed on Khar'kov begin
8 February	Soviet forces recapture Kursk
14 February	Soviet forces of the Southern *Front* recapture Rostov-on-Don
16 February	Khar'kov recaptured by Soviet forces of the Voronezh *Front*
20 February	German forces begin withdrawal from the Demiansk salient
1 March	German forces begin withdrawal from the Rzhev–Viaz'ma salient
3 March	Soviet forces of the Western *Front* recapture Rzhev
12 March	Soviet forces of the Western *Front* recapture Viaz'ma
16 March	German forces recapture Khar'kov
13 May	Axis forces in North Africa surrender
4 July	German forces begin Operation 'Citadel' against the Soviet Kursk salient
10 July	British and US forces invade Sicily
11–12 July	Major tank battle near Prokhorovka on the southern side of the Kursk salient
12 July	Soviet forces of the Central, Briansk and Western *Fronts* begin Operation 'Kutuzov' or the 'Orel Strategic Offensive' Operation to the north of the Kursk salient
13 July	German forces go over to the defensive in the Kursk region
14 July	Major partisan offensive against German lines of communication, that would later be described as the 'War of the Rails', ordered to begin on 21 July for Orlov partisans and 3 August for Leningrad, Kalinin, Smolensk and Belorussian partisans
3 August	Soviet forces of the Voronezh and Steppe *Fronts* begin Operation 'Rumiantsev' or the 'Belgorod–Khar'kov Strategic Offensive' Operation to the south of the Kursk salient
5 August	Soviet forces of the Briansk *Front* recapture Orel
7 August	Soviet forces of the Kalinin and Western *Fronts* begin Operation 'Suvorov' in the Smolensk region
12 August	Hitler takes the decision to form a defensive line, the *Ostwall*, along the Dnepr River
13 August	Start of the Soviet 'Donbass Strategic Offensive' Operation (to 22 September 1943)
28 August	Khar'kov recaptured for the final time by Soviet forces and remains in Soviet hands

9 September	British and American landings on mainland Italy at Salerno
15 September	German forces start to withdraw behind the so-called *Ostwall*
16 September	The Black Sea port of Novorossiisk is finally recaptured by Soviet forces
17 September	Briansk recaptured by Soviet forces
22 September	Soviet forces of the Central and Voronezh *Fronts* seize a number of bridgeheads over the Dnepr River that are contained by German forces
25 September	Smolensk recaptured by Soviet forces of the Western *Front*
26 September	Soviet forces make major gains on the western bank of the lower Dnepr River during the 'Lower Dnepr Strategic Offensive' Operation (to 20 December 1943)
20 October	Major renaming of Soviet *Fronts*: the Kalinin, Baltic and Central *Fronts* become the 1st and 2nd Baltic and Belorussian *Fronts* respectively, and the Voronezh, Steppe, South-Western and Southern *Fronts* become the 1st–4th Ukrainian *Fronts* respectively
2 November	Forces of the 1st Ukrainian *Front* seize a substantial bridgehead over the Dnepr to the north of Kiev and begin to break out the following day
6 November	Soviet forces of the 1st Ukrainian *Front* recapture Kiev
12 November	Soviet forces of the 1st Ukrainian *Front* recapture Zhitomir
19 November	German forces recapture Zhitomir
24 December	Start of the Soviet 'Dnepr'–Carpathian Strategic Offensive' Operation (to 17 April) by the 1st–4th Ukrainian *Fronts* that sees the liberation of much of the remainder of the Ukraine on the western side of the Dnepr River and Soviet forces penetrating Romanian territory
31 December	Zhitomir recaptured by Soviet forces of 1st Ukrainian *Front*

1944

24 January	'Korsun'–Shevchenkovskii Offensive' Operation, part of the 'Dnepr–Carpathian Strategic Offensive' Operation, of forces of the 1st and 2nd Ukrainian *Fronts* (to 17 February 1944)

27 January	Blockade of Leningrad formally lifted during the 'Leningrad–Novgorod Strategic Offensive' Operation by forces of the Leningrad and Volkhov *Fronts*
8 March	German Führer order on the holding of *feste Plätze* or 'fortified places' for the slowing down of the Soviet advance
10 May	Soviet forces recapture Sevastopol' during the 'Crimean Strategic Offensive' Operation by forces of the 4th Ukrainian *Front* and Independent Maritime Army
6 June	D-Day landings in Normandy by British, Canadian and US troops
10 June	Soviet forces of the Leningrad and Karelian *Fronts* begin the 'Viborg–Petrozavodsk Strategic Offensive' Operation against Finnish forces (to 9 August 1944) that is crucial in forcing Finland out of the war
23 June	Soviet forces of the 1st Baltic and 1st, 2nd and 3rd Belorussian *Fronts* begin the 'Belorussian Strategic Offensive' Operation (to 29 August 1944) that saw the liberation of Belorussia, the destruction of much of the German Army Group Centre and Soviet forces penetrate Polish territory
3 July	Minsk is recaptured by Soviet forces of the 2nd and 3rd Belorussian *Fronts*
13 July	Soviet forces of the 1st Ukrainian *Front* begin the 'L'vov–Sandomierz Strategic Offensive' Operation (to 29 August) that sees Soviet forces seize a bridgehead over the Vistula River
21 July	Pskov recaptured by Soviet forces of the 3rd Belorussian *Front*
24 July	Lublin captured by Soviet forces of the 1st Belorussian *Front*
1 August	Start of the abortive Warsaw uprising by the Polish Home Army (to 2 October 1944)
20–29 August	The brief Soviet 'Iassi–Kishinev Strategic Offensive' Operation sees the Soviet liberation of Moldavia and tears open German–Rumanian defences in the south
23 August	Coup in Bucharest sees overthrow of Marshal Antonescu in favour of king
29 August	Start of the abortive Slovak uprising (to 27 October 1944)
8 and 28 September	Soviet forces begin the 'East Carpathian

1944	Strategic Offensive' (to 28 October 1944) and 'Belgrade Strategic Offensive' (to 20 October 1944) Operations respectively that saw Soviet troops entering Czechoslovakia and clear German forces from much of Yugoslavia in liaison with Yugoslav forces
5 September	Ceasefire between Soviet and Finnish forces
13 October	Riga recaptured by Soviet forces of the 2nd and 3rd Baltic *Fronts*
20 October	Yugoslav partisans and Soviet forces of 3rd Ukrainian *Front* capture Belgrade
29 October	Soviet forces of the 2nd and 3rd Ukrainian *Fronts*, with the participation of Rumanian troops, launch the 'Budapest Strategic Offensive' Operation (to 13 February 1945)
16 December	German forces in the West launch an offensive in the Ardennes region, which is halted by 24 December 1944
1945	
12 January	Soviet forces of the 1st Belorussian and 1st Ukrainian *Fronts* launch the 'Vistula–Oder Strategic Offensive' Operation (to 18 February 1945) that saw Soviet forces seize a number of bridgeheads over the Oder River and the destruction of considerable German forces
13 January	Soviet forces of the 2nd and 3rd Belorussian *Fronts* (to 25 April 1945) saw Soviet forces capture much of East Prussia at considerable cost
10 February	Official start of the Soviet 'East Pomeranian Strategic Offensive' Operation (to 4 April 1945) that saw Soviet forces, initially of 2nd Belorussian *Front*, clear much of the Baltic coastlines of Poland and eastern Germany and any threat to Soviet forces on the Berlin axis from the north
16–20 February	German counter-attack near Stargard in Pomerania further diverts Soviet attention from the Berlin axis
1 March	Soviet forces of 1st Belorussian *Front* start participation in the 'East Pomeranian Strategic Offensive' Operation
6–15 March	German offensive by 6th SS Panzer Army near Lake Balaton in Hungary
16 March	Soviet forces of 3rd Ukrainian with elements of 1st

	Ukrainian *Front* launch the 'Vienna Strategic Offensive' Operation (to 15 April 1945)
10 April	Königsberg captured by Soviet forces of 3rd Belorussian *Front*
16 April	Soviet forces of 1st Belorussian along with 1st Ukrainian and 2nd Belorussian *Fronts* launch the 'Berlin Strategic Offensive' Operation (to 8 May 1945)
26 April	Meeting of Soviet and US forces in the region of Torgau on the Elbe River
2 May	Berlin garrison surrenders
6 May	Forces of 1st, 2nd and 4th Ukrainian *Fronts* launch the last Soviet operation of the war in Europe with the 'Prague Strategic Offensive' Operation (to 11 May)
7 May	'Initial' German surrender to the Allies takes place at Rheims, to take effect the following day
8 May	'Final' German surrender to the Allies takes place at Karlshorst to take effect the following day
9 May	Soviet troops land on the Danish island of Bornholm
11 May	Conclusion of Soviet operations against residual German opposition in the Prague region
6 and 9 August	United States drops atomic bombs on the Japanese cities of Hiroshima and Nagasaki
9 August	Soviet forces of the Trans-Baikal and 1st and 2nd Far-Eastern *Fronts* launch the 'Manchurian Strategic Offensive' Operation against Japanese forces in Manchuria, on South Sakhalin and the Kurile Islands (to 2 September)
2 September	Japanese surrender

Glossary

AA	Anti-aircraft	
ACV	Armoured Command Vehicle	
AK	*armeiskii korpus*	Army corps
army		Military formation typically consisting of a number of corps and supporting units
army group		German military formation consisting of a number of armies; until late in the war, equivalent in strength to more than one or a large Soviet *front*
ASDIC	Allied Submarine Detection Investigation Committee	British term for what is now more typically called SONAR
ASSR	*Avtonomnaia Sovetskaia Sotsialisticheskaia Respublika*	Autonomous Soviet Socialist Republic
AT	Anti-tank	
battalion		Military unit typically consisting of a number of companies or equivalent (for most German unit types an *Abteilung*)
Bolsheviks		Informal title for VKP(b)
brigade		Military unit typically consisting of a number of battalions or equivalent
boekomplekt	*boevoi komplekt*	A quantity of munitions for a given weapon or tank or other weapons systems (e.g. for a tank the maximum number of shells and machine-gun ammunition

		that could be carried), or indeed requirement for a whole units or formation
ChF	*Chernomorskii flot*	Soviet Black Sea Fleet
commissar		Political officer, formally down to battalion level, with shared responsibility for decision-making with a commanding officer between 16 July 1941 and 9 October 1942. Below battalion level political officers were known as *politruki*.
company		Military unit consisting of a number of platoons or equivalent
Comintern	Communist International	Organization established by the Bolsheviks in 1919 for the co-ordination of the activities of foreign communist parties. Disbanded in 1943
corps		Military formation typically consisting of a number of divisions or equivalent and supporting units
DBAK/DBAD	*dal'nebombardirovochnii aviatsionnii korpus/ dal'nebombardirovochnaia aviatsionnaia diviziia*	Long-Range Bomber Aviation Corps/Long-Range Bomber Aviation Division
DDRudZW8	*Das Deutsche Reich und der Zweite Weltkrieg. Band 8*	See Bibliography
division		Military unit typically consisting of a number of brigades or equivalent. A full-strength German infantry division was larger than a Soviet infantry division, particularly during late 1941 and early 1942
DOT/DZOT	*dolgovremennaia ognevaia tochka/derevo-zemlianaia ognevaia tochka*	Permanent Fire-Point/Wood-Earth Fire-Point
Einsatzgruppe		National Socialist field formation under the authority of the *Reichsführer SS* for the

		elimination of enemies of National Socialism, on Soviet territory initially in particular commissars and Party officials, but increasingly involved in the killing of Jews and anti-partisan warfare
EKA	*Einwohner-Kampf-Abteilung*	Locally recruited militia-type units for security duties on German-occupied territory
fortified district	*ukreplennii raion*	Prior to and on the outbreak of the Great Patriotic War, these were frontier-defence zones manned at brigade or regimental strength whose principal unit was the machine-gun battalion. From 1942 fortified regions served as low-manpower high-firepower formations for the holding of quiet sectors of the front
front		Soviet military formation consisting of a number of armies and typically equivalent in strength to an early-war German army or later-war German army group
FSB	*Federal'naia Sluzhba Bezopasnosti*	Federal Security Service – Russian successor to the KGB
GABTU	*Glavnoe avtobronetankovoe upravlenie*	Main Auto-Armour Board of the Red Army
GAU	*Glavnoe artilleriiskoe upravlenie*	Main Artillery Board of the Red Army
Guards		First given as an honorary title to Soviet units that had excelled in battle in September 1941, as the war progressed guards units and formations made up an increasing proportion of Soviet forces and tended to be larger and better-equipped than their regular counterparts
GAZ	*Gosudarstvennii avtomobil'nii zavod*	State Automobile Factory

Genshtab – see **GSh KA**

Glossary

GKO/GOKO	*Gosudarstvennii Komitet Oboroni*	State Defence Committee – effectively the Soviet war cabinet, chaired by Stalin
GlavPU KA	*Glavnoe politicheskoe upravlenie Krasnoi armii*	Main Political Directorate of the Red Army. Responsible for ideological work within the Red Army, which to a large extent meant discipline, including the appointment and supervision of political officers below *front* level and appointing political members to military soviets
Gosplan	*Gosudarstvennii planovaia komissia {pri Sovnarkome SSSR}*	State Planning Commission (attached to the Council of People's Ministers of the USSR)
GRU	*Glavnoe razvedivatel'noe upravlenie*	Main Reconnaissance Board (of the Red Army)
GSh KA	*General'nii shtab Krasnoi armii*	General Headquarters of the Red Army
GU	*Glavnoe upravlenie*	Main Board or Central Administration of ...
GUGVF	*Glavnoe upravlenie Grazhdanskogo vozdushnogo flota*	Central Administration of the Civilian Air Fleet
Gulag	*Glavnoe upravlenie ispravitel'no-trudovikh lagerei i kolonii*	Central Administration for Corrective Labour Camps and Colonies
GUSKA	*Glavnoe upravlenie sviazi Krasnoi armii*	Main Board of Communications of the Red Army
GVKhU	*Glavnoe voenno-khimicheskoe upravlenie*	Main Military Chemical Board (of the Red Army)
HMG	Heavy machine gun	
ITB		Independent Tank Battalion
Jaeger	[Regiment/Division]	German 'light' infantry
JSMS	*Journal of Slavic Military Studies*	See Bibliography
KB-70		70-octane fuel, used by Soviet aircraft and with imported motor vehicles. Imported aircraft demanded 80–100 octane fuel
KBF	*Krasnoznamennii Baltiiskii flot*	Soviet Baltic Fleet
KGB	*Komitet Gosudarstvennoi Bezopasnosti*	

Glossary

KMG	*konno-mekhanizirovannaia kruppa*	Cavalry-Mechanized Group
kolkhoz	*kollektivnoe khoziaistvo*	Collective farm
Komsomol – see also **VLKSM**	*Kommunisticheskii soiuz molodozhi*	Communist Youth League
KV	Kliment Voroshilov	Soviet heavy tank named after a Soviet marshal and close associate of Stalin
Lend-Lease		US system of providing aid without payment or credit introduced in March 1941 with Britain in mind and extended to the Soviet Union in November 1941
LMG	Light machine gun	
Luftwaffe		The German air force
Luftwaffe field division		Infantry divisions organized by the Luftwaffe from surplus personnel that proved less effective than most *Wehrmacht* divisions and tended to be relegated to second-line and security duties
MID	*Ministerstvo inostrannikh del*	Ministry of Foreign Affairs
military soviet		Councils at *front* and army level consisting of military and political members, the latter functioning as the equivalent of commissars in providing Party supervision over decision-making. They did, however, at times serve a useful role as bridges between civilian organizations and the Red Army, in particular in providing material support. Military Soviets also played a role in the development and effective functioning of the partisan movement, the latter organized under Party auspices, in particular in facilitating partisan co-operation with the Red Army

Narodnoe opolchenie – see *opolchenie*

NCO		Non-commissioned officer
NEP		The New Economic Policy from 1921
NK/*Narkom*	*Narodnii komissar* or *Narodnii komissariat*	People's Commissar or People's Commissariat – equivalent of a minister or ministry
NKO	*Narodnii komissariat oboroni*	
NKGB	*Narodnii komissariat gosudarstvennii bezopasnosti*	People's Commissariat for State Security – a new ministry that acquired responsibilities, including foreign intelligence and counter-espionage on Soviet territory, from the NKVD for a brief period in early 1941 and then again from 1943–46
NKPS	*Narodnii komissariat putei soobshcheniia*	People's Commissariat for Transport [lit. Routes of Communication]
NKVD	*Narodnii komissariat vnutrennikh del*	People's Commissariat for Internal Affairs
OATB	*Otdel'naia avto-transportnaia brigada*	Independent Auto-Transport Brigade
oblast'		Soviet administrative region
OD	*Ordnungsdienst*	Local 'police' on German-occupied territory
OKH	*Oberkommando des Heeres*	German High Command of the Army, increasingly as the war progressed only concerned with the Eastern Front
OO NKVD	*Osobii otdel* NKVD	Special Section of the NKVD – responsible for counter-intelligence in military units from 1941–43. Replaced by SMERSH
opolchenie		Hastily trained Soviet militia units thrown before the German advance in 1941
OVO	*Osobii voennii okrug*	Special military district – a military district located in sensitive border regions
Ostarbeiter		Workers, initially recruited and

		then conscripted from German-occupied territories in the East for labour in Germany
Panzerfaust		German recoil-less hollow-charge disposable infantry anti-tank weapon responsible for the destruction of huge numbers of Soviet tanks in 1944–45
People's Commissariat – see **NK**		
POW	Prisoner of War	
PVO	*protivovozdushnaia oborona*	Air defence – Soviet air defence forces – including anti-aircraft guns and fighter aircraft
PzKpfw	*Panzerkampfwagen*	Tank
raion		Soviet administrative district
rasputitsa		Russian term for the period in autumn and spring when dirt roads became difficult going due to rain and the spring thaw respectively
RDF	Radio-Direction Finding	
regiment		Military unit consisting of more than one battalion or equivalent, often with supporting units, and roughly equivalent in strength to a brigade
Reichsführer SS		Head of the SS
RGAE	*Rossiiskii gosudarstvennii arkhiv economiki*	Russian State Archive for the Economy
RGASPI	*Rossiiskii gosudarstvennii arkhiv sotsial'no-politicheskoi istorii*	Russian State Archive for Socio-Political History
RKKA	*Rabochaia i krest'ianskaia krasnaia armiia*	Workers' and Peasants' Red Army
RS	*Reaktivnie snariadi*	Soviet rocket artillery, typically known as *katiusha*
RSFSR	*Rossiiskaia Sotsialisticheskaia Federativnaia Sovetskaia Respublika*	Russian Socialist Federated Soviet Republic – formally incorporated in to the USSR in 1924
RVGK	*Rezerv Verkhovnogo Glavnokomandovaniia*	Reserve of the Supreme High Command
SAU	*samokhodnaia artilleriiskaia ustanovka*	Self-propelled, typically tracked, artillery or anti-tank gun
SBD	*Sbornik boevikh dokumentov*	See Bibliography

SF	*Severnii flot*	Soviet Northern Fleet
SMERSH	*Smert' spionam*	Lit. death to spies – Soviet military counter-intelligence from 1943
SMG	Sub-machine gun	
SNK – see *Sovnarkom*		
SONAR	Sound Navigation And Ranging	Underwater detection device
Sovinformburo		News and propaganda agency formed on the outbreak of the Great Patriotic War that subsequently became the Novosti news agency
Sovnarkom	*Sovet narodnikh komissarov*	Council of People's Commissars – effectively the highest tier for the Soviet governmental, as opposed to Party, structure
sovkhoz	*sovetskoe khoziaistvo*	Soviet farm on which those working the land were not stakeholders as in a *kolkhoz*, but were paid wages
SP – see SAU		
SS	*Schutzstaffel*	German National Socialist security, and increasingly military organization (see **Waffen** SS)
SSSR – see USSR		
Stavka GK	*Stavka Glavnogo Komandovaniia*	Headquarters of the High Command (established 23 June 1941)
Stavka VK	*Stavka Verkhovnogo Komandovanniia*	Headquarters of the Supreme Command (established 10 July 1941)
Stavka VGK	*Stavka Verkhovnogo Glavnogo Komandovanniia*	Headquarters of the Supreme High Command (established 8 August 1941)
STZ	*Stalingradskii traktornii zavod*	Stalingrad Tractor Factory
Supreme Soviet		The equivalent of the Soviet parliament, to which the *Sovnarkom* was theoretically answerable
SVE	*Sovetskaia Voennaia Entsiklopediia*	See Bibliography
T-34		Legendary Soviet medium tank

		in production throughout the war that proved far superior to available German types when first encountered during 1941
TA	Tank Army	
TASS	*Telegraf'noe agenstvo Sovetskogo Souiza*	Telegraph Agency of the Soviet Union – responsible for the dissemination of news outside the USSR
TB	Tank Battalion	
TsGA SPb	*Tsentral'nii gosudarstvennii arkhiv Sankt Peterburga*	Central State Archive of St Petersburg
TsK	*Tsentral'nii komitet*	Central Committee (of the Communist Party) – Party equivalent of the Supreme Soviet
TsMVS	*Tsentral'nii muzei vooruzhennikh sil*	Central Museum of the Armed Forces (photograph source)
TsShPD	*Tsentral'nii shtab partisanskogo dvizheniia*	Central Headquarter of the Partisan Movement
TsVMM	*Tsentral'nii voenno-morskoi muzei*	Central Naval Museum (photograph source)
US NA	United States National Archives	
USG KA	*Upravlenie snabzhennia goriuchim*	Board of Fuel Supply of the Red Army
USSR	Union of Soviet Socialist Republics	Formed in 1924
Vizh	*Voenno-istoricheskii zhurnal*	See Bibliography
VKP(b)	*Vsesoiuznaia kommunisticheskaia partiia (bolshevikov)*	All-Union Communist Party (Bolsheviks)
VLKSM	*Vsesoiuznii Leninskii kommunisticheskii soiuz molodezhi*	All-Union Leninist Communist Union of Young People – see also **Komsomol**
VMF	*Voenno-morskoi flot*	The Soviet navy
VO	*voennii okrug*	Military district – military-administrative region, converted to a *front* if playing a front-line role in wartime
voenkomat	*voennii komissariat*	Military Commissariat – local organs responsible for the registration and mobilization of conscripts in to the Red Army

Volksturm		German equivalent of the *opolchenie*
VVS	*Voenno-vozdushnie sili*	Soviet air forces
Waffen SS		Conventional armed forces formed under the auspices of the *Reichsführer SS* even if under *Wehrmacht* operational control. Increasingly prevalent from 1943 onwards
Wehrmacht		The German armed forces, although often used with reference to the army (*Heer*)
WiIn	*Wirtschaftsinspektion*	Army-Group level military-economic organ with responsibilities for the economic exploitation of occupied territories in the interests of the *Wehrmacht*

Notes

Introduction

1 It is worth mentioning David M. Glantz, *Companion to Colossus Reborn: Key Documents and Statistics* (Lawrence, KS: University Press of Kansas, 2005), as one of the few useful collections of documents and statistics available in English.
2 Good examples being H.R. Trevor-Roper (ed.), *Hitler's War Directives, 1939–1945* (London: Sidgwick and Jackson Ltd, 1964) and J. Noakes and G. Pridham (eds), *Nazism 1919–1945 – A Documentary Reader. Volume 3: Foreign Policy, War and Racial Extermination* (Exeter: University of Exeter Press, 1988).

1 Lenin, Stalin and the West 1917–39

1 This chapter is based on material first presented as 'Stalin and the West', in Gordon Martel (ed.), *A Companion to International History, 1900–2001* (Oxford: Blackwell, 2007), pp. 257–268.
2 On the conflict between diplomatic stability and destabilization of, in this instance, Poland in the early–mid 1920s, see D. Stone, 'The August 1924 Raid on Stolpce, Poland, and the Evolution of Soviet Active Intelligence', *Intelligence and National Security*, Volume 21, Number 2 (Spring 2006), pp. 331–341.
3 See H. Flory, 'The Arcos Raid and the Rupture of Anglo-Soviet Relations, 1927', *Journal of Contemporary History*, Volume 12, Number 4 (October 1977), pp. 707–723.
4 See N.S. Simonov, '"Strengthen the Defence of the Land of the Soviets": The 1927 "War Alarm" and its Consequences', *Europe–Asia Studies*, Volume 48, Number 8 (1996), pp. 1355–1364. See also Lennart Samuelson, *Plans for Stalin's War Machine: Tukhachevskii and Military-Economic Planning, 1925–1941* (Basingstoke: Palgrave, 2000).
5 On the issue of the location of defence industries, see David Stone, 'The First Five-Year Plan and the Geography of Soviet Defence Industry', *Europe–Asia Studies*, Volume 57, Number 7 (November 2005), pp. 1047–1063.
6 Gordon W. Morrell, 'Redefining Intelligence and Intelligence Gathering: The Industrial Intelligence Centre and the Metro-Vickers Affair, Moscow 1933', *Intelligence and National Security*, Volume 9, Number 3 (July 1994), pp. 520 and 531 note 6.
7 O.N. Ken, *Mobilizatsionnoe planirovanie i politicheskie resheniia (konets 1920 – seredina 1930-Kh godov)* (St Petersburg: Izdatel'stvo Evropeiskovogo universiteta v Sankt Peterburge, 2002). For an English-language overview of this important work, see my review in *Journal of Strategic Studies*, Volume 28, Number 5 (October 2005), pp. 894–895.
8 [N252/40/38] 'Viscount Chilston to Mr Eden. – (Received January 15.), Moscow, January 12, 1937', in D. Cameron Watt (ed.), *British Documents on Foreign Affairs: Reports and Papers from the Foreign Office Confidential Print. Part II. From the First to Second World War. Series A. The Soviet Union, 1917–1939. Volume 14. The Soviet Union, Jan.1937–Dec.1938* (Frederick, MD: University Publications of America, 1986), pp. 6–7.

9 J. Rohwer and M.S. Monakov, *Stalin's Ocean Going Fleet: Soviet Naval Strategy and Shipbuilding Programmes, 1935–1953* (London: Frank Cass, 2001), pp. 34–35, 45–46, 51–52.
10 See Peter Jackson, 'France', in Robert Boyce and Joseph A. Maiolo (eds), *The Origins of World War Two: The Debate Continues* (Basingstoke: Palgrave Macmillan, 2003), pp. 94–98.
11 A.J.P. Taylor, *The Origins of the Second World War* (London: Hamish Hamilton, 1961); J. Haslam, *The Soviet Union and the Struggle for Collective Security in Europe, 1933–39* (London: Macmillan Press Ltd, 1984); G. Roberts, *The Soviet Union and the Origins of the Second World War: Russo-German Relations and the Road to War, 1933–1941* (London: Macmillan Press Ltd, 1995); M.J. Carley, 'Behind Stalin's Moustache: Pragmatism in Early Soviet Foreign Policy, 1917–1941', *Diplomacy and Statecraft*, Volume 12, Number 3 (September 2001), pp. 159–174.
12 Roberts, *The Soviet Union and the Origins of the Second World War*, pp. 3–4.
13 J. Hochman, *The Soviet Union and the Failure of Collective Security, 1934–1938* (Ithaca, NY: Cornell University Press, 1984); A.M. Nekrich, *Pariahs, Partners, Predators: German Soviet Relations, 1922–1941* (New York: Columbia University Press, 1997).
14 Silvio Pons, *Stalin and the Inevitable War 1936–1941* (London: Frank Cass, 2002).
15 John Ferris, 'Image and Accident: Intelligence and the Origins of World War II, 1933–1941', in John Robert Ferris, *Intelligence and Strategy – Selected Essays* (Abingdon: Routledge, 2005), p. 107.
16 See Keith Neilson, *Britain, Soviet Russia and the Collapse of the Versailles Order, 1919–1939* (Cambridge: Cambridge University Press, 2006).
17 Zara Steiner, 'The Soviet Commissariat of Foreign Affairs and the Czechoslovakian Crisis in 1938: New Material from the Soviet Archives', *Historical Journal*, Volume 42, Number 3 (1999), pp. 751–779; Hugh Ragsdale, *The Soviets, the Munich Crisis, and the Coming of World War II* (New York: Cambridge University Press, 2004), p. 120.
18 O. Khlevniuk, 'The Objectives of the Great Terror, 1937–38', in D.L. Hoffmann (ed.), *Stalinism: The Essential Readings* (Malden, MA.: Blackwell Publishing, 2003) and in J. Cooper, M. Perrie and E.A. Rees (eds), *Soviet History 1917–1953: Essays in Honour of R.W. Davies* (New York: St Martin's Press, 1995).
19 Albert Resis, 'The Fall of Litvinov: Harbinger of the German-Soviet Non-aggression Pact', *Europe-Asia Studies*, Volume 52, Number 1 (2000), pp. 33–56.
20 Press interview by Voroshilov, Commissar for War, on the Anglo-French–Soviet military negotiations, 27 August 1939 (Mirovoe khoziaistvo, 1939, 9, p. 11), in J. Degras (ed.), *Soviet Documents on Foreign Policy. Volume III 1933–1941* (London: Oxford University Press, 1953), pp. 361–362.
21 Taylor, *The Origins of the Second World War*, p. 231.
22 See, for instance, from a largely German perspective, T.R. Philbin III, *The Lure of Neptune: German-Soviet Naval Collaboration and Ambitions, 1919–1941* (Columbia, SC: University of South Carolina, 1994).
23 Ken, *Moblilizatsionnoe planirovanie*, p. 365.
24 See for instance V. Sipols, *Taini diplomaticheskie: Kanun Velikoi Otechestvennoi voinoi. 1939–1941* (Moscow: TOO 'Novina', 1997), pp. 160–165.
25 For an illustration of this regarding Finland, see M. Jakobsen, *The Diplomacy of the Winter War: an Account of the Russo-Finnish War, 1939–1940* (Cambridge, MA: Harvard University Press, 1961), pp. 115–119.
26 Ken, *Moblilizatsionnoe planirovanie*, p. 366

2 The Icebreaker controversy and Soviet intentions in 1941

1 Elements of this chapter were first published as 'The Icebreaker Controversy and Soviet Intentions in 1941: The Plan for the Strategic Deployment of Soviet Forces of 15 May and Other Key Documents', *JSMS*, Volume 21, Number 1 (January–March 2008), pp. 1–16.

2 See Alexander Hill, 'The Birth of the Soviet Northern Fleet 1937–1942', *JSMS*, Volume 16, Number 2 (June 2003), pp. 70–71. For a broader perspective on British, German and Soviet interests in the region, see Patrick Salmon, *Scandinavia and the Great Powers, 1890–1940* (Cambridge: Cambridge University Press, 1997).
3 V. Suvorov (pseud.), 'Who was Planning to Attack Whom in June 1941, Hitler or Stalin?', *Journal of the Royal United Services Institute for Defence Studies*, Volume 130, Number 2 (1985), pp. 50–55.
4 Available in English is V. Suvorov, *Icebreaker: Who Started the Second World War?* (London: Hamish Hamilton, 1990). His work in this field continued in Russian with *Den'-M* (Moscow: AST, 1995).
5 J. Hoffmann, *Stalin's War of Extermination, 1941–1945: Planning, Realization, and Documentation* (Capshaw, AL: Theses & Dissertations Press, 2001). See also J. Hoffmann, 'The Red Army until the Beginning of the German-Soviet War', in H. Boog, J. Forster, J. Hoffmann, E. Klink, R.-D. Muller, G.R. Ueberschar and E. Osers (eds), *Germany and the Second World War. Volume IV. The Attack on the Soviet Union* (Oxford: Clarendon Press, 1998), pp. 72–93.
6 D. Glantz, *Stumbling Colossus: The Red Army on the Eve of War* (Lawrence, KS: University Press of Kansas, 1998).
7 I.e. in particular into Poland.
8 G. Gorodetsky, *Grand Delusion. Stalin and the German Invasion of Russia* (New Haven, CT: Yale University Press, 1999).
9 See Jürgen Förster and Evan Mawdsley, 'Hitler and Stalin in Perspective: Secret Speeches on the Eve of Barbarossa', *War in History*, Volume 11, Number 1 (2004), pp. 61–103.
10 V.A. Nevezhin, 'The Pact with Germany and the Idea of an 'Offensive War'', *JSMS*, Volume 8, Number 4 (December 1995), pp. 809–843. See also V.A. Nevezhin, *Sindrom nastupatel'noi voini. Sovetskaia propaganda v predverii 'sviashchennikh boev', 1939–1941 gg.* (Moscow: 'AIRO-XX', 1997).
11 Evan Mawdsley, 'Crossing the Rubicon: Soviet Plans for Offensive War in 1940–1941', *International History Review*, Volume 25, Number 4 (2003), pp. 837–838. See also P.N. Bobilev, 'Tochku v diskussii stavit' rano. K voprosu o planirovanii v General'nom shtabe RKKA vozmozhnoi voini s Germaniei v 1940–1941 godakh', *Otechestvennaia istoriia*, Number 1 (2000), pp. 41–64.
12 For a useful discussion of such intelligence in decision making in Europe prior to the outbreak of the Second World War and the Axis invasion of the Soviet Union, see John Ferris, 'Image and Accident: Intelligence and the Origins of World War II, 1933–1941', in John Robert Ferris, *Intelligence and Strategy – Selected Essays* (Abingdon: Routledge, 2005), pp. 99–137.

3 Barbarossa

1 David Glantz and Jonathan House, *When Titans Clashed: How the Red Army Stopped Hitler* (Lawrence, KS: University Press of Kansas, 1995), p. 49.
2 According to V.P. Naumov (ed.), *1941 god: V 2 kn. Kn.1 and Kn.2* (Moscow: Mezhdunarodnii fond 'Demokratiia', 1998), pp. 439–430, which also provides this document in Russian, on the document it was noted 'sent at 21:15 on 22 June 1941'.
3 See David Glantz, *Colossus Reborn: The Red Army at War, 1941–1943* (Lawrence, KA: University Press of Kansas, 2005), pp. 382–383.
4 Ibid., pp. 379–382.
5 See Evan Mawdlsey, *Thunder in the East: The Nazi-Soviet War 1941–1945* (London: Hodder Arnold, 2005), p. 65.
6 See Glantz, *Colossus Reborn*, pp. 370–373.
7 K.K. Rokossovskii, *Soldatskii dolg* (Moscow: Voennoe izdatel'stvo Ministerstva oboroni SSSR, 1968), pp. 22–23.
8 A total of 3,648 tanks, self-propelled guns and other armoured vehicles were initially

committed by the *Wehrmacht* to Operation 'Barbarossa' (see Table 8, Chapter 4), compared to a Red Army tank strength of 22,600 tanks on 22 June 1941 according to Krivosheev (500 'heavy', 900 'medium' and 21,200 'light' – although the latter included BT-7 'cruiser' tanks that could have been classified as 'medium' and certainly had armament to challenge the PzKpfw 38(t) and PzKpfw III, even if their armour was light). G.F. Krivosheev (ed.), *Soviet Casualties and Combat Losses in the Twentieth Century* (London: Greenhill Books, 1997), p. 252.
9 Glantz, *Colossus Reborn*, p. 265 and Rokossovskii, *Soldatskii dolg*, p. 13.
10 On this and other counter-attacks in the region, see Glantz and House, *When Titans Clashed*, pp. 53–55.
11 Ibid., p. 58.
12 K.A. Kalashnikov et al. (eds), *Krasnaia armiia v iiune 1941 goda (statisticheskii sbornik)* (Novosibirsk: 'Novosibirskii khronograf', 2003), p. 155 and M.A. Bobrov, 'Strategicheskoe razvertivanie VVS Krasnoi armii na zapade strani pered Velikoi Otechestvennoi voinoi', *VIZh*, Number 5 (2006), p. 5.
13 A different extract from this document also appears in Chapter 9.
14 See Chapter 8.
15 See Nachal'nikam shtabov frontov o zapreshchenii peregovorov otkritim tekstom po telefonu i apparati morze, 19 iiulia 1941 g., in *RA T.23 (12–1)*, p. 73.
16 *Velikaia Otechestvennaia voina 1941–1945 gg.: Deistvuiushchaia armiia* (Moscow: Animi Fortitudo, Kuchkovo pole, 2005), p. 165.
17 21st Tank Division actually started the war with 200 tanks rather than the 375 required for it to be full strength. See Glantz, *Colossus Reborn*, p. 265.
18 See Mawdsley, *Thunder in the East*, pp. 79–81 and Krivosheev, *Soviet Casualties and Combat Losses*, p. 114. On the disparity between German and Soviet figures for POWs taken in such instances, see the Conclusion.

4 The Battle of Moscow

1 Evan Mawdlsey, *Thunder in the East: The Nazi-Soviet War 1941–1945* (London: Hodder Arnold, 2005), pp. 94–100 and 105, and David Glantz and Jonathan House, *When Titans Clashed: How the Red Army Stopped Hitler* (Lawrence, KS: University Press of Kansas, 1995), pp. 79–81.
2 Glantz and House, *When Titans Clashed*, p. 68.
3 Glantz and House, *When Titans Clashed*, pp. 81–82.
4 P.A. Rotmistrov, *Vremia i tanki* (Moscow: Voenizdat, 1972), p. 113.
5 Not including 9th, 17th and 24th Tank Brigades. 'Moskovskaia bitva v tsifrakh (period kontrnastupleniia)', *Vizh*, Number 1 (1967), p. 92.
6 'Moskovskaia bitva v tsifrakh (period oboroni)', *Vizh*, Number 3 (1967), p. 71.
7 Celebrated in November due to the shift from the Gregorian calendar in use at the time of the Revolution.
8 Mawdsley, *Thunder in the East*, p. 90.
9 V.M. Safir, 'Oborona Moskvi. Narofominskii proriv 1–5 dekabria 1941 goda (chto bilo i chego ne bilo v deistvitelnosti)', *Voenno-istoricheskii arkhiv*, Vipusk 1 (1997), p. 83.
10 N.S. Simonov, *Voenno-promishlennii kompleks SSSR v 1920–1950-e godi: tempi ekonomicheskogo rosta, struktura, organizatsiia proizvodstva i upravlenie* (Moscow: ROSSPEN, 1996), p. 164.
11 M. Suprun, *Lend-liz i severnie konvoi 1941–1945* (Moscow: Andreevskii flag 1997) p. 358.
12 Simonov, *Voenno-promishlennii kompleks SSSR*, p. 162.
13 Ibid., pp. 163–164.
14 Postanovlenie Gosudarstvennogo Komiteta Oboroni 'Ob organizatsii proizvodstva srednikh tankov T-34 na zavode "Krasnoe Sormovo", No. 1 ss, 1 iiulia 1941 g.', in I.A. Gor'kov (ed.), *Gosudarstvennii Komitet Oboroni postanovliaet (1941-1945). Tsifri, dokumenti* (Moscow: OLMA-PRESS, 2002), pp. 495–497 and GKO. Postanovlenie No. GOKO-

82/ss ot 9 iiulia 1941 g. Moskva, Kreml'. Ob obespechenii proizvodstva tankov T-34 na zavode 'Krasnoe Sormovo', RGASPI f.644.o.1.d.1.l.272.
15 Simonov, *Voenno-promishlennii kompleks SSSR*, p. 163.
16 GKO. Postanovlenie No. GOKO-1880/ss ot 5 iiunia 1942 g. Moskva, Kreml'. O proizvodstve tankov T-34. RGASPI f.644.o.1.d.38.l.266 and Simonov, *Voenno-promishlennii kompleks SSSR*, p. 163.
17 Along with 2,400 light tanks. G.F. Krivosheev (ed.), *Soviet Casualties and Combat Losses in the Twentieth Century* (London: Greenhill Books, 1997), p. 252 and Simonov, *Voenno-promishlennii kompleks SSSR*, p. 162.
18 Simonov, *Voenno-promishlennii kompleks SSSR*, p. 162 and Suprun, *Lend-liz i severnie konvoi 1941–1945*, p. 52.
19 N. Biriukov, *Tanki – frontu! Zapiski sovetskogo generala* (Smolensk: Rusich, 2005), pp. 55 and 71.
20 It was, for instance, soon identified that the pneumatic transmission on Matildas could not stand up to the temperatures to which they were subjected in Russia, and required replacement with mechanical alternatives. Not only were the track plates on Valentines considered too narrow, and suitable only for summer conditions, but spurs were considered necessary in Russian conditions and had to be manufactured locally. British-supplied track pins were considered weak and difficult to replace. Ibid., pp. 62 and 68–69 and Secret Cipher Telgram. From: 30 Military Mission. To: The War Office. Recd 22/11/41. TNA WO193/580.
21 Suprun, *Lend-liz i severnie konvoi 1941–1945*, p. 52.
22 Krivosheev, *Soviet Casualties and Combat Losses*, p. 252 and Suprun, *Lend-liz i severnie konvoi 1941–1945*, p. 52.
23 Suprun, *Lend-liz i severnie konvoi 1941–1945*, pp. 49 and 52.
24 Krivosheev, *Soviet Casualties and Combat Losses*, p. 252 and Suprun, *Lend-liz i severnie konvoi 1941–1945*, p. 53.
25 Biriukov, *Tanki – frontu!*, pp. 16 and 47.
26 Ibid., pp. 51–55.
27 Secret Cipher Telegram. From: 30 Military Mission. To: The War Office. Recd 11/12/41. TNA WO193/580.
28 Rotmistrov, *Vremia i tanki*, pp. 106–119.
29 See David Glantz, 'Forgotten Battles of the German-Soviet War (1941–1945), Part 3: The Winter Campaign (5 December-April 1942): The Moscow Counteroffensive', *JSMS*, Volume 13, Number 2 (June 2000), pp. 139–185.
30 See Chapter 8.
31 It is important to note that the key issue here, as can be noted in Document 64, was disclosing information by radio that the enemy had time to act on.
32 See Chapter 7.
33 Telephone here need not, and most probably does not, refer to a land-line.

5 The tide turns – the Battle for Stalingrad

1 N.A. Kirsanov, 'Mobilizatsiia zhenshchin v Krasnuiu armiiu v godi fashistskogo nashestviia', *Vizh*, Number 5 (2007), pp. 15–17 and Gosudarstvennii Komitet Oboroni. Postanovlenie No. GOKO-1618ss ot '18' aprelia 1942 g.... O zamene v tilovikh chastiakh i uchrezhdeniiakh VVS KA voenno-sluzhashchikh muzhchin zhenshchinami. Online. Available www.soldat.ru/gko/scans/1618-01-1.jpg (accessed 2 May 2008).
2 N.A. Kirsanov, 'Mobilizatsiia zhenshchin v Krasnuiu armiiu', pp. 15–16.
3 Ibid., p. 16.
4 Gosudarstvennii Komitet Oboroni. Postanovlenie No. GOKO-2470ss ot '3' noiabria 1942 g.... O formirovanii zhenskoi dobrovol'cheskoi strelkovoi brigade. Online. Available www.soldat.ru/gko/scans/2470-01-1.jpg (accessed 2 May 2008).
5 Evan Mawdlsey, *Thunder in the East: The Nazi-Soviet War 1941–1945* (London: Hodder

Arnold, 2005), pp. 136–151 and David Glantz and Jonathan House, *When Titans Clashed: How the Red Army Stopped Hitler* (Lawrence, KS: University Press of Kansas, 1995), pp. 105–116.
6 Mawdsley, *Thunder in the East*, pp. 152–155 and Glantz and House, *When Titans Clashed*, pp. 136–139.
7 Mawdsley, *Thunder in the East*, pp. 178–179 and Glantz and House, *When Titans Clashed*, p. 107.
8 Mawdsley, *Thunder in the East*, pp. 157–159 and Glantz and House, *When Titans Clashed*, pp. 117–122.
9 A *versta* was equivalent to 3,500 feet or just over 1,000 metres.
10 Glantz and House, *When Titans Clashed*, p. 117.
11 Mawdsley, *Thunder in the East*, pp. 161–162 and 176. Glantz and House, *When Titans Clashed*, pp. 133–134, 139–141, 158.
12 Glantz and House, *When Titans Clashed*, p. 141.
13 *SVE* 7, p. 660.
14 *SVE* 5, p. 271.
15 Including both anti-tank guns, known as 'anti-tank artillery', and other artillery resources.
16 *SVE* 7, p. 660.
17 David M. Glantz, *Zhukov's Greatest Defeat: The Red Army's Epic Disaster in Operation Mars, 1942* (Lawrence, KS: University Press of Kansas, 1999), pp. 18–24.
18 Ibid., p. 319.
19 See David Glantz, *Colossus Reborn: The Red Army at War, 1941–1943* (Lawrence, KA: University Press of Kansas, 2005), pp. 475–476.
20 On the contribution made by Rumanian forces to the Axis effort on the Eastern Front, see Mark Axworthy, Cornel Scafeş and Cristian Craciunoiu, *Third Axis, Fourth Ally: Romanian Armed Forces in the European War, 1941–1945* (London: Arms and Armour, 1995). On the Italian contribution see MacGregor Knox, *Hitler's Italian Allies: Royal Armed Forces, Fascist Regime and the War of 1940–1943* (Cambridge: Cambridge University Press, 2000).

6 The Battle of Kursk and the race for the Dnepr

1 See Evan Mawdlsey, *Thunder in the East: The Nazi-Soviet War 1941–1945* (London: Hodder Arnold, 2005), pp. 249–262.
2 Ibid., pp. 263–264.
3 David M. Glantz and Harold S. Orenstein (trans. and eds.), *The Battle for Kursk, 1943: The Soviet General Staff Study* (London: Frank Cass, 2001), pp. 17 and 25.
4 *Velikaia Otechestvennaia voina. 1941–1945.... Kniga vtoraia. Perelom*, p. 259.
5 See David Glantz and Jonathan House, *When Titans Clashed: How the Red Army Stopped Hitler* (Lawrence, KS: University Press of Kansas, 1995), p. 166 and Mawdsley, *Thunder in the East*, p. 266.
6 Some idea of the scale of Soviet tank losses at Prokhorovka and in subsequent operations can be gleaned from Glantz, *Stumbling Colossus*, pp. 245–246. For a German analysis highlighting how heavy Soviet losses were compared to German, see *DDRudZW8*, pp. 120–135.
7 Glantz and House, *When Titans Clashed*, pp. 168–170.
8 S.M. Shtemenko, *The Soviet General Staff at War, 1941–1945* (Moscow: Progress Publishers, 1970), pp. 116–117 and 140–143.
9 According to orders of the end of September forcing the Dnepr on a 'wide front' in order to limit German ability to concentrate against particular bridgeheads, whilst at the same time destroying any German footholds on the Soviet side of the river to prevent German counter-attacks on Soviet flanks and into the Soviet rear. 'Bitva za Dnepr v dokumentakh', *Vizh*, 1983, Number 10, pp. 35–36.

10 V. Kazantsev, 'Melitopol'skaia nastupatel'naia operatsiia (v tsifrakh)', *Vizh*, Number 7 (1977), p. 69 and *DDRudZW8*, p. 382 and map p. 352.
11 See 'Kievskaia nastupatel'naia operatsiia v dokumentakh', *Vizh*, Number 11 (1983), pp. 54–59.
12 See Glantz and House, *When Titans Clashed*, pp. 172–174; *DDRudZW8*, maps pp. 350 and 352; *Velikaia Otechestvennaia voina. 1941–1945.... Kniga vtoraia. Perelom*, pp. 291–323; and Mawdsley, *Thunder in the East*, pp. 277–278.
13 V.A. Zolotarev and I.A. Kozlov, *Tri stoletiia Rossiiskogo flota, 1941–1945* (Moscow: AST; St Petersburg: Poligon, 2005), pp. 517–519 and A.B. Shirokorad, *Korabli i katera VMF SSSR 1939–45 gg. Spravochnik* (Minsk: Kharvest, 2002), pp. 240 and 248.
14 *SVE* 4, pp. 147–148.
15 *Velikaia Otechestvennaia voina. 1941–1945.... Kniga vtoraia. Perelom*, p. 300 and *DDRudZW8*, pp. 364–366 and map p. 351.
16 Glantz, *Colossus Reborn*, p. 280.

7 The siege of Leningrad

1 Mawdsley, *Thunder in the East*, pp. 81–83 and David Glantz and Jonathan House, *When Titans Clashed: How the Red Army Stopped Hitler* (Lawrence, KS: University Press of Kansas, 1995), pp. 51–52, 63, 75–77. Reference has been made in this chapter to F.F. Viktorov *et al.*, *Istoriia Ordena Lenina Leningradskogo voennogo okruga* (Moscow: Voennoe izdatel'stvo Ministerstva oboroni SSSR, 1974).
2 Mawdsley, *Thunder in the East*, pp. 84–85.
3 Mawdsley, *Thunder in the East*, pp. 90–91 and 129–131.
4 See Harrison E. Salisbury, *The 900 Days: The Siege of Leningrad* (New York and Evanston: Harper and Row, 1969), pp. 288–295.
5 See N.L. Lomagin, *Neizvestnaia blokada. Kn. 1. (2-e izd)* (St Petersburg: Izdatel'skii Dom 'Neva', 2004), pp. 126–128.
6 Ibid., p. 130.
7 Ibid., p. 131.
8 Ibid.
9 For a sympathetic treatment of Vlasov, see Catherine Andreyev, *Vlasov and the Russian Liberation Movement: Soviet Reality and Émigré Theories* (Cambridge: Cambridge University Press, 1987).
10 Mawdsley, *Thunder in the East*, pp. 178–180.

8 Lend-Lease aid, the Soviet economy and the Soviet Union at war

1 M. Harrison, *Accounting for War. Soviet Production, Employment and the Defence Burden, 1940–1945* (Cambridge: Cambridge University Press, 1996), p. 134.
2 Igor Kaberov, *Swastika in the Gunsight: Memoirs of a Russian Fighter Pilot 1941–1943* (Stroud: Sutton Publishing, 1999), p. 141. First published in Russian in 1975.
3 See A.P. Dobson, *US Wartime Aid to Britain* (London: Croom Helm, 1986), Chapters 1 and 2 and R.H. Jones, *The Roads to Russia: United States Lend-Lease to the Soviet Union* (Norman, OK: University of Oklahoma Press, 1969), Chapter 1.
4 See Jones, *The Roads to Russia*, Chapter 2.
5 'Most Secret. Hist. (R) 1. September 18, 1941. War Cabinet. Assistance to Russia. 29th June. TNA PREM 3/401/1'.
6 'Most Secret. Hist. (R) 1. September 18, 1941. War Cabinet. Assistance to Russia. 25th July and 4th September. Foreign Office to Moscow. TNA PREM 3/401/1'.
7 Destroyers would in fact only be supplied to the Soviet Union in summer 1944 in lieu of the Soviet share of the Italian fleet. The Soviet Northern Fleet received Town Class ships that had been supplied to Britain under the 'destroyers for bases' agreement, albeit with weapons and electronics fits appropriate to that stage of the war. See Arnold Hague,

Destroyers for Great Britain: A History of the 50 Town Class Ships Transferred from the United States to Great Britain in 1940 (London: Greenhill Books, 1990).
8   'Secret. D.O. (41) 11. September 22, 1941. War Cabinet. Conference on British-United States Production and Assistance to Russia. TNA PREM 3/401/7'.
9   Ibid., Enclosure IV.
10 Jones, *The Roads to Russia*, Chapter 2.
11 Accessible accounts of these convoys are provided in Paul Kemp, *Convoy! Drama in Arctic Waters* (London: Brockhampton Press, 1999) and Richard Woodman, *Arctic Convoys* (London: John Murray Ltd, 1994).
12 '(Cypher). Special (Lord Beaverbrook). From British Supply Mission, Moscow, to Foreign Office. Lord Beaverbrook. No. 42 Linen. 3rd October, 1941. TNA WO193/580', and 'Secret. W.P. (41) 238. October 8, 1941. War Cabinet. Moscow Conference. TNA PREM 3/401/7'.
13 N. Biriukov, *Tanki – frontu! Zapiski sovetskogo generala* (Smolensk: Rusich, 2005), pp. 148–149.
14 M. Suprun, *Lend-liz i severnie konvoi 1941–1945* (Moscow: Andreevskii flag 1997), p. 123.
15 Ibid., p. 52.
16 M. Harrison, *Soviet Planning in Peace and War, 1938–1945* (Cambridge: Cambridge University Press, 1985), p. 251. See also G.F. Krivosheev (ed.), *Soviet Casualties and Combat Losses in the Twentieth Century* (London: Greenhill Books, 1997), p. 254.
17 'Most Secret. W.P. (42) 417. September 17, 1942. War Cabinet. Report on fulfillment of the Moscow Protocol, October, 1941 – June, 1942. TNA PREM 3/401/7', p. 17.
18 A.G. Federov, *Aviatsiia v bitve pod Moskvoi* (Moscow: Nauka, 1975), pp. 92–93.
19 Ibid., and V. Romanenko's clearly well-informed but unfootnoted 'P-40 v Sovetskoi aviatsii'. Online. Available http://lend-lease.airforce.ru/articles/romanenko/p-40/index.htm (accessed 2 May 2008).
20 Romanenko, 'P-40 v Sovetskoi aviatsii' and A.A. Novikov, *V nebe Leningrada (zapiski komanduiushchego aviatsiei)* (Moscow: Nauka, 1970), p. 230.
21 Nonetheless, by late 1942 they were being supplied in small numbers. On 3 November 1942, 49 of 150 promised had been dispatched to the Soviet Union, with the remainder due to be sent by the end of the month. Extract from 'A.B.E. (42) 21st meeting held on Tuesday, 3rd November, 1942. Supplies of Aircraft to the USSR. TNA AIR 20/3904'.
22 'Secret Cipher Telgram. Recd. AMCS 0112 hrs. 4.7.42. To: Air Ministry. From: 30 Mission. TNA AIR 20/3904' and 'Gosudarstvennii Komitet Oboroni. Postanovlenie No. GKO-1291ss ot 16 favralia 1942 g. Moskva, Kreml'. O perevooruzhenii samolotov "Kharrikein". RGASPI f.644.o.1.d.21.l.96'.
23 Suprun, *Lend-liz i severnie konvoi*, p. 51.
24 Known as Kittyhawk with the British. A P-40 airframe with an up-rated engine and additional armament over P-40A-Cs.
25 Popular with Soviet forces in part by virtue of being geared towards low-level performance, and with a heavy armament including a 37 mm cannon firing through the propeller hub.
26 The Valentine-equipped tank brigades mentioned in the document eventually found their way, in the first instance, into the following units: 170th–40th Army, Briansk *Front* as of 1 June 1942; 59th–(11th TK) 5th Tank Army, Briansk *Front* as of 1 July 1942 (in some sources from 6 June 1942); 201st–61st Army, Briansk *Front* as of 1 May 1942; 177th–53rd Army, North-Western *Front* as of 1 June; 103rd–3rd Tank Corps, Briansk *Front* as of 1 June then 3rd Tank Corps, 61st Army, Western *Front* as of 1 July 1942. See Voenno-nauchnoe upravlenie General'nogo shtaba – Voenno-istoricheskii otdel, *Boevoi sostav Sovetskoi armii, chast' II (Ianvar'-dekabr' 1942 goda)* (Moscow: Voennoe izdatel'stvo Ministerstva oboroni SSSR, 1966).
27 The Matilda-equipped tank brigades mentioned in the document eventually found their way, in the first instance, into the following units: 186th–10th Tank Corps, 16th Army, Western *Front* as of 1 August 1942; 184th–3rd Shock Army, Kalinin *Front* as of 1 June

1942; 140th–51st Army, North Caucasus *Front* as of 1 June 1942; 136th–14th Tank Corps, North Caucasus *Front* as of 1 August 1942. See *Boevoi sostav*.

28 The M3 Light-equipped tank brigades mentioned in the document eventually found their way, in the first instance, into the following units: 137th–51st Army, North Caucasus *Front* as of 1 June 1942; 179th–3rd Tank Army, Western *Front* as of 1 August 1942. See *Boevoi sostav*.

29 Evacuation companies. Part of a broader drive in early 1942 to improve the recovery and repair of tanks from the battlefield, including the creation of 63 mobile repair bases in a GKO decree of 15 February 1942. 'Gosudarstvennii Komitet Oboroni. Postanovlenie No. GKO-1287ss ot 15 fevralia 1942 g. Moskva, Kreml'. O formirovanii ... 63 podvizhnikh remontnikh baz no polevomu remontu tankov.... RGASPI f. 644.o.1.d.21.ll.87-8'.

30 Bantam BRC quarter-ton 'jeep'.

31 The British equivalent of SONAR. Prior to the war Soviet destroyers were not fitted with any form of active underwater detection device. Repair offered an opportunity for the fitting of ASDIC sets to Soviet vessels, the destroyer *Gromkii* for instance being fitted with ASDIC during repairs at Factory No. 402 at Molotovsk from 20 June to 9 October 1942. See L.G. Shmigel'skii, 'Molotovskii zavod No. 402 i severnie konvoi', in *Severnie konvoi: Issledovaniia, vospominaniia, dokumenti. Vip. 3* (Moscow: Andreevskii flag, 2000), p. 82 and A.V. Platonov, *Entsiklopediia Sovetskikh nadvodnikh korablei 1941–1945* (St Petersburg: Izdatel'stvo 'Poligon', 2002), p. 178. By this point the Soviet 'guardship' *Groza* had apparently used ASDIC (Drakon-128s) to locate, attack and damage a German U-boat on 10 September 1942. See R.I. Larintsev, 'Lend-lizovskie postavki na Severnii flot i ikh effektivnost'', in M.N. Suprun (ed.), *Voina v Arktike (1939–1945 gg.)* (Arkhangel'sk: Pomorskii gosudarstvennii universitet, 2001), p. 268 and Platonov, op. cit., pp. 254 and 259.

32 Trawlers were in short supply in the Soviet Navy, and both trawlers and sweep gear were requested under 'Lend-Lease'. See Hill, 'The Birth of the Soviet Northern Fleet 1937–1942', pp. 65–82. In March 1942 the first of seven British 'TAM' type trawler conversions delivered in February–March 1942 were incorporated into the Northern Fleet, with the first 'MMS' type purpose-built naval trawlers arriving with the convoy PQ-18 in September 1942. See Shirokorad, *Korabli i katera VMF SSSR*, pp. 500–503.

33 Principal base of the Northern Fleet, near Murmansk.

34 A high-strength alloy of aluminium, manganese, magnesium and copper used in aircraft manufacture.

35 Amongst other things of considerable value in aircraft manufacturing, 18,000 tons of aluminium was promised by Britain and the Commonwealth during the First Moscow Protocol period to the end of June 1942, of which 14,147 tons had been supplied by the end of June 1942. 'Most Secret. W.P. (42) 417. September 17, 1942. War Cabinet. Report on fulfillment of the Moscow Protocol, October, 1941 – June, 1942. TNA PREM 3/401/7', p. 18 and Harrison, *Accounting for War*, p. 195.

36 A solvent used in the manufacture of TNT.

37 Used for the manufacture of aircraft canopies and other similar applications.

38 *Narodnii Komissariat Zagotovok* – People's Commissariat for Procurement.

39 V.F. Vorsin, 'Motor Vehicle Transport Deliveries through "Lend-Lease"', *JSMS*, Volume 10, Number 2 (June 1997), pp. 153–175.

40 During March, 750 imported 'Studebaker' and 'International' lorries were allocated to the formation of artillery regiments for the High Command (RVGK) reserve. 'Gosudarstvennii Komitet Oboroni. Postanovlenie No. GKO-1421ss ot 11 marta 1942 g. Moskva, Kreml'. Ob obespechenii mekhtiagoi i avtotransportom formiruemikh artilleriiskikh polkov reserva Glavnogo komandovanii. RGASPI f.644.o.1.d.24.l.47'.

41 'Most Secret. W.P. (42) 417. September 17, 1942. War Cabinet. Report on fulfillment of the Moscow Protocol, October, 1941 – June, 1942. TNA PREM 3/401/7', p. 18 and Harrison, *Accounting for War*, p. 195. Whilst not within the scope of this reader, it is worth noting that raw materials were provided to the Western Allies under reverse Lend-

Lease. To 30 June 1942, these included 20,243 tons of chrome ore and 10,000 railway sleepers, excluding supplies for the Middle East. 'War Cabinet. Report on fulfillment of the Moscow Protocol, October, 1941 – June, 1942', p. 25.
42 'Gosudarstvennii Komitet Oboroni. Postanovlenie No. GKO-227ss ot 20 iiulia 1941 g. Moskva, Kreml'. O postavke Narkomatu Oboroni sredstv sviazi.RGASPI f.644.o.1.d.3.l.209'.
43 'Gosudarstvennii Komitet Oboroni. Postanovlenie No. GKO-998ss ot 6 dekabria 1941 g. Moskva, Kreml'. O plane proizvodstva i postavkakh osnovnikh sredstv sviazi dlia Glavnogo Upravleniia Sviazi KA v dekabria 1941 goda. RGASPI f.644.o.1.d.16.l.62'.
44 *Severnie konvoi: Issledovaniia, vospominaniia, dokumenti. Vip. 3*, p. 328 and 'Secret Cipher Telegram. To: No. 30, Military Mission, Moscow. From: The War Office. Recd. 1435/30/9/41. TNA WO 193/580'.
45 'Secret Cipher Telegram. From: The War Office. To: No. 30 Military Mission, Moscow. Desp. 2145 1/10/41. TNA WO 193/580'.
46 'Secret Cipher Telgram. From: Beaverbrook Mission. To: The War Office. Recd 2225 2/10/41. WO 193/580' and 'Most Secret. W.P. (42) 417. September 17, 1942. War Cabinet. Report on fulfillment of the Moscow Protocol, October, 1941 – June, 1942. TNA PREM 3/401/7 p. 19'.
47 *Severnie konvoi: Issledovaniia, vospominaniia, dokumenti. Vip. 2* (Moscow: Nauka, 1994), p. 220.
48 Krivosheev, *Soviet Casualties and Combat Losses*, p. 258.
49 *Severnie konvoi: Issledovaniia, vospominaniia, dokumenti. Vip. 3*, p. 328.
50 'Most Secret. W.P. (42) 417. September 17, 1942. War Cabinet. Report on fulfillment of the Moscow Protocol, October, 1941 – June, 1942. TNA PREM 3/401/7', p. 22 and Harrison, *Accounting for War*, p. 196.
51 Suprun, *Lend-liz i severnie konvoi*, p. 122.
52 Louis Brown, *A Radar History of World War II – Technical and Military Imperatives* (Bristol and Philadelphia: Institute of Physics Publishing, 1999), pp. 59–60.
53 'Gosudarstvennii Komitet Oboroni. Postanovlenie No. GKO-1266ss ot 10 fevralia 1942 g. Moskva, Kreml'. O priniatii na vooruzhenie voisk PVO Krasnoi Armii i Voenno-Morskogo Flota Stantsii Orudiinoi Navodki (SON-2) i organizatsii otechestvennogo proizvodstva SON-2. RGASPI f.644.o.1.d.21.l.31'.
54 *Severnie konvoi: Issledovaniia, vospominaniia, dokumenti. Vip. 2*, p. 220.
55 Barber and Harrison, *The Soviet Home Front*, pp. 79–87.
56 Roger Munting, 'Soviet Food Supply and Allied Aid in the War, 1941–1945', *Soviet Studies*, Volume XXXVI, Number 4 (October 1984), p. 588. For more information on 'Lend-Lease' food supplies to the Soviet Union in Russian, see M.N. Suprun, 'Prodovol'stvennie postavki v SSSR po Lend-lizu v godi Vtoroi mirovoi voini', *Otechesvennaia istoriia*, Number 3 (1996), pp. 46–54.
57 A good example here would be the production of boots for Red Army troops increasingly well-supplied with weapons.

9 The Soviet Partisan Movement

1 See Alexander Hill, *The War Behind the Eastern Front: The Soviet Partisan Movement in North-West Russia, 1941–1944* (London: Frank Cass, 2005), Chapter 3.
2 'Postanovlenie Politbiuro TsK VKP(b) o meropriiatiiakh po bor'be s parashiutnimi desantami i diversantami protivnika v prifrontovoi polose, 24 iiunia 1941 g.', and 'Prikaz NKVD SSSR No. 00804 o meropriiatiiakh po bor'be s parashiutnimi desantami i diversantami protivnika v prifrontovoi polose, 25 iiunia 1941 g.', in Eroshin *et al.* (eds), *Organi gosudarstvennoi bezopasnosti.... Tom II. Nachalo. Kniga pervaia (22 iiunia – 31 avgusta 1941 goda)*, pp. 64, 77.
3 I.P. Petrov, *Partisanskoe dvizhenie v Leningradskoi oblasti* (Leningrad: Lenizdat, 1973), p. 22.

4 According to Petrov, prior to the order of 18 July, the Leningrad *obkom* VKP(b) had ordered the evacuation of Party personnel with Soviet forces. Ibid., p. 25 note 1.
5 Sekretariu Kalininskogo obkoma VKP(b) tov.Vorontsovu, ot sekretaria Sebezhskogo RK VKP(b) Petrova, V.E., pred. RUK'a Sebezhskogo raiona Feshchenko T.S., nach. Sebezhskogo NKVD Vinogradova V.Ia. 15 noiabria 1941 g., gor. Kashin. Dokladnaia zapiska. RGASPI f.69.o.1.d.347.l.25.
6 'Direktiva UNKGB i UNKVD po Kalininskoi oblasti No. 807 nachal'nikam MRO NKGB, GO i RO NKVD o merakh po uluchsheniiu organizatsii partisanskikh otriadov i diversionnikh grupp, napravliaemikh v til protivnika, 29 iiulia 1941 g.', in Eroshin *et al.* (eds), *Organi gosudarstvennoi bezopasnosti.... Tom II. Nachalo. Kniga pervaia (22 iiunia – 31 avgusta 1941 goda)*, p. 417.
7 'Prikaz NKVD SSSR No. 001151 ob organizatsii 4-x otdelov pri NKVD-UNKVD respublik, kraev i oblastei, 25 avgusta', in Eroshin *et al.* (eds), *Organi gosudarstvennoi bezopasnosti.... Tom II. Nachalo. Kniga pervaia (22 iiunia – 31 avgusta 1941 goda)*, p. 158.
8 V otdel kadrov Obkoma VKP(b) [Kalininskoi oblasti]. Ot komandira partisano-diversionnoi gruppi Timofeeva I.V. 29.XI.41g. RGASPI f.69.o.1.d.347.l.46.
9 *SVE 2*, pp. 201–202. In English, see C. Van Dyke, *The Soviet Invasion of Finland 1939–1940* (London: Frank Cass, 1997), p. 208.
10 G.A. Kumanev, 'Otvet P.K. Ponomarenko na voprosi G.A. Kumaneva. 2 noiabria 1978 g.', *Otechestvennaia istoriia*, Number 6 (1998), p. 141.
11 Ibid.
12 David Glantz, 'Boldin', in H. Shukman (ed.), *Stalin's Generals* (New York: Grove Press, 1993), pp. 48–49.
13 Kumanev, 'Otvet P.K. Ponomarenko ...', p. 141.
14 Hill, *The War Behind the Eastern Front*, Chapter 9.
15 Ponomarenko, 'Bor'ba sovetskogo naroda ...', p. 34.
16 See R. Stephan, 'Smersh: Soviet Military Counter-intelligence during the Second World War', *Journal of Contemporary History*, Volume 22 (1987), pp. 585–613.
17 V.I. Boiarskii, *Partisani i armiia: Istoriia uteriannikh vozmozhnostei* (Minsk: Kharvest; Moscow: AST, 2003), p. 260.
18 *Istoriia Velikoi Otechestvennoi voini Sovetskogo Soiuza 1941–1945. Tom vtoroi (iiun' 1941 g. – noiabr' 1942 g.)* (Moscow: Voennoe izdatel'stvo Ministerstva oboroni SSSR, 1961), p. 119.
19 Drawing on summary data from the Leningrad Headquarters of the Partisan Movement. Petrov, *Partisanskoe dvizhenie v Leningradskoi oblasti*, p. 437.
20 P.K. Ponomarenko, *Vsenarodnaia bor'ba v tilu nemetsko-fashistskikh zakhvatchikov 1941–1944* (Moscow: Nauka, 1985), p. 434.
21 Petrov, *Partisanskoe dvizhenie v Leningradskoi oblasti*, p. 439.
22 'Iz otcheta o rabote Otdela kadrov Tsentral'nogo shtaba partisanskogo dvizheniia za period s 15 iiunia 1942 g. po 15 fevralia 1944 g., 28 fevralia 1944 g.', in *RA T.20 (9)*, p. 485 and Hill, *The War Behind the Eastern Front*, p. 176.
23 *RA T.20 (9)*, p. 480.
24 *RA T.20 (9)*, pp. 481 and 485–486.
25 Hannes Heer, 'The Logic of the War of Extermination', in Hannes Heer and Klaus Naumann (eds), *War of Extermination: The German Military in World War II, 1941–1944* (London: Berghahn Books, 2004), p. 95.
26 281. Sicherungs-Division. Abt. Ia Tgb.Nr. 88/43 gKdos. Ostrow, den 14. April 1943. Betr.: Unternehmen 'Frühjahrsbestellung'. Divisionsbefehl. US NA T-315 1872 102-3.
27 According to partisan sources supported by three aircraft, probably primarily for reconnaissance. NKO SSSR. Shtab voiskovoi chasti No. 00128. 12 maia 1943. Nachal'niku Tsentral'nogo shtaba partisanskogo dvizheniia ... Donesenie o partisanskikh brigadakh Bobakova, Karlikova, Maksimenko. RGASPI f.69.o.1.d.353.l.14.
28 Operativnaia svodka No. 39 Kalininskogo shtaba partisanskogo dvizheniia, 3.5.1943. RGASPI f.69.o.1.d.345.l.67ob.

29 Brigade of Bobakov, 364; Karlikov (Boidin) 956; Maksimenko, 347; Moiseenko (Lazarenko), 143; Shapovalov, 645. Vedomost' boevogo i chislennogo sostava partisanskikh otriadov Kalininskogo fronta, po sostoianiiu na 1 marta 1943g. Kalininskaia oblast'. RGASPI f.69.o.1.d.359.l.13. It is worth noting that the brigade led on 1 March 1943 by Boidin had only a single radio set, with the the brigade of Lazarenko being without radio communications.
30 281. Sicherungs-Division. Abt. Ia. Ostrow, den 25.4.1943. Divisions-Tagesbefehl. US NA T-315 1872 82.
31 Hill, *The War Behind the Eastern Front*, pp. 140–141.
32 281 Sicherungs-Division. Abt. 1a. Tgb.Nr 642/43 geh. Ostrow, den 24.4.1943. Betr.: Unternehmen 'Holzktion'. Divisionsbefehl. US NA T-315 1872 90.
33 Hill, *The War Behind the Eastern Front*, p. 86.
34 *V tilu vraga: Bor'ba partisan i podpol'shchikov na okkupirovannoi territorii Leningradskoi oblasti. 1944 g.: Sbornik dokumentov* (Leningrad: Lenizdat, 1985), p. 249 and Hill, *The War Behind the Eastern Front*, p. 176.
35 Hill, *The War Behind the Eastern Front*, p. 117.
36 Ibid., p. 48.
37 N. Miuller [Müller], *Vermakht i okkupatsiia (1941–1944)* (Moscow: Voenizdat, 1974), p. 107.
38 Hill, *The War Behind the Eastern Front*, p. 48.
39 Ibid., p. 86.
40 E.M. Howell, *The Soviet Partisan Movement 1941–1944. DA Pam 20–244* (Washington, DC: Department of the Army, 1956), p. 73.
41 See, for instance, Hill, *The War Behind the Eastern Front*, pp. 47–48 and B. Shepherd, *War in the Wild East: The German Army and Soviet Partisans* (Cambridge, MA: Harvard University Press, 2004), pp. 76–77, 104–105.
42 Howell, *The Soviet Partisan Movement*, p. 85 and Hill, *The War Behind the Eastern Front*, p. 94.
43 Ponomarenko, *Vsenarodnaia bor'ba*, p. 377.
44 Reconnaissance summary material, presumably of the Central Headquarters of the Partisan Movement, in the personal fund of Panteleimon Ponomarenko, RGASPI f.625.o.1.d.38.l.332 and S.W. Mitchum, *Hitler's Legions: German Army Order of Battle, World War II* (London: Leo Cooper/Secker and Warburg, 1985), p. 174.
45 Hill, *The War Behind the Eastern Front*, p. 160.
46 Reconnaissance summary material, presumably of the Central Headquarters of the Partisan Movement, in the personal fund of Panteleimon Ponomarenko, RGASPI f.625.o.1.d.38.l. 337 and Mitchum, op. cit., p. 50.
47 Howell, *The Soviet Partisan Movement*, p. 73 and Shepherd, *War in the Wild East*, p. 92.
48 Hill, *The War Behind the Eastern Front*, p. 95.
49 Reconnaissance summary material, presumably of the Central Headquarters of the Partisan Movement, in the personal fund of Panteleimon Ponomarenko, RGASPI f.625.o.1.d.38.l.331.
50 Ponomarenko, *Vsenarodnaia bor'ba*, p. 434.
51 *V tilu vraga ... 1944*, p. 249.
52 Howell, *The Soviet Partisan Movement*, p. 76.
53 Howell, *The Soviet Partisan Movement*, p. 94 and Hill, *The War Behind the Eastern Front*, p. 132.
54 Hill, *The War Behind the Eastern Front*, pp. 132–133 and 139.
55 Howell, *The Soviet Partisan Movement*, pp. 163–165.
56 Howell, *The Soviet Partisan Movement*, pp. 173–180 and Hill, *The War Behind the Eastern Front*, pp. 154–160.
57 Hill, *The War Behind the Eastern Front*, pp. 75 and 121–122.
58 Reconnaissance summary material, presumably of the Central Headquarters of the

Partisan Movement, in the personal fund of Panteleimon Ponomarenko, RGASPI f.625.o.1.d.38.l. 337.
59 See Howell, *The Soviet Partisan Movement*, p. 168.
60 See, for example, G.L. Weinberg, 'The Yelnya-Dorogobuzh area of Smolensk Oblast', in J. Armstrong (ed.), *Soviet Partisans in World War II* (Madison, WI: University of Wisconsin Press, 1964) pp. 411–422; Howell, *The Soviet Partisan Movement*, pp. 77–80 and 182–188; and Shepherd, *War in the Wild East*, p. 122.
61 V. Andrianov, 'Operativnoe ispol'zovanie partisanskikh sil', *Vizh*, Number 7 (1969), pp. 24–27.
62 Hill, *The War Behind the Eastern Front*, pp. 100–102.
63 Krivosheev, *Soviet Casualties and Combat Losses*, pp. 166, 175, 179 and W. Haupt, *Army Group North – The Wehrmacht in Russia 1941–1945* (Atglen, PA: Schiffer Military History, 1997), p. 382.

10 The 'Ten "Stalinist" Crushing Blows' of 1944

1 Evan Mawdsley, *Thunder in the East: The Nazi-Soviet War 1941–1945* (London: Hodder Arnold, 2005), p. 270 and *DDRudZW8*, map p. 347.
2 *DDRudZW8*, p. 294.
3 See Mawdsley, *Thunder in the East*, pp. 288–289 and David Glantz and Jonathan House, *When Titans Clashed: How the Red Army Stopped Hitler* (Lawrence, KS: University Press of Kansas, 1995), pp. 192–193.
4 Mawdsley, *Thunder in the East*, p. 278 and *DDRudZW8*, pp. 394–419 and map p. 354.
5 Document 4 of 12 February 1944, in 'Korsun'-Shevchenkovskaia operatsiia v dokumentakh (24 ianvaria-17 fevralia 1944 g.)', *Vizh*, Number 2 (1984), p. 43.
6 Mawdsley, *Thunder in the East*, pp. 285–286 and Glantz and House, *When Titans Clashed*, p. 191 and *DDRudZW8*, pp. 486–490.
7 'Postanovlenie GOKO No. 5859ss "O Krimskikh Tatarakh", 11 maia 1944 g.', in N.L. Pobol' and P.M. Polian (eds), *Stalinskie deportatsii. 1928–1953* (Moscow: MFD: Materik, 2005), pp. 497–499.
8 Mawdsley, *Thunder in the East*, pp. 292–295.
9 Mawdsley, *Thunder in the East*, pp. 270–271 and G.F. Krivosheev (ed.), *Soviet Casualties and Combat Losses in the Twentieth Century* (London: Greenhill Books, 1997), pp. 134–135.
10 Glantz and House, *When Titans Clashed*, p. 203.
11 Mawdsley, *Thunder in the East*, pp. 299–307 and Glantz and House, *When Titans Clashed*, pp. 204–210 and *DDRudZW8*, p. 532.
12 *DDRudZW8*, p. 556, 'Belorusskaia operatsiia v tsifrakh', *Vizh*, Number 6 (1964), p. 82 and Krivosheev, *Soviet Casualties and Combat Losses*, pp. 145 and 263.
13 See Mawdsley, *Thunder in the East*, pp. 324–333.
14 *DDRudZW8*, pp. 692–694.
15 Krivosheev, *Soviet Casualties and Combat Losses*, p. 101.
16 See Mawdsley, *Thunder in the East*, pp. 338–343 and *DDRudZW8*, map p. 794 and pp. 736 and 739, and 'Iassko-Kishinevskaia operatssia v tsifrakh', *Vizh*, Number 8 (1964), p. 89.
17 Mawdsley, *Thunder in the East*, pp. 310–313 and Glantz and House, *When Titans Clashed*, pp. 226–229.
18 Mawdsley, *Thunder in the East*, pp. 353–355 and *SVE 2*, pp. 375–376.
19 On the campaign in Hungary, see Mawdsley, *Thunder in the East*, pp. 348–351.
20 See Earl F. Ziemke, *The German Northern Theater of Operations 1940–1945* [German Report Series] (Eastbourne: Antony Rowe Ltd, undated), pp. 300–301.
21 See Mikhail Suprun, 'Operation "West": The Role of the Northern Fleet and its Air Forces in the Liberation of the Russian Arctic in 1944', *JSMS*, Volume 20, Number 3 (July–September 2007), pp. 433–447.

11 From the Vistula to Berlin – the end of the Reich

1. For Rokossovskii at least, as his memoirs suggest, this transfer constituted a demotion, despite Stalin's apparent reassurance that 'if you and Konev don't advance, then Zhukov won't either'. Rokossovskii's reminiscence of his days commanding the 7th Samara Cavalry Division on the same page, during which period Zhukov was one of his brigade commanders, is quite possibly a veiled means of highlighting his chagrin at being replaced by Zhukov. See K.K. Rokossovskii, *Soldatskii dolg* (Moscow: Voennoe izdatel'stvo Ministerstva oboroni SSSR, 1968), p. 297.
2. S.M. Shtemenko, *The Soviet General Staff at War, 1941–1945* (Moscow: Progress Publishers, 1970), p. 310.
3. See David Glantz and Jonathan House, *When Titans Clashed: How the Red Army Stopped Hitler* (Lawrence, KS: University Press of Kansas, 1995), pp. 241–247.
4. See Evan Mawdlsey, *Thunder in the East: The Nazi-Soviet War 1941–1945* (London: Hodder Arnold, 2005), pp. 366–370.
5. Shtemenko, *The Soviet General Staff at War*, pp. 309–311, 315.
6. G.K. Zhukov, *Vospominaniia i razmishleniia. V trekh tomakh. Tom 3 – 12-e izdanie* (Moscow: AO Izdatel'stvo 'Novosti', 1995), pp. 202–203.
7. Where the German *Panzerfaust* was effectively a miniature recoil-less gun, the US Bazooka and German *Panzerschreck* launched rocket-propelled projectiles. The British PIAT relied on a large spring and small explosive charge, meaning no backblast as the *Panzerfaust* and no smoke as the Bazooka and *Panzershreck*, although range was short.
8. See Mawdsley, *Thunder in the East*, pp. 386–390.
9. Mawdsley, *Thunder in the East*, p. 390 and 'Berlinskaia operatsiia v tsifrakh', *Vizh*, Number 4 (1965), p. 81.
10. By now standard Soviet practice whereby Soviet rifle battalions would penetrate German defences across a broad front (so that the enemy would not be able to identify where the main blow would fall), in order not only to clarify the nature of the German first line of defence, but where applicable to occupy it where German troops had fallen back to positions to their rear. See *SVE* 7, p. 33.
11. See Mawdsley, *Thunder in the East*, p. 390; Glantz and House, *When Titans Clashed*, p. 263; and Zhukov, *Vospominaniia i razmishleniia.... Tom 3*, p. 244.
12. See Robert Stephan, 'Smersh: Soviet Military Counter-intelligence during the Second World War', *Journal of Contemporary History*, Volume 22 (1987), pp. 585–613.
13. Particularly useful in the preparation of this section was analysis provided in I.A. Gor'kov, 2002 and Viktor Cherepantov, *Vlast' i voina. Stalinskii mekhanizm gosudarstvennogo upravleniia v Velikoi Otechestvennoi voine* (Moscow: Izdatel'stvo 'Izvestiia', 2006).
14. O.A. Rzheshevskii (gen. ed.), *Velikaia Otechestvennaia voina 1941–1945. Sobitiia. Liudi. Dokumenti* (Moscow: Izdatel'stvo politicheskoi literature, 1990), p. 264.
15. See Mawdsley, *Thunder in the East*, pp. 394–395.

12 The Soviet invasion of Manchuria

1. *Velikaia Otechestvennaia voina. 1941–1945.... Kniga tret'ia. Osvobozhdenie*, p. 388.
2. Even the dropping of the first US atomic bomb on Hiroshima on 6 August did not apparently raise Japanese readiness. See Edward J. Drea, 'Missing Intentions: Japanese Intelligence and the Soviet Invasion of Manchuria, 1945', *Military Affairs*, April 1984, pp. 66–70.
3. O.A. Rzheshevskii (gen. ed.), *Velikaia Otechestvennaia voina 1941–1945. Sobitiia. Liudi. Dokumenti* (Moscow: Izdatel'stvo politicheskoi literature, 1990), p. 458. On 5 August the Primorskaia Group had become 1st Far-Eastern *Front* and the Far-Eastern *Front* had become 2nd Far-Eastern *Front*. *Velikaia Otechestvennaia voina. 1941–1945.... Kniga tret'ia. Osvobozhdenie*, p. 391.

4 G.F. Krivosheev (ed.), *Soviet Casualties and Combat Losses in the Twentieth Century* (London: Greenhill Books, 1997), pp. 160–161.
5 Glantz, *August Storm: The Soviet 1945 Strategic Offensive in Manchuria*, Leavenworth Paper Number 7 (Fort Leavenworth, KS: Combat Studies Institute, US Army Command and General Staff College, February 1983), p. 32.
6 V. Ezhakov, 'Boevoe primenenie tankov v gorno-taezhnoi mestnosti po opitu 1-go Dal'nevostochnogo fronta', *Vizh*, Number 1 (1974), p. 78.
7 Glantz, *August Storm: The Soviet 1945 Strategic Offensive in Manchuria*, p. 32.
8 Drea, 'Missing Intentions: Japanese Intelligence and the Soviet Invasion of Manchuria, 1945', p. 68.
9 'Primenenie aviatsii v Man'chzhurskoi operatsii' [interview with Marshal of Aviation P.S. Kirsanov], *Vizh*, Number 8 (1985), pp. 22–24.
10 Glantz, *August Storm: The Soviet 1945 Strategic Offensive in Manchuria*, p. 71.
11 Ibid., pp. 72–77.
12 See *SVE* 8, pp. 635–636 and *SVE* 4, pp. 531–532.
13 Drea, 'Missing Intentions: Japanese Intelligence and the Soviet Invasion of Manchuria, 1945', p. 69.
14 Glantz, *August Storm: The Soviet 1945 Strategic Offensive in Manchuria*, p. 33.
15 Ibid., pp. 92–94.
16 'Kampaniia Sovetskikh Vooruzhennikh Sil na Dal'nem Vostoke', p. 68.
17 Glantz, *August Storm: The Soviet 1945 Strategic Offensive in Manchuria*, p. 138.
18 *SVE* 5, p. 130.
19 Krivosheev, *Soviet Casualties and Combat Losses*, pp. 161 and 264.
20 I.M. Tret'iak, 'Razgrom Kvantungskoi armii na Dal'nem Vostoke', *Vizh*, Number 8 (1985), p. 17.
21 Glantz, *August Storm: The Soviet 1945 Strategic Offensive in Manchuria*, p. 219.
22 Ibid., pp. 156–158.

Conclusion

1 G.F. Krivosheev (ed.), *Soviet Casualties and Combat Losses in the Twentieth Century* (London: Greenhill Books, 1997), pp. 96, 252, 257.
2 Some idea of the views of German officers of the Red Army can be gleaned from Chapter 19 of B.H. Liddell Hart's *The Other Side of the Hill: The Classic Account of Hitler's War through the Eyes of German Generals* (London: Pan Books Ltd, 1983), pp. 329–339, first published in 1948, with a revised and enlarged edition in 1951. In the examples cited there was certainly agreement on an improvement in Soviet staff work and the use of tanks over time, with the use of infantry on the offensive being singled out for widespread criticism.
3 Or at least, if talk of continuing the war from Canada was more than rhetoric, seizing the British mainland that would prove to be such a useful staging post for US military might.
4 Richard Overy, *Why the Allies Won* (London: Pimlico, 1996), p. 320.
5 A particularly strong case for the importance of the Allied air war for the defeat of Nazi Germany is made by Philips P. O'Brien in, 'East versus West in the Defeat of Nazi Germany', *Journal of Strategic Studies*, Volume 23, Number 2 (June 2000), pp. 89–113. O'Brien suggests, for example, that between January and November 1943 3,936 German aircraft were lost in the Mediterranean theatre, compared to 3,773 on the Eastern Front, with over 54 per cent of Luftwaffe operational front-line strength in the West by 1 January 1944 with a further 10 per cent in the Mediterranean, with the air war against the Western Allies soaking up an even more substantial proportion of productive efforts when AA guns are included. For a more moderate relative assessment of the importance of the Allied air war compared to the fighting on the ground on the Eastern Front, see Overy, *Why the Allies Won*, pp. 321–323.

6 Figures for 1945 are overall German losses without distinction between the 'East' and 'other fronts'. See Evan Mawdlsey, *Thunder in the East: The Nazi-Soviet War 1941–1945* (London: Hodder Arnold, 2005), p. 404 and below.
7 The Soviet 12-volume Brezhnev-era official history of the war, cited in a later article, gives a total of 190 German and allied divisions in the East for 22 June 1941, peaking at 266 for November 1942, with 245 for 1 January 1944. Subtracting the appropriate figures in Table C.1 from the above gives 27.5 German-allied divisions for 22 June 1941 and 44 for 1 January 1944 (the Khrushchev-era Soviet official history notes a peak of 72.5 non-German Axis divisional equivalents operating on the Eastern Front in November 1942). However, only Italian forces were theoretically redeployable to other theatres at the beginning of the war (and indeed in November 1942). As Knox notes, in August–September 1942 the Italian 8th Army had a significant 229,000 men in southern Russia, along with 18,000 lorries and artillery tractors, 946 artillery pieces, almost 300 47 mm anti-tank guns, 52 modern anti-aircraft guns and around 50 MC200 and MC202 fighter aircraft. As Knox goes on to add,

> even a fraction of the materiel and skilled manpower deployed in Russia would have significantly increased the mobility, firepower, and tactical skill of the experienced but attenuated Italian divisions and air units that accompanied Rommel in the final Axis drive on Egypt.

A not dissimilarly sized force was finally lost to Anglo-American forces in Tunisia in May 1943. With only very limited German-allied Italian forces fighting the Allies after September 1943, almost none of the German-allied divisions in the later figure were even theoretically redeployable to face the Western Allies.

See A.V. Usikov and V.T. Iminov, 'Rol' i mesto sovetsko-germanskogo fronta v Vtoroi Mirovoi voine', *Vizh*, Number 5 (2005), p. 5; *Istoriiia Velikoi Otechestvennoi voini.... Tom shestoi. Itogi...*, p. 26; and Knox, *Hitler's Italian Allies*, pp. 83–86.
8 *Velikaia Otechestvennaia voina. 1941–1945. Voenno-istoricheskie ocherki. Kniga chetvertaia. Narod i voina* (Moscow: Nauka, 1999), pp. 282–284.
9 Krivosheev, *Soviet Casualties and Combat Losses*, p. 96.
10 Ibid., p. 235 and Boog et al., *Germany and the Second World War. Volume IV*, p. 1176.
11 See, for example, Hill, *The War Behind the Eastern Front*, p. 38.
12 Krivosheev, pp. 235–237 and Boog et al., *Germany and the Second World War. Volume IV*, p. 1172.
13 The above figures, for example, perhaps incorrectly list some of those POWs (along with other Soviet citizens, e.g. *Ostarbeiter*) who remained in the West after the war as having been killed. Indeed, post-war Soviet statistics suggested 451,000 did not return to the Soviet Union, according to alternative figures perhaps as many as 688,000. See A.A. Sherviakov, 'Gitlerovskii genotsid i repatriatsiia sovetskogo nasileniia', in *Liudskie poteri SSSR v period vtorio mirovoi voini. Sbornik statei* (St Petersburg: Izdatel'stvo 'Russki-Baltiiskii informatsionnii tsentr BLITS', 1995), p. 180.
14 During the war mortality rates amongst the civilian population in Soviet rear areas rose across the board according to statistics provided by registry offices (ZAGS), with 1942 unsurprisingly being particularly bad. Poor diet and nutrition certainly contributed to higher mortality rates. See various articles on civilian losses in the Soviet rear in *Liudskie poteri SSSR*, pp. 124–173. Calculating civilian deaths on Axis-occupied territory, particularly in the light of forced-labour recruitment from these areas and the issue of living non-returnees to the Soviet Union at the end of the war, is particularly difficult. The situation in the Gulag camps is easier to assess, with mortality rates leaping at the beginning of the war before declining as the war progressed and arguably the food situation, particularly bad in 1942, improved. In 1940 46,665 Gulag prisoners died, compared to 100,997 for 1941 and 248,887 in 1942 (where the camp population was 1,500,524 on 1 January 1941, 1,415,596 on 1 January 1942 and 983,974 on 1 January 1943). See V.N.

Zemskov, 'Smertnost' zakliuchennikh v 1941–1945 gg.', in *Liudskie poteri SSSR*, pp. 174–175.

15 At the beginning of the war there were 4,826,907 personnel, largely men, in the Red Army and navy with a further 74,945 servicemen and 'military-construction' workers serving in formations under civilian departments but being provided rations by the People's Commissariat for Defence. During the war, a further 29,574,900 personnel, largely men, were called up/mobilized. See Krivosheev, *Soviet Casualties and Combat Losses*, p. 91.

16 Also many existing tractors, particularly tracked, were used by the Red Army. On the use of horses by the *Wehrmacht*, see R.L. Dinaro and Austin Bay, 'Horse-Drawn Transport in the German Army', *Journal of Contemporary History*, Volume 23 (1988), pp. 129–142. Other than cavalry, of decreasing importance as the war progressed, photographs rarely show horses in use by the Red Army. However, in June 1941 a Soviet rifle division alone had a list strength of more than 3,000 horses and in September 1943 the Soviet Southern Front had 62,121 horses accounted for. See Kalashnikov *et al.*, *Krasnaia armiia v iiune 1942 goda*, p. 62 and Kazantsev, 'Melitopol'skaia nastupatel'naia operatsiia v tsifrakh', p. 67.

17 *Velikaia Otechestvennaia voina. 1941–1945.... Kniga chetvertaia. Narod i voina*, p. 294.

18 As a starting point in English, see Susan J. Linz (ed.), *The Impact of World War II on the Soviet Union* (Totowa, NJ: Rowman and Allanheld, 1985) and more recently, Juliane Fürst (ed.), *Late Stalinist Russia: Society Between Reconstruction and Reinvention* (Abingdon: Routledge, 2006).

19 Mawdsley, *Thunder in the East*, pp. 403–405.

20 See Krivosheev, *Soviet Casualties and Combat Losses*, pp. 272–278.

21 Krivosheev gives those killed, died of wounds and missing in action on the Eastern Front as 863,700 for Hungary, 93,900 for Italy, 681,800 for Rumania and 86,400 for Finland. Ibid., p. 278.

22 For biographies of these figures see, in the first instance, Shukman (ed.), *Stalin's Generals*.

23 For a positive assessment of Stalin's wartime leadership, see Geoffrey Roberts, *Stalin's Wars: From World War to Cold War, 1939–1953* (New Haven, CT: Yale University Press, 2006). More critical but nonetheless balanced is Evan Mawdsley, 'Stalin: Victors are not Judged', *JSMS*, Volume 19, Number 4 (December 2006), pp. 705–725. For an extremely negative and academically weak but nonetheless influential assessment see Dmitrii Volkogonov, *Stalin: Triumph and Tragedy* (ed. and trans. Harold Shukman) (London: Weidenfeld and Nicolson, 1991). Nikita Khrushchev's memoirs have also had a significant impact on assessments of Stalin's leadership. See Nikita Khrushchev, *Khrushchev Remembers* (Boston, MA: Little, Brown and Company, 1970) and other editions.

24 The Russian term *narod* was arguably more akin to the German *Volk*, even if with less of a racial component, than the people as in 'the British people'. On Soviet and Russian nationalism and other motivating factors during the war, see Geoffrey Hosking, 'The Second World War and Soviet National Consciousness', *Past and Present*, Volume 175, Number 1 (2002), pp. 162–187 and Roger Reese, 'Motivations to Serve: The Soviet Soldier in the Second World War', *JSMS*, Volume 20, Number 2 (April–June 2007), pp. 263–282.

Bibliography

Materials consulted in the writing of this documentary reader are listed below. Additional materials may be found in the introduction and further reading sections for each chapter.

Archival materials

Central State Archive for St Petersburg (TsGA SPb):

f.9789.o.1 – Agricultural directorate of the German economic inspectorate 'Nord' [WiIn Nord]

Russian State Archive for Socio-Political History (RGASPI):

f.69.o.1 – Central Headquarters of the Partisan Movement
f.644.o.1 – State Defence Committee
f. 625.o.1 – Ponomarenko, Panteleimon Kondrat'evich (1946–1981).

Russian State Archive for the Economy (RGAE):

f.413.o.9 – Ministry of Foreign Trade of the USSR

United Kingdom National Archives (UK TNA):

AIR 20 – Air Ministry, and Ministry of Defence: Papers accumulated by the Air Historical Branch
FO 371 – Foreign Office: Political Departments: General Correspondence from 1906–1966
PREM 3 – Prime Minister's Office: Operational Correspondence and Papers
WO 193 – War Office: Directorate of Military Operations and Plans, later Directorate of Military Operations: Files concerning Military Planning, Intelligence and Statistics (Collation Files)

United States National Archives (US NA):

T-315 German Field Commands: Divisions

Documents in Russian available on the internet

[Postanovlenie GKO]. Online. Available www.soldat.ru/doc/gko/gko1942.html, www.soldat.ru/doc/gko/gko1943.html (accessed 2 May 2008).
Prikaz Verkhovnogo ... 25 ianvaria 1943 goda. Online. Available www.soldat.ru/doc/vgk/unnum1.html (accessed 2 May 2008).

Published documents in Russian

N. Biriukov, *Tanki – frontu! Zapiski sovetskogo generala* (Smolensk: Rusich, 2005).
'Bitva za Dnepr v dokumentakh', *Vizh*, 1983, Number 10, pp. 35–39.
Blokadnie dnevniki i dokumenti (seriia: 'Arkhiv Bol'shogo Doma') (St Petersburg: Evropeiskii Dom, 2004).
V.P. Eroshin, I.N. Stepanov, S.B. Shurigin and V.P. Iampol'skii (eds), *Organi gosudarstvennoi bezopasnosti.... Tom I. Nakanune. Kniga vtoraia (1 ianvaria – 21 iiunia 1941 g.)* (Moscow: A/O 'Kniga i biznes', 1995).
V.P. Eroshin, A.A. Zdanovich and V.P. Iampol'skii (eds), *Organi gosudarstvennoi bezopasnosti... . Tom II. Nachalo. Kniga pervaia (22 iiunia – 31 avgusta 1941 goda)* (Moscow: Izdatel'stvo 'Rus'', 2000).
V.P. Gusachenko, V.V. Korovin, I.I. Avdeev, V.P. Iampol'skii (eds), *Organi gosudarstvennoi bezopasnosti SSSR.... Tom II. Nachalo. Kniga vtoraia. 1 sentiabria-31 dekabria 1941 goda* (Moscow: Izdatel'stvo 'Rus'', 2000).
'Keivskaia nastupatel'naia operatsiia v dokumentakh', *Vizh*, Number 11 (1983), pp. 54–59.
A.F. Kiselev and E.M. Shchagin (eds), *Khrestomatiia po otechestvennoi istorii (1914–1945 gg.): Uchebnoe posobie dlia studentov vuzov* (Moscow: Gumanitarnii izdatel'skii tsentr VLADOS, 1996).
P.N. Knishevskii, O.I. Vasil'eva, V.V. Visotskii, S.A. Solomatin (eds), *Skritaia pravda voini: 1941 god. Neizvestnie dokumenti* (Moscow: 'Russkaia kniga', 1992).
'Korsun'-Shevchenkovskaia operatsiia v dokumentakh (24 ianvaria-17 fevralia 1944 g.)', *Vizh*, Number 2 (1984), pp. 41–44.
KPSS o Vooruzhennikh Silakh Sovetskogo Soiuza: Dokumenti 1917–1981 (Moscow: Voennoe izdatel'stvo Ministerstva Oboroni SSSR, 1981).
I.N. Kuznetsov (ed.), *Bez grifa 'Sekretno'* (Novosibirsk: 1997).
N.A. Lomagin, *Neizvestnaia blokada. Dokumenti, prilozheniia. Kn. 2. (2-e izd)* (St Petersburg: Izdatel'skii Dom 'Neva', 2004).
Lubianka. Stalin i NKVD-NKGB-GUKR 'Smersh'. 1939-mart 1946 (Moscow: MFD: Materik, 2006).
V.P. Naumov (ed.), *1941 god: V 2 kn. Kn.1* and *Kn.2* (Moscow: Mezhdunarodnii fond 'Demokratiia', 1998).
A.A. Pechenkin, 'Po zakonam voennogo vremeni. Iiun'-dekabr' 1941 g.', *Istoricheskii arkhiv* 3 (2000), pp. 66–81.
N.L. Pobol' and P.M. Polian (eds), *Stalinskie deportatsii. 1928–1953* (Moscow: MFD: Materik, 2005).
'Prikaz Narodnogo komissara oboroni ot 5 sentiabria 1942 goda "O zadachakh partisanskogo dvizheniia"', *Vizh*, Number 8 (1975), pp. 61–65.
Russkii arkhiv: Velikaia Otechestvennaia:
T.12(1). *Nakanune voini. Materiali soveshchaniia visshego rukovodiashchego sostava RKKA 23–31 dekabria 1940 g.* (Moscow: 'Terra', 1993).
T.13 (2–2). *Prikazi Narodnogo komissara oboroni SSSR 22 iiunia 1941 g. – 1942 g.* (Moscow: TERRA, 1997).

T.15 (4–4). Kurskaia bitva. Dokumenti i materiali 27 marta – 23 avgusta 1943 g. (Moscow: TERRA, 1997).
T.16 (5–1). Stavka VGK. Dokumenti i materiali. 1941 god. (Moscow: TERRA, 1998).
T.16 (5–3). Stavka VGK. Dokumenti i materiali. 1943 god. (Moscow: TERRA, 1999).
T.16 (5–4). Stavka VGK: Dokumenti i materiali 1944–1945 (Moscow: TERRA, 1999),
T.18 7 (2). Sovetsko-iaponskaia voina 1945 goda... (Moscow: TERRA, 2000).
T.20 (9). Partisanskoe dvizhenie v godi Velikoi Otechestvennoi voini 1941–1945 gg.: Dokumenti i materiali (Moscow: Terra, 1999).
T.21 (10). Prikazi i direktivi narodnogo komissara VMF v godi Velikoi Otechestvennoi voini. (Moscow: TERRA, 1996).
T.23 (12–1). General'nii shtab v godi Velikoi Otechestvennoi voini: Dokumenti i materiali. 1941 god. (Moscow: TERRA, 1998).
T.23 (12–2). General'nii shtab v godi Velikoi Otechestvennoi voini: Dokumenti i materiali. 1942 god. (Moscow: TERRA, 1999).
T.23 (12–3). General'nii shtab v godi Velikoi Otechestvennoi voini: Dokumenti i materiali. 1943 god. (Moskva: TERRA, 1999).
T.25 (14). Til Krasnoi Armii v Velikoi Otechestvennoi voine 1941–1945 gg.: ... (Moscow: TERRA, 1998).
O.A. Rzheshevskii (gen. ed.), *Velikaia Otechestvennaia voina 1941–1945. Sobitiia. Liudi. Dokumenti* (Moscow: Izdatel'stvo politicheskoi literature, 1990).
Sbornik boevikh dokumentov Velikoi Otechestvennoi voini. Vipusk 1, 4, 5, 10, 11, 13, 21, 24, 27, 30, 38 (Moscow: Voennoe izdatel'stvo Ministerstva Oboroni Soiuza SSR, 1947–1959).
Sbornik zakonov SSSR v dvukh tomakh. Tom 2. Sbornik zakonov SSSR i ukazov Presidiuma Verkhovnogo Soveta SSSR, 1938–1967 (Moscow: Izdatel'stvo 'Izvestiia Sovetov deputatov trudiashchikhsia SSSR', 1968).
G.N. Sevost'ianov (ed.), *Sovetsko-amerikanskie otnosheniia. 1939–1945* (Moscow: MFD, 2004).
Stalingradskaia epopeia: ... (Moscow: 'Zvonnitsa-MG', 2000).
N.L. Volkovskii (ed.), *Blokada Leningrada v dokumentakh rassekrechennikh arkhivov* (Moscow: OOO 'Izdatel'stvo AST; St Petersburg: OOO 'Izdatel'stvo 'Poligon'', 2004).
V tilu vraga: Bor'ba partisan i podpol'shchikov na okkupirovannoi territorii Leningradskoi oblasti. 1944 g.: Sbornik dokumentov (Leningrad: Lenizdat, 1985).

Published documents in German

Hitlers Weisungen für die Kriegsführung, 1939–1945: Dokumente des Oberkommandos der Wehrmacht (Munich: Deutscher Taschenbuch Verlag, 1965).
Norbert Müller, *Okkupation, Raub, Vernichtung – Dokumente zur Besatzungspolitik der faschistischen Wehrmacht auf Sowjetischem Territorium 1941 bis 1944* (Berlin: Militärverlag der DDR, 1980).
R.-D. Müller, *Die deutsche Wirtschaftspolitik in den besetzten sowjetischen Gebieten 1941–1943 – Der Abschlussbericht der Wirtschaftstabes Ost ...* (Boppard: Harald Boldt Verlag, 1991).

Published documents in English

D. Cameron Watt (ed.), *British Documents on Foreign Affairs: Reports and Papers from the Foreign Office Confidential Print. Part II. From the First to Second World War. Series A. The Soviet Union, 1917–1939. Volume 14. The Soviet Union, Jan.1937-Dec.1938* (Frederick, MD: University Publications of America, 1986).

Correspondence between the Chairman of the Council of Ministers of the USSR and the Presidents of the USA and Prime Ministers of Great Britain during the Great Patriotic War of 1941–1945. Volume 1. Correspondence with Winston S. Churchill and Clement R. Attlee (July 1941-November 1945) (Moscow: Progress Publishers, 1957).

J. Degras (ed.), *Soviet Documents on Foreign Policy. Volume III 1933–1941* (London: Oxford University Press, 1953).

Jürgen Förster and Evan Mawdsley, 'Hitler and Stalin in Perspective: Secret Speeches on the Eve of Barbarossa', *War in History*, Volume 11, Number 1 (2004), pp. 61–103.

David M. Glantz and Harold S. Orenstein (trans. and eds.), *Belorussia 1944: The Soviet General Staff Study* (London/Portland, OR: Frank Cass, 2001).

David M. Glantz and Harold S. Orenstein (trans. and eds.), *The Battle for Kursk, 1943: The Soviet General Staff Study* (London: Frank Cass, 2001).

David M. Glantz and Harold S. Orenstein (trans. and eds.), *The Battle for L'vov, July 1944: The Soviet General Staff Study* (London/Portland, OR: Frank Cass, 2002).

David M. Glantz and Harold S. Orenstein (trans. and eds.), *The Battle for the Ukraine: The Red Army's Korsun'-Shevchenkovskii Offensive, 1944* (The Soviet General Staff Study) (London/Portland, OR: Frank Cass, 2003).

Alexander Hill, 'The Allocation of Allied "Lend-Lease" Aid to the Soviet Union Arriving with Convoy PQ-12, March 1942 – A State Defense Committee Decree', *JSMS*, Volume 19, Number 4 (December 2006), pp. 727–738.

Alexander Hill, 'The Icebreaker Controversy and Soviet Intentions in 1941: The Plan for the Strategic Deployment of Soviet Forces of 15 May and Other Key Documents', *JSMS*, Volume 21, Number 1 (January–March 2008), pp. 1–16.

Joseph Stalin, *Order of the Day. The Speeches and Important Orders of the Day made by Marshal Joseph Stalin* (Toronto: Progress Books, 1944).

J.V. Stalin, *On the Great War of the Soviet Union* (Moscow: Foreign Languages Publishing House, 1947).

J.V. Stalin, *Works. Volume 9. December 1926-July 1927* and *Volume 13. July 1930-January 1934* (Moscow: Foreign Languages Publishing House, 1954).

Memoirs in Russian

I.S. Konev, *Sorok piatii* (Moscow: Voennoe izdatel'stvo Ministerstva oboroni SSSR, 1966).

A.A. Novikov, *V nebe Leningrada (zapiski komanduiushchego aviatsiei)* (Moscow: Nauka, 1970).

K.K. Rokossovskii, *Soldatskii dolg* (Moscow: Voennoe izdatel'stvo Ministerstva oboroni SSSR, 1968).

G.K. Zhukov, *Vospominaniia i razmishleniia. V trekh tomakh. Tom 2* and *Tom 3 – 12-e izdanie* (Moscow: AO Izdatel'stvo 'Novosti', 1995).

Memoirs in English

Igor Kaberov, *Swastika in the Gunsight: Memoirs of a Russian Fighter Pilot 1941–1943* (Stroud: Sutton Publishing, 1999).

S.M. Shtemenko, *The Soviet General Staff at War, 1941–1945* (Moscow: Progress Publishers, 1970).

Other books in Russian

Atlas ofitsera (Moscow: Voenno-topograficheskoe upravlenie, 1947).
Bitva pod Kurskom: ot oboroni k nastupleniiu (Moscow: AST: B66 Khranitel', 2006).
Boevoi sostav Sovetskoi armii, chast' II (Ianvar'-dekabr' 1942 goda) (Moscow: Voennoe izdatel'stvo Ministerstva oboroni SSSR, 1966).
V.I. Boiarskii, *Partisani i armiia: Istoriia uteriannikh vozmozhnostei* (Minsk: Kharvest; Moscow: AST, 2003),
Viktor Cherepantov, *Vlast' i voina. Stalinskii mekhanizm gosudarstvennogo upravleniia v Velikoi Otechestvennoi voine* (Moscow: Izdatel'stvo 'Izvestiia', 2006).
A.G. Federov, *Aviatsiia v bitve pod Moskvoi* (Moscow: 'Nauka', 1971).
I.A. Gor'kov, *Kreml'. Stavka. Genshtab* (Tver': 'RIF LTD', 1995).
I.A. Gor'kov, *Gosudarstvennii Komitet Oboroni postanovliaet (1941–1945). Tsifri, dokumenti* (Moscow: OLMA-PRESS, 2002).
A.A. Gorter, V.T. Gorter and M.N. Suprun, *Osvobozhdenie Vostochnogo Finnmarka, 1944–1945/Frigjøringen av Øst-Finnmark 1944–1945* (Arkhangel'sk-Vadsø: Arkhangel'sk-Pomor, 2005).
Istoriia Velikoi Otechestvennoi voini Sovetskogo Soiuza 1941–1945. Tom vtoroi (iiun' 1941 g. – noiabr' 1942 g.) (Moscow: Voennoe izdatel'stvo Ministerstva oboroni SSSR, 1961).
Istoriia Velikoi Otechestvennoi voini Sovetskogo Soiuza 1941–1945. Tom shestoi. Itogi Velikoi Otechestvennoi voini (Moscow: Voennoe izdatel'stvo Ministerstva oboroni Soiuza SSR, 1965).
K.A. Kalashnikov, V.I. Fes'kov, A.I. Chmikhalo, V.I. Golikov (eds), *Krasnaia armiia v iiune 1941 goda (statisticheskii sbornik)* (Novosibirsk: 'Novosibirskii khronograf', 2003).
O.N. Ken, *Mobilizatsionnoe planirovanie i politicheskie resheniia (konets 1920 – seredina 1930-Kh godov)* (St Petersburg: Izdatel'stvo Evropeiskovogo universiteta v Sankt Peterburge, 2002).
Liudskie poteri SSSR v period vtorio mirovoi voini. Sbornik statei (St Petersburg: Izdatel'stvo 'Russki-Baltiiskii informatsionnii tsentr BLITS', 1995).
N.L. Lomagin, *Neizvestnaia blokada. Kn. 1. (2-e izd)* (St Petersburg: Izdatel'skii Dom 'Neva', 2004).
N. Miuller [Müller], *Vermakht i okkupatsiia (1941–1944)* (Moscow: Voenizdat, 1974).
V.A. Nevezhin, *Sindrom nastupatel'noi voini. Sovetskaia propaganda v predverii 'sviashchennikh boev', 1939–1941 gg.* (Moscow: AIRO-XX', 1997).
I.P. Petrov, *Partisanskoe dvizhenie v Leningradskoi oblasti* (Leningrad: Lenizdat, 1973).
A.V. Platonov, *Entsiklopediia Sovetskikh nadvodnikh korablei 1941–1945* (St Petersburg: Izdatel'stvo 'Poligon' 2002).
P.K. Ponomarenko, *Vsenarodnaia bor'ba v tilu nemetsko-fashistskikh zakhvatchikov 1941–1944* (Moscow: Nauka, 1985).
P.A. Rotmistrov, *Vremia i tanki* (Moscow: Voenizdat, 1972).
Severnie konvoi: Issledovaniia, vospominaniia, dokumenti. Vip. 2 (Moscow: Nauka 1994).
Severnie konvoi: Issledovaniia, vospominaniia, dokumenti. Vip. 3 (Moscow: 'Andreevskii flag', 2000).
A.B. Shirokorad, *Korabli i katera VMF SSSR 1939–45 gg.* Spravochnik (Minsk: Kharvest, 2002).
N.S. Simonov, *Voenno-promishlennii kompleks SSSR v 1920–1950-e godi: tempi ekonomicheskogo rosta, struktura, organizatsiia proizvodstva i upravlenie* (Moscow: ROSSPEN, 1996).
V. Sipols, *Taini diplomaticheskie: Kanun Velikoi Otechestvennoi voinoi. 1939–1941* (Moscow: TOO 'Novina', 1997).
Sovetskaia Voennaia Entsiklopediia: {v 8 tomakh} (Moscow: Voennoe izdatel'stvo Ministerstva oboroni, 1976–1980).

M. Suprun, *Lend-liz i severnie konvoi 1941–1945* (Moscow: Andreevskii flag 1997).
O.F. Suvenirov, *Tragediia RKKA 1937–1938* (Moscow: Terra, 1998).
Velikaia Otechestvennaia voina. 1941–1945. Voenno-istoricheskie ocherki. Kniga vtoraia. Perelom (Moscow: Nauka, 1998).
Velikaia Otechestvennaia voina. 1941–1945. Voenno-istoricheskii ocherki. Kniga tret'ia. Osvobozhdenie (Moscow: Nauka, 1999).
Velikaia Otechestvennaia voina. 1941–1945. Voenno-istoricheskie ocherki. Kniga chetvertaia. Narod i voina (Moscow: Nauka, 1999).
Velikaia Otechestvennaia voina 1941–1945 gg.: Deistvuiushchaia armiia (Moscow: Animi Fortitudo, Kuchkovo pole, 2005).
F.F. Viktorov, N.I. Barishnikov, N.F. Vargin, L.G. Vinnitskii, I.I. Evstiukhin, O.S. Zhitskov et al., *Istoriia Ordena Lenina Leningradskogo voennogo okruga* (Moscow: Voennoe izdatel'stvo Ministerstva oboroni SSSR, 1974).
V.A. Zolotarev and I.A. Kozlov, *Tri stoletiia Rossiiskogo flota, 1941–1945* (Moscow: AST; St Petersburg: Poligon, 2005).

Other books in German

Karl Heinz Frieser, K. Shmider, K. Schönherr, G. Schreiber, K. Ungváry, B. Wegner, *Das Deutsche Reich und der Zweite Weltkrieg. Band 8. Die Ostfront 1943/44* (München: Deutsche Verlags-Anstalt, 2007).

Other books in English

John Barber and Mark Harrison, *The Soviet Home Front, 1941–1945* (London: Longman, 1991).
H. Boog, J. Forster, J. Hoffmann, E. Klink, R.-D. Muller, G.R. Ueberschar and E. Osers (eds), *Germany and the Second World War. Volume IV. The Attack on the Soviet Union* (Oxford: Clarendon Press, 1998).
Louis Brown, *A Radar History of World War II – Technical and Military Imperatives* (Bristol and Philadelphia, PA: Institute of Physics Publishing, 1999).
A.P. Dobson, *US Wartime Aid to Britain* (London: Croom Helm 1986).
C. Van Dyke, *The Soviet Invasion of Finland 1939–1940* (London: Frank Cass, 1997).
J. Haslam, *The Soviet Union and the Struggle for Collective Security in Europe, 1933–39* (London: Macmillan Press Ltd, 1984).
David Glantz, *August Storm: The Soviet 1945 Strategic Offensive in Manchuria*, Leavenworth Paper Number 7 (Fort Leavenworth, KS: Combat Studies Institute, US Army Command and General Staff College, February 1983).
David Glantz, *Stumbling Colossus: The Red Army on the Eve of War* (Lawrence, KS: University Press of Kansas, 1998).
David M. Glantz, *Zhukov's Greatest Defeat: The Red Army's Epic Disaster in Operation Mars, 1942* (Lawrence, KS: University Press of Kansas, 1999).
David Glantz, *Colossus Reborn: The Red Army at War, 1941–1943* (Lawrence, KA: University Press of Kansas, 2005).
David Glantz and Jonathan House, *When Titans Clashed: How the Red Army Stopped Hitler* (Lawrence, KS: University Press of Kansas, 1995).
G. Gorodetsky, *Grand Delusion. Stalin and the German Invasion of Russia* (New Haven, CT: Yale University Press, 1999).

Arnold Hague, *Destroyers for Great Britain: A History of the 50 Town Class Ships Transferred from the United States to Great Britain in 1940* (London: Greenhill Books, 1990).

M. Harrison, *Soviet Planning in Peace and War, 1938–1945* (Cambridge: Cambridge University Press, 1985).

M. Harrison, *Accounting for War. Soviet Production, Employment and the Defence Burden, 1940–1945* (Cambridge: Cambridge University Press, 1996).

W. Haupt, *Army Group North – The Wehrmacht in Russia 1941–1945* (Atglen, PA: Schiffer Military History, 1997).

Hannes Heer, 'The Logic of the War of Extermination', in Hannes Heer and Klaus Naumann (eds), *War of Extermination: The German Military in World War II, 1941–1944* (London: Berghahn Books, 2004), pp. 92–126.

Alexander Hill, *The War Behind the Eastern Front: The Soviet Partisan Movement in North-West Russia, 1941–1944* (London: Frank Cass, 2005).

J. Hochman, *The Soviet Union and the Failure of Collective Security, 1934–1938* (Ithaca, NY: Cornell University Press, 1984).

J. Hoffmann, *Stalin's War of Extermination, 1941–1945: Planning, Realization, and Documentation* (Capshaw, Ala.: Theses & Dissertations Press, 2001).

E.M. Howell, *The Soviet Partisan Movement 1941–1944. DA Pam 20-244* (Washington DC: Department of the Army, 1956).

M. Jakobsen, *The Diplomacy of the Winter War: an Account of the Russo-Finnish War, 1939–1940* (Cambridge, MA: Harvard University Press, 1961).

R.H. Jones, *The Roads to Russia: United States Lend-Lease to the Soviet Union* (Norman, OK: University of Oklahoma Press, 1969).

MacGregor Knox, *Hitler's Italian Allies: Royal Armed Forces, Fascist Regime and the War of 1940–1943* (Cambridge: Cambridge University Press, 2000).

G.F. Krivosheev (ed.), *Soviet Casualties and Combat Losses in the Twentieth Century* (London: Greenhill Books, 1997).

B.H. Liddell Hart, *The Other Side of the Hill: The Classic Account of Hitler's War through the Eyes of German Generals* (London: Pan Books Ltd, 1983).

R.C. Lucas, *The Army Air Forces and the Soviet Union, 1941–1945* (Tallahassee, Florida: Florida State University, 1970).

Evan Mawdlsey, *Thunder in the East: The Nazi-Soviet War 1941–1945* (London: Hodder Arnold, 2005).

S.W. Mitchum, *Hitler's Legions: German Army Order of Battle, World War II* (London: Leo Cooper/Secker and Warburg, 1985).

Keith Neilson, *Britain, Soviet Russia and the Collapse of the Versailles Order, 1919–1939* (Cambridge: Cambridge University Press, 2006).

A.M. Nekrich, *Pariahs, Partners, Predators: German Soviet Relations, 1922–1941* (New York: Columbia University Press, 1997).

Office, Chief of Finance, War Department, *Lend-Lease Shipments. World War II* (Washington DC: 31 December 1946).

Richard Overy, *Why the Allies Won* (London: Pimlico, 1996).

T.R. Philbin III, *The Lure of Neptune: German-Soviet Naval Collaboration and Ambitions, 1919–1941* (Columbia, SC: University of South Carolina, 1994).

Silvio Pons, *Stalin and the Inevitable War 1936–1941* (London: Frank Cass, 2002).

Hugh Ragsdale, *The Soviets, the Munich Crisis, and the Coming of World War II* (New York: Cambridge University Press, 2004).

G. Roberts, *The Soviet Union and the Origins of the Second World War: Russo-German Relations and the Road to War, 1933–1941* (London: Macmillan Press Ltd, 1995).

J. Rohwer and M.S. Monakov, *Stalin's Ocean Going Fleet: Soviet Naval Strategy and Shipbuilding Programmes, 1935–1953* (London: Frank Cass, 2001).
Harrison E. Salisbury, *The 900 Days: The Siege of Leningrad* (New York and Evanston: Harper and Row, 1969).
Patrick Salmon, *Scandinavia and the Great Powers, 1890–1940* (Cambridge: Cambridge University Press, 1997).
Lennart Samuelson, *Plans for Stalin's War Machine: Tukhachevskii and Military-Economic Planning, 1925–1941* (Basingstoke: Palgrave, 2000).
B. Shepherd, *War in the Wild East: The German Army and Soviet Partisans* (Cambridge, MA: Harvard University Press, 2004).
H. Shukman (ed.), *Stalin's Generals* (New York: Grove Press, 1993).
A.J.P. Taylor, *The Origins of the Second World War* (London: Hamish Hamilton, 1961).
Earl F. Ziemke, *The German Northern Theater of Operations 1940–1945* [German Report Series] (Eastbourne, UK: Antony Rowe Ltd, undated).

Journal articles and selected book chapters in Russian

V. Andrianov, 'Operativnoe ispol'zovanie partisanskikh sil', *Vizh*, Number 7 (1969), pp. 24–27.
'Belorusskaia operatsiia v tsifrakh', *Vizh*, Number 6 (1964), pp. 74–86.
'Berlinskaia operatsiia v tsifrakh', *Vizh*, Number 4 (1965), pp. 79–88.
P.N. Bobilev, 'Tochku v diskussii stavit' rano. K voprosu o planirovanii v General'nom shtabe RKKA vozmozhnoi voini s Germaniei v 1940–1941 godakh', *Otechestvennaia istoriia*, Number 1 (2000), pp. 41–64.
M.A. Bobrov, 'Strategicheskoe razvertivanie VVS Krasnoi armii na zapade strani pered Velikoi Otechestvennoi voinoi', 2006, Number 5 (2006), pp. 3–7.
V. Ezhakov, 'Boevoe primenenie tankov v gorno-taezhnoi mestnosti po opitu 1-go Dal'nevostochnogo fronta', *Vizh*, Number 1 (1974), pp. 77–81.
'Iassko-Kishinevskaia operatssia v tsifrakh', *Vizh*, Number 8 (1964), pp. 36–41.
I. Izotikov, 'Na kakikh samoletakh letal Pokrishkin, ili ne boites' britantsev, dari prinosiashchikh?', *Vestnik protivovozdushnoi oboroni*, Number 4 (1991), pp. 33–36.
'Kampaniia Sovetskikh Vooruzhennikh Sil na Dal'nem Vostoke v 1945 g. (Fakti i tsifri)', *Vizh*, Number 8 (1965), pp. 64–73.
V. Kazantsev, 'Melitopol'skaia operatsiia (v tsifrakh)', *Vizh*, Number 7 (1977), pp. 63–71.
N.A. Kirsanov, 'Mobilizatsiia zhenshchin v Krasnuiu armiiu v godi fashistskogo nashestviia', *Vizh*, Number 5 (2007), pp. 15–17.
G.A. Kumanev 'Otvet P.K. Ponomarenko na voprosi G.A. Kumaneva. 2 noiabria 1978 g.', *Otechestvennaia istoriia*, Number 6 (1998), pp. 133–149.
R.I. Larintsev, 'Lend-lizovskie postavki na Severnii flot i ikh effektivnost'', in M.N. Suprun (ed.), *Voina v Arktike (1939–1945 gg.)* (Arkhangel'sk: Pomorskii gosudarstvennii universitet, 2001), 263–270.
'Moskovskaia bitva v tsifrakh (period kontrnastupleniia)', *Vizh*, Number 1 (1967), pp. 89–101.
'Moskovskaia bitva v tsifrakh (period oboroni)', *Vizh*, Number 3 (1967), pp. 69–79.
P.K. Ponomarenko, 'Bor'ba Sovetskogo naroda v tilu vraga', *Vizh*, Number 4 (1965), 26–36.
'Primenenie aviatsii v Man'chzhurskoi operatsii' [Interview with Marshal of Aviation P.S. Kirsanov], *Vizh*, Number 8 (1985), pp. 20–24.

V.M. Safir, 'Oborona Moskvi. Narofominskii proriv 1–5 dekabria 1941 goda (chto bilo i chego ne bilo v deistvitelnosti)', *Voenno-istoricheskii arkhiv*, Vipusk 1 (1997), pp. 77–125.

A.A. Sherviakov, 'Gitlerovskii genotsid i repatriatsiia sovetskogo nasileniia', in *Liudskie poteri SSSR v period vtorio mirovoi voini. Sbornik statei* (St Petersburg: Izdatel'stvo 'Russki-Baltiiskii informatsionnii tsentr BLITS', 1995), pp. 178–181.

L.G. Shmigel'skii, 'Molotovskii zavod No. 402 i severnie konvoi', in *Severnie konvoi: Issledovaniia, vospominaniia, dokumenti. Vip. 3* (Moscow: Andreevskii flag 2000), pp. 68–102.

M.N. Suprun, 'Prodovol'stvennie postavki v SSSR po Lend-lizu v godi Vtoroi mirovoi voini', *Otechesvennaia istoriia*, Number 3 (1996), pp. 46–54.

I.M. Tret'iak, 'Razgrom Kvantungskoi armii na Dal'nem Vostoke', *Vizh*, Number 8 (1985), pp. 9–19.

'Vislo-Oderskaia operatsiia v tsifrakh', *Vizh*, Number 1 (1965), pp. 71–81.

Vostochno-Prusskaia operatsiia v tsifrakh', *Vizh*, Number 2 (1965), pp. 80–90.

A.V. Usikov and V.T. Iminov, 'Rol' i mesto sovetsko-germanskogo fronta v Vtoroi Mirovoi voine', *Vizh*, Number 5 (2005), pp. 3–8.

V.N. Zemskov, 'Smertnost' zakliuchennikh v 1941–1945 gg.', in *Liudskie poteri SSSR v period vtorio mirovoi voini. Sbornik statei* (St Petersburg: Izdatel'stvo 'Russki-Baltiiskii informatsionnii tsentr BLITS', 1995), pp. 174–177.

Articles in Russian available through the internet

V. Romanenko, 'P-40 v Sovetskoi aviatsii'. Online. Available http://lend-lease.airforce.ru/articles/romanenko/p-40/index.htm (accessed 2 May 2008).

Journal articles in English

M.J. Carley, 'Behind Stalin's Moustache: Pragmatism in Early Soviet Foreign Policy, 1917–1941', *Diplomacy and Statecraft*, Volume 12, Number 3 (September 2001), pp. 159–174.

Edward J. Drea, 'Missing Intentions: Japanese Intelligence and the Soviet Invasion of Manchuria, 1945', *Military Affairs* (April 1984), pp. 66–73.

John Ferris, 'Image and Accident: Intelligence and the Origins of World War II, 1933–1941', in John Robert Ferris, *Intelligence and Strategy – Selected Essays* (Abingdon: Routledge, 2005), pp. 99–137.

H. Flory, 'The Arcos Raid and the Rupture of Anglo-Soviet Relations, 1927', *Journal of Contemporary History*, Volume 12, Number 4 (October 1977), pp. 707–723.

David Glantz, 'Forgotten Battles of the German-Soviet War (1941–1945), Part II', *JSMS*, Volume 13, Number 1 (March 2000), pp. 172–237.

David Glantz, 'Forgotten Battles of the German-Soviet War (1941–1945), Part 3: The Winter Campaign (5 December-April 1942): The Moscow Counteroffensive', *JSMS*, Volume 13, Number 2 (June 2000), pp. 139–185

Alexander Hill, 'The Birth of the Soviet Northern Fleet 1937–1942', *JSMS*, Volume 16, Number 2 (June 2003), pp. 65–82.

Alexander Hill, 'British "Lend-Lease" Tanks and the Battle for Moscow, November–December 1941 – A Research Note', *JSMS*, Volume 19, Number 2 (June 2006), pp. 289–294.

Alexander Hill, 'British Lend-Lease Aid and the Soviet War Effort, June 1941-June 1942', *Journal of Military History*, Volume 71, Number 3 (July 2007), pp. 773–808.

Alexander Hill, 'Stalin and the West', in Gordon Martel (ed.), *A Companion to International History, 1900–2001* (Oxford: Blackwell, 2007), pp. 257–268.

Peter Jackson, 'France', in Robert Boyce and Joseph A. Maiolo (eds), *The Origins of World War Two: The Debate Continues* (Basingstoke: Palgrave Macmillan, 2003), pp. 86–110.

O. Khlevniuk, 'The Objectives of the Great Terror, 1937–38', in D.L. Hoffmann (ed.), *Stalinism: The Essential Readings* (Malden, MA: Blackwell Publishing, 2003), pp. 83–104.

Evan Mawdsley, 'Crossing the Rubicon: Soviet Plans for Offensive War in 1940–1941', *International History Review*, Volume 25, Number 4 (2003), pp. 818–865.

Gordon W. Morrell, 'Redefining Intelligence and Intelligence Gathering: The Industrial Intelligence Centre and the Metro-Vickers Affair, Moscow 1933', *Intelligence and National Security*, Volume 9, Number 3 (July 1994), pp. 520–533.

Roger Munting, 'Soviet Food Supply and Allied Aid in the War, 1941–1945', *Soviet Studies*, Volume XXXVI, Number 4 (October 1984), pp. 582–593.

V.A. Nevezhin, 'The Pact with Germany and the Idea of an "Offensive War"', *JSMS*, Volume 8, Number 4 (December 1995), pp. 809–843.

Philips P. O'Brien, 'East versus West in the Defeat of Nazi Germany', *The Journal of Strategic Studies*, Volume 23, Number 2 (June 2000), pp. 89–113.

Albert Resis, 'The Fall of Litvinov: Harbinger of the German-Soviet Non-aggression Pact', *Europe–Asia Studies*, Volume 52, Number 1 (2000), pp. 33–56.

N.S. Simonov, '"Strengthen the Defence of the Land of the Soviets": The 1927 "War Alarm" and its Consequences', *Europe–Asia Studies*, Volume 48, Number 8 (1996), pp. 1355–1364.

Zara Steiner, 'The Soviet Commissariat of Foreign Affairs and the Czechoslovakian Crisis in 1938: New Material from the Soviet Archives', *Historical Journal*, Volume 42, Number 3 (1999), pp. 751–779.

R. Stephan, 'Smersh: Soviet Military Counter-intelligence during the Second World War', *Journal of Contemporary History*, Volume 22 (1987), pp. 585–613.

D. Stone 'The August 1924 Raid on Stolpce, Poland, and the Evolution of Soviet Active Intelligence', *Intelligence and National Security*, Volume 21, Number 2 (Spring 2006), pp. 331–341.

David Stone, 'The First Five-Year Plan and the Geography of Soviet Defence Industry', *Europe–Asia Studies*, Volume 57, Number 7 (November 2005), pp. 1047–1063.

Mikhail Suprun, 'Operation "West": The Role of the Northern Fleet and its Air Forces in the Liberation of the Russian Arctic in 1944', *JSMS*, Volume 20, Number 3 (July–September 2007), pp. 433–447.

V. Suvorov (pseud.), 'Who was Planning to Attack Whom in June 1941, Hitler or Stalin?', *Journal of the Royal United Services Institute for Defence Studies*, Volume 130, Number 2 (1985), pp. 50–55.

V.F. Vorsin, 'Motor Vehicle Transport Deliveries through "Lend-Lease"', *JSMS*, Volume 10, Number 2 (June 1997), pp. 153–175.

Index

aircraft, German: Bf109 176
aircraft, Soviet: Ar-2 53; DB-3 51;
  I-15/I-153 53, 146, *175*; I-16 *53*, 146,
  175; Il-2 51, *53*; Il-4 51; LaGG-3 51,
  175, 176; LaGG-5 *175*; LaGG-7 *175*;
  Li-2 ('Dakota') 148–9; MiG-1 51;
  MiG-3 51, *53*, *175*, 176; Pe-2 *53*;
  PS-84 146; SB *53*; Su-2 *53*; TB-3 51,
  148; TB-7 51; U-2 112; Yak-1 51,
  53, *175*; Yak-2 *53*; Yak-4 *53*; Yak-7
  175; Yak-9 *175*; *see also* VVS
aircraft, Soviet – Lend-Lease: Aerocobra
  (P-39) 171, *174–5*, 177; Hurricane
  164, *174–5*, 176, *177*, 180; P-40
  167, 170, 174, *174–5*, 176–7,
  321n19; Spitfire *175*, 176, 180
Antonescu, I. 240, 301
Antonov, A.I. 131, 138, 225, 265,
  269–70, 274
Arkhangel'sk 12, **52**, 84, 98, **107**, **124**,
  170, 180, 182, **229**, 295, 297

Baltic–White Sea Canal 9, 11–12
Beria, L.P. 36, 44–8, 68, 71, 92, 105,
  152, 199, 227, 244, 248, 269–71
Berlin **229**, 264; *see also* Red Army
  (operations)
blocking detachments 56, 68–9, 102–3,
  247–8
Brest 30, **52**, **52**, **107**, 213
Brezhnev, L.I. 287, 329n7
Briansk 33, **52**, 68–9, **107**, 117,
  213–14, 295, 300
Brodi 42, 50, **237**, 294
Budapest **229**, 241–3, 251, 253, 260,
  284
Budennii, S.M. 44, 47, 290, 294
Bulganin, N.A. 47, 72, 81, 269, 271
Bulgaria 221

Cherniakhovskii, I.D. 255, 257
Churchill, W. 49, 166–7, 290
Comintern 6, 9, 14, 46, 305
command and control (Soviet) 51–2, 61,
  78, 190, 197; and radio
  communications *38*, 50, 61, 88, 178,
  182, 190, 216, 262–3, 318, 325
commissars *see* institute of commissars
convoys (Northern) 170, *185*, 295, 297,
  321n11; PQ-12 177, 181–2; PQ-13
  184; PQ-17 98, 297; PQ-18 322n32
counter intelligence (Soviet): and
  German stay-behind agents 229;
  responsibility for in military units
  54–5, 114, 271

deception *see maskirovka*
Demiansk 98, 117, **124**, 216, 299

Einsatzgruppen 208, 305–6
El'nia **52**, 64–5, 72, **107**, 294–5
evacuation, civilian: German 262; of
  Leningrad 145, 149–52; of Moscow
  70–1, 296; Soviet 56–7, 180, 294,
  296, 324n4

feste Plätze 231, 301
Final Solution 287–9
Finnish forces 30, 36, 42, 62, 115,
  142–3, 145–7, 220, 228, 285, 296,
  301–2, 330n21
Führer directives: Number 21 293;
  Number 34 295; Number 41 297;
  Number 45 99, 297; *see also feste
  Plätze*

Genshtab (GSh KA), role and
  significance of 131–2, 270–1
German Army *see Wehrmacht*

GKO (State Defence Committee): composition 45, 270–1; creation and function 45, 48, 50, 294, 307
Great Britain *see* Churchill; Stalin, and the Allies
guards units, Soviet: creation of 161, 306
Guderian, H. 63
Gulag 12, 92, 307, 329n14

Halder, F. 51
Hitler, A.: and delay to 'Citadel' 125; leadership 290; no retreat 79, 108, 224–6, 231, 239, 296; sanctioned withdrawals 132, 222, 227, 298–9; suicide 271; *see also feste Plätze*; Führer directives
Holocaust *see* Final Solution
horses, transport role: German *210*, 223, 231, 239, 245–6, 253, 330n16; Japan 281; Soviet 60, 94–5, 186, 205–6, 235, 239, 281, 273, 288, 330n16
Horthy, M. 241
Hungarian forces 30, 36, 208, 221, 240–2, *252*, 285, 298, 330n21

institute of commissars: and dual command 24, 52–6; and unitary command 24, 113–14
intelligence: German 35–6, 61, 216, 228–9; Soviet 29–30, 35, 41–2, 51–2, 72, 125, 129, 134, 139, 209, 215–16, 236, 238–9, 254, 271, 277, 280, 307, 309 (and deployment tanks 86–7, 96, 110; partisans and 198, 200, 209, 215–16; and urban warfare 258–9)
Italian forces 115, 285, 298, 329–30n14

Kaganovich, L.M. 44, 46
Kalinin, M.I. 24, 114
Katiusha see RS
Kerch' 97–8, **107**, **124**, 138, 226, 288
Khar'kov 52, 97–8, **107**, 117, 123, **124**, 125, 129, 131, 160, 186, 296–7, 299
Khrushchev, N.S. 79, 163–4, 269, 284, 286, 287, 329n7, 330n23
Kiev 30, 50–1, **52**, 63, 66, 68, **107**, 135, **124**, 223, **237**, 238, 290, 295, 300
Komsomol 45, 54, 62, 93, 194–5, 308, 312

Konev, I.S. 225–6, 247, 253, 265, 267–8, 271–2, 290, 327n1
Königsberg 42, **229**, 255–7, 260, 284, 303
Krebs, H. 271
Kronstadt 12, 137, 144–5, 152, 260
Kulik, G.I. 44, 46, 48
Kursk 51, 117, **124**, 125–6, **127–8**, 130–2, **133**, 214, **229**, 299
Küstrin 254, 264, *264*, 266
Kuznetsov, A.A. 46–7, 150, 158
Kuznetsov, N.G. 41, 44, 46–7, 92, 269–70

labour camps *see* Gulag
Lend-Lease *see* aircraft; motor vehicles; PVO; railways; tanks; United States
Lenin, V.I. 5, 48, 76, 292
Leningrad 52, **107**, **124**, 144, 204; siege of 97–8, 115, 143–61, 186, 221–3, 295–8, 301; significance 9, 141, 144; threat to through Finland 19–20, 141; *see also* motor vehicles; railways; Red Army (operations)
logistics *see* supply
lorries *see* motor vehicles
Lublin 30, 32–3, 42, 235–6, 301
Luftwaffe 249, 254, 308; air assets drawn to West 328n5: first days 'Barbarossa' 41, 50; overflights Soviet territory pre-'Barbarossa' 35–6; and siege of Leningrad 149; and Soviet naval losses 137–8
Luga (line) 62, 142, 294
L'vov 30, 34, 220, **229**, **237**, 238

Malenkov, G.M. 42, 44–8, 152, 248, 269–71
maskirovka 110, 224, 229
Mekhlis, L.Z. 44, 46, 197, 270
Meretskov, K.A. 27, 44, 223, 281
Merkulov, V.N. 46–7, 271
Mikoian, A.I. 44, 46–7, 171–2, 269, 271
military soviets 24, 41–4, 65, 77, 79, 87–8, 92, 96, 102, 141–3, 149–50, 152, 161, 176, 197, 236, 274, 307–8; and military rule (*voennoe polozhenie*) 43–4; and the partisan movement 197, 216
Minsk 33, 47, 50, **52**, **107**, **124**, 213, 220, **229**, **229**, 231, 294, 301

Index

Molotov, V.M. 45–8, 70–1, 149, 171, 194, 248, 270–1
Moscow **52**, **107**, **124**, **229**; 7 November 1941 parade 296; siege and evacuation 70–1; *see also* Red Army (operations)
motor vehicles, Soviet: availability *38*, 60, 94–6, 111, 113, 119, 121–2, 165, 178–9, 181, 186–7, *188*, 190–1, *232*, 235, 238–9, *251*, *267*, 273, 283, 322n39; and siege Leningrad **144**, 149–50
Mozhaisk (line) 62–3, 68–70, 295
Murmansk 32, **52**, 98, **107**, **124**, 170, 181–2, 184, **229**, 322n32

narodnoe opolchenie 50, 61–3, 195, 248, 294, 309, 313
Narva 63, 132, 142, 204, 213, 223, 240
Nationalism, Soviet/Russian: in propaganda 50, 76
navy *see* Soviet Navy
NKGB 195–6, 227, 271, 309
NKVD 36, 46–7, 54–6, 62–3, 68–9, 71, 91–2, 102–3, 105, 113–14, 152–3, 155, 157–8, 195–9, 215, 227, 248, 269–71, 288, 295, 309; and the partisan movement 195–9; *see also* Beria; blocking detachments; special sections
Novgorod 52, 59, 63, **107**, **124**, 142–3, **204**, 220, 222
Novikov, A.A. 176, 270
Novorossiisk 288, 298, 300

Odessa 52, **107**, **124**, 137, 220, **229**, 296
OKH 51, 289, 309
OO/NKVD *see* special sections
operations, German: 'Barbarossa' 35, 40–67, **52**, 115, 141, 207, 270, 293–4, 317n8; '*Blau*' 99, 105, 297; '*Braunschweig*' 99, 297; 'Citadel' 125–32, 139, 216, 299; 'Kremlin' 97; 'Northern Lights' 161; 'Spring Clean' 202–6, 217; 'Typhoon' 66, 68–81, 295
operations, Soviet:
'Bagration/Belorussian' 229, *233*, 235, 237, 240, 301; 'Baltic' *234*; 'Belgrade' *234*, 241, 302; 'Berlin' 264, *267*, 303; 'Bolkhov' 86; 'Budapest' *234*, 241, 302; 'Crimean' *233*, 301; 'Dnepr–Carpathian' 223–4, *233*, 300; 'Donbass' 131, 299; 'East Carpathian' *234*, 241, 301; 'East Pomeranian' 261, 262, 302; 'East Prussian' 249, *251*, *261*, 262; 'Iassi–Kishinev' *234*, 239, 301; 'Jupiter' 113; 'Kerch–Feodosiia' *91*, 137, 296; 'Kiev Defensive' 66; 'Kirovgrad' 223; 'Korsun–Shevchenkovskii' 223–4, 300; 'Kursk Defensive' *133*; 'Kutuzov/Orel' 130, *133*, 299; 'Leningrad–Novgorod' 221, *233*, 301; 'Little Saturn' 108, 298; 'Lower Dnepr' 300; 'Lublin–Brest' 235; 'L'vov–Sandomierz/L'vov Peremishl'' *233*, 236–7, **237**, 241, 301; 'Manchurian' 275, *276*, 277, **278**, 280, 282; 'Mars/Rzhev–Sichevka' 107, 113, 297–8; 'Moscow Defensive', 295; 'Moscow Offensive' 81, *91*, **107**, 296–7; 'Nikopol'sk–Krivoi Rog' 223; 'North Caucasus Defensive' 297; 'Oboian–Kursk (Belgorod)' 85; 'Orel–Bolkhov' 85; 'Petsamo–Kirkenes' 137, *234*, 243; 'Prague' 303; 'Rostov' *91*, 296; 'Rovno–Lutsk' 223; 'Rumiantsev/Belgorod–Khar'kov' 130, 131, *133*, 299; 'Rzhev–Viaz'ma' *91*, 297; 'Sandomierz–Silesian' 249; 'Siniavino' 161, 297; 'Spark' 161, 298; 'Stalingrad Defensive' 99, 297; 'Stalingrad Strategic' **107**, **124**, 298; 'Suvorov' 228, 299; 'Tikhvin' *91*; 'Uranus' 107, 298; 'Viborg–Petrozavodsk' 228, *233*, 301; 'Vienna' 302; 'Vistula–Oder' 248–9, *250*, 251, *252*, *261*, 262, 302; 'Voronezh–Khar'kov' 298; 'Voronezh–Voroshilovgrad Defensive' 99, 297; 'War of the Rails' 209, 211–13, 216, 299; 'West' 326n21; 'Zhitomir-Berdichevskaia' 223
opolchenie see *narodnoe opolchenie*
Order Number 189 (NKO) 199–200, 211, 215, 298
Order Number 227 (NKO) 100–3, 297
Order Number 270 (*Stavka* VGK) 55–6, 100, 248, 295
Orel 85, **107**, 117, **124**, 130, 296, 299
Ostarbeiter 218, 248, 309, 329n13

Ostwall 132, 222, 299–300

Panzerfaust 257–9, 263, 310, 327n7
Panzerschreck 263, 327n7
Paulus, F. 108
Petsamo 23, 228, 243–4
Polish forces 23, 235–6, 301
Ponomarenko, P.K. 193, 197–9, 204, 208, 211–12
prisoners of war (POWs): Soviet in German hands (fate of 248, 287–9, 329n13: and major encirclements 66, 68, 317n13: as source intelligence 128); German in Soviet hands (fate of 289; Stalingrad 108)
propaganda, Soviet: and abortive preparation for war 29, 35; lack of realism in early war 75–6; *see also* Nationalism
Pskov 52, **107**, 141–2, **204**, 210–11, 213, 223, 294, 301
PVO 310; ground use AA guns 63; Lend-Lease aircraft and 174, *175*, 177; women serving in 93

radio communications, Soviet: Lend-Lease and 176, 178, 182, 190; procedures 61, 88, 262–3, 318n31; shortages in 38, 50, 61, 88, 182, 216, 325n29
railways: availability of rolling stock 187, *188*, *191*; importance for logistics 27, 32, 34, 57, 101, 119, 122, 187, **204**, 217, 223, 237–8, **237**, 266, 273; partisan ops versus German 199–200, **204**, 209–14, *210*; and siege of Leningrad 143, 144, 147, 152, 161
reconnaissance *see* intelligence
Red Army, formations and units, armies: 1st Czechoslovak *234*; 1st Guards 118; 1st Polish 236; 1st Shock *233*, 262; 2nd Shock 88, 159–60, 222, 297; 2nd Tank 126; 3rd Guards 118; 3rd Guards Tank 135, 268; 3rd Shock 321; 3rd Tank 322n26; 4th Air 138, *233*; 4th Guards 136; 4th Guards Tank 272; 4th Tank 268; 5th Guards 136; 5th Guards Tank 136, 139, 224, 226, 239; 5th Shock 254; 5th Tank 118–19, 136, 321n26; 6th 118–19, 122, 258; 6th Guards 129; 6th Guards Tank 242, 279; 6th Tank 240; 7th 142; 7th Guards 136; 7th Independent 178; 8th 142, 248; 8th Guards 254, 259; 9th 79; 9th Air 277; 10th Air 277; 11th 59; 11th Guards 229, *230*, 256; 12th Air 277; 13th 127, 134–5; 14th 244; 15th 274; 16th 85, 279; 16th Air 125; 18th Long-Range Air 267; 20th 82; 24th 64–5; 27th 225–6; 30rh 85; 33rd 79; 34th 59; 37th 136; 38th 129, 135; 39th 234; 40th 129, 321n26; 43rd 64, 235, 251; 46th 242; 47th *250*; 48th 59–61, *127*; 50th 79, 85; 51st 322n27; 52nd 136; 53rd 136, 321n26; 54th 61, 144, 146–7, 159; 56th 79; 57th 131, 136; 59th 160, 297; 60th 127, *250*; 61st 82, 321n26; 62nd 100, 103, 105; 65th 127; 67th 161; 70th *127*; Coastal (Primorskaia) 98; Independent Maritime 226, *233*, 301
Red Army, formations and units, battalions: 23rd Ski 80, 82; 24th Ski 80, 82; 126th ITB 85; 131st ITB 85, *85*; 132nd ITB 85; 136th ITB 79–82, 85, *85*; 137th Tank *85*; 138th ITB 85, *85*; 139th Tank 85; 140th ITB 80–1; 145th ITB *85*; 302nd Machine-Gun 70; 305th Machine-Gun 70; 467th Indep Sapper 70; 538th Sapper 70
Red Army, formations and units, brigades: 1st Guards Tank 87; 1st Mountain Rifle 59–61; 2nd Guards Mech 242; 2nd Guards Tank 87; 3rd Rifle 159; 9th Tank 72, 317n5; 17th OATB 150; 17th Rifle 82; 17th Tank 72, 87, 317n5; 18th Rifle 80, 82; 18th Tank 72, 87; 19th Tank 72; 20th Tank 70, 72, 81, 87; 21st Tank 72; 22nd Rifle 159; 22nd Tank 72; 24th Rifle 159; 24th Tank 85, 317n5; 25th Rifle 159; 32nd Tank 87; 53rd Rifle 159; 57th Rifle 159; 58th Rifle 159; 59th Rifle 159; 59th Tank 177; 62nd Tank 272; 63rd Tank 272; 68th Tank 87; 70th SP Artillery 272; 84th Rifle 82; 103rd Tank 177; 136th Tank 177; 137th Tank 177; 140th Tank 177; 145th Tank 85; 146th Tank 85, *85*, 87; 170th Tank 177; 177th Tank 177;

179th Tank 177; 184th Tank 177; 186th Tank 177; 201st Tank 177

Red Army, formations and units, corps: 1st Mech 136; 2nd DBAK 51; 2nd Guards Mech 242–3; 3rd Bomber Air 125; 3rd Tank 123, 321n26; 4th Guards Mech 242; 5th Guards Cav 226, 243; 5th Guards Tank 129, 130; 5th Mech 268; 6th Fighter Air 125; 6th Mixed Air 125; 7th Mech 136, 243; 9th Mech 50–1; 9th Tank 126; 10th Tank 123, 272, 275, 321n27; 11th Tank 321n26; 14th Tank 321n27; 15th Mech 51; 15th Rifle 134; 17th Guards Rifle 134; 18th Tank 123, 130, 139, 240, 243; 19th Tank 126; 23rd Tank 240; 28th Rifle 134; 29th Tank 130, 139; Czechoslovak 234

Red Army, formations and units, divisions: 7th Breakthrough Artillery 242; 7th Cavalry 327n1; 18th DBAD 51; 21st Tank 59–61, 317n17; 31st Indep Artillery 70; 32nd Rifle 70; 41st Indep AA 70; 59th Indep AA 70; 63rd Guards Rifle 161; 66th Cavalry 79; 68th Cavalry 79; 110th Rifle 80; 113th Rifle 80; 312th Rifle 70; 128th Rifle 59–61; 180th Rifle 226; 204th Rifle 129; 309th Rifle 129; 311th Rifle 59–61; 316th Rifle 70; 327th Rifle 88, 159

Red Army, formations and units, fortified districts 33–4, 40, 94; Maloiaroslavets 72; Pskov-Ostrov 141

Red Army, formations and units, *fronts*: 1st Baltic 231, *231*, *233–4*, *251*, 300–1; 1st Belorussian 231, *231*, 236, 247–9, 253–4, 263–8, **264**, *267*, 271–2, 301–2; 1st Far Eastern 275, *276*, 277, *277*, **278**, 303; 1st Ukrainian 134–5, 223–5, *233–4*, 237–8, 247–9, 253–4, **264**, 265–8, *267*, 271–2, 300–3; 2nd Baltic 223, *233–4*, 300–2; 2nd Belorussian 231, *231*, *233–4*, 247, 249, *251*, 254, **264**, 265–8, *267*, 301–3; 2nd Far Eastern 275, *276*, 277, **278**, 278–9, 303; 2nd Ukrainian 135, 139, 224–6, *233–4*, 239–40, 242–3, 251, 260, 300, 302–3; 3rd Baltic 223, *233–4*, 300–2; 3rd Belorussian 229, *230*, 231, *231–4*, 249, *251*, 254–5, 257, 301–3; 3rd Ukrainian 135, *233–4*, 239–40, 242–3, 300, 302; 4th Ukrainian 132, 226–7, *233–4*, *252*, 300–1, 303; Baltic 300; Belorussian 300; Briansk 69, 75, 86, *133*, 172, 298–9, 321n26; Central 69, 125, 126, *126–8*, *133*, 299–300; Don 103, 108, 115, 297; Far Eastern 274; Kalinin 73, 75, 106, 113, 115, 172, 211, 221, 296–8, 300, 321n27; Karelian 69, 143, 177–8, *233–4*, 301; Leningrad 59, 69, 115, 143–4, 146, *148*, 149–50, 152, *153*, 159, 161, 176–7, 218, 222–3, *233–4*, 240, 297–8, 301; North Caucasus 115, 138, 322n27; Northern 31–2, 69, 142–3; North-Western 31–2, 42, 45, 59, 61, 69, 218, 321n26; Reserve 64–5, 70, 146, 295; Southern 42, 69, 78–9, 101, 115, 131–2, 296, 299–300, 330n16; South-Western 30–3, 42, 45, 51, *53*, 66, 69, 73, 75, 81, 107, 115, 118–23, 125, 131, 135, 294, 298, 300; Stalingrad 103–4, 106, 108, 297; Steppe 126, 129–31, *133*, 135, 299–300; Trans-Baikal 274–5, *276*, *277*, 277–80, *278*, 303; Transcaucasian 92, 296; Volkhov 88, 115, 159–61, 218, 222–3, *233*, 297–8, 301; Voronezh 115, 125–6, *128*, 128–31, *133*, 134, 298–300; Western 30–2, 42, 45, 47–8, 65, 69–70, 72–3, 75, 79, 81–2, 85–9, 106, 113, *133*, 141,143, 146, 294–300, 321–2n26

Red Army, formations and units, military districts: Arkhangel'sk 32; Central Asian 32; Far Eastern 31; Kiev Special 40, 51; Leningrad 32, 40, 141–2; Moscow 63; Odessa 40–1; Pribaltic Special 32, 40; Trans-Baikal 31–2; Transcaucasus 32; Western Special ('Belorussian') 32, 40, 47–8

Red Army, formations and units, *napravlenii*: North-Western 142–3, 294; South-Western 78–9, 172, 294; Western 294

Red Army, formations and units, regiments: 22nd Reserve Air 177; 27th Reserve Air 174, 177; 27th Reserve Rifle 70; 121st AT Artillery 70; 126th Fighter Air 174, 177; 154th Fighter Air 176; 159th Fighter

Red Army *continued*
  Air 176; 222nd Rifle 70; 230th Reserve Rifle 70; 367th AT Artillery 70; 395th AT Artillery 70; 382nd Rifle 70; 408th AT Artillery 70; 421st AT Artillery 70; 452nd Rifle 70; 584th AT Artillery 70; 587th Air 94; 588th Air 94
Riga 30, 32, 221, **229**, 240, 302
Rikov, A.I. 6
Rokossovskii, K.K. 50–1, 108, 247, 249, 265, 267, 271, 290, 327n1
Roosevelt, F.D. 165, 170, 290
Rostov-on-Don **52**, 79, 99, 101, **107**, 108, **124**, 290, 296–7, 299
Rovno 30, 50, **229**, **237**, 294
RS (*Katiusha*) 310; use 70, 72, 81, 111, 129–30, 138, *230–1*, *251*, 266, *267*, *276*
Rumanian forces 30, 33, 35–6, 42, 107–8, 115, 208, 221, 226–7, 239–41, 285, 296, 301–2, 319n20, 330n21
Rundstedt, G. von 79
Rzhev 91, 98, **107**, 113, 117, **124**, 299

'scorched-earth' policy: German 134, 187, 288; Soviet 49, 57, 71, 77–8, 144–5, 288, 296
Sevastopol' **52**, 98, **107**, 137, 227, **229**, 288, 297, 301
Shaposhnikov, B.M. 44–6, 65–6, 78, 143, 159–60
Shcherbakov, A.S. 47, 71
Shtemenko, S.M. 3, 131–2, 248, 253–4, 269–70
Slovak/Slovakia 208, 241, 301
SMERSH 217, 271, 309, 311
Smolensk **52**, 63, **107**, **124**, 213, 228, 294–5, 300
Soviet Navy (VMF): limited use of assets 137, 260, 262; requests for vessels to Allies 168, 322n32; SONAR/ASDIC and 166, 183–4, 322n31
Soviet Navy (VMF) fleets: Baltic 12, 32, 41, 137, 142, 144–5, 176, *233–4*, 260, 307; Black Sea 41, 99, 137–8, 226–7, *233–4*, 305; Northern 32, 41, 137, 142, 178, 184, *234*, 244, 311, 322n32: Pacific 277–8, 279
Soviet Navy (VMF), vessels: battleship *Arkhangel'sk* 244; *Besposhchadnii* 137; cruiser *Murmansk* 244; *Gromkii* 322n31; guardship *Groza* 322n31; *Khar'kov* 137; *Leningrad* 12; *Sposobnii* 137; submarines 83, 184, 262; *Tashkent* 13; Town Class destroyers 165, 320n7; Type-7 destroyers 13
special sections 54–6, 68–9, 103, 114, 199, 271, 295, 309
SPs, German, (*Sturmgeschütze*): Ferdinand 126
SPs, Soviet: SU-76 96, 275; SU-100 275; ISU-122 257; ISU-152 257, 275
Stalin, I.V. 1, 3, 5–9, 14–15, 17, 19, 27, 29, 36–7, 40–1, 43–50, 54–6, 58, 61, 63, 71, 75–7, 82, 86, 89, 91–5, 97, 100, 102–4, 106, 108, 111, 113, 115–16, 123–5, 131–2, 137–9, 142–3, 146, 148, 159–60, 163, 167, 171, 179, 183, 193–4, 197–200, 211, 220–1, 225, 247–8, 263, 267–71, 274, 285, 287, 289–91, 293–5, 307–8, 327n1; 5 May 1941 speech 29, 293; 3 July 1941 speech 49–50, 294; and the Allies 49–50, 76–7, 123, 166–7, 183, 263, 285; confidence in officer corps 113–14, 132, 268–71, 290; military leadership 58, 86, 91, 123, 146, 290, 294–5, 330n18: reaction to loss of communications with W. *Front* 47–8, 294
Stalingrad **52**, 77–8, 97–101, 103–9, **107**, 113, 115, 117, 123, **124**, 132, 186, 225, 229, 239, 256, 285, 288, 297–9
Staraia Russa **52**, 59, 143, 211, 295
Stargard 254, **264**, 302
State Defence Committee *see* GKO
Stavka GK: composition 44; formation 44–5
Stavka VGK: formation 45; increased realism in operational planning 108; late-war composition 268–9; role *Stavka* reps to *fronts* 131–2
Stavka VK: formation 45
supply, as limiting factor in ops: German 98, 100, 210, 214; Soviet 98, 112, 117–23, 214, 235–6, 249, 254–5, 279; *see also* horses; motor vehicles; railways

Tallin **52**, 137, 221, **229**, 240
tanks, German: PzKpfw I 74; PzKpfw II 50, 74; PzKpfw III 50, 74, 317n8:

PzKpfw IV 74, 38, 50, 74: V Panther 84, 130; VI Tiger 125–6, 130; see also SPs
tanks, Soviet: BT series 8, 50, 275, 317n8: IS series 257; KV series 38, 51, 58, 73, 75, 83–4, 147, 275, 308; production of 83–4, 95, 186; T-18 8; T-24 8; T-26 8, 50, 275; T-27 8; T-28 38; T-34 311; T-35 8, 38; T-37 8; T-70 112; use 38, 51, 73, 75, 112, 130, 275
tanks, Soviet – Lend-Lease: Matilda (MK II) 82–5, 172, 173, 177, 318n20, 321–2n27; Valentine (MK III) 83–5, 173, 177, 318n20, 321n26; M3 173, 322n28
Tikhvin 52, 107, 146–7, 152, 290, 296
Timoshenko, S.K. 24–5, 34, 40–2, 44–8, 79, 99, 271, 294
trucks see motor vehicles
Tula 52, 79, 85, 107

United Kingdom see Great Britain
United States see Roosevelt; Stalin, and the Allies
urban warfare 104–5, 77–8, 243, 249, 251, 254–60, 262, 283–4

Vasilevskii, A.M. 82, 86, 96, 100, 105–6, 130–1, 257, 269, 290
Vatunin, N.F. 44–8, 141, 255, 271
Viaz'ma 33, 52, 68–9, 91, 98, 106–7, 107, 117, 296, 299
Vishinskii, A.I. 46, 269–70
VLKSM see *Komsomol*
VMF see Soviet Navy
Volksturm 248, 313
Voronezh 52, 101, 107, 115, 117, 124, 297–8
Voronov, K.E. 18, 44–6, 48, 142–4, 270–1, 290, 294, 308
VVS 313; and '*Doroga zhizni*' 146, 148, 176; early-war losses 41, 51, 53, 174; early-war reorganization 58–9; and Kursk salient 126–8; see also aircraft

Waffen SS 117, 236, 240, 313
Warsaw 7, 30, 32, 52, 107, 229, 235–6, 247, 253, 301
Wehrmacht, formations and units, army groups: Army Group A 99–100, 108, 117, 249, 251, 252, 253, 297–8; Army Group B 99, 108, 298; Army Group Centre 50–1, 63, 98, 113, 117, 128, 208–9, 214, 218, 221, 228–9, 231, 231, 240, 251, 254–5, 294–5, 297–8, 301; Army Group Kurland 241, 254; Army Group North 51, 117, 141, 147, 202, 206–8, 211, 216, 217, 218, 218, 221, 223, 228, 240–1, 255, 294–5; Army Group South 79, 99, 128, 208, 218, 294, 296–7; Army Group South Ukraine 240
Wehrmacht, formations and units, brigades: 2nd SS 208–9
Wehrmacht, formations and units, Panzer groups: 1st 51, 294; 2nd 68, 79, 295–6; 3rd 68, 79, 295–6; 4th 68, 79, 143, 295
Wehrmacht, formations and units, regiments: 20th SS Police 272; 27th Infantry 209, 216; 356th Infantry 208; 368th Infantry 207; 639th Field Training 222; 691st Infantry 209; Cavalry 'Nord' 222; SS Führer [*begleit*] 272
Wehrmacht and allies, formations and units, armies: 1st Hungarian 252; 2nd Hungarian 298; 1st Panzer 252; 2nd 128; 3rd Panzer 231, 231, 265; 4th 231, 231, 252; 4th Panzer 109, 117, 128, 223, 249, 256, 265, 298; 6th 109, 113, 115, 117, 132, 239, 253, 256, 296–7, 299; 6th SS Panzer 253, 302; 8th Italian 329n7; 9th 113, 128, 231, 252, 265; 11th 297; 16th 59, 143, 211, 222; 17th 227, 252; 18th 142, 160, 222–3; 20th Mountain 244
Wehrmacht and allies, formations and units, battalions (*Abteilung*): 73rd Fortress Machine-Gun 256; 74th Fortress Machine-Gun 256; 273rd Latvian Police 209; 515th Latvian Police 209; 615th Latvian Police 209; 651st Special Punishment 222; 656th Pioneer 222; 657th Pioneer 222; 676th Pioneer 222
Wehrmacht and allies, formations and units, corps: 3rd Panzer 136, 224; 3rd Rumanian Mountain 208; 4th Infantry (Army) 108; 4th SS Panzer 251; 8th Infantry 108; 11th Infantry 108; 13th Infantry 236; 14th Panzer 108; 17th Panzer 136; 24th Panzer

Wehrmacht and allies *continued*
139, 251; 39th Panzer 228; 40th Panzer 136; 48th Panzer 108, 128–9; 51st Infantry 108; Grossdeutschland Panzer 253; 'Slovak Corps' 241; SS Panzer 128–9

Wehrmacht and allies, formations and units, divisions: 1st *Luftwaffe* Field 222; 1st Rumanian Armoured 240; 1st Rumanian Cavalry 108; 2nd *Luftwaffe* Field 222; 2nd Panzer 74, 75; 3rd Panzer 128; 5th Panzer 74, 75; 6th Panzer 256; 8th 'Light' 222; 10th Panzergrenadier 240; 12th Infantry 209, 216, 228; 13th *Luftwaffe* Field 222; 14th Panzer 108; 14th Waffen SS 'Galicia' 236; 15th Latvian 222; 16th Panzer 108, 251; 17th Panzer 129, 251; 19th Panzer 128, 139; 20th Rumanian Infantry 108; 21st 'Light' 222; 24th *Luftwaffe* Field 222; 24th Panzer 108; 28th 'Light' 222; 30th *Jaeger* 207; 44th 'Light' 108; 56th Infantry 256; 69th Infantry 256; 71st 'Light' 108; 76th 'Light' 108; 94th 'Light' 108; 95th Infantry 222; 100th 'Light' 108; 101st Infantry 222; 113th Infantry 108; 121st Construction 222; 121st 'Light' 222; 137th Infantry 64; 141st Reserve Infantry 208; 143rd Reserve Infantry 208; 147th Reserve Infantry 208; 151st Reserve Infantry 208; 153rd Field Training 208; 197th Infantry 51; 201st Security 208; 203rd Security 208; 207th Security *202*, 208; 212th *Luftwaffe* Field 222; 213th Security 207; 221st Security 208; 228th Infantry 208; 232nd Security 222; 236th Security 222; 281st Security 201–2, *202*, 206–10; 285th Security *202*, 208; 286th Security 207–8; 290th *Luftwaffe* Field 222; 295th Infantry 108; 297th Infantry 108; 305th Infantry 108; 339th Infantry 209; 371st Infantry 108; 376th Infantry 108; 384th Infantry 108; 388th Field Training 208; 389th Infantry 108; 390th Field Training 208; 391st Field Training 208; 401st Infantry 222; 403rd Security 207; 444th Security 208; 454th Security 208; 549th Infantry 256; 625th Infantry 222; 657th Security 222; 661st Infantry 222; Das Reich Panzer 272; Grossdeutschland Panzer 256; Spanish 'Blue' 222; SS Police 222

Weidling, H. 271

women: in military service 92–4; and the partisan war 123, *202*

Zhdanov, A.A. 44, 146–7, 150, 152, 157, 161

Zhigarev, P.F. 44, 46–7, 146, 148, 270

Zhitomir 135, 238, 300

Zhukov, G.K. 34, 40, 42, 44–8, 64–6, 72, 81–2, 87, 89, 103, 106, 113, 131, 142, 144, 225, 247, 253–4, 263, 265, 266–7, 269, 271–2, 290, 294, 327n1; 15 May war plan and 34; and El'nia counterattack 64–6; and Moscow counterattack 82; and Stalingrad encirclement and Operation 'Mars' 106–7, 113

eBooks – at www.eBookstore.tandf.co.uk

A library at your fingertips!

eBooks are electronic versions of printed books. You can store them on your PC/laptop or browse them online.

They have advantages for anyone needing rapid access to a wide variety of published, copyright information.

eBooks can help your research by enabling you to bookmark chapters, annotate text and use instant searches to find specific words or phrases. Several eBook files would fit on even a small laptop or PDA.

NEW: Save money by eSubscribing: cheap, online access to any eBook for as long as you need it.

Annual subscription packages

We now offer special low-cost bulk subscriptions to packages of eBooks in certain subject areas. These are available to libraries or to individuals.

For more information please contact webmaster.ebooks@tandf.co.uk

We're continually developing the eBook concept, so keep up to date by visiting the website.

www.eBookstore.tandf.co.uk

An environmentally friendly book printed and bound in England by www.printondemand-worldwide.com

PEFC Certified
This product is from sustainably managed forests and controlled sources
www.pefc.org
PEFC/16-33-415

Mixed Sources
Product group from well-managed forests, and other controlled sources
www.fsc.org Cert no. TT-COC-002641
© 1996 Forest Stewardship Council

This book is made entirely of chain-of-custody materials

#0490 - 021111 - C0 - 234/156 - PB